SALLY HEATHCOTE SUFFRAGETTE

MARY M TALBOT
KATE CHARLESWORTH
BRYAN TALBOT

DARK HORSE BOOKS

Publication Design
BRYAN TALBOT with NICK JAMES

Publisher
MIKE RICHARDSON

US Editor
CHRIS WARNER

US Assistant Editor
EVERETT PATTERSON

———————◆◆◆———————

SALLY HEATHCOTE, SUFFRAGETTE

Dark Horse Books
A division of Dark Horse Comics, Inc.
10956 SE Main Street
Milwaukie OR 97222

Darkhorse.com

To find a comics shop in your area, call the Comic Shop
Locator Service toll-free at 1-888-266-4226

First edition: September 2014
ISBN 978-1-61655-547-4

1 3 5 7 9 10 8 6 4 2

Printed in China

———————◆◆◆———————

MIKE RICHARDSON President and Publisher • NEIL HANKERSON Executive Vice President • TOM WEDDLE Chief
Financial Officer • RANDY STRADLEY Vice President of Publishing • MICHAEL MARTENS Vice President of Book
Trade Sales • ANITA NELSON Vice President of Business Affairs • SCOTT ALLIE Editor in Chief • MATT PARKINSON
Vice President of Marketing • DAVID SCROGGY Vice President of Product Development • DALE LAFOUNTAIN Vice
President of Information Technology • DARLENE VOGEL Senior Director of Print, Design, and Production • KEN
LIZZI General Counsel • DAVEY ESTRADA Editorial Director • CHRIS WARNER Senior Books Editor • DIANA SCHUTZ
Executive Editor • CARY GRAZZINI Director of Print and Development • LIA RIBACCHI Art Director • CARA NIECE
Director of Scheduling • MARK BERNARDI Director of Digital Publishing

A maiming subserviency had for ages held
the spirit of the mass of women in thrall.
The militant suffrage movement broke
that thralldom ... They laughed at danger.

Emmeline Pethick-Lawrence

To our niece, Emma Atherton—stay radical!

Mary and Bryan Talbot

For Dianne Barry, for endless patience and support.

Kate Charlesworth

Acknowledgements

Chaz Brenchley, Meg Davis, Al Davison, Dan Franklin, Dr Mel Gibson, Stephen Holland, Pádraig Ó Méalóid, William Proctor, Dr Angela Smith, Jessica Talmage at the Mary Evans Picture Library, Chester West, John Woody at the *Illustrated London News* Archive, the staff of the Newcastle Local Studies Centre and the Women's Library at London Metropolitan University.

Page 128 Hand lettering: Katy Rodda.

PART ONE

RISE UP!

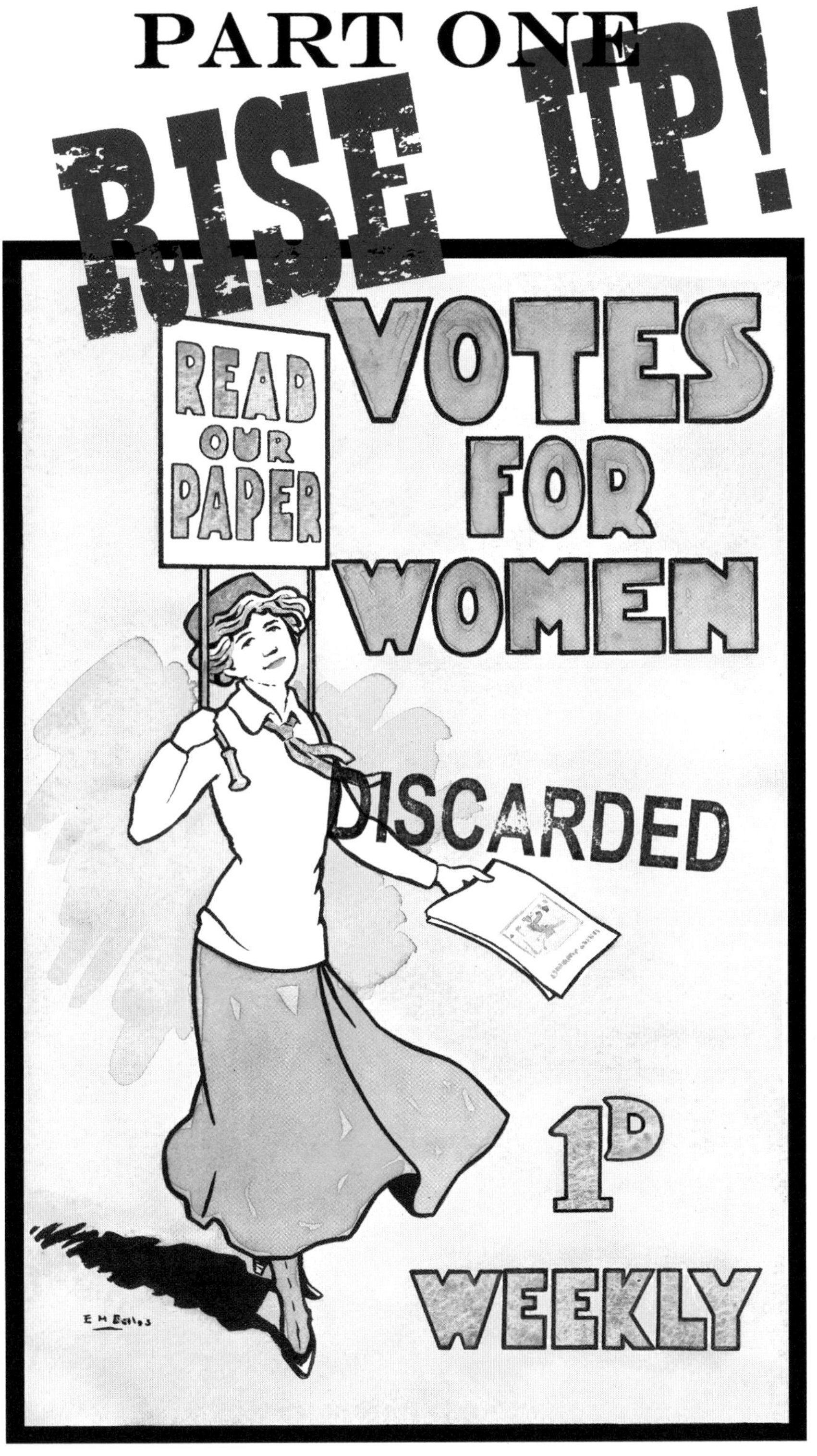
READ OUR PAPER
VOTES FOR WOMEN
1D
WEEKLY

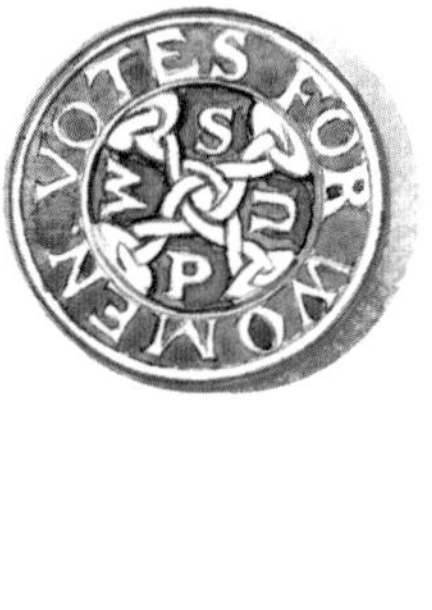
VOTES FOR WOMEN
W S P U

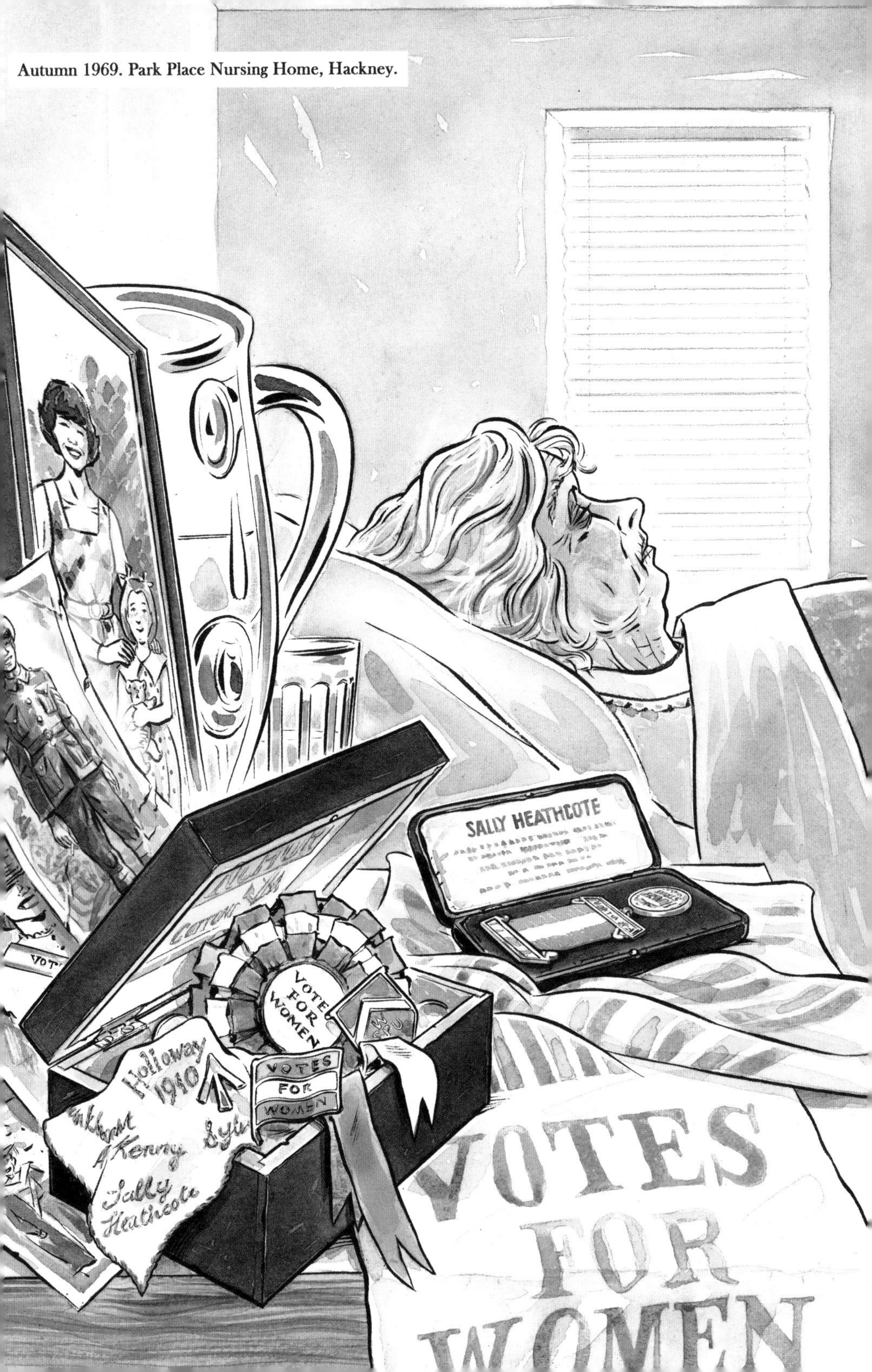
Autumn 1969. Park Place Nursing Home, Hackney.
SALLY HEATHCOTE
VOTES FOR WOMEN
VOTES FOR WOMEN
Holloway 1910
Kenny
Sally Heathcote
VOTES FOR WOMEN

July 15th, 1912. Oxford Crown Court.
Your Honour, when apprehended, the defendant, Miss Helen Millar Craggs of Hampstead, was found to have the following items in her possession...
...one bottle and two cans inflammable oil, two boxes matches, four tapers, nine picklocks...
VOTES FOR WOMEN
...twelve firelighters wrapped in tow, one hammer, head wrapped in kid glove, one electric torch, one glass-cutter, thirteen keys...
...one handwritten note.
Sir,
I myself have taken part in every peaceful method of propagan
and petition but I have been driven to realise that it is all to no avail. Women see around them the most appalling evils in the social order; they see childr
born into conditions which maim them, physically and mentally, for life; they see their fellow-women working in the sweated industries at a wage which makes their life a living death
— or sacrificed

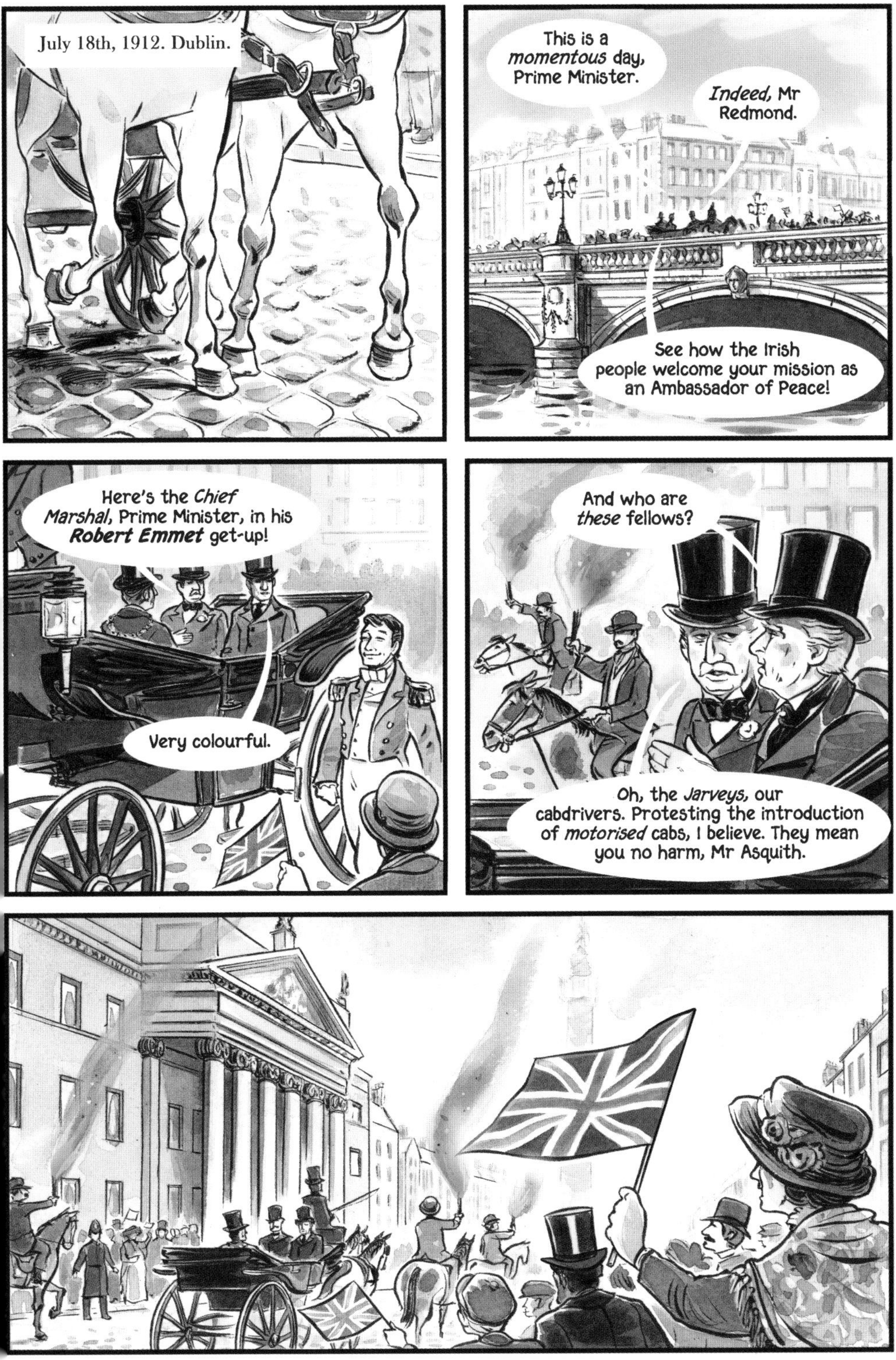

July 18th, 1912. Dublin.
This is a *momentous* day, Prime Minister.
Indeed, Mr Redmond.
See how the Irish people welcome your mission as an Ambassador of Peace!
Here's the *Chief Marshal,* Prime Minister, in his ***Robert Emmet*** get-up!
Very colourful.
And who are *these* fellows?
Oh, the *Jarveys,* our cabdrivers. Protesting the introduction of *motorised* cabs, I believe. They mean you no harm, Mr Asquith.

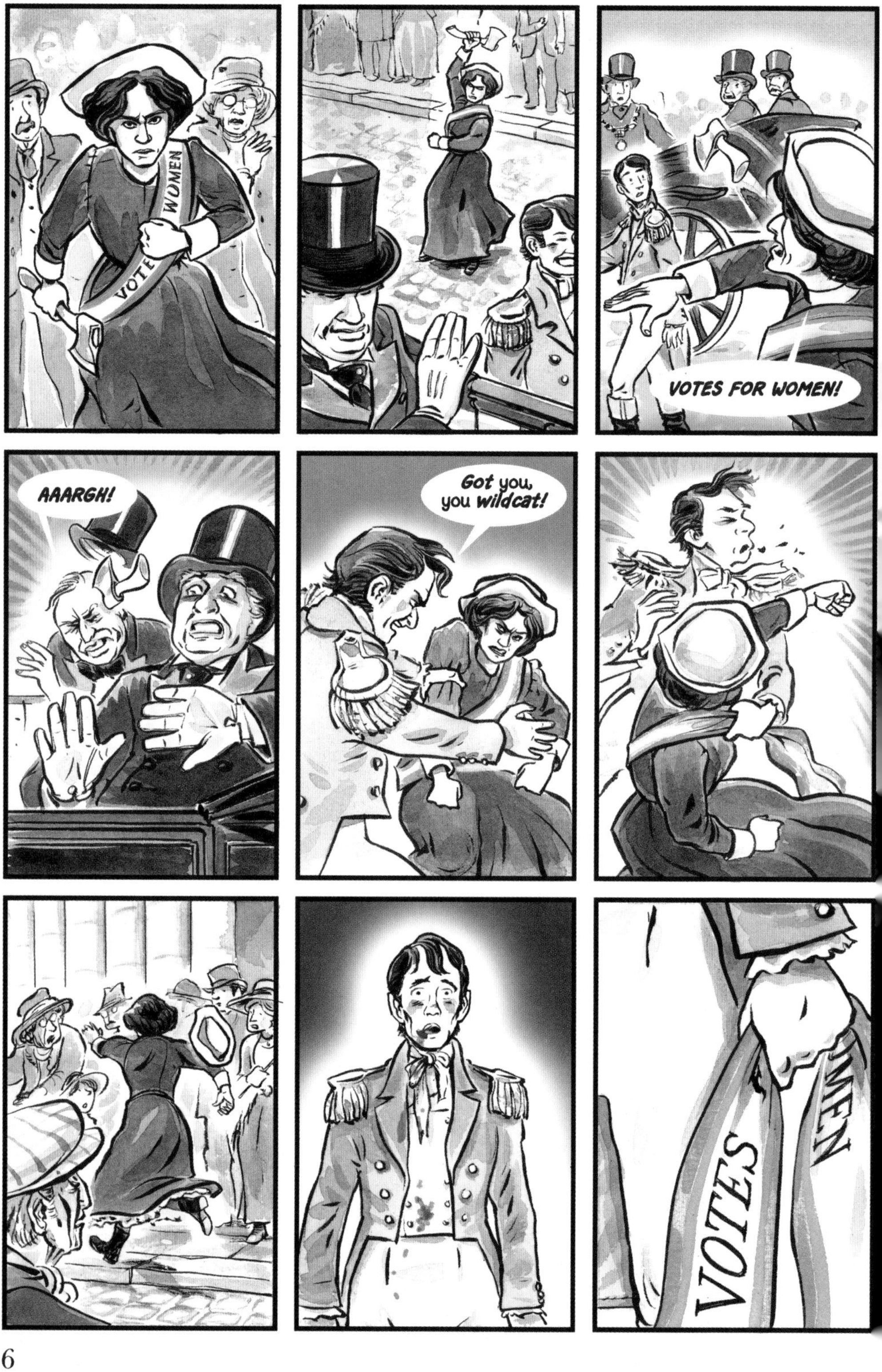
VOTE
WOMEN
VOTES FOR WOMEN!
AAARGH!
Got you, you wildcat!
VOTES
MEN

October 1st, 1912. RMS *Campania*, North Atlantic.

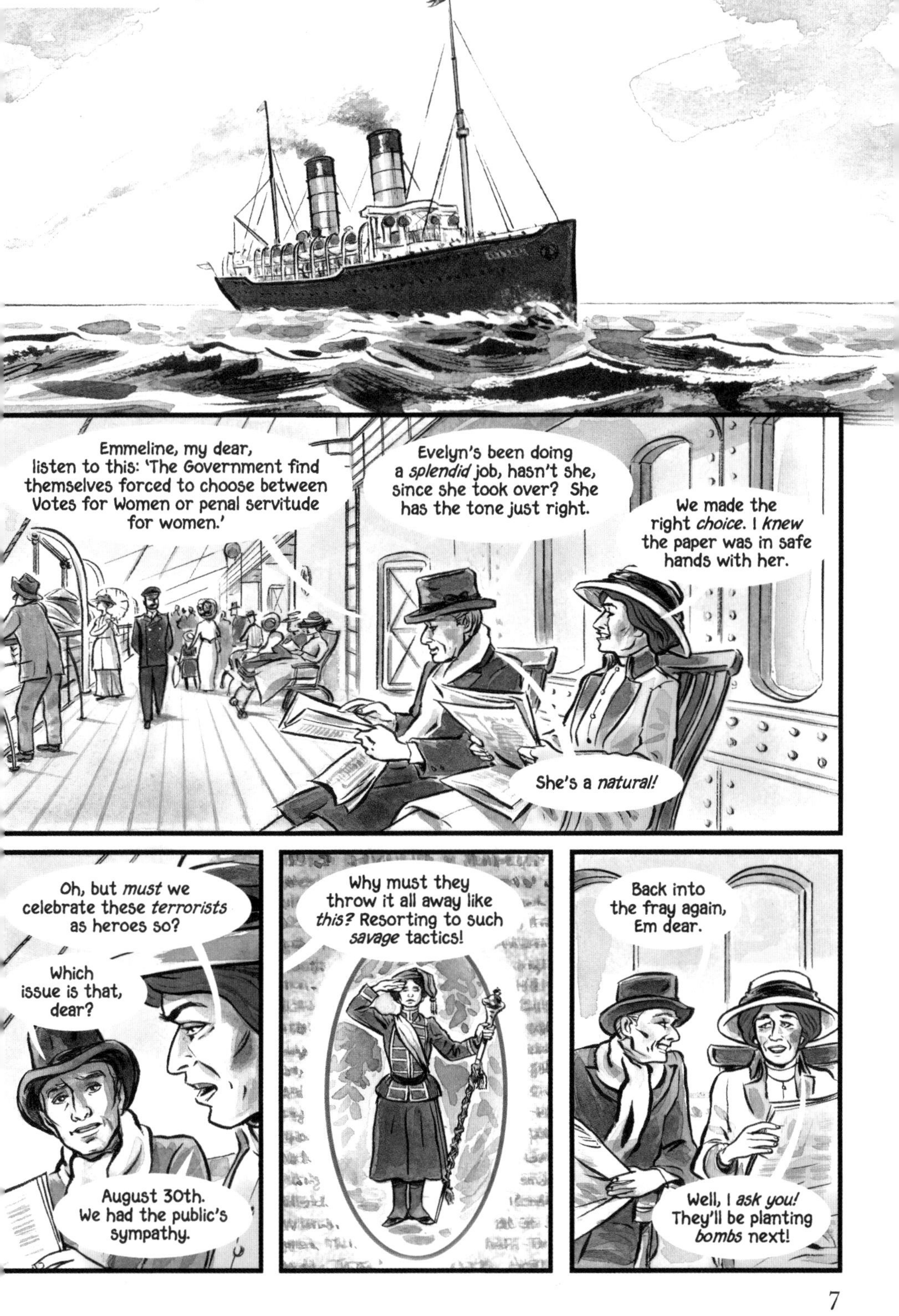

Emmeline, my dear, listen to this: 'The Government find themselves forced to choose between Votes for Women or penal servitude for women.'
Evelyn's been doing a *splendid* job, hasn't she, since she took over? She has the tone just right.
We made the right *choice*. I *knew* the paper was in safe hands with her.
She's a *natural!*
Oh, but *must* we celebrate these *terrorists* as heroes so?
Which issue is that, dear?
August 30th. We had the public's sympathy.
Why must they throw it all away like *this?* Resorting to such *savage* tactics!
Back into the fray again, Em dear.
Well, I *ask you!* They'll be planting *bombs* next!

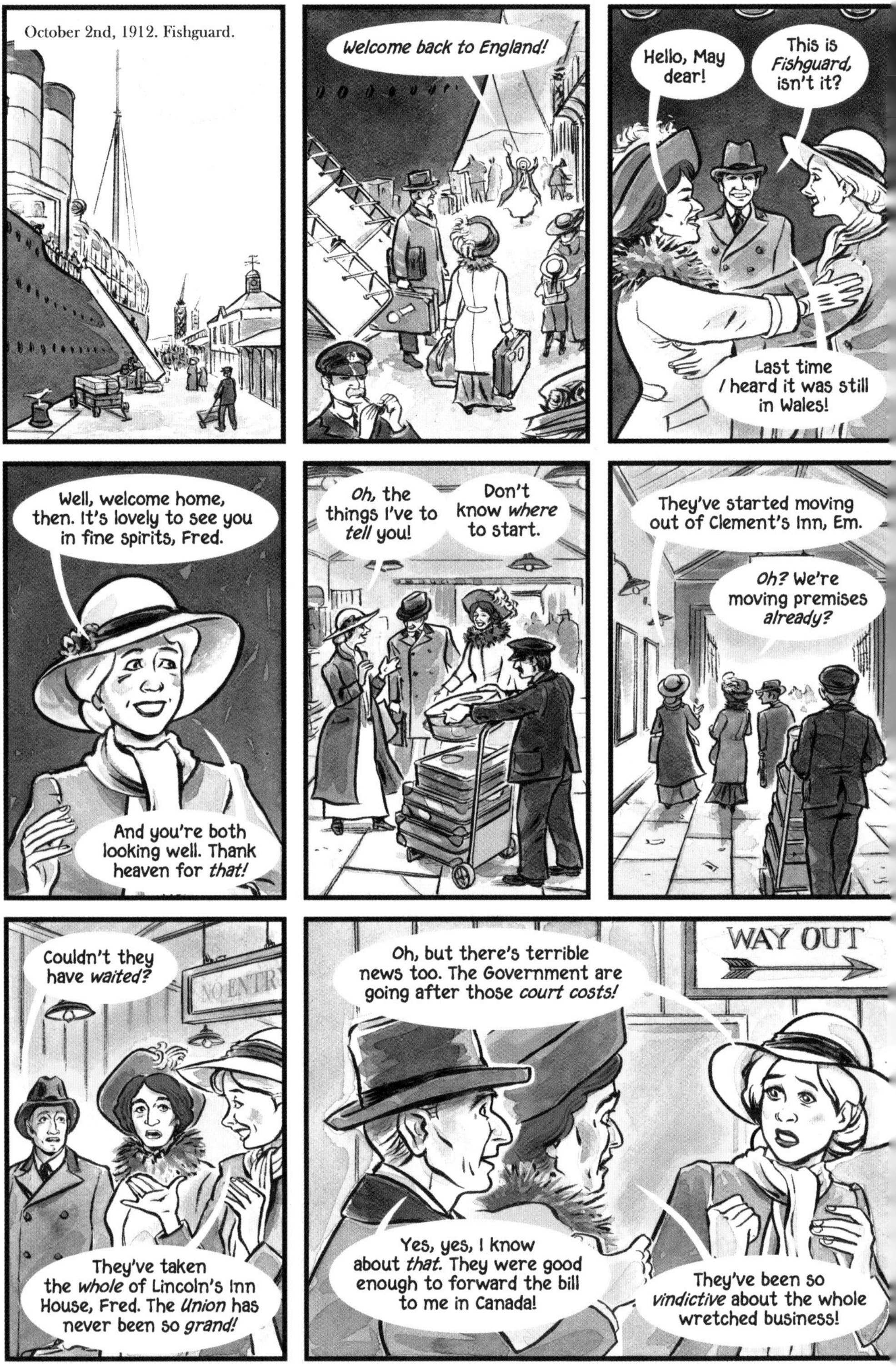
October 2nd, 1912. Fishguard.
Welcome back to England!
Hello, May dear!
This is Fishguard, isn't it?
Last time I heard it was still in Wales!
Well, welcome home, then. It's lovely to see you in fine spirits, Fred.
And you're both looking well. Thank heaven for that!
Oh, the things I've to tell you!
Don't know where to start.
They've started moving out of Clement's Inn, Em.
Oh? We're moving premises already?
Couldn't they have waited?
NO ENTRY
They've taken the whole of Lincoln's Inn House, Fred. The Union has never been so grand!
WAY OUT
Oh, but there's terrible news too. The Government are going after those court costs!
Yes, yes, I know about that. They were good enough to forward the bill to me in Canada!
They've been so vindictive about the whole wretched business!

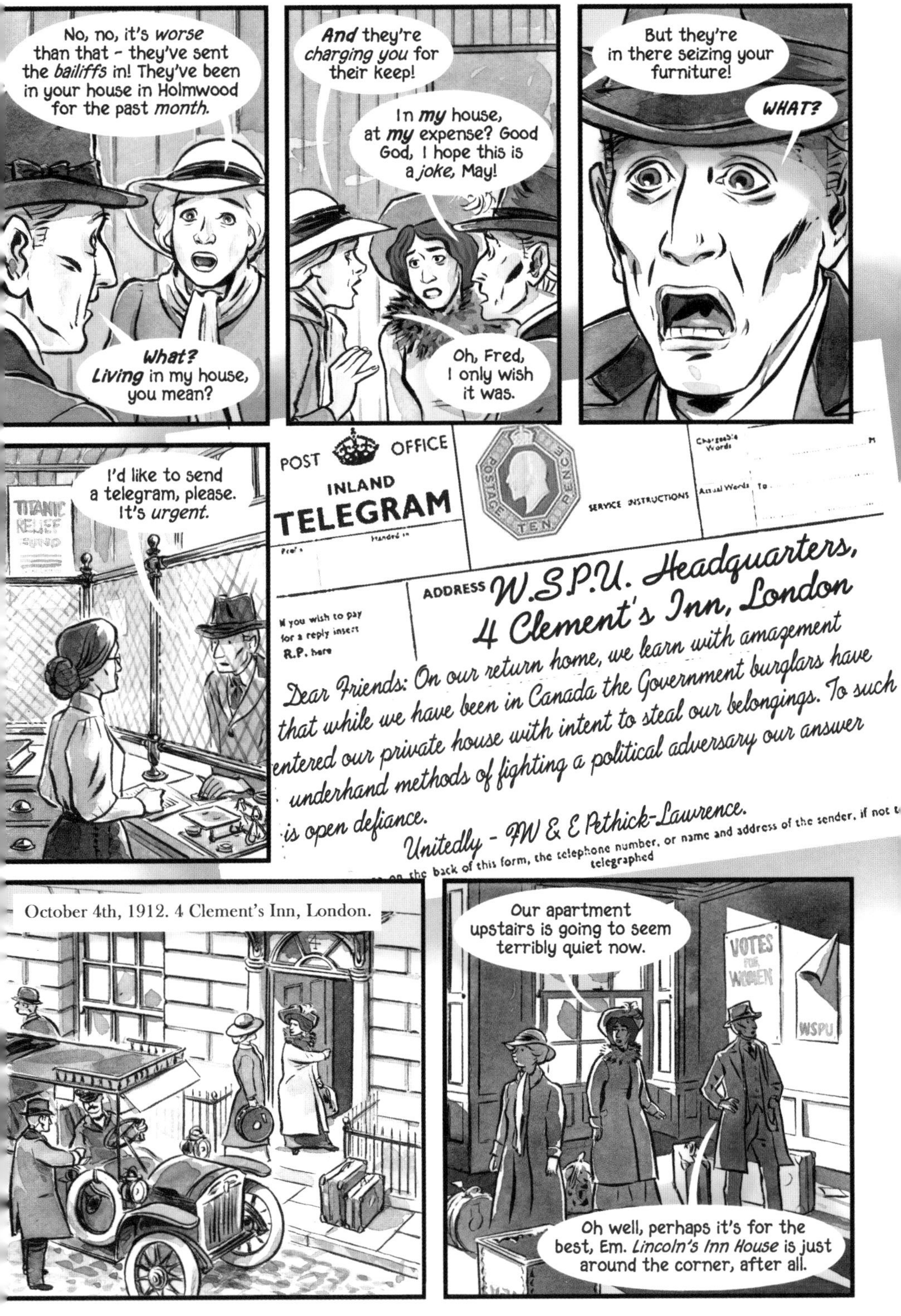
No, no, it's *worse* than that – they've sent the *bailiffs* in! They've been in your house in Holmwood for the past *month*.
What? *Living* in my house, you mean?
And they're *charging you* for their keep!
In *my* house, at *my* expense? Good God, I hope this is a *joke*, May!
Oh, Fred, I only wish it was.
But they're in there seizing your furniture!
WHAT?
I'd like to send a telegram, please. It's *urgent*.
TITANIC RELIEF FUND
POST OFFICE
INLAND
TELEGRAM
POSTAGE TEN PENCE
SERVICE INSTRUCTIONS
Chargeable Words
Actual Words
To
If you wish to pay for a reply insert R.P. here
ADDRESS W.S.P.U. Headquarters, 4 Clement's Inn, London
Dear Friends: On our return home, we learn with amazement that while we have been in Canada the Government burglars have entered our private house with intent to steal our belongings. To such underhand methods of fighting a political adversary our answer is open defiance.
Unitedly – FW & E Pethick-Lawrence.
the back of this form, the telephone number, or name and address of the sender, if not telegraphed
October 4th, 1912. 4 Clement's Inn, London.
Our apartment upstairs is going to seem terribly quiet now.
VOTES FOR WOMEN
WSPU
Oh well, perhaps it's for the best, Em. *Lincoln's Inn House* is just around the corner, after all.

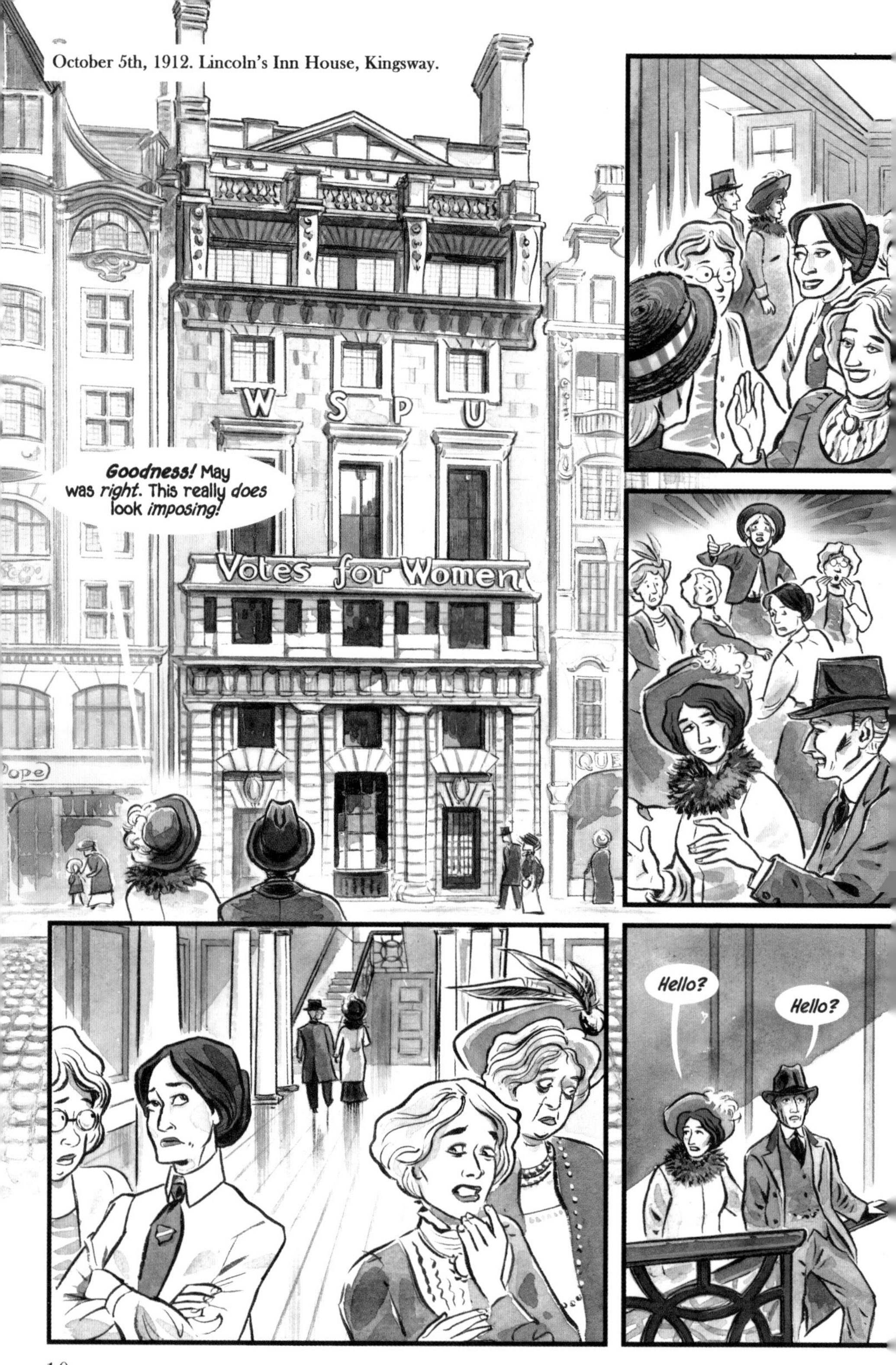
October 5th, 1912. Lincoln's Inn House, Kingsway.
WSPU
Votes for Women
Goodness! May was right. This really does look imposing!
Hello?
Hello?

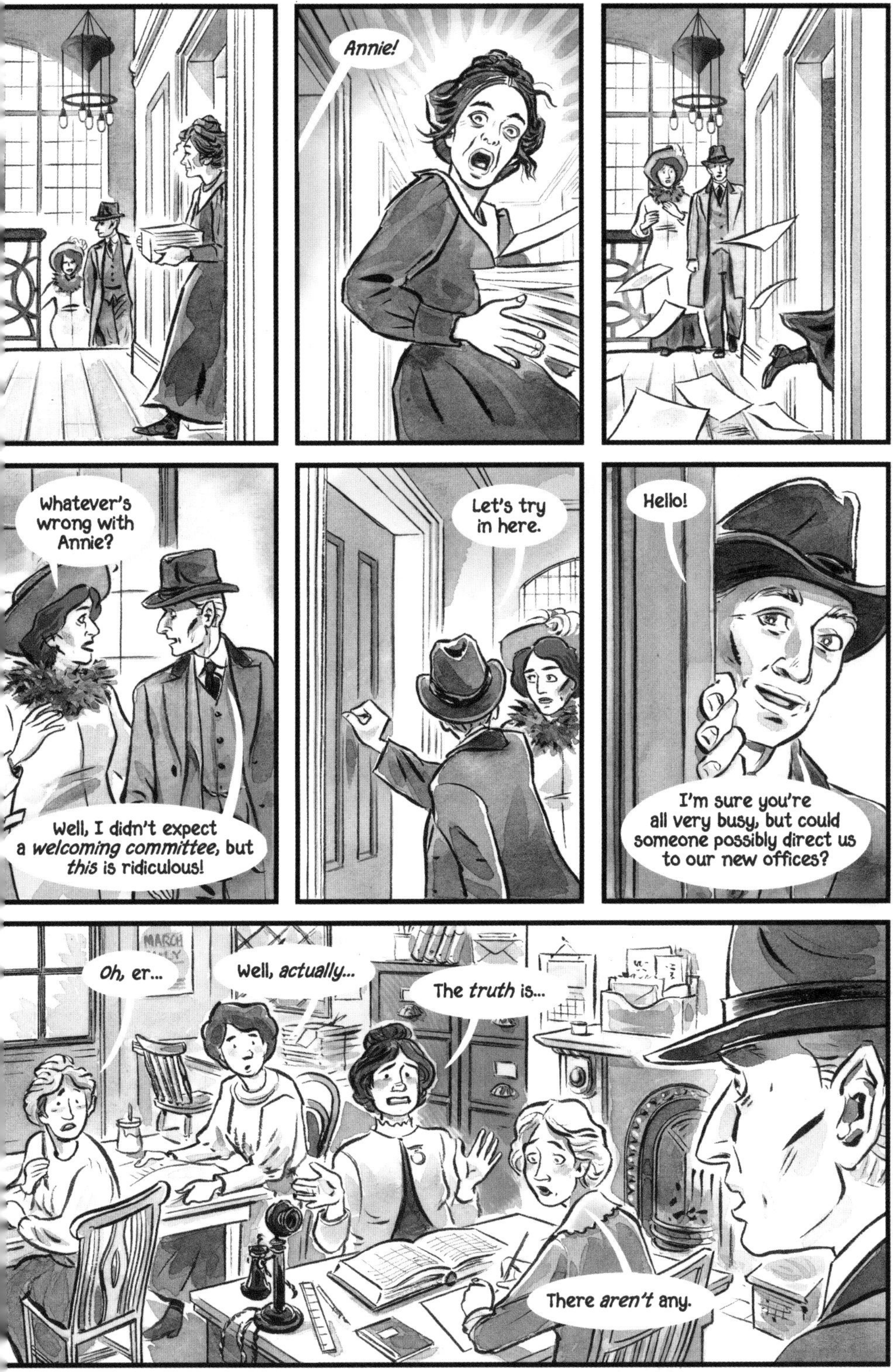
Annie!
Whatever's wrong with Annie?
Well, I didn't expect a *welcoming committee*, but *this* is ridiculous!
Let's try in here.
Hello!
I'm sure you're all very busy, but could someone possibly direct us to our new offices?
Oh, er...
Well, *actually*...
The *truth* is...
There *aren't* any.

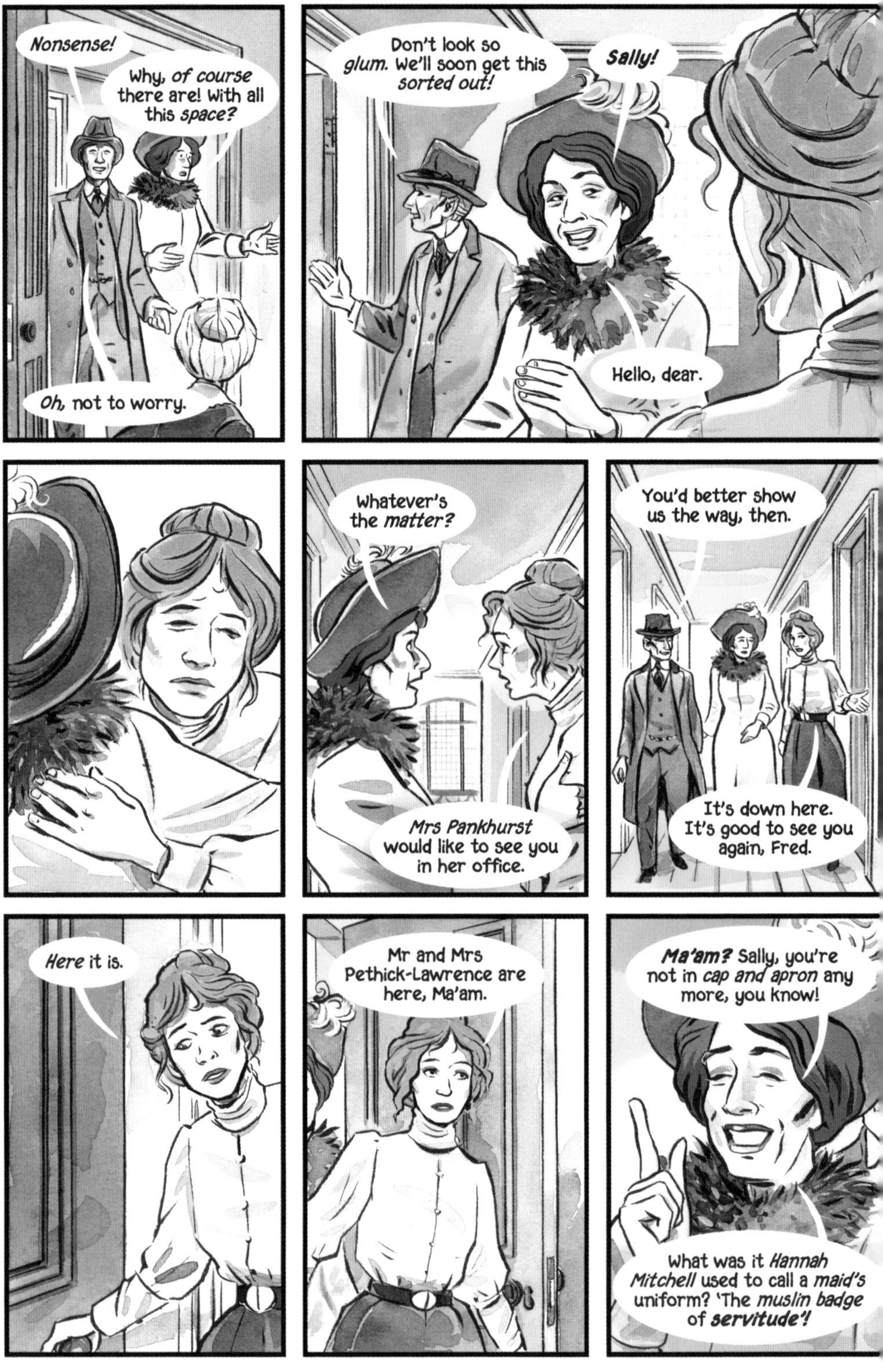
Nonsense!
Why, of course there are! With all this space?
Oh, not to worry.
Don't look so glum. We'll soon get this sorted out!
Sally!
Hello, dear.
Whatever's the matter?
Mrs Pankhurst would like to see you in her office.
You'd better show us the way, then.
It's down here. It's good to see you again, Fred.
Here it is.
Mr and Mrs Pethick-Lawrence are here, Ma'am.
Ma'am? Sally, you're not in cap and apron any more, you know!
What was it Hannah Mitchell used to call a maid's uniform? 'The muslin badge of servitude'!

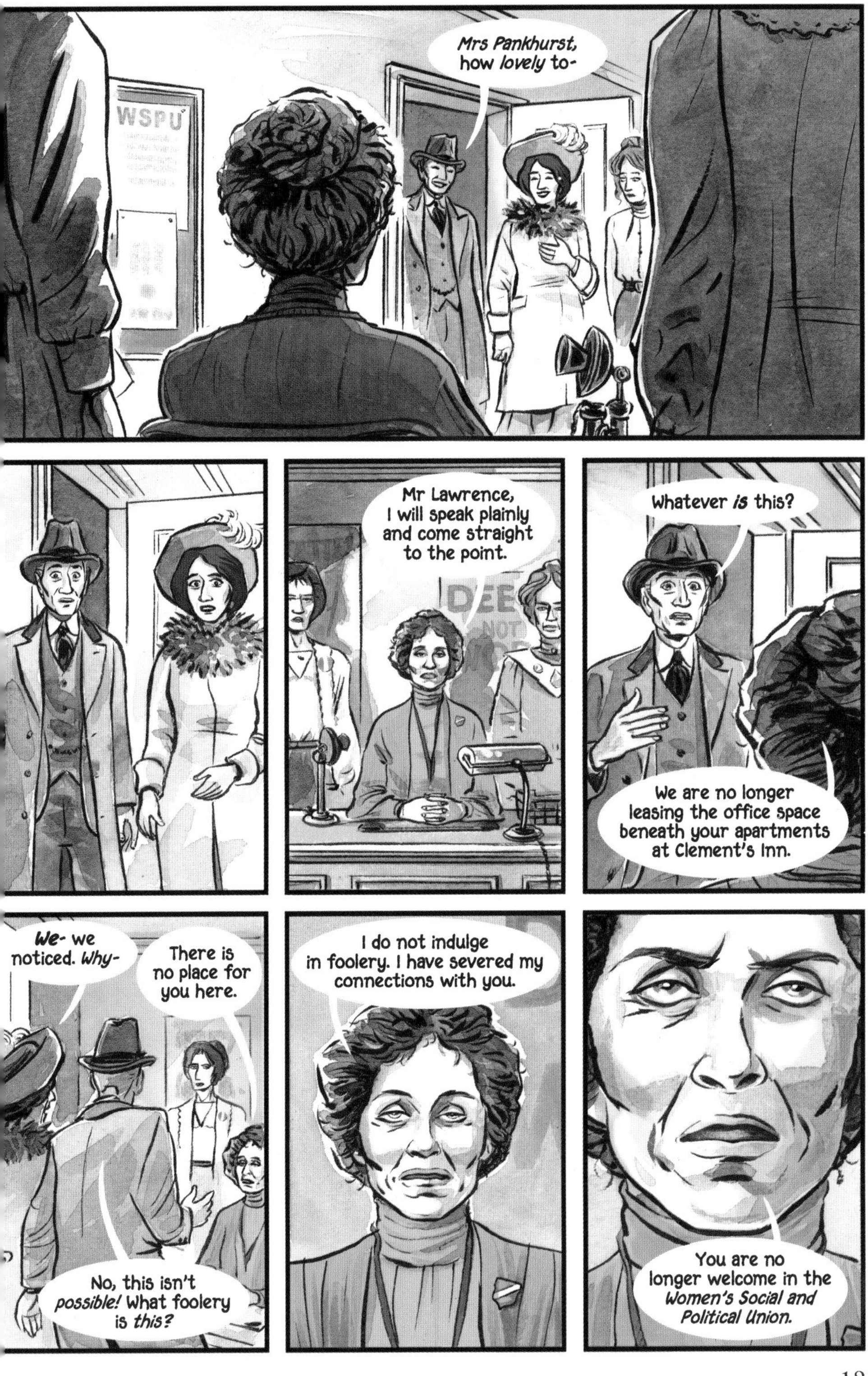
WSPU
Mrs Pankhurst, how lovely to-
Mr Lawrence, I will speak plainly and come straight to the point.
Whatever is this?
We are no longer leasing the office space beneath your apartments at Clement's Inn.
We- we noticed. Why-
There is no place for you here.
No, this isn't possible! What foolery is this?
I do not indulge in foolery. I have severed my connections with you.
You are no longer welcome in the Women's Social and Political Union.

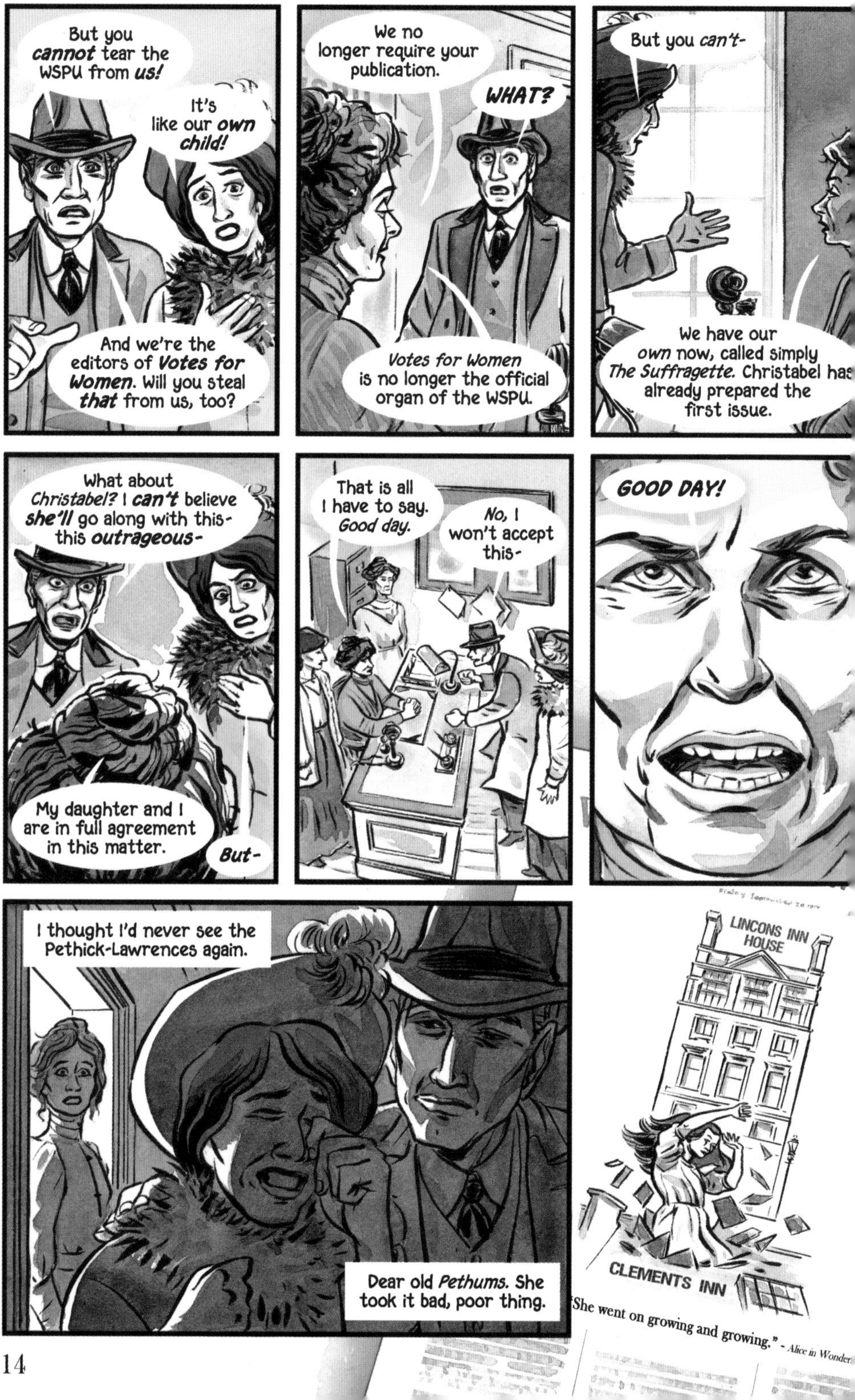

But you *cannot* tear the WSPU from *us!*
It's like our *own child!*
And we're the editors of *Votes for Women*. Will you steal *that* from us, too?
We no longer require your publication.
WHAT?
Votes for Women is no longer the official organ of the WSPU.
But you *can't*-
We have our *own* now, called simply *The Suffragette*. Christabel has already prepared the first issue.
What about *Christabel?* I *can't* believe *she'll* go along with this- this *outrageous*-
My daughter and I are in full agreement in this matter.
But-
That is all I have to say. *Good day.*
No, I won't accept this-
GOOD DAY!
I thought I'd never see the Pethick-Lawrences again.
Dear old *Pethums*. She took it bad, poor thing.
LINCONS INN HOUSE
CLEMENTS INN
"She went on growing and growing." - Alice in Wonder

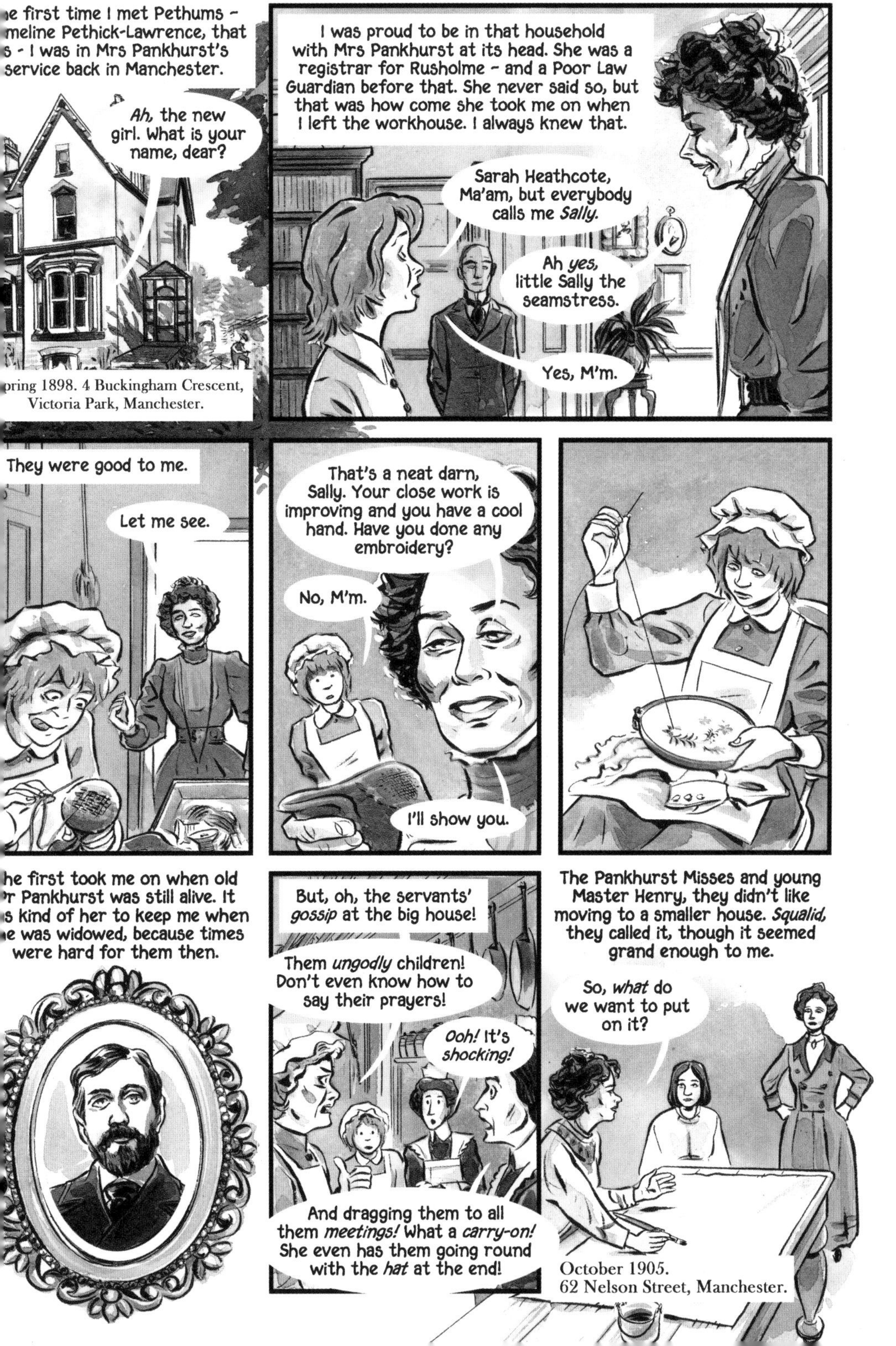

ne first time I met Pethums - meline Pethick-Lawrence, that s - I was in Mrs Pankhurst's service back in Manchester.
Ah, the new girl. What is your name, dear?
pring 1898. 4 Buckingham Crescent, Victoria Park, Manchester.
I was proud to be in that household with Mrs Pankhurst at its head. She was a registrar for Rusholme - and a Poor Law Guardian before that. She never said so, but that was how come she took me on when I left the workhouse. I always knew that.
Sarah Heathcote, Ma'am, but everybody calls me Sally.
Ah yes, little Sally the seamstress.
Yes, M'm.
They were good to me.
Let me see.
That's a neat darn, Sally. Your close work is improving and you have a cool hand. Have you done any embroidery?
No, M'm.
I'll show you.
he first took me on when old r Pankhurst was still alive. It s kind of her to keep me when e was widowed, because times were hard for them then.
But, oh, the servants' gossip at the big house!
Them ungodly children! Don't even know how to say their prayers!
Ooh! It's shocking!
And dragging them to all them meetings! What a carry-on! She even has them going round with the hat at the end!
The Pankhurst Misses and young Master Henry, they didn't like moving to a smaller house. Squalid, they called it, though it seemed grand enough to me.
So, what do we want to put on it?
October 1905. 62 Nelson Street, Manchester.

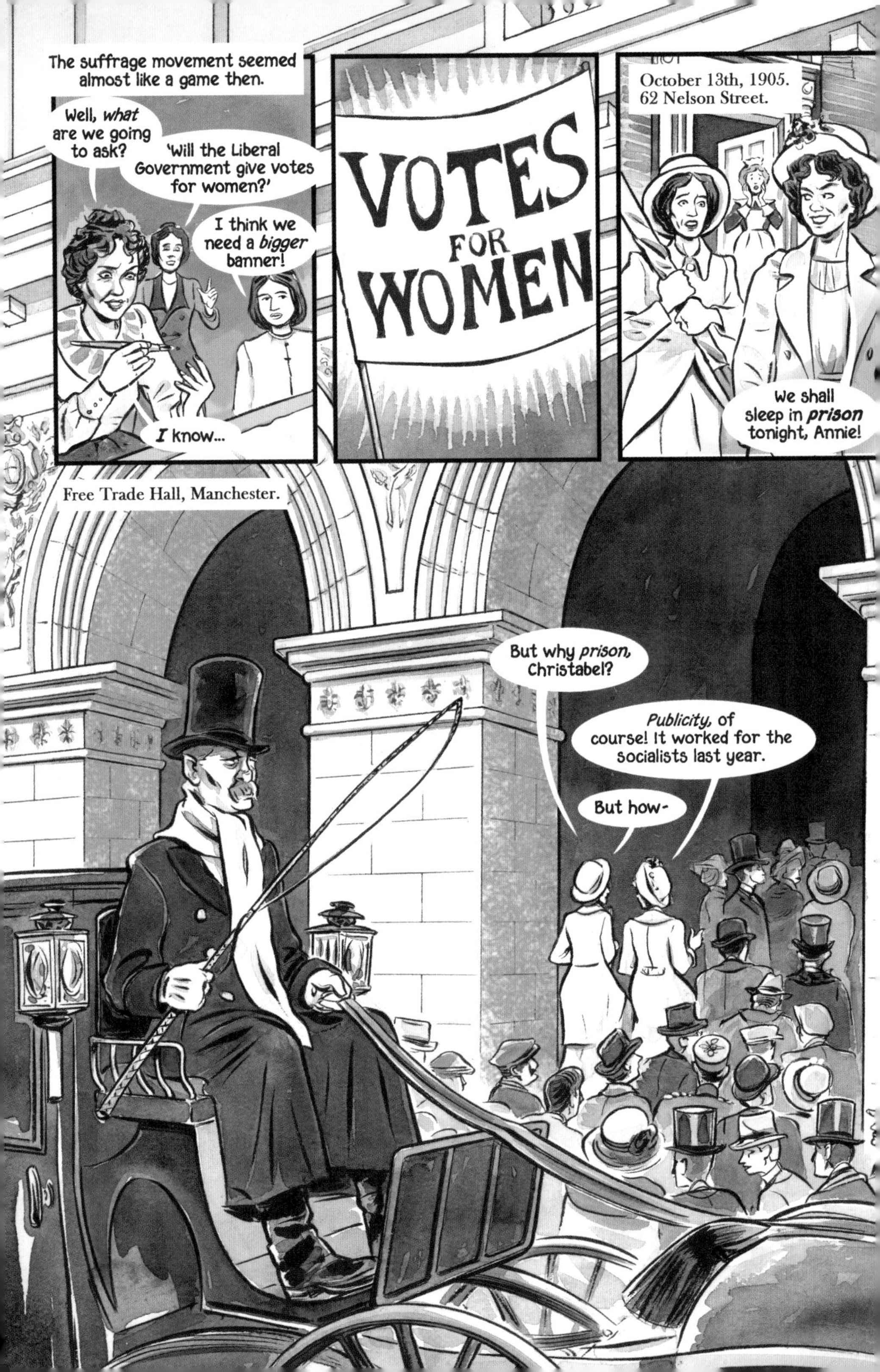
The suffrage movement seemed almost like a game then.
Well, *what* are we going to ask?
'Will the Liberal Government give votes for women?'
I think we need a *bigger* banner!
I know...
VOTES FOR WOMEN
October 13th, 1905. 62 Nelson Street.
We shall sleep in ***prison*** tonight, Annie!
Free Trade Hall, Manchester.
But why *prison,* Christabel?
Publicity, of course! It worked for the socialists last year.
But how-

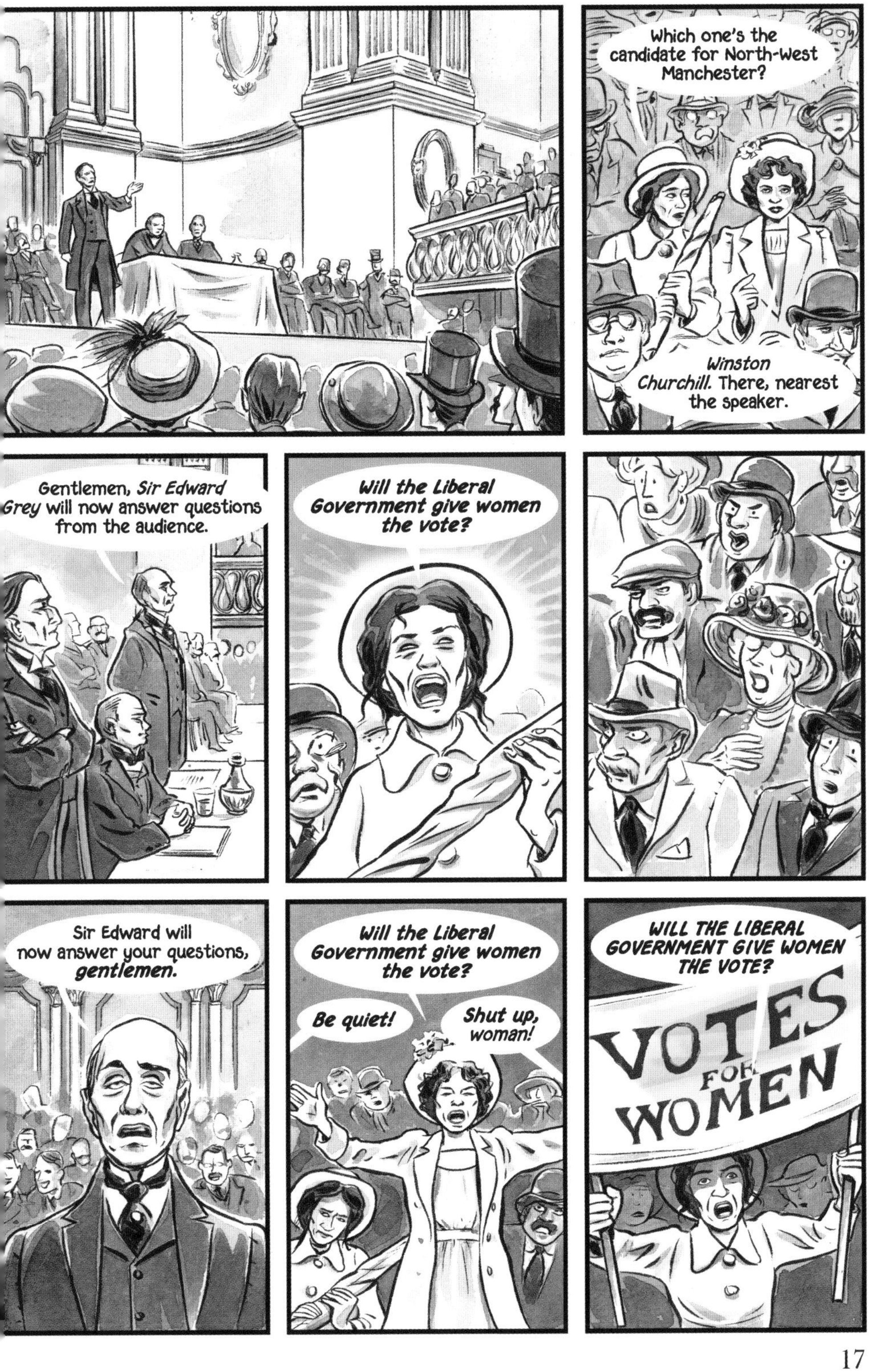
Which one's the candidate for North-West Manchester?
Winston Churchill. There, nearest the speaker.
Gentlemen, *Sir Edward Grey* will now answer questions from the audience.
Will the Liberal Government give women the vote?
Sir Edward will now answer your questions, ***gentlemen.***
Will the Liberal Government give women the vote?
Be quiet!
Shut up, woman!
WILL THE LIBERAL GOVERNMENT GIVE WOMEN THE VOTE?
VOTES FOR WOMEN

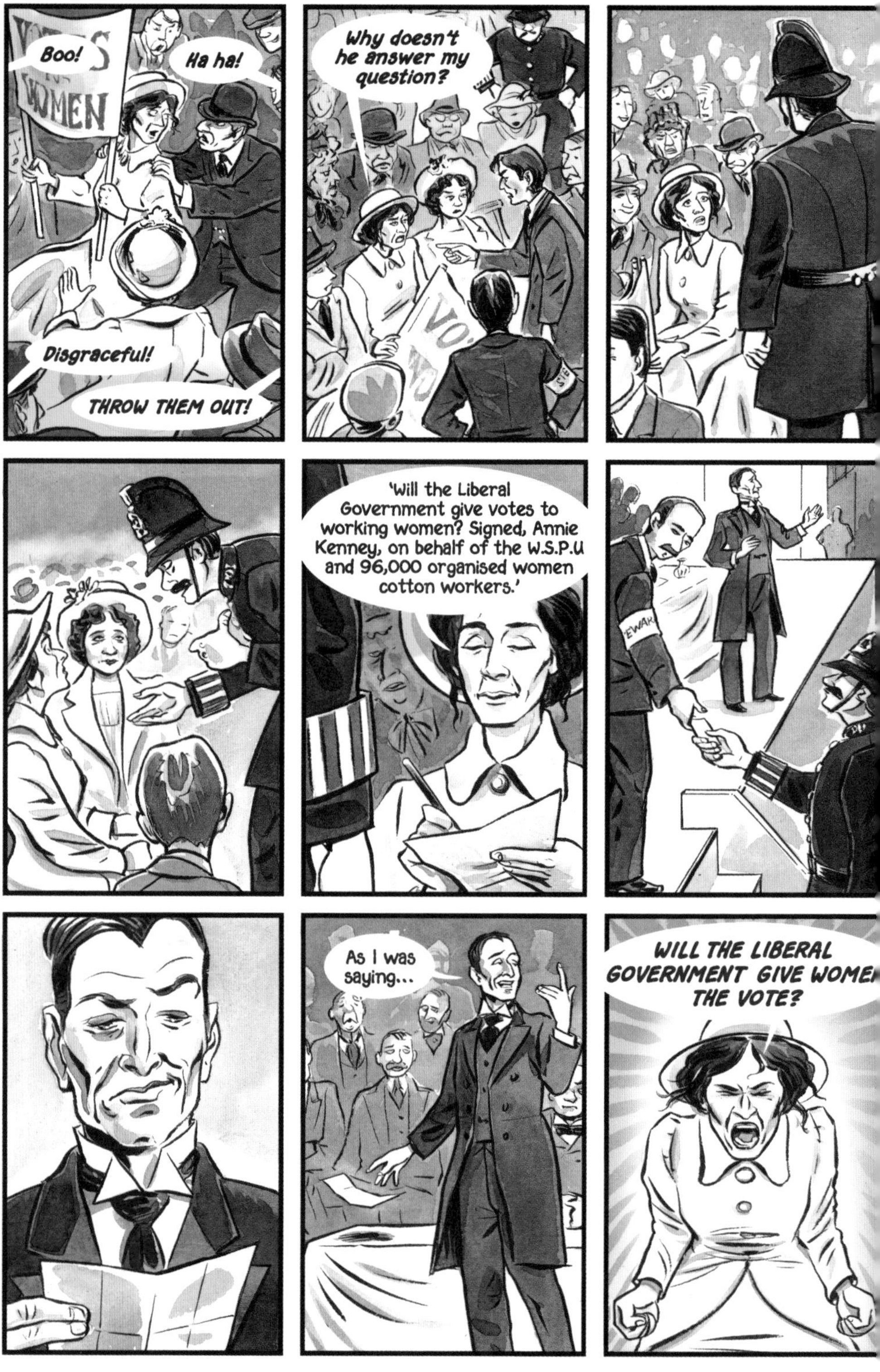
Boo!
Ha ha!
Disgraceful!
THROW THEM OUT!
Why doesn't he answer my question?
'Will the Liberal Government give votes to working women? Signed, Annie Kenney, on behalf of the W.S.P.U and 96,000 organised women cotton workers.'
As I was saying...
WILL THE LIBERAL GOVERNMENT GIVE WOMEN THE VOTE?

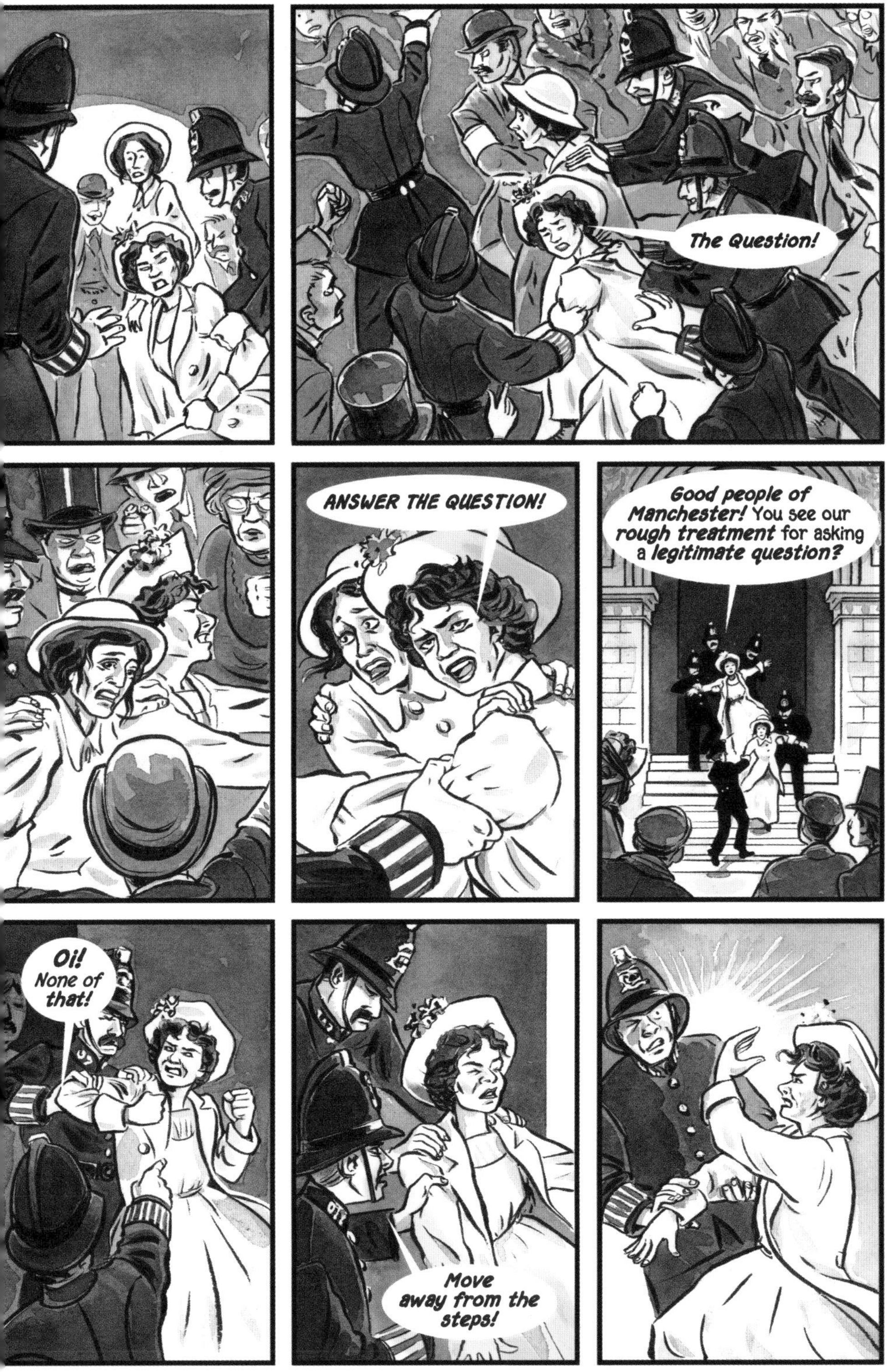
The Question!
ANSWER THE QUESTION!
Good people of Manchester! You see our rough treatment for asking a legitimate question?
Oi! None of that!
Move away from the steps!

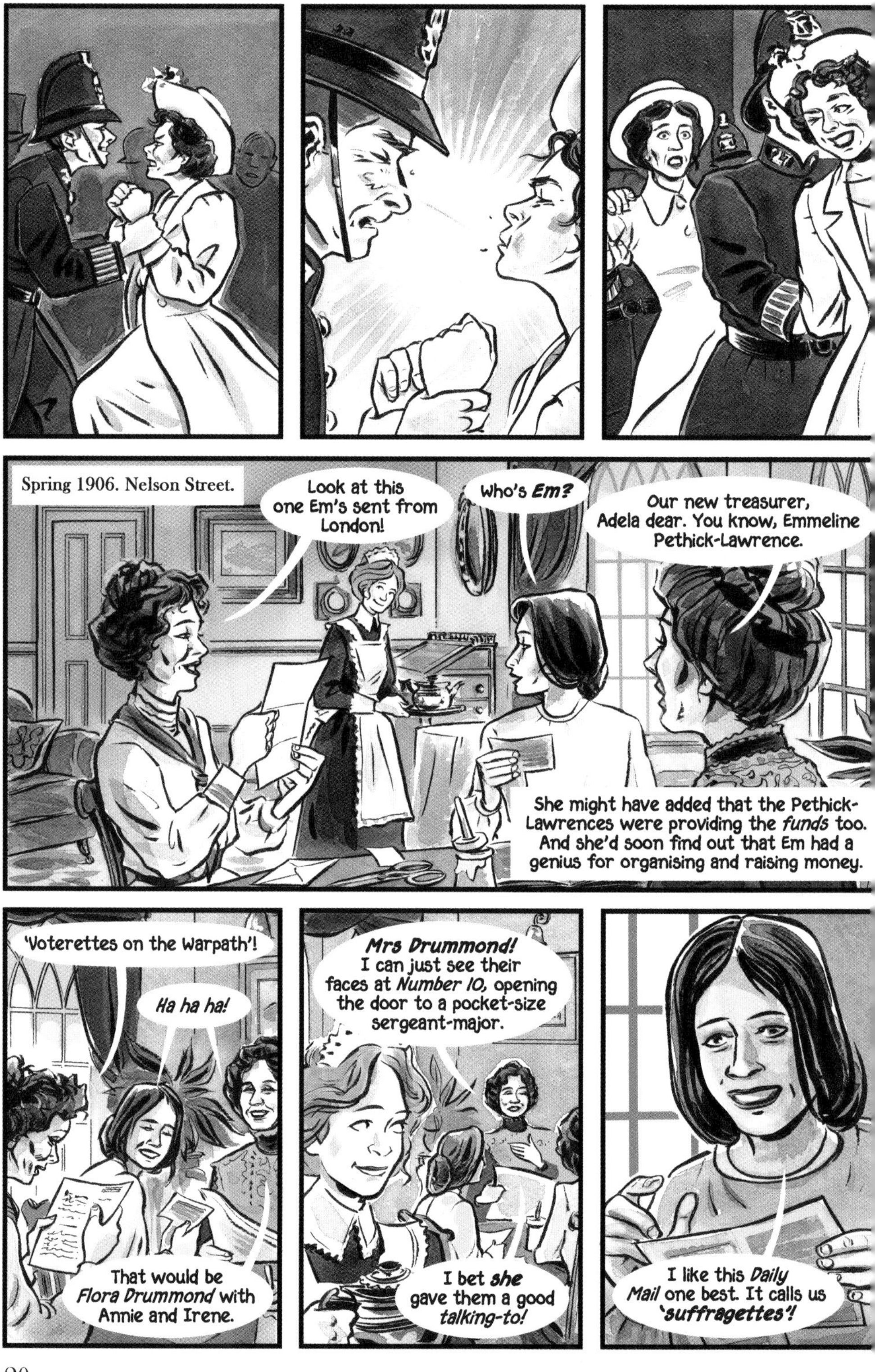
Spring 1906. Nelson Street.
Look at this one Em's sent from London!
Who's *Em?*
Our new treasurer, Adela dear. You know, Emmeline Pethick-Lawrence.
She might have added that the Pethick-Lawrences were providing the *funds* too. And she'd soon find out that Em had a genius for organising and raising money.
'Voterettes on the Warpath'!
Ha ha ha!
That would be *Flora Drummond* with Annie and Irene.
Mrs Drummond! I can just see their faces at *Number 10,* opening the door to a pocket-size sergeant-major.
I bet *she* gave them a good *talking-to!*
I like this *Daily Mail* one best. It calls us *'suffragettes'!*

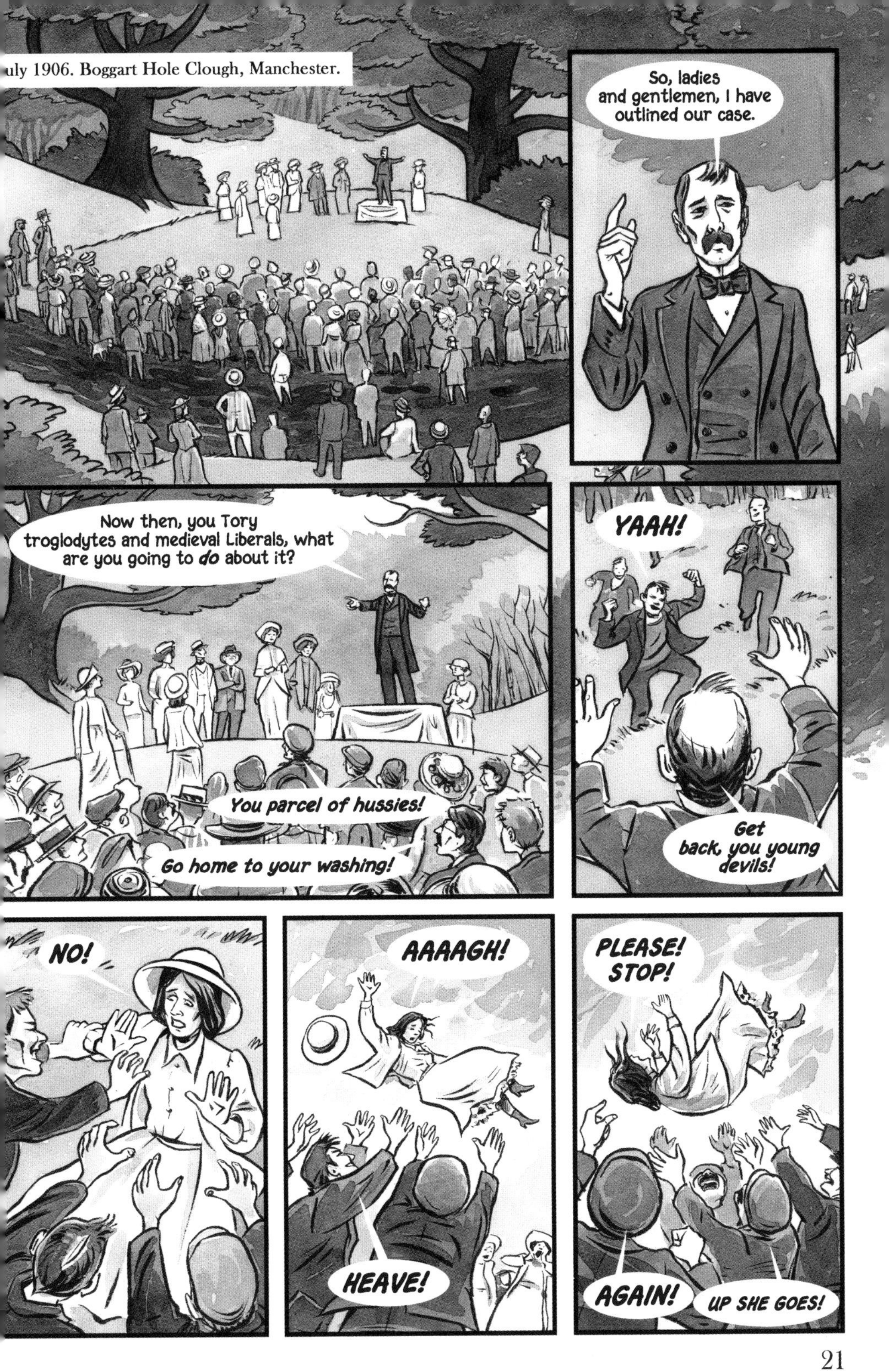
uly 1906. Boggart Hole Clough, Manchester.
So, ladies and gentlemen, I have outlined our case.
Now then, you Tory troglodytes and medieval Liberals, what are you going to *do* about it?
You parcel of hussies!
Go home to your washing!
YAAH!
Get back, you young devils!
NO!
AAAAGH!
HEAVE!
PLEASE! STOP!
AGAIN!
UP SHE GOES!

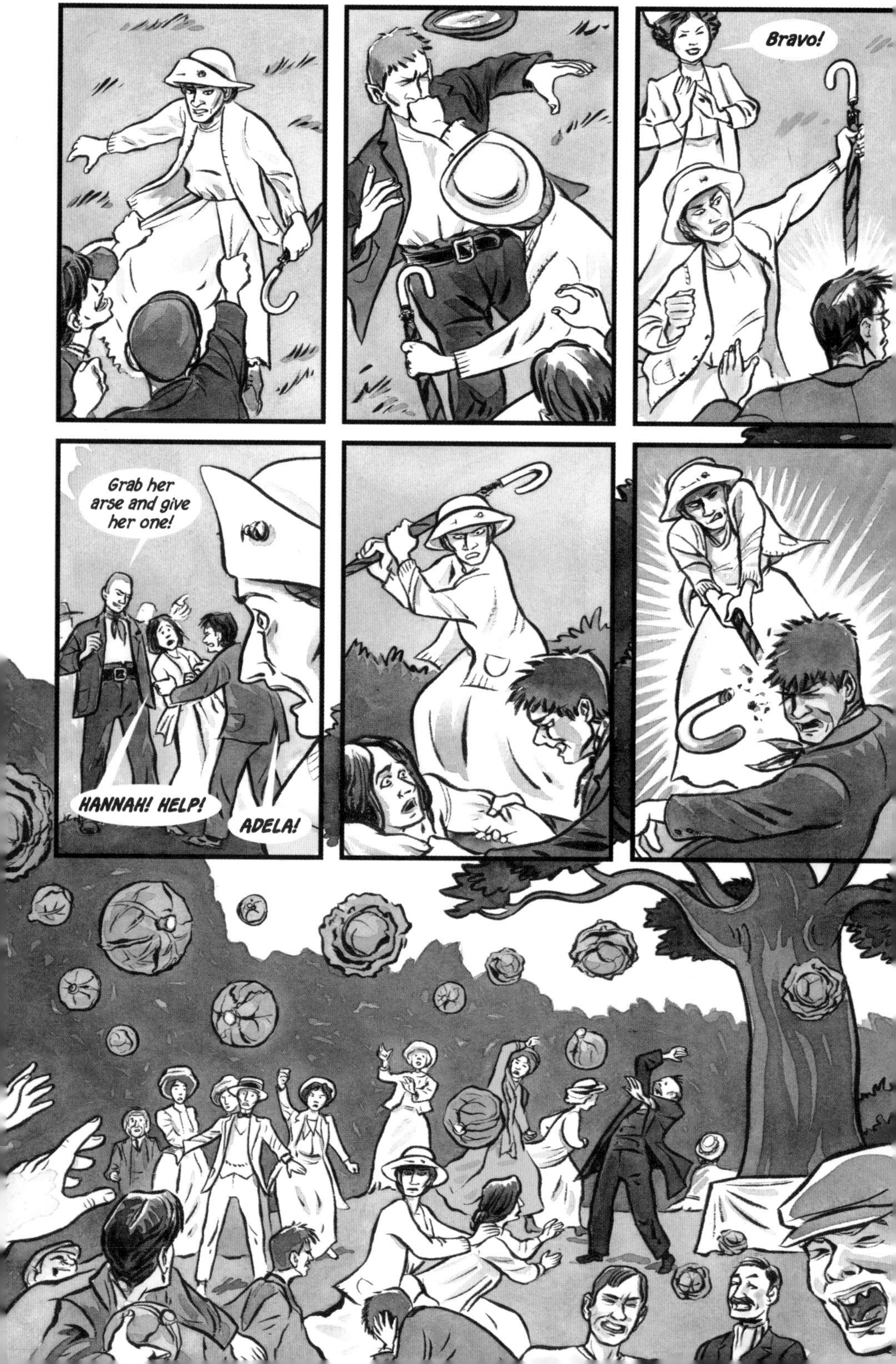
Bravo!
Grab her arse and give her one!
HANNAH! HELP!
ADELA!

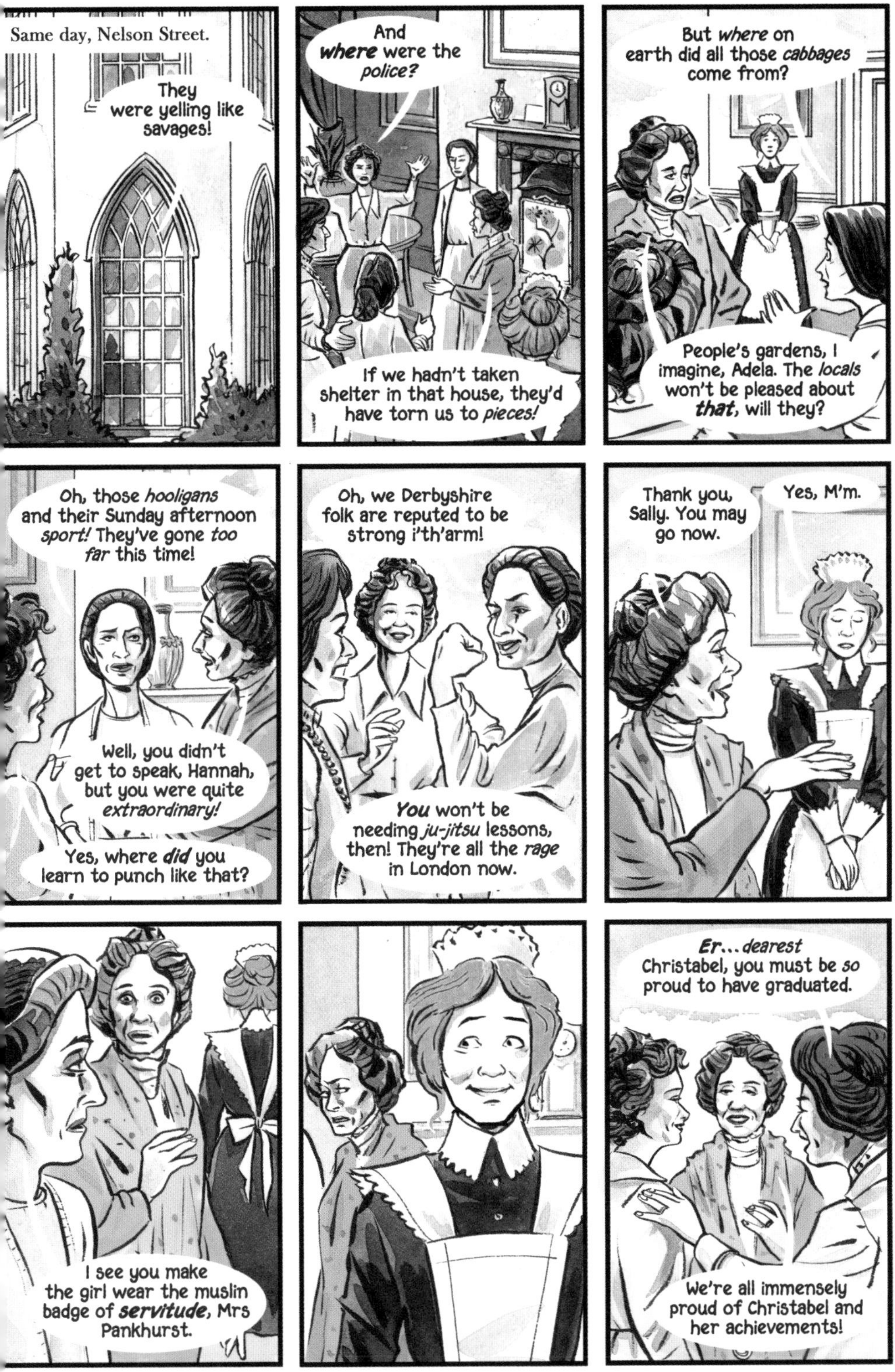
Same day, Nelson Street.
They were yelling like savages!
And *where* were the *police?*
If we hadn't taken shelter in that house, they'd have torn us to *pieces!*
But *where* on earth did all those *cabbages* come from?
People's gardens, I imagine, Adela. The *locals* won't be pleased about ***that***, will they?
Oh, those *hooligans* and their Sunday afternoon *sport!* They've gone *too far* this time!
Well, you didn't get to speak, Hannah, but you were quite *extraordinary!*
Yes, where *did* you learn to punch like that?
Oh, we Derbyshire folk are reputed to be strong i'th'arm!
You won't be needing *ju-jitsu* lessons, then! They're all the *rage* in London now.
Thank you, Sally. You may go now.
Yes, M'm.
I see you make the girl wear the muslin badge of ***servitude***, Mrs Pankhurst.
Er... dearest Christabel, you must be *so* proud to have graduated.
We're all immensely proud of Christabel and her achievements!

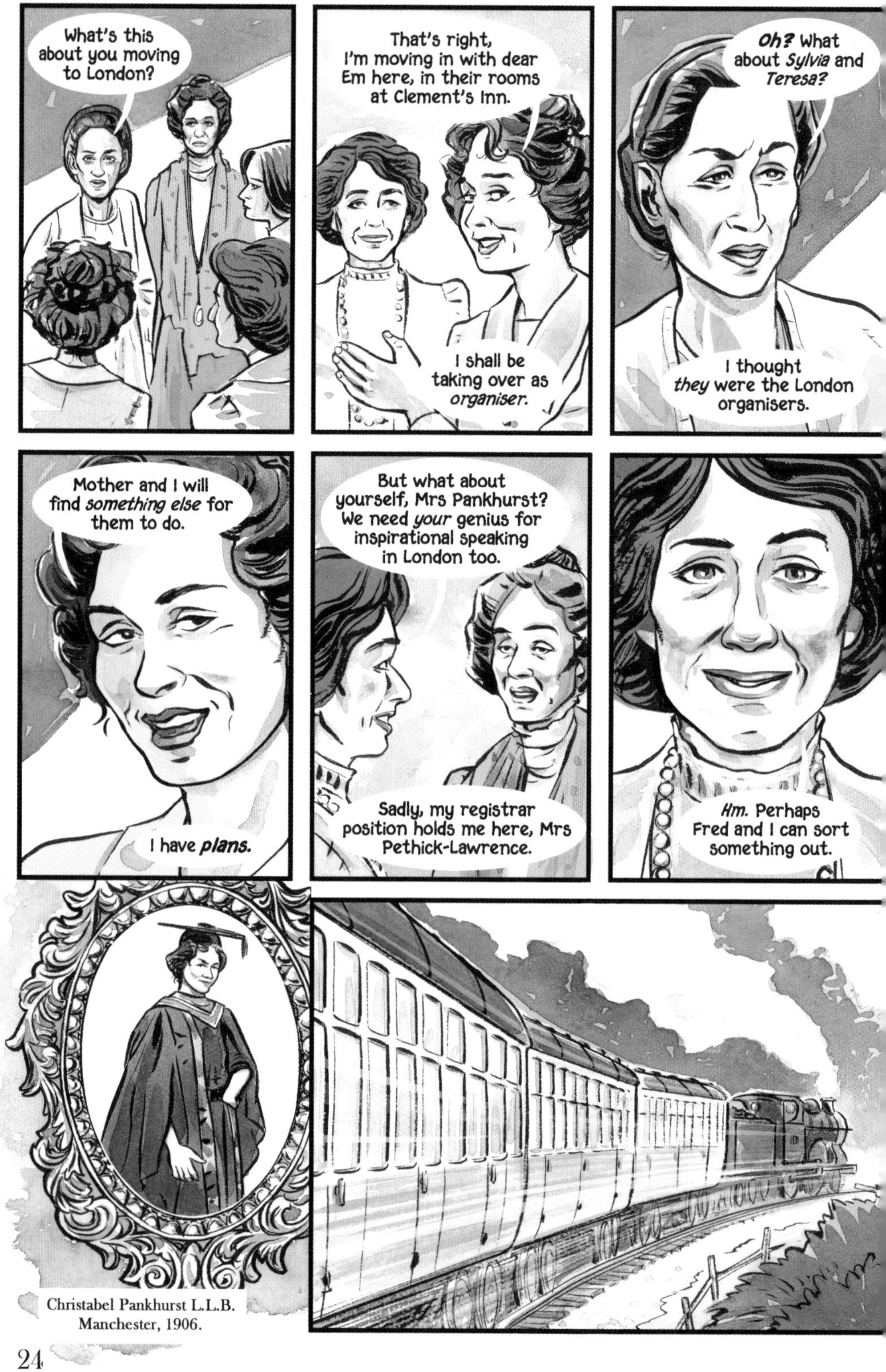
What's this about you moving to London?
That's right, I'm moving in with dear Em here, in their rooms at Clement's Inn.
I shall be taking over as *organiser.*
Oh? What about *Sylvia* and *Teresa?*
I thought *they* were the London organisers.
Mother and I will find *something else* for them to do.
I have ***plans.***
But what about yourself, Mrs Pankhurst? We need *your* genius for inspirational speaking in London too.
Sadly, my registrar position holds me here, Mrs Pethick-Lawrence.
Hm. Perhaps Fred and I can sort something out.

Christabel Pankhurst L.L.B.
Manchester, 1906.

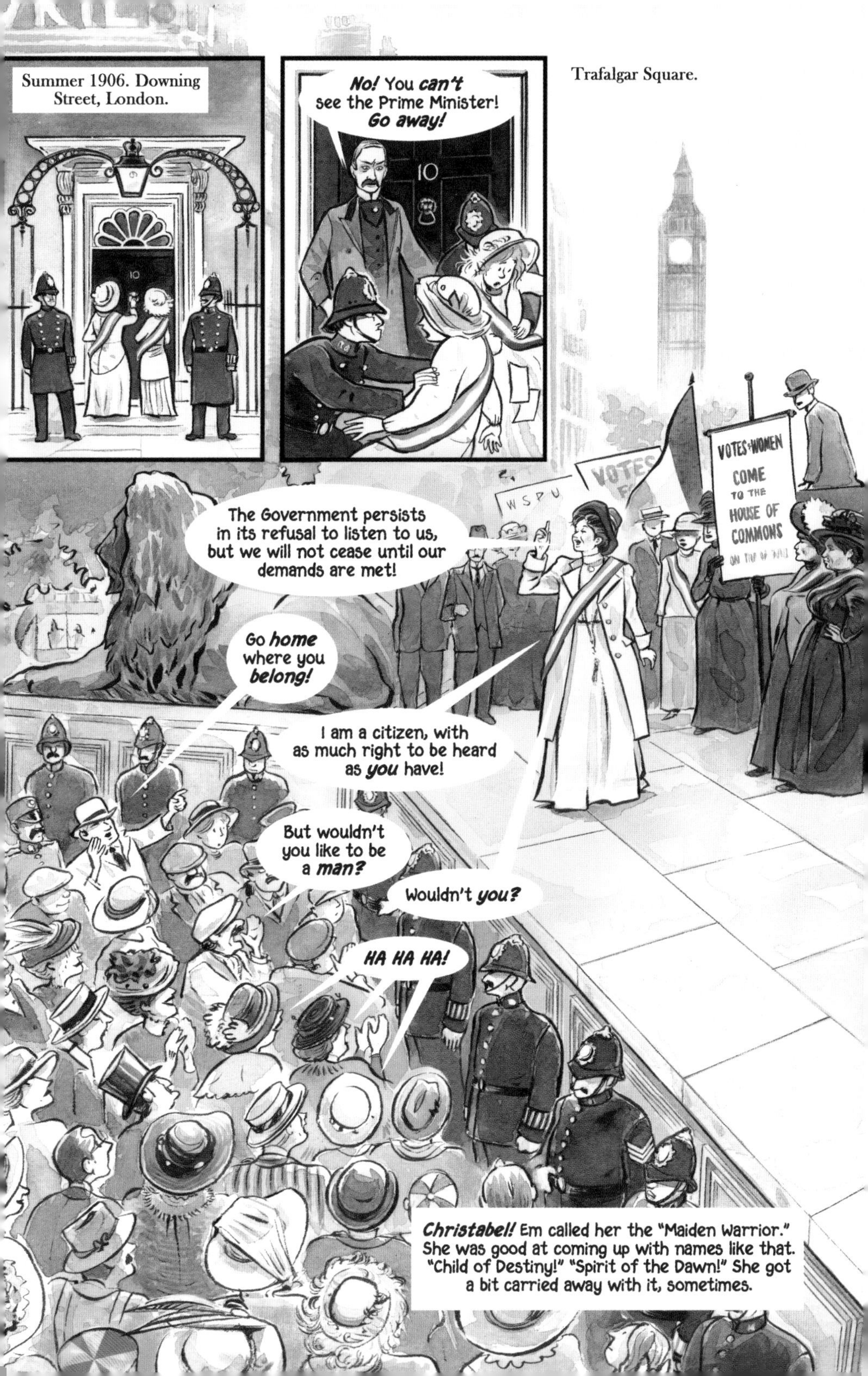
Summer 1906. Downing Street, London.
10
No! You can't see the Prime Minister! Go away!
10
Trafalgar Square.
W S P U
VOTES
VOTES FOR WOMEN
COME TO THE HOUSE OF COMMONS
The Government persists in its refusal to listen to us, but we will not cease until our demands are met!
Go home where you belong!
I am a citizen, with as much right to be heard as you have!
But wouldn't you like to be a man?
Wouldn't you?
HA HA HA!
Christabel! Em called her the "Maiden Warrior." She was good at coming up with names like that. "Child of Destiny!" "Spirit of the Dawn!" She got a bit carried away with it, sometimes.

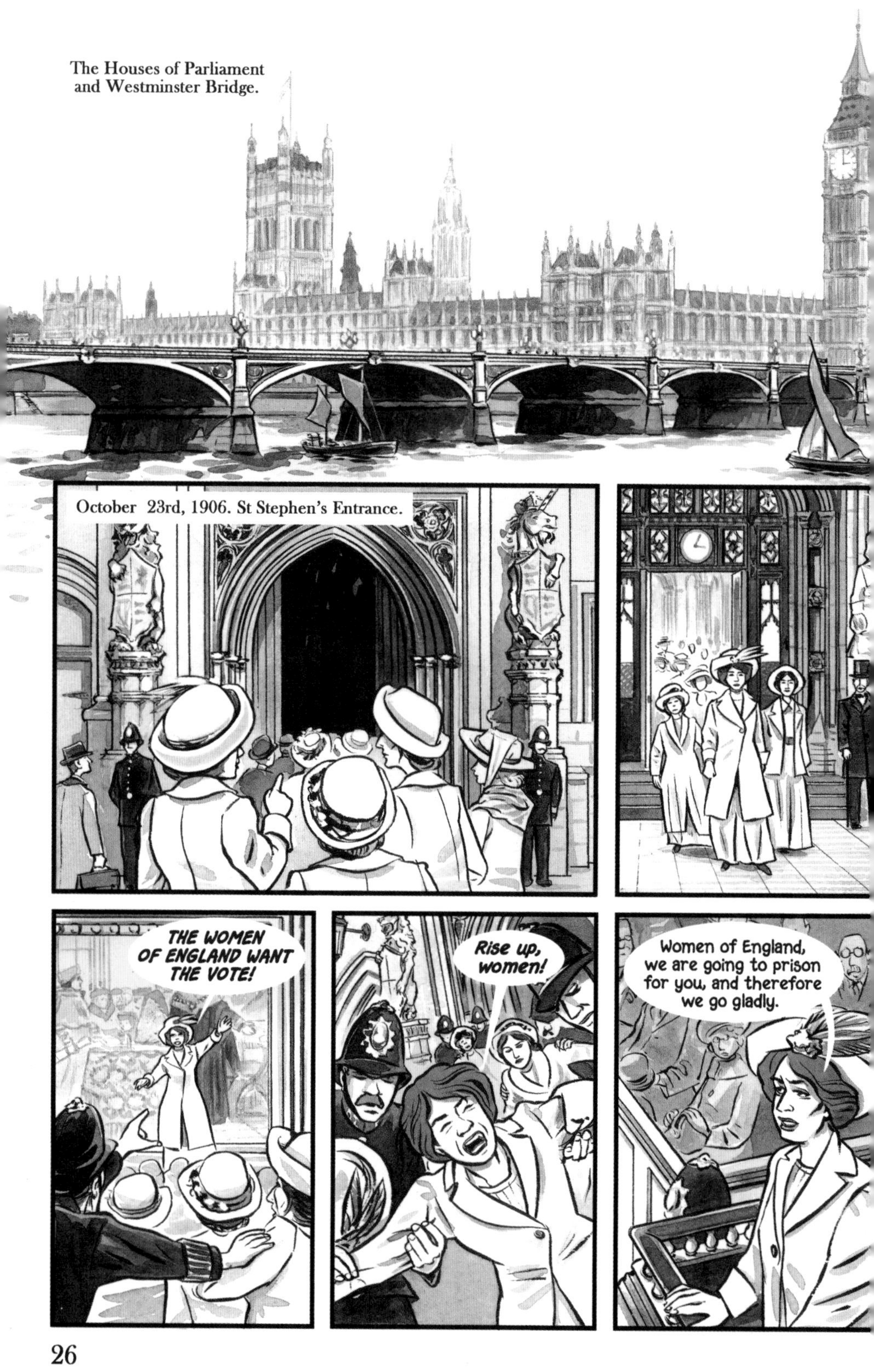
The Houses of Parliament
and Westminster Bridge.
October 23rd, 1906. St Stephen's Entrance.
THE WOMEN OF ENGLAND WANT THE VOTE!
Rise up, women!
Women of England, we are going to prison for you, and therefore we go gladly.

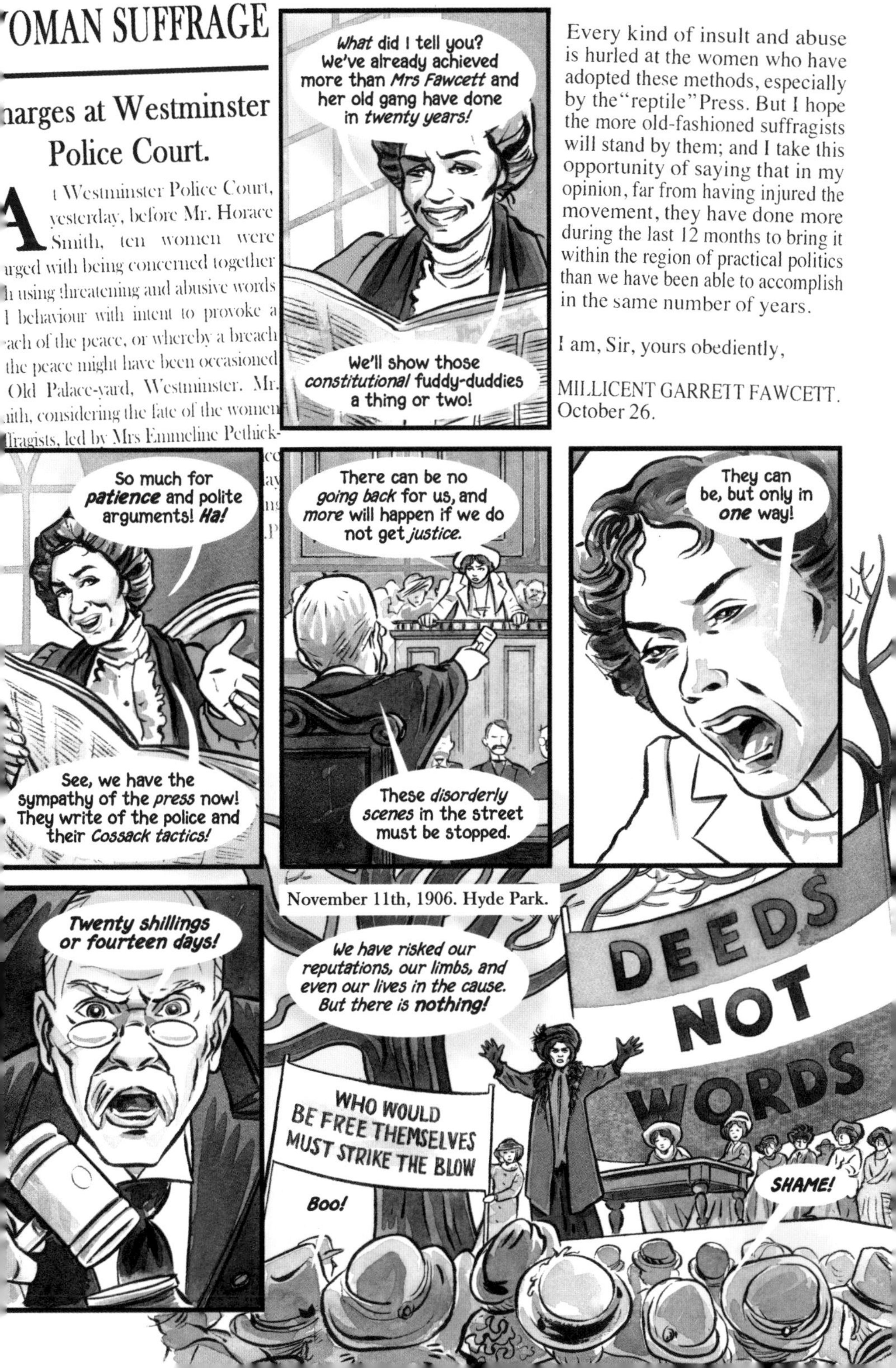

OMAN SUFFRAGE
harges at Westminster
Police Court.
A t Westminster Police Court, yesterday, before Mr. Horace Smith, ten women were
rged with being concerned together
h using threatening and abusive words
l behaviour with intent to provoke a
each of the peace, or whereby a breach
the peace might have been occasioned
Old Palace-yard, Westminster. Mr.
ith, considering the fate of the women
ffragists, led by Mrs Emmeline Pethick-
What did I tell you? We've already achieved more than Mrs Fawcett and her old gang have done in twenty years!
We'll show those constitutional fuddy-duddies a thing or two!
Every kind of insult and abuse is hurled at the women who have adopted these methods, especially by the "reptile" Press. But I hope the more old-fashioned suffragists will stand by them; and I take this opportunity of saying that in my opinion, far from having injured the movement, they have done more during the last 12 months to bring it within the region of practical politics than we have been able to accomplish in the same number of years.
I am, Sir, yours obediently,
MILLICENT GARRETT FAWCETT.
October 26.
So much for patience and polite arguments! Ha!
See, we have the sympathy of the press now! They write of the police and their Cossack tactics!
There can be no going back for us, and more will happen if we do not get justice.
These disorderly scenes in the street must be stopped.
They can be, but only in one way!
Twenty shillings or fourteen days!
November 11th, 1906. Hyde Park.
We have risked our reputations, our limbs, and even our lives in the cause. But there is nothing!
DEEDS NOT WORDS
WHO WOULD BE FREE THEMSELVES MUST STRIKE THE BLOW
Boo!
SHAME!

ENTERTAINMENTS, BALLS, &c.

DINNER TO RELEASED SUFFRAGISTS

A complimentary dinner to the woman suffragists recently released from Holloway Gaol was given at the Savoy Hotel last night. Mrs. Fawcett presided, and all the released prisoners, with the exception of Mrs. Pethick Lawrence were present. The company, numbering about 250, also included Mr. and Mrs George Bernard Shaw, Sir Charles

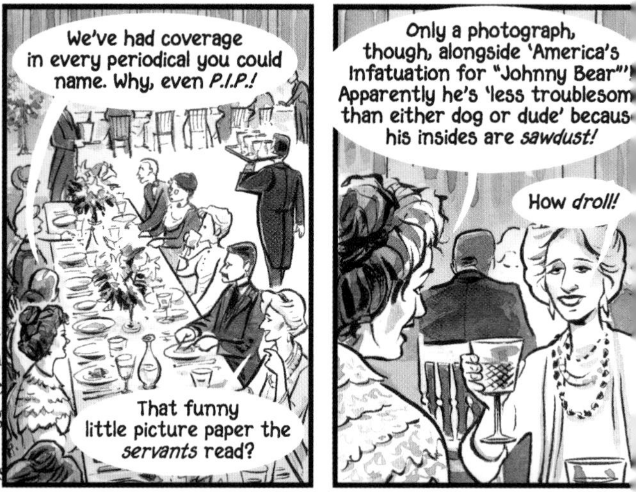
We've had coverage in every periodical you could name. Why, even *P.I.P.!*
That funny little picture paper the *servants* read?
Only a photograph, though, alongside 'America's Infatuation for "Johnny Bear"'! Apparently he's 'less troublesom than either dog or dude' becaus his insides are *sawdust!*
How *droll!*

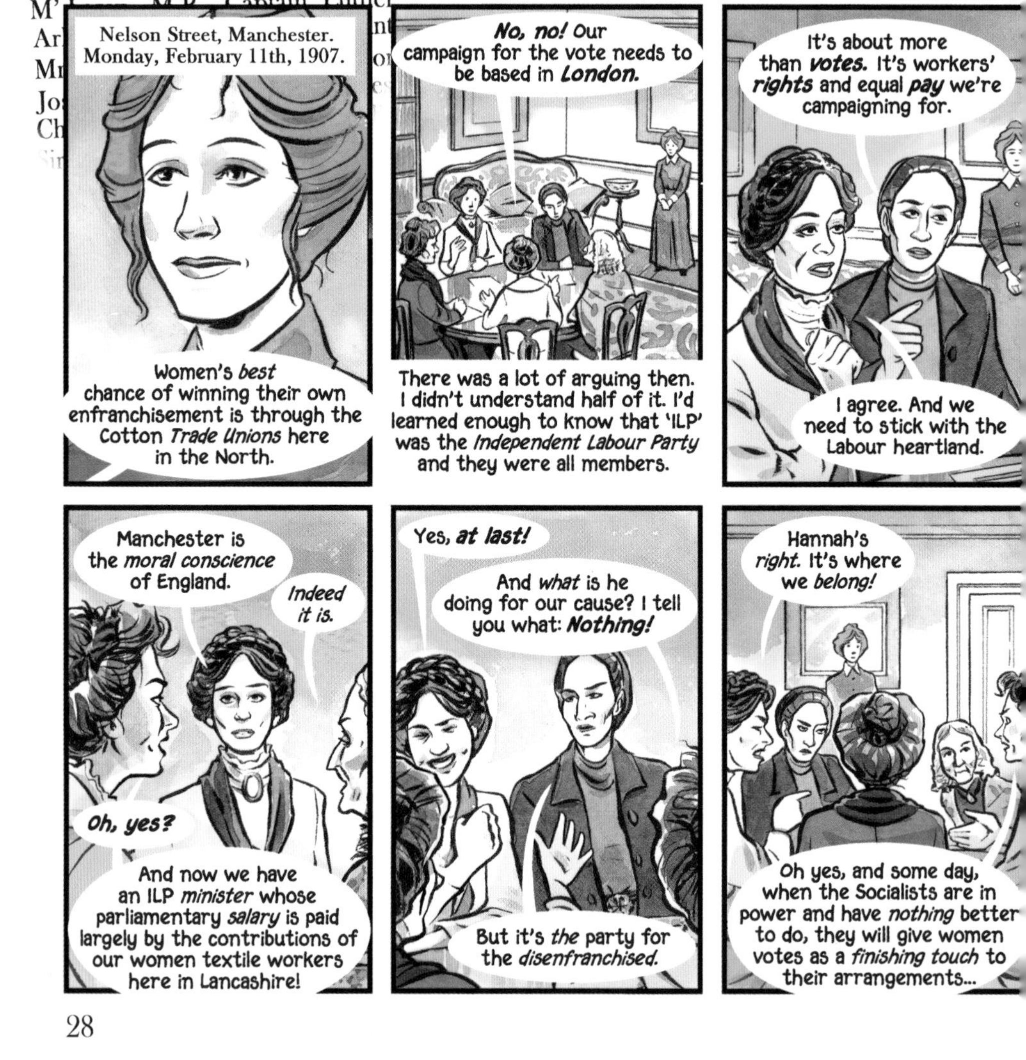
Nelson Street, Manchester. Monday, February 11th, 1907.
Women's *best* chance of winning their own enfranchisement is through the Cotton *Trade Unions* here in the North.
No, no! Our campaign for the vote needs to be based in *London.*
There was a lot of arguing then. I didn't understand half of it. I'd learned enough to know that 'ILP' was the *Independent Labour Party* and they were all members.
It's about more than *votes.* It's workers' *rights* and equal *pay* we're campaigning for.
I agree. And we need to stick with the Labour heartland.
Manchester is the *moral conscience* of England.
Indeed it is.
Oh, yes?
And now we have an ILP *minister* whose parliamentary *salary* is paid largely by the contributions of our women textile workers here in Lancashire!
Yes, *at last!*
And *what* is he doing for our cause? I tell you what: *Nothing!*
But it's *the* party for the *disenfranchised.*
Hannah's *right.* It's where we *belong!*
Oh yes, and some day, when the Socialists are in power and have *nothing* better to do, they will give women votes as a *finishing touch* to their arrangements...

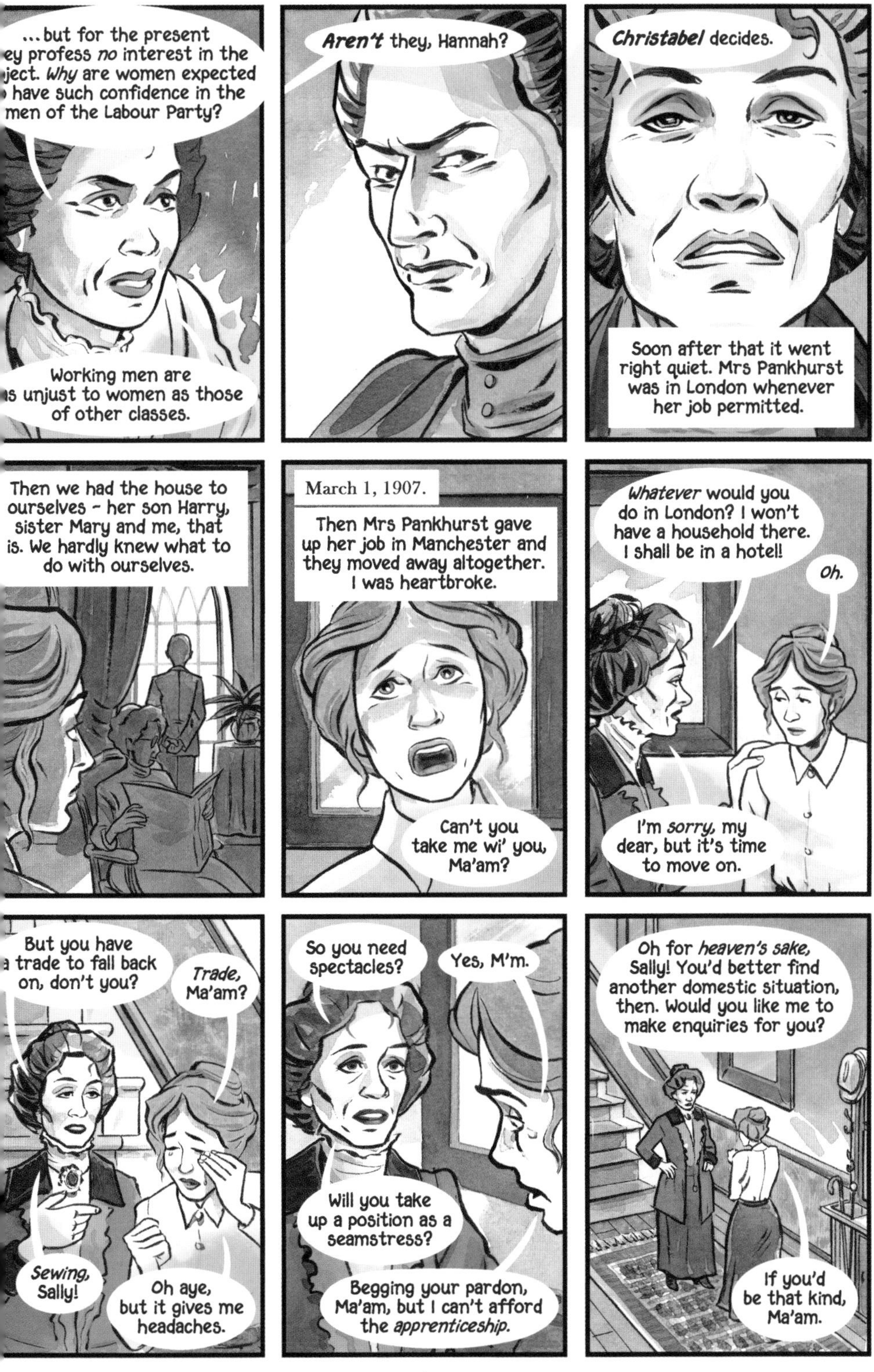
...but for the present
ey profess *no* interest in the
ject. *Why* are women expected
have such confidence in the
men of the Labour Party?
Working men are
is unjust to women as those
of other classes.
Aren't they, Hannah?
Christabel decides.
Soon after that it went
right quiet. Mrs Pankhurst
was in London whenever
her job permitted.
Then we had the house to
ourselves - her son Harry,
sister Mary and me, that
is. We hardly knew what to
do with ourselves.
March 1, 1907.
Then Mrs Pankhurst gave
up her job in Manchester and
they moved away altogether.
I was heartbroke.
Can't you
take me wi' you,
Ma'am?
Whatever would you
do in London? I won't
have a household there.
I shall be in a hotel!
Oh.
I'm *sorry*, my
dear, but it's time
to move on.
But you have
a trade to fall back
on, don't you?
Trade,
Ma'am?
Sewing,
Sally!
Oh aye,
but it gives me
headaches.
So you need
spectacles?
Yes, M'm.
Will you take
up a position as a
seamstress?
Begging your pardon,
Ma'am, but I can't afford
the *apprenticeship.*
Oh for *heaven's sake,*
Sally! You'd better find
another domestic situation,
then. Would you like me to
make enquiries for you?
If you'd
be that kind,
Ma'am.

Summer 1907. Huddersfield.

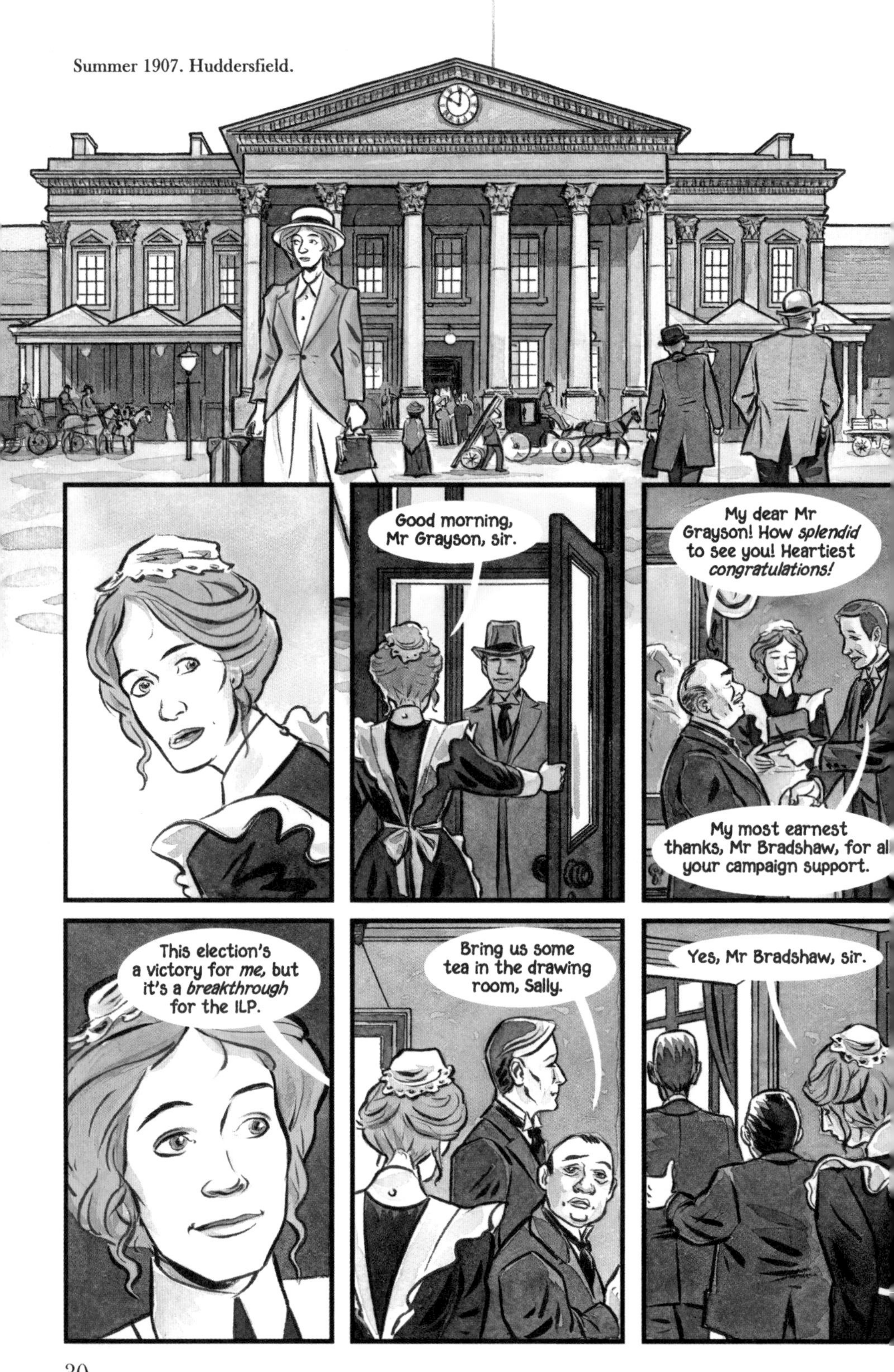
Good morning, Mr Grayson, sir.
My dear Mr Grayson! How *splendid* to see you! Heartiest *congratulations!*
My most earnest thanks, Mr Bradshaw, for all your campaign support.
This election's a victory for *me*, but it's a *breakthrough* for the ILP.
Bring us some tea in the drawing room, Sally.
Yes, Mr Bradshaw, sir.

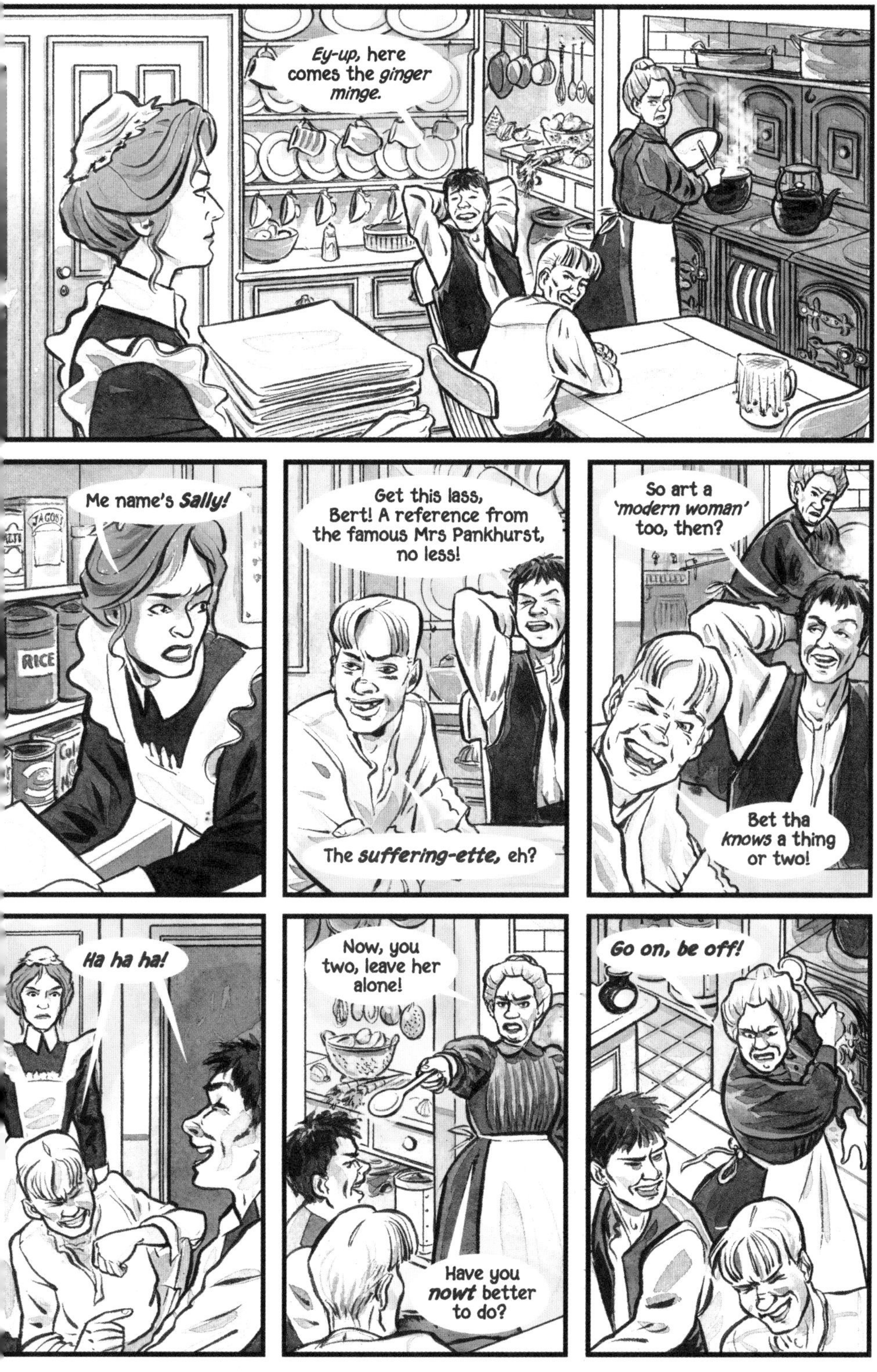
Ey-up, here comes the ginger minge.
Me name's Sally!
Get this lass, Bert! A reference from the famous Mrs Pankhurst, no less!
The suffering-ette, eh?
So art a 'modern woman' too, then?
Bet tha knows a thing or two!
Ha ha ha!
Now, you two, leave her alone!
Have you nowt better to do?
Go on, be off!

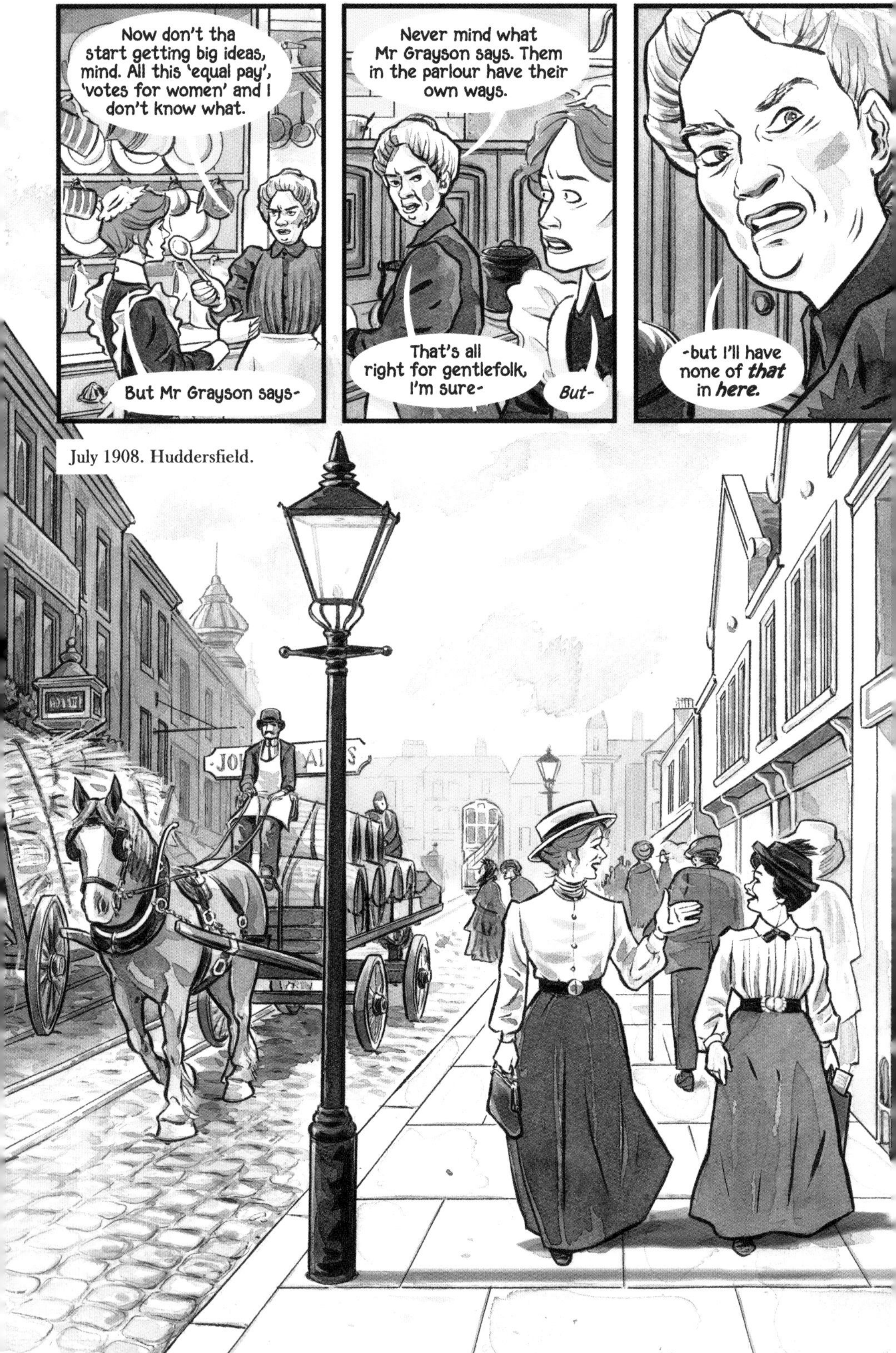
Now don't tha start getting big ideas, mind. All this 'equal pay', 'votes for women' and I don't know what.
But Mr Grayson says-
Never mind what Mr Grayson says. Them in the parlour have their own ways.
That's all right for gentlefolk, I'm sure-
But-
-but I'll have none of *that* in *here.*
July 1908. Huddersfield.

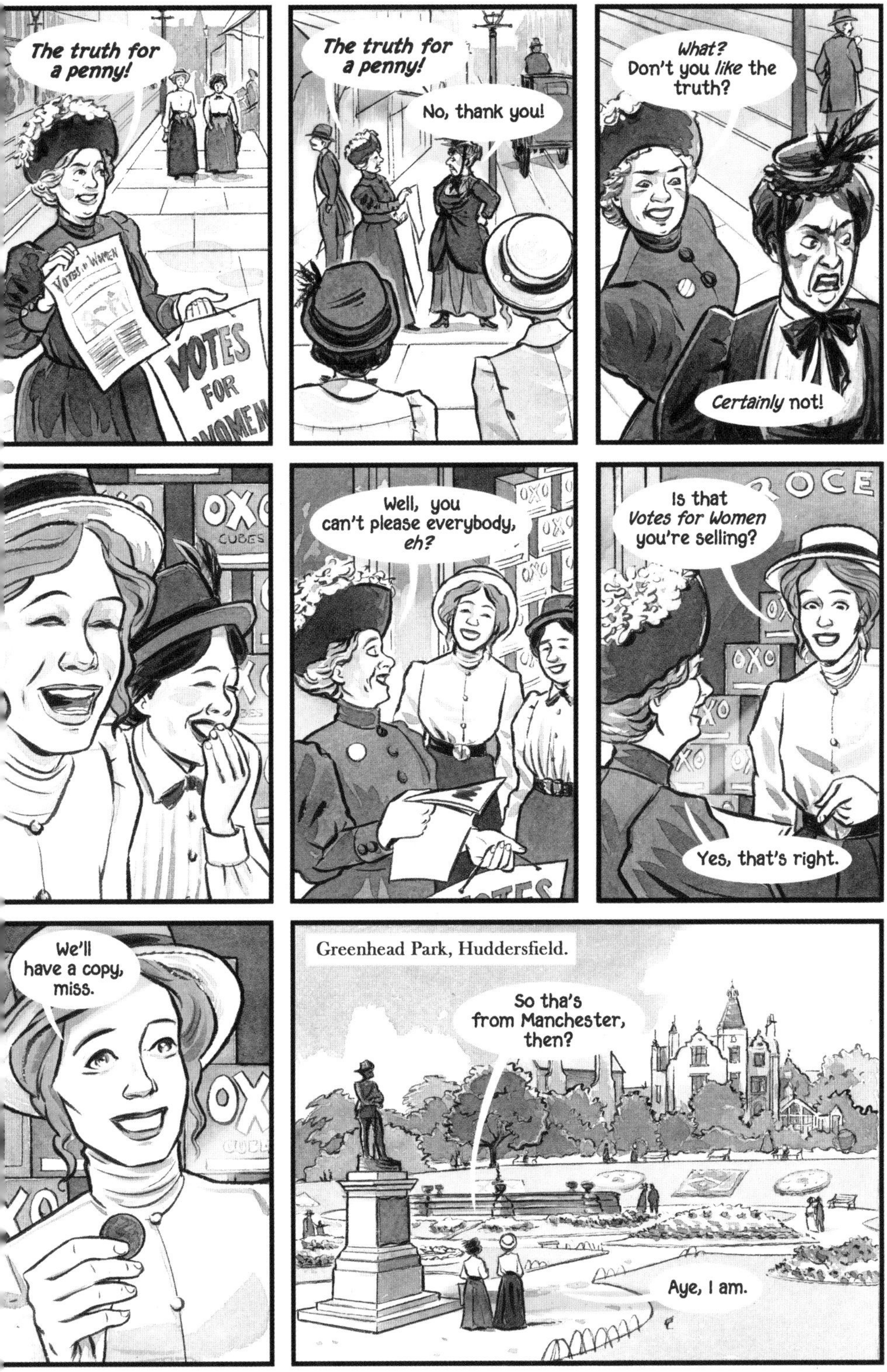
The truth for a penny!
VOTES FOR WOMEN
VOTES FOR WOMEN
The truth for a penny!
No, thank you!
What? Don't you *like* the truth?
Certainly not!
OXO CUBES
Well, you can't please everybody, *eh?*
Is that *Votes for Women* you're selling?
Yes, that's right.
We'll have a copy, miss.
Greenhead Park, Huddersfield.
So tha's from Manchester, then?
Aye, I am.

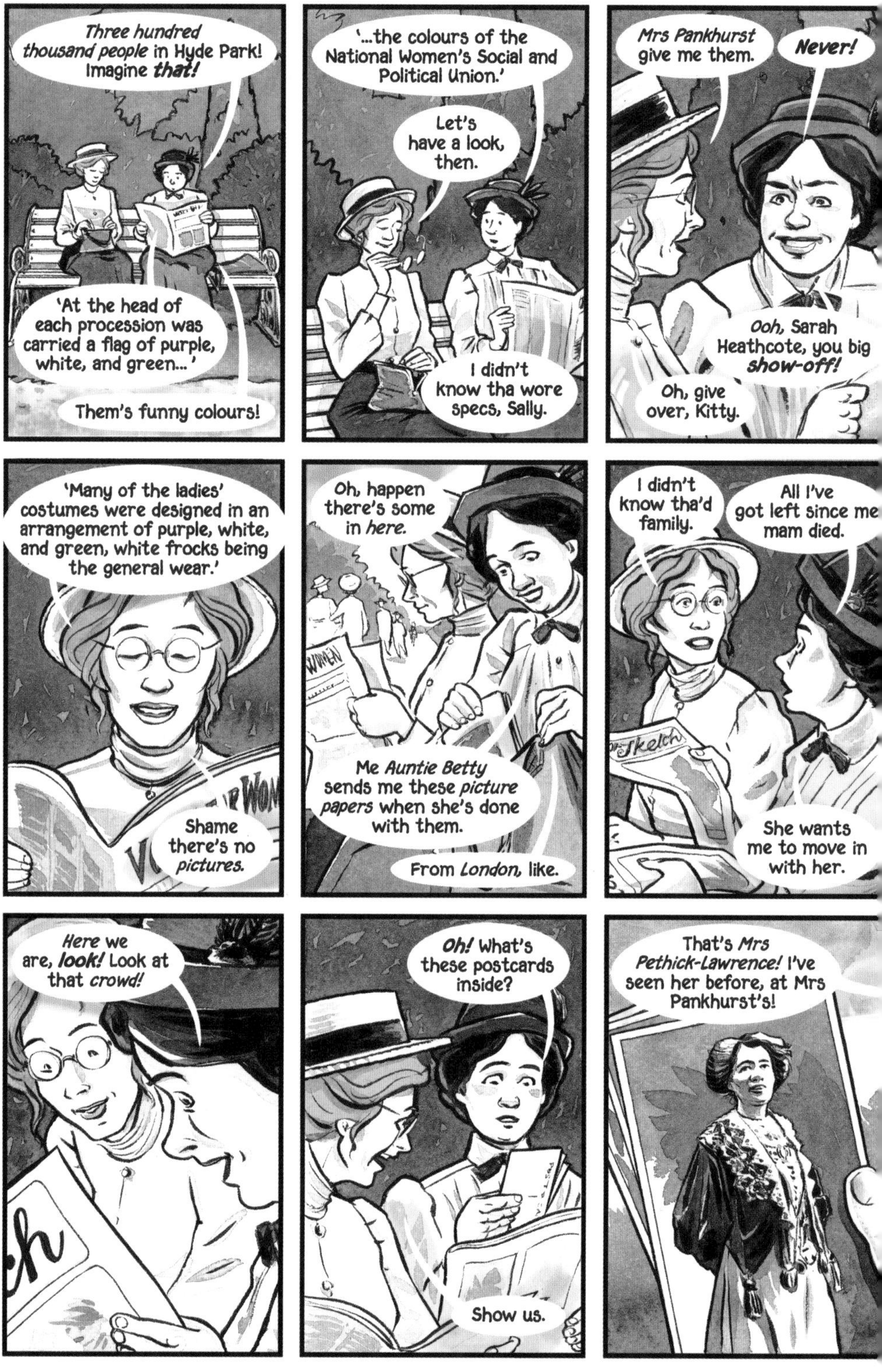
Three hundred thousand people in Hyde Park! Imagine that!
'At the head of each procession was carried a flag of purple, white, and green...'
Them's funny colours!
'...the colours of the National Women's Social and Political Union.'
Let's have a look, then.
I didn't know tha wore specs, Sally.
Mrs Pankhurst give me them.
Never!
Ooh, Sarah Heathcote, you big show-off!
Oh, give over, Kitty.
'Many of the ladies' costumes were designed in an arrangement of purple, white, and green, white frocks being the general wear.'
Shame there's no pictures.
Oh, happen there's some in here.
Me Auntie Betty sends me these picture papers when she's done with them.
From London, like.
I didn't know tha'd family.
All I've got left since me mam died.
She wants me to move in with her.
Here we are, look! Look at that crowd!
Oh! What's these postcards inside?
Show us.
That's Mrs Pethick-Lawrence! I've seen her before, at Mrs Pankhurst's!

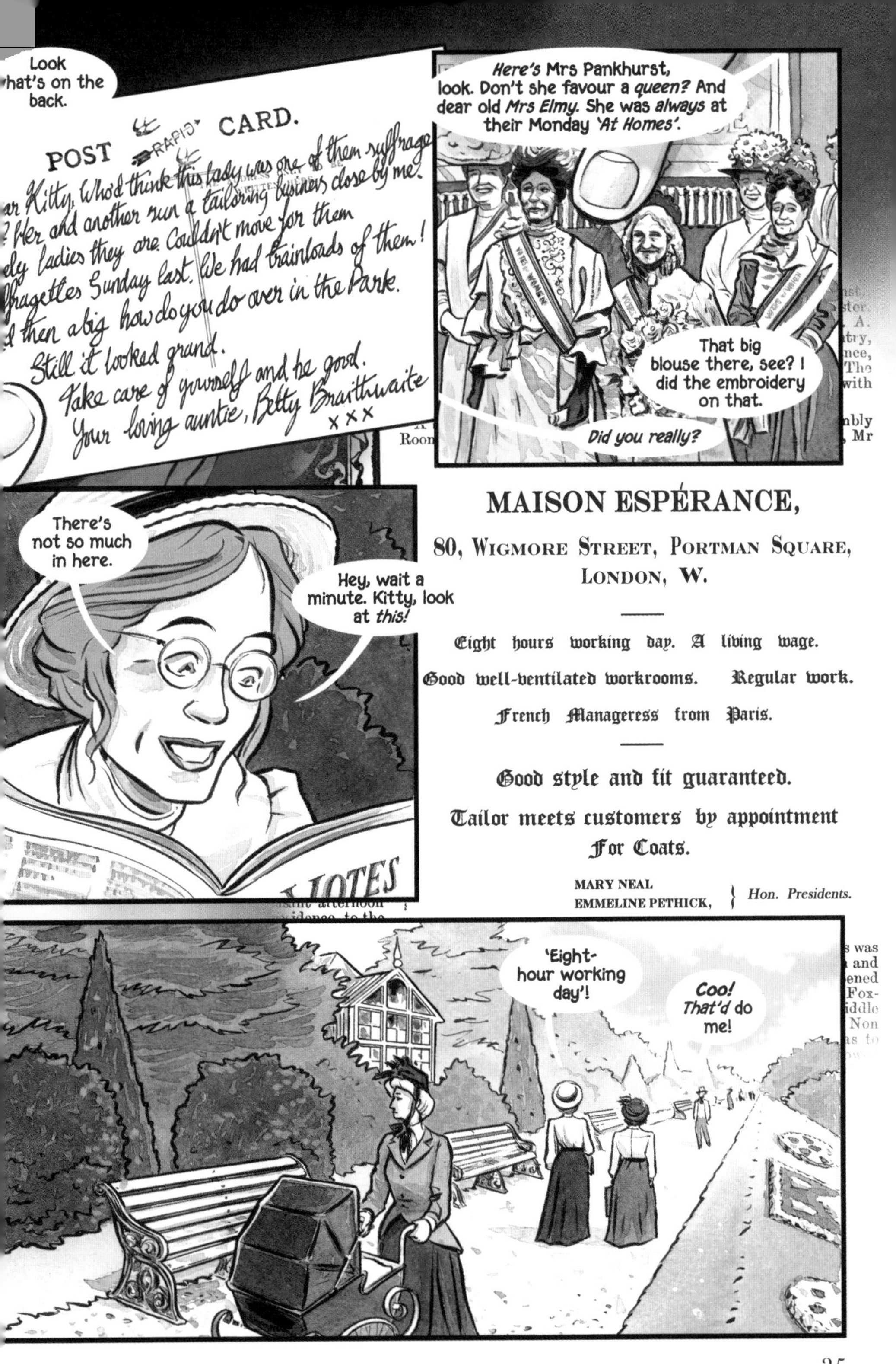
Look
what's on the back.
POST CARD.
ar Kitty, Who'd think this lady was one of them suffrag
? Her and another run a tailoring business close by me.
ly ladies they are. Couldn't move for them
ffragettes Sunday last. We had trainloads of them!
l then a big how do you do over in the Park.
Still it looked grand.
Take care of yourself and be good.
Your loving auntie, Betty Braithwaite
xxx
Here's Mrs Pankhurst, look. Don't she favour a *queen?* And dear old *Mrs Elmy*. She was *always* at their Monday *'At Homes'*.
That big blouse there, see? I did the embroidery on that.
Did you really?
There's not so much in here.
Hey, wait a minute. Kitty, look at *this!*
MAISON ESPÉRANCE,
80, WIGMORE STREET, PORTMAN SQUARE, LONDON, W.
Eight hours working day. A living wage.
Good well-ventilated workrooms. Regular work.
French Manageress from Paris.
Good style and fit guaranteed.
Tailor meets customers by appointment For Coats.
MARY NEAL, EMMELINE PETHICK, } *Hon. Presidents.*
'Eight-hour working day'!
Coo! That'd do me!

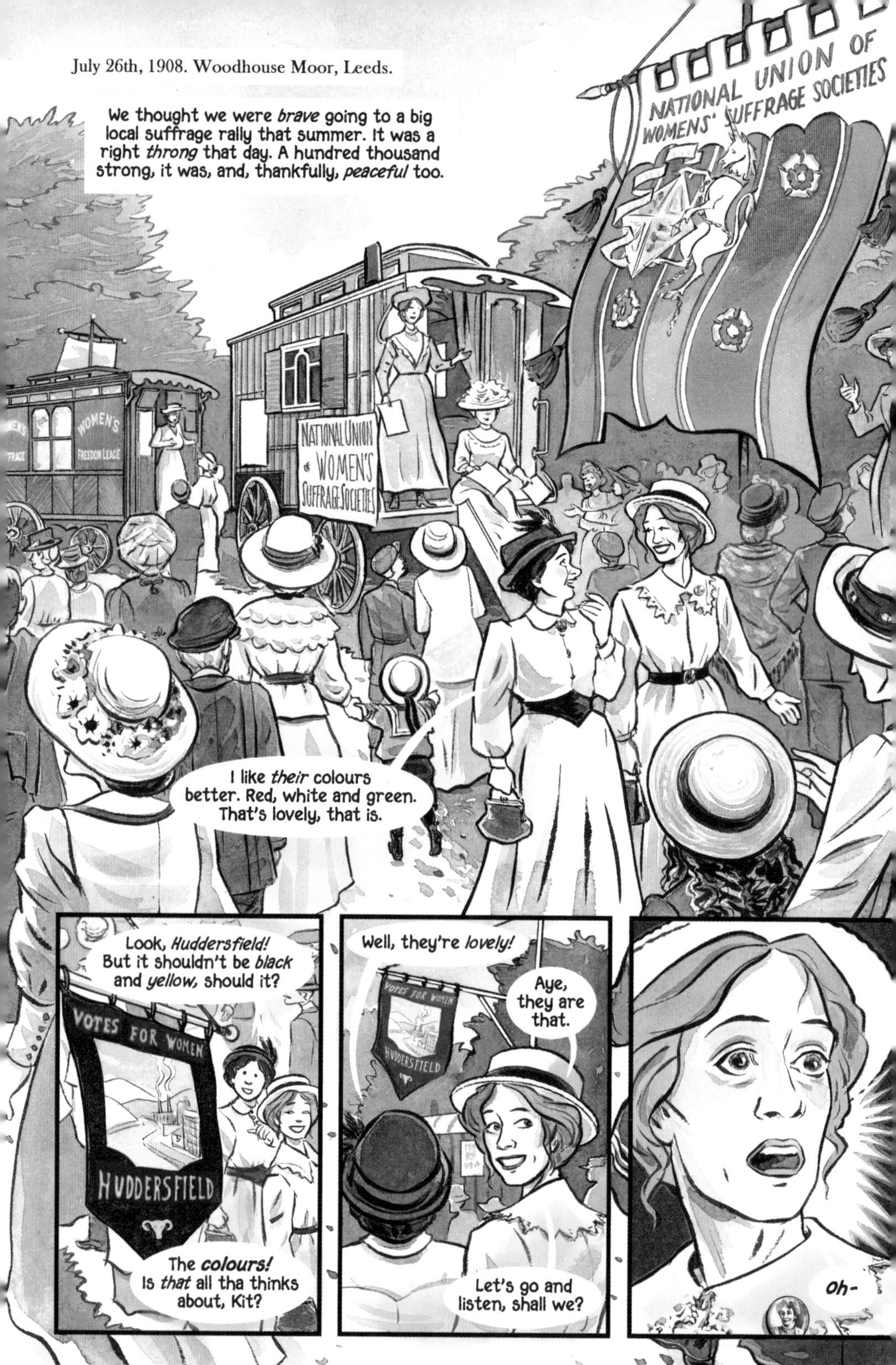
July 26th, 1908. Woodhouse Moor, Leeds.
We thought we were *brave* going to a big local suffrage rally that summer. It was a right *throng* that day. A hundred thousand strong, it was, and, thankfully, *peaceful* too.
NATIONAL UNION OF WOMENS' SUFFRAGE SOCIETIES
WOMEN'S FREEDOM LEAGE
NATIONAL UNION of WOMEN'S SUFFRAGE SOCIETIES
I like *their* colours better. Red, white and green. That's lovely, that is.
Look, *Huddersfield!* But it shouldn't be *black* and *yellow,* should it?
VOTES FOR WOMEN
HUDDERSFIELD
The ***colours!*** Is *that* all tha thinks about, Kit?
Well, they're *lovely!*
Aye, they are that.
Let's go and listen, shall we?
Oh-

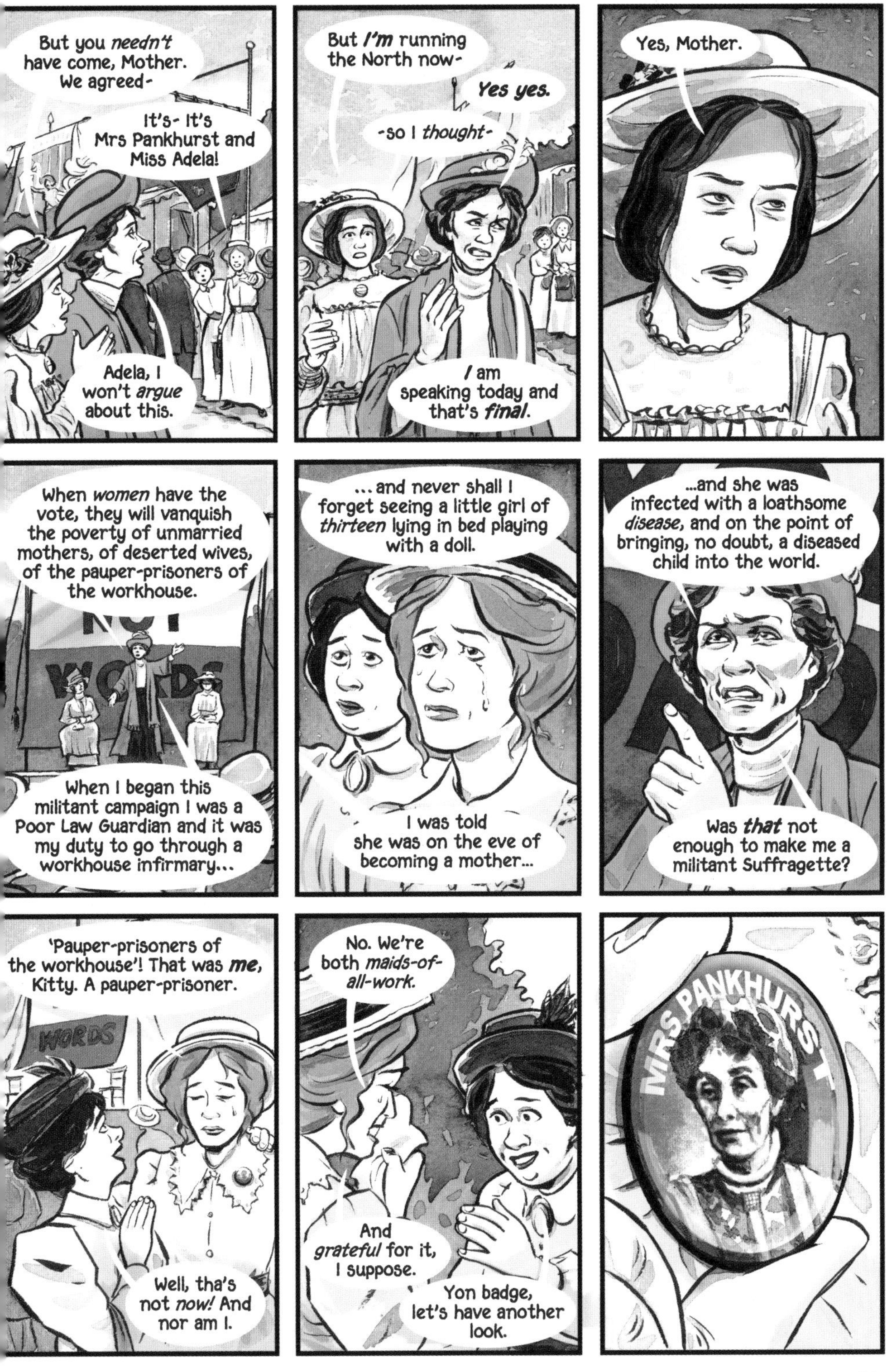

But you *needn't* have come, Mother. We agreed-
It's- It's Mrs Pankhurst and Miss Adela!
Adela, I won't *argue* about this.
But *I'm* running the North now-
Yes yes.
-so I *thought*-
I am speaking today and that's *final*.
Yes, Mother.
When *women* have the vote, they will vanquish the poverty of unmarried mothers, of deserted wives, of the pauper-prisoners of the workhouse.
WORDS
When I began this militant campaign I was a Poor Law Guardian and it was my duty to go through a workhouse infirmary...
...and never shall I forget seeing a little girl of *thirteen* lying in bed playing with a doll.
I was told she was on the eve of becoming a mother...
...and she was infected with a loathsome *disease*, and on the point of bringing, no doubt, a diseased child into the world.
Was *that* not enough to make me a militant Suffragette?
'Pauper-prisoners of the workhouse'! That was *me*, Kitty. A pauper-prisoner.
WORDS
Well, tha's not *now!* And nor am I.
No. We're both *maids-of-all-work*.
And *grateful* for it, I suppose.
Yon badge, let's have another look.
MRS PANKHURST

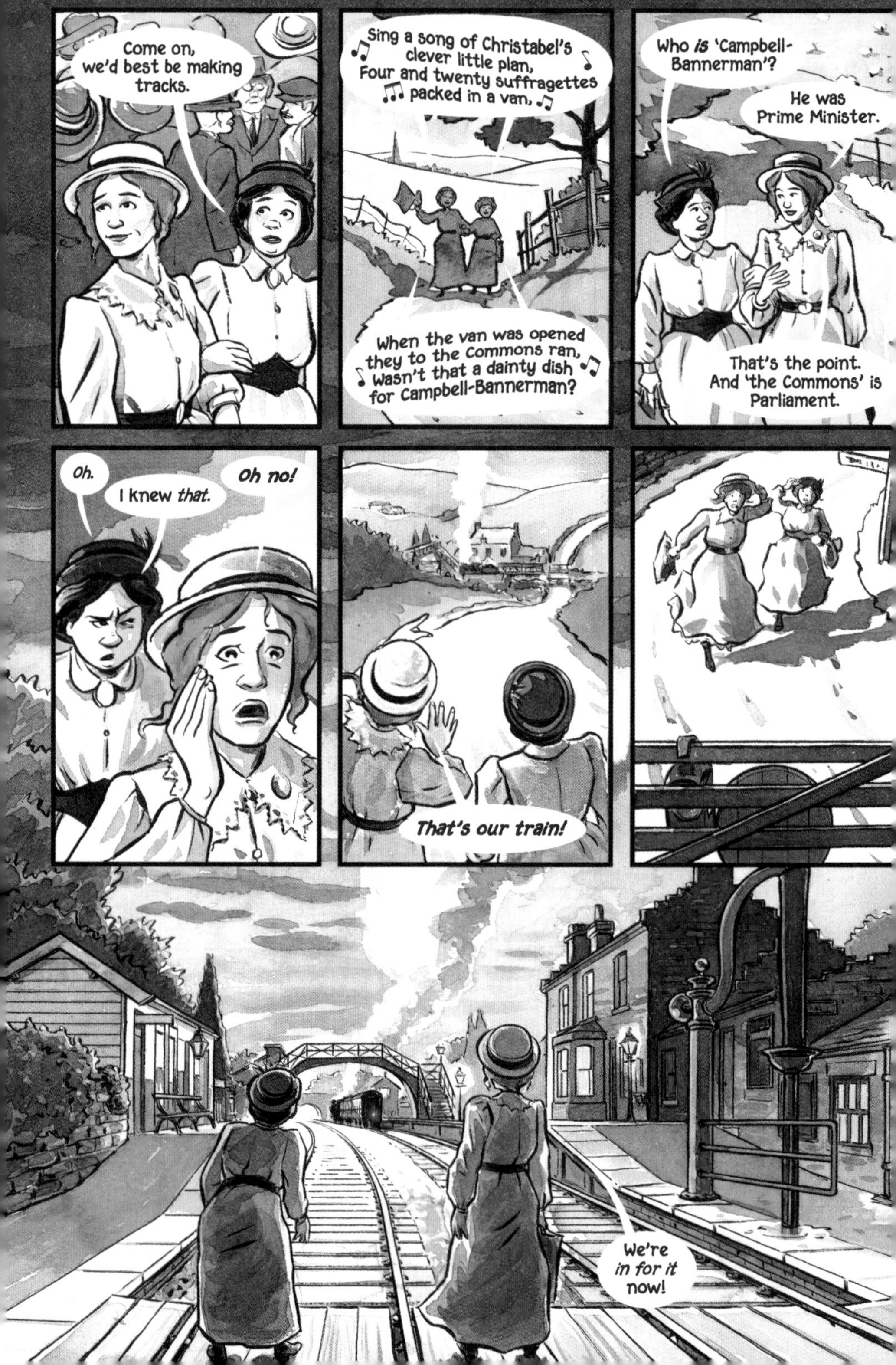
Come on, we'd best be making tracks.
Sing a song of Christabel's clever little plan, Four and twenty suffragettes packed in a van,
When the van was opened they to the Commons ran, Wasn't that a dainty dish for Campbell-Bannerman?
Who *is* 'Campbell-Bannerman'?
He was Prime Minister.
That's the point. And 'the Commons' is Parliament.
Oh.
I knew *that.*
Oh no!
That's our train!
We're *in for it* now!

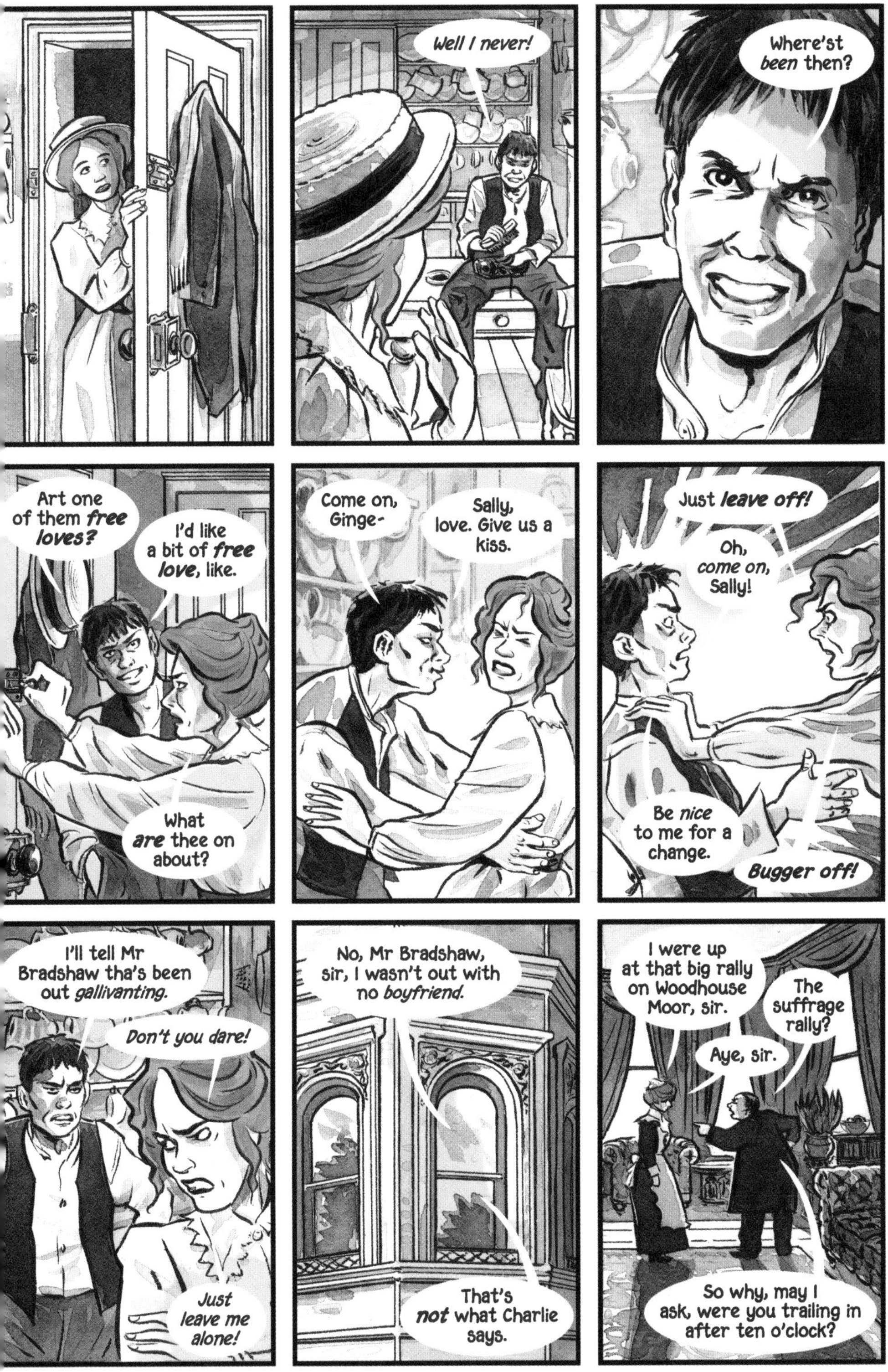
Well I never!
Where'st been then?
Art one of them free loves?
I'd like a bit of free love, like.
What are thee on about?
Come on, Ginge-
Sally, love. Give us a kiss.
Just leave off!
Oh, come on, Sally!
Be nice to me for a change.
Bugger off!
I'll tell Mr Bradshaw tha's been out gallivanting.
Don't you dare!
Just leave me alone!
No, Mr Bradshaw, sir, I wasn't out with no boyfriend.
That's not what Charlie says.
I were up at that big rally on Woodhouse Moor, sir.
The suffrage rally?
Aye, sir.
So why, may I ask, were you trailing in after ten o'clock?

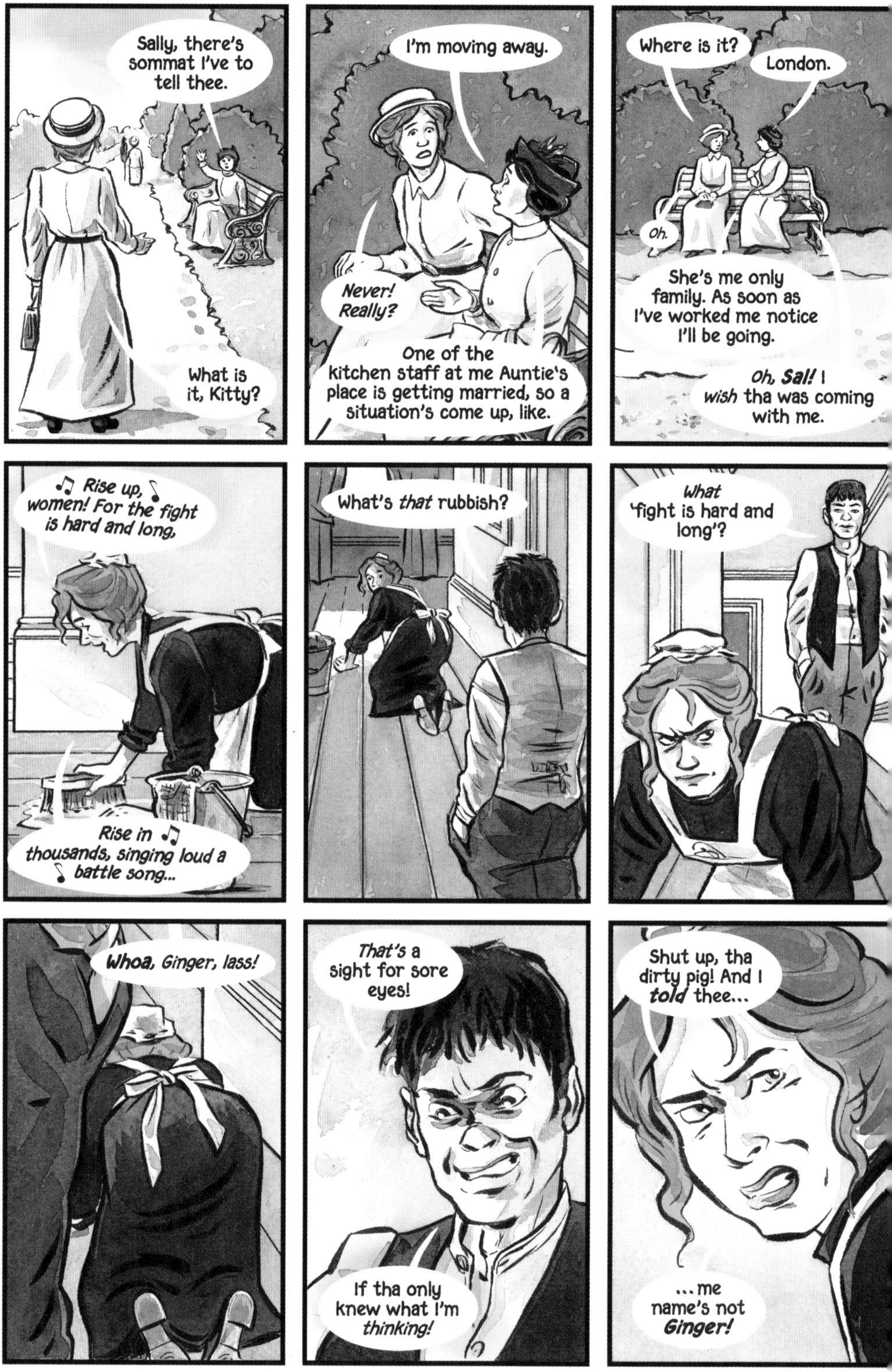

Sally, there's sommat I've to tell thee.
What is it, Kitty?
I'm moving away.
Never! Really?
One of the kitchen staff at me Auntie's place is getting married, so a situation's come up, like.
Where is it?
London.
Oh.
She's me only family. As soon as I've worked me notice I'll be going.
Oh, Sal! I *wish* tha was coming with me.
♫ *Rise up, women! For the fight is hard and long,*
Rise in thousands, singing loud a battle song...
What's *that* rubbish?
What 'fight is hard and long'?
Whoa, *Ginger, lass!*
That's a sight for sore eyes!
If tha only knew what I'm *thinking!*
Shut up, tha dirty pig! And I ***told*** thee...
...me name's not ***Ginger!***

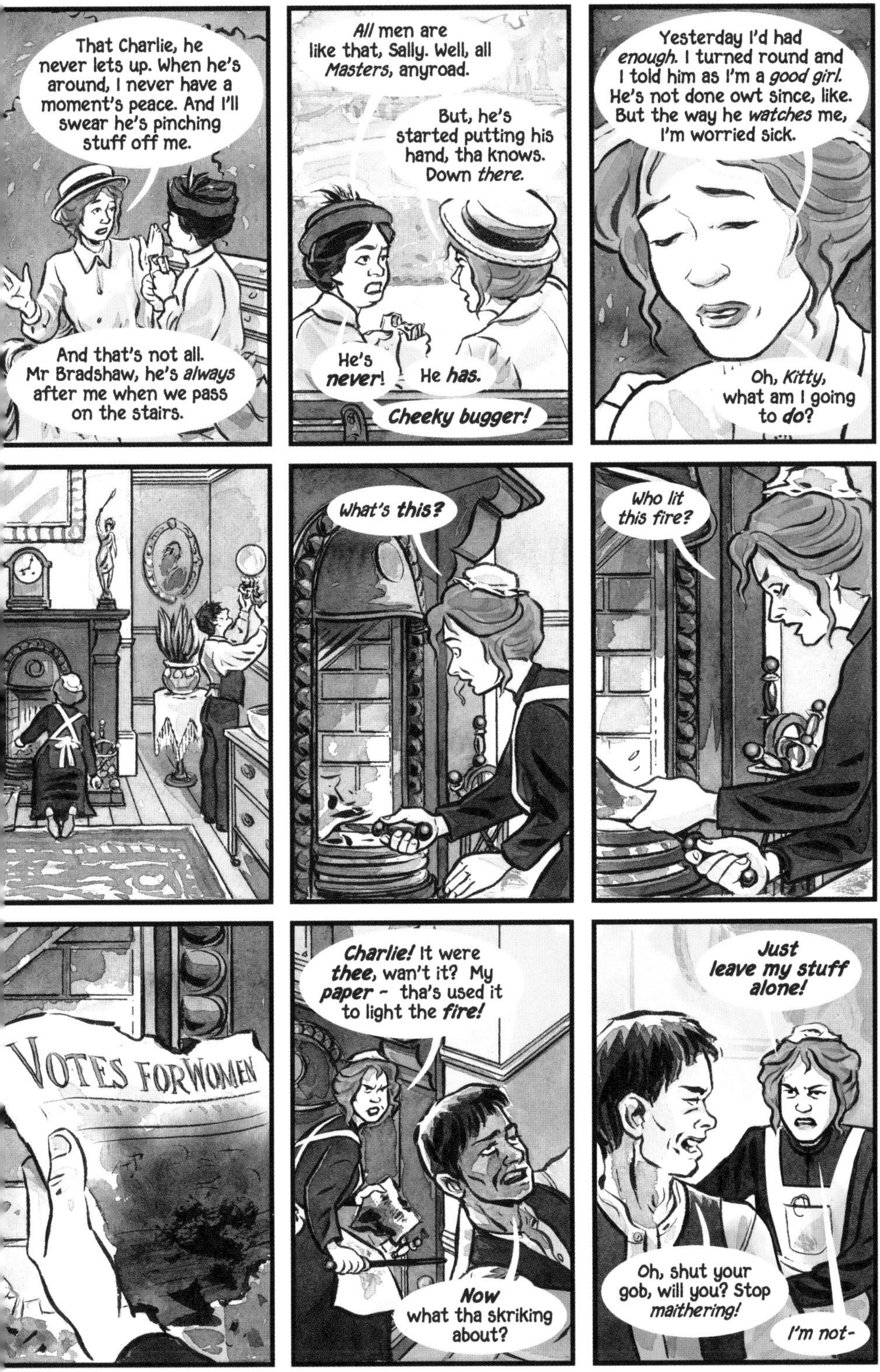
That Charlie, he never lets up. When he's around, I never have a moment's peace. And I'll swear he's pinching stuff off me.
And that's not all. Mr Bradshaw, he's *always* after me when we pass on the stairs.
All men are like that, Sally. Well, all *Masters*, anyroad.
But, he's started putting his hand, tha knows. Down *there*.
He's **never**!
He **has**.
Cheeky bugger!
Yesterday I'd had *enough*. I turned round and I told him as I'm a *good girl*. He's not done owt since, like. But the way he *watches* me, I'm worried sick.
Oh, *Kitty*, what am I going to *do*?
What's **this?**
Who lit this fire?
VOTES FOR WOMEN
Charlie! It were ***thee***, wan't it? My ***paper*** - tha's used it to light the ***fire!***
Now what tha skriking about?
Just leave my stuff alone!
Oh, shut your gob, will you? Stop *maithering!*
I'm not-

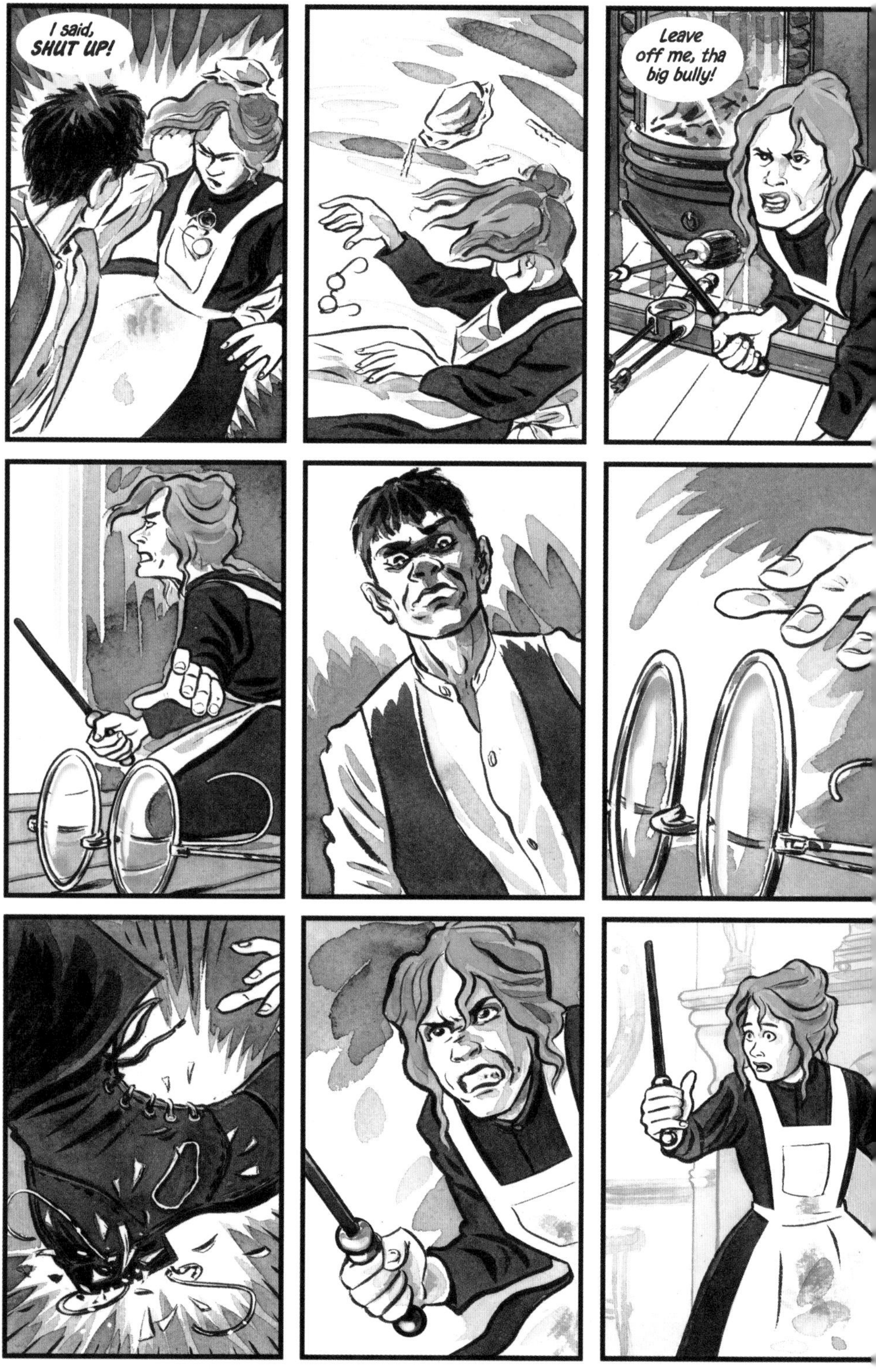
I said, SHUT UP!
Leave off me, tha big bully!

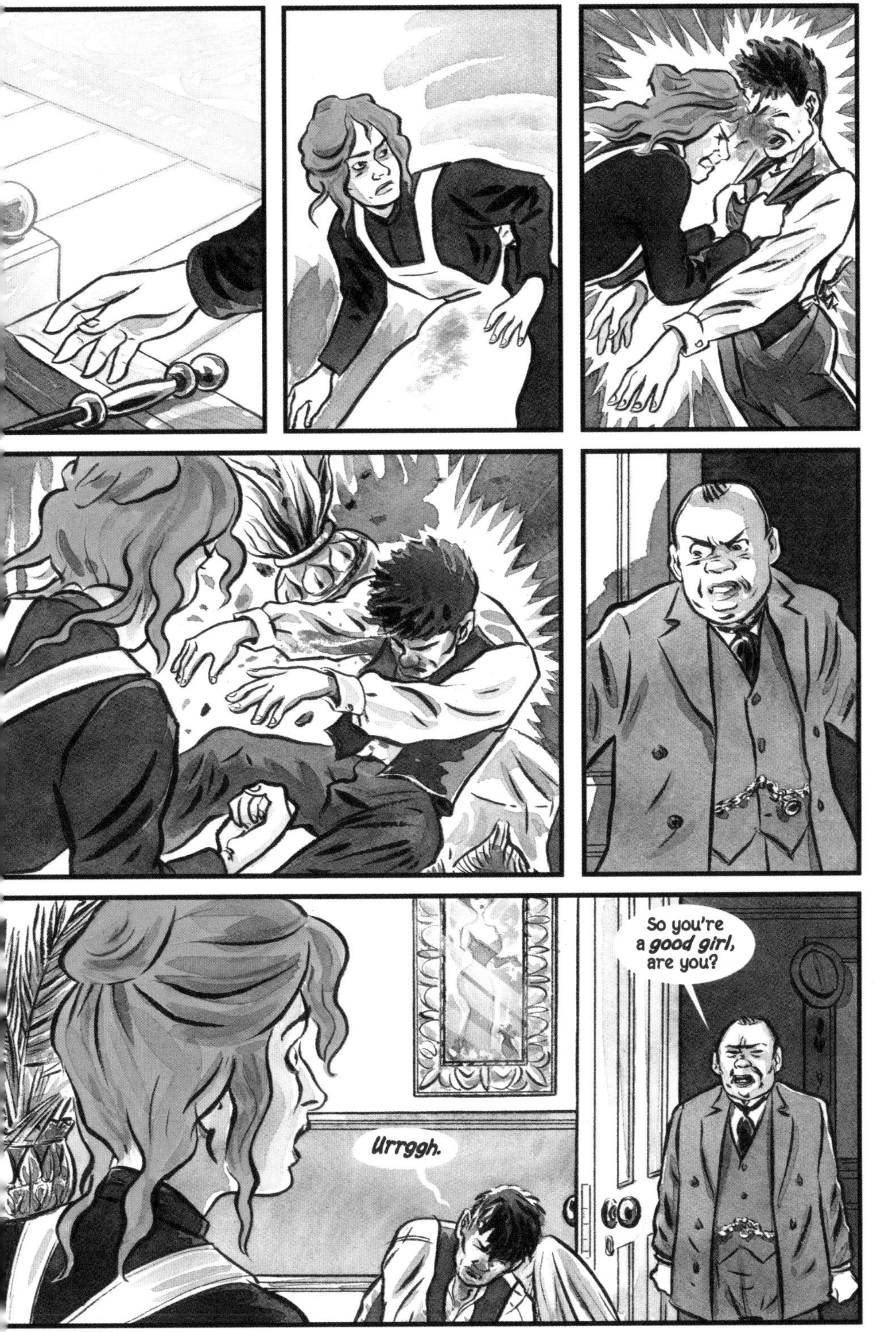
So you're a *good girl,* are you?
Urrggh.

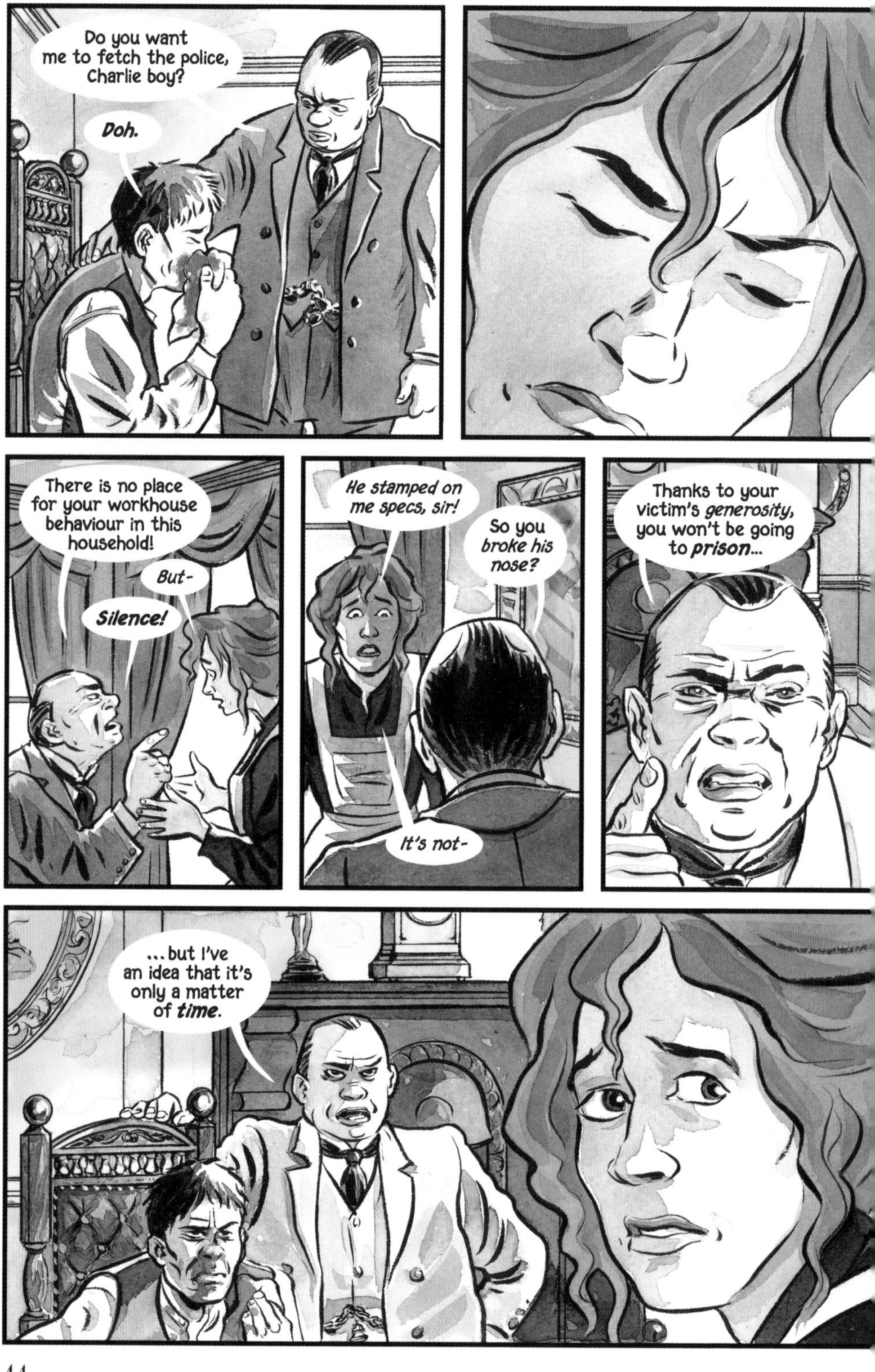
Do you want me to fetch the police, Charlie boy?
Doh.
There is no place for your workhouse behaviour in this household!
But-
Silence!
He stamped on me specs, sir!
So you broke his nose?
It's not-
Thanks to your victim's *generosity*, you won't be going to ***prison***...
...but I've an idea that it's only a matter of ***time***.

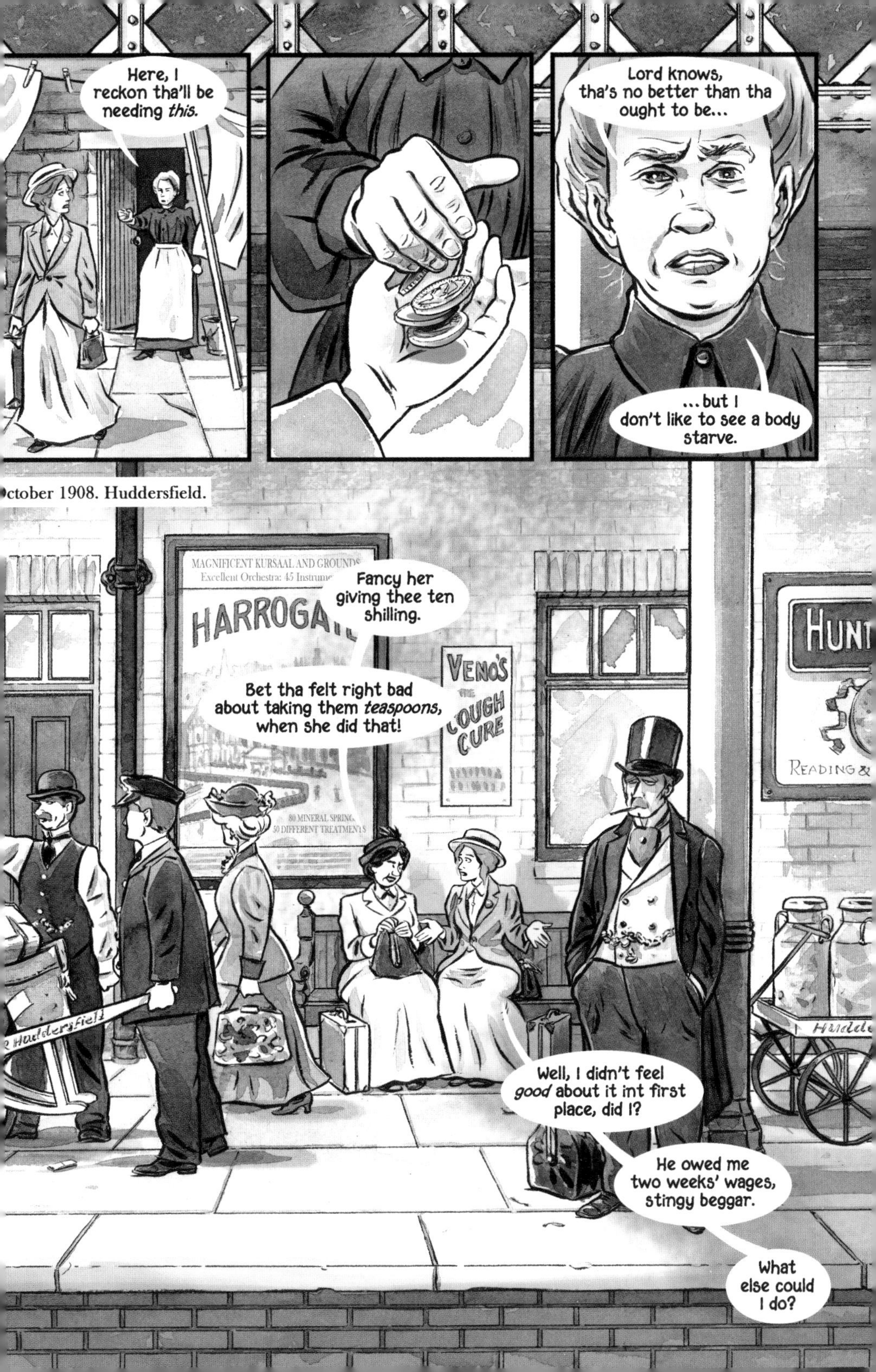
Here, I reckon tha'll be needing *this.*
Lord knows, tha's no better than tha ought to be...
...but I don't like to see a body starve.
October 1908. Huddersfield.
MAGNIFICENT KURSAAL AND GROUNDS
HARROGATE
80 MINERAL SPRINGS
50 DIFFERENT TREATMENTS
VENO'S THE COUGH CURE
HUNT
READING &
Fancy her giving thee ten shilling.
Bet tha felt right bad about taking them *teaspoons,* when she did that!
Huddersfield
Well, I didn't feel *good* about it int first place, did I?
He owed me two weeks' wages, stingy beggar.
What else could I do?

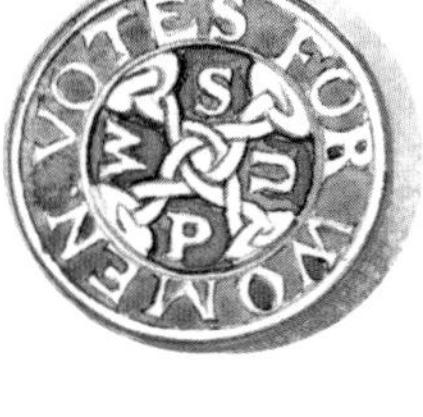
VOTES FOR WOMEN
W S P U

PART TWO
THE MARCH OF THE WOMEN

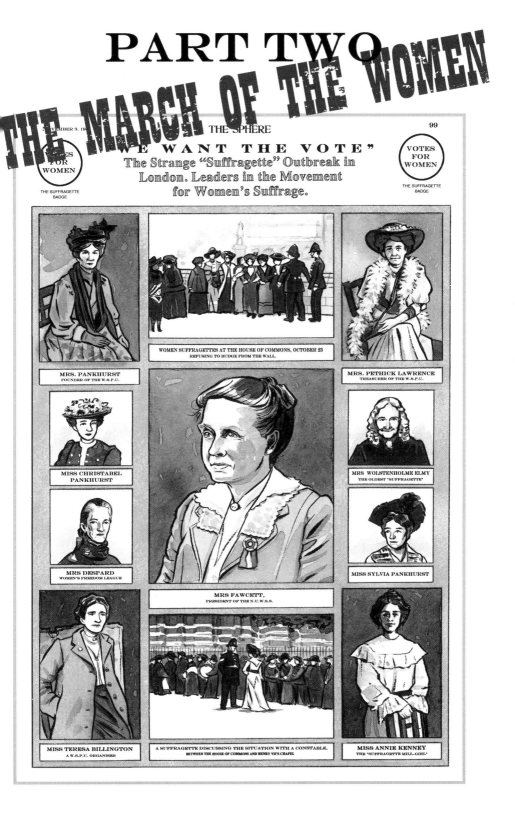

VOTES FOR WOMEN

THE SUFFRAGETTE BADGE

"WE WANT THE VOTE"
The Strange "Suffragette" Outbreak in London. Leaders in the Movement for Women's Suffrage.

VOTES FOR WOMEN

THE SUFFRAGETTE BADGE

MRS. PANKHURST
FOUNDER OF THE W.S.P.U.

WOMEN SUFFRAGETTES AT THE HOUSE OF COMMONS, OCTOBER 23
REFUSING TO BUDGE FROM THE WALL.

MRS. PETHICK LAWRENCE
TREASURER OF THE W.S.P.U.

MISS CHRISTABEL PANKHURST

MRS WOLSTENHOLME ELMY
THE OLDEST "SUFFRAGETTE"

MRS DESPARD
WOMEN'S FREEDOM LEAGUE

MRS FAWCETT,
PRESIDENT OF THE N.U.W.S.S.

MISS SYLVIA PANKHURST

MISS TERESA BILLINGTON
A W.S.P.U. ORGANISER

A SUFFRAGETTE DISCUSSING THE SITUATION WITH A CONSTABLE,
BETWEEN THE HOUSE OF COMMONS AND HENRY VII'S CHAPEL.

MISS ANNIE KENNEY
THE "SUFFRAGETTE MILL-GIRL"

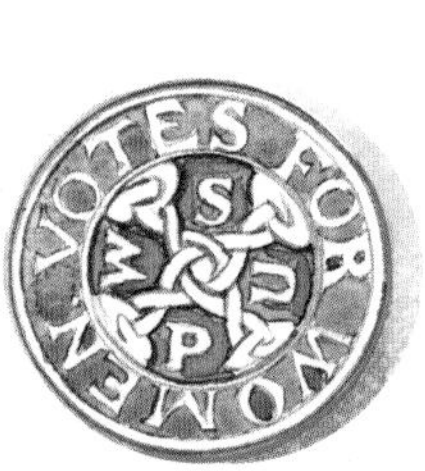
VOTES FOR WOMEN
W S P U

ctober 1908. Stafford Terrace, London W8.

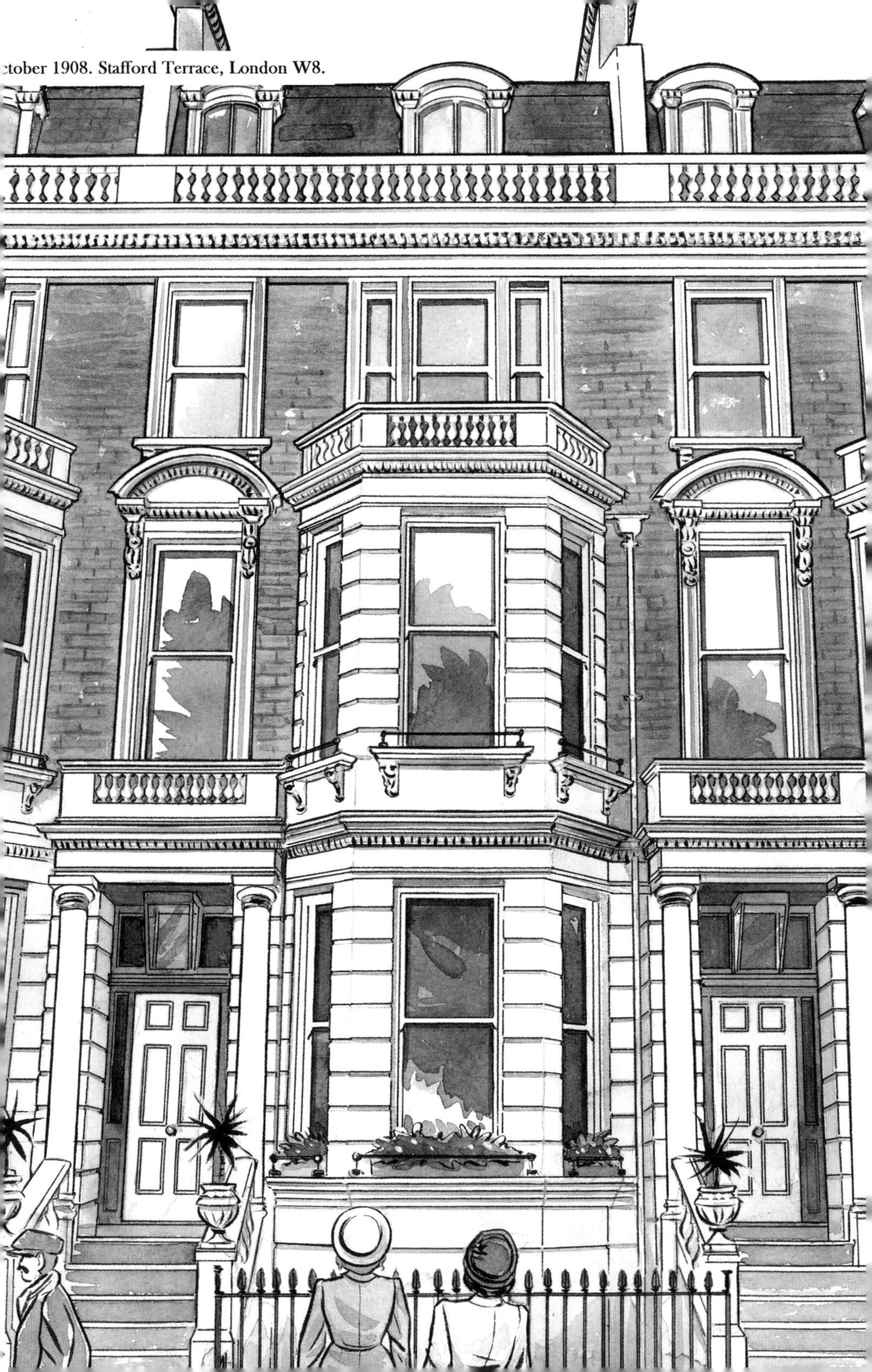

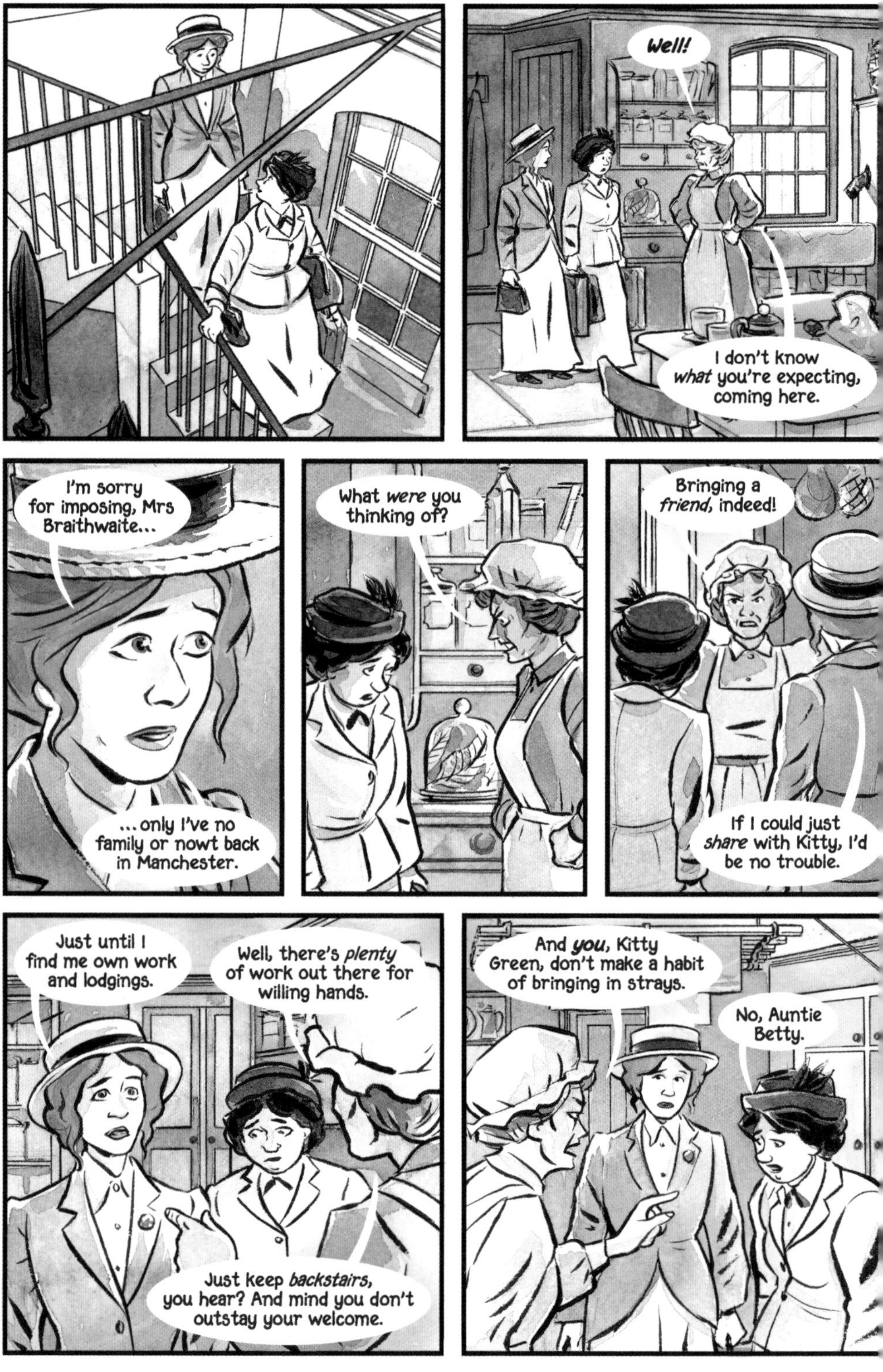
Well!
I don't know *what* you're expecting, coming here.
I'm sorry for imposing, Mrs Braithwaite...
...only I've no family or nowt back in Manchester.
What *were* you thinking of?
Bringing a *friend*, indeed!
If I could just *share* with Kitty, I'd be no trouble.
Just until I find me own work and lodgings.
Well, there's *plenty* of work out there for willing hands.
Just keep *backstairs*, you hear? And mind you don't outstay your welcome.
And **you**, Kitty Green, don't make a habit of bringing in strays.
No, Auntie Betty.

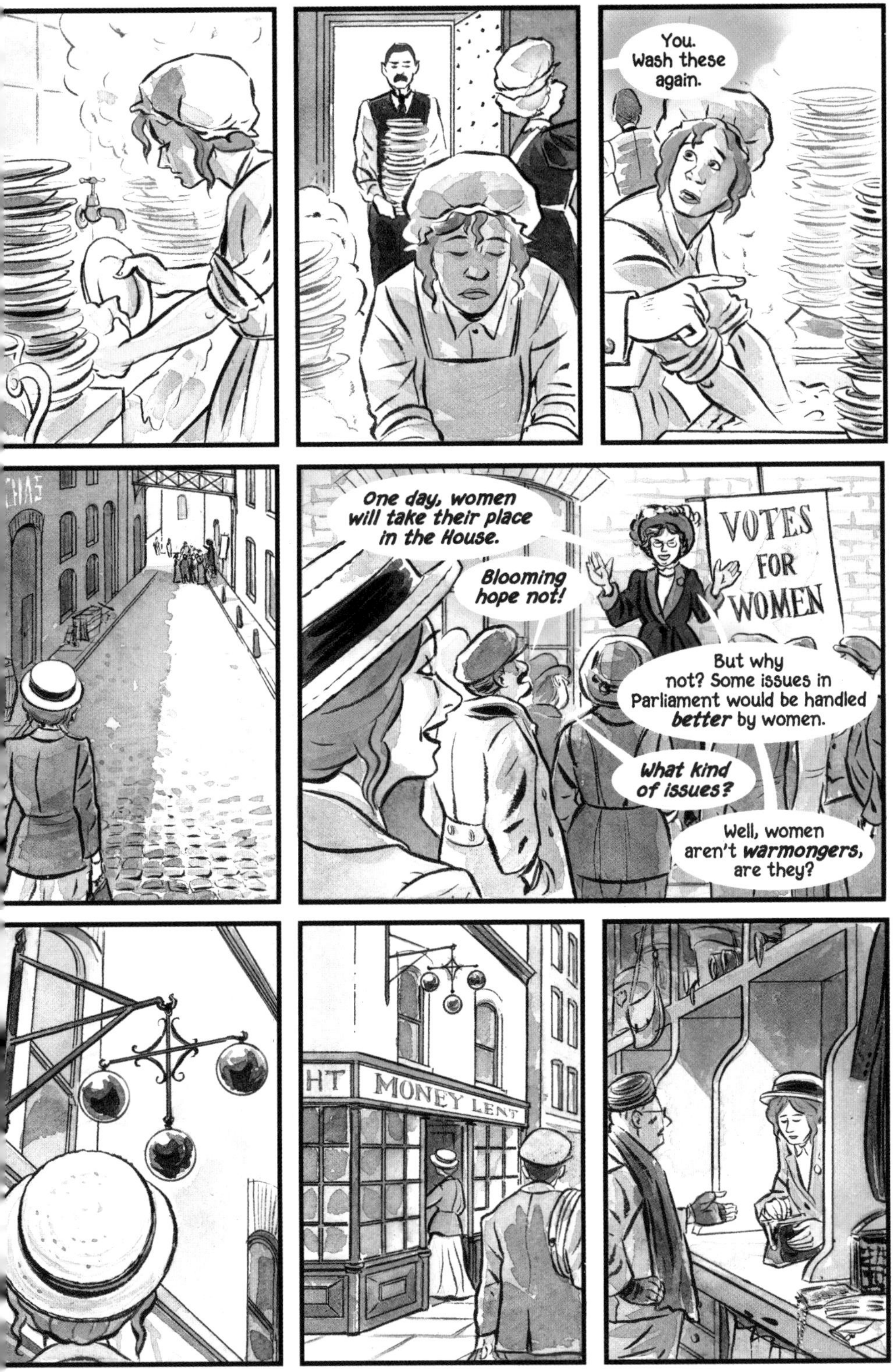
You. Wash these again.
One day, women will take their place in the House.
Blooming hope not!
VOTES FOR WOMEN
But why not? Some issues in Parliament would be handled better by women.
What kind of issues?
Well, women aren't warmongers, are they?
MONEY LENT

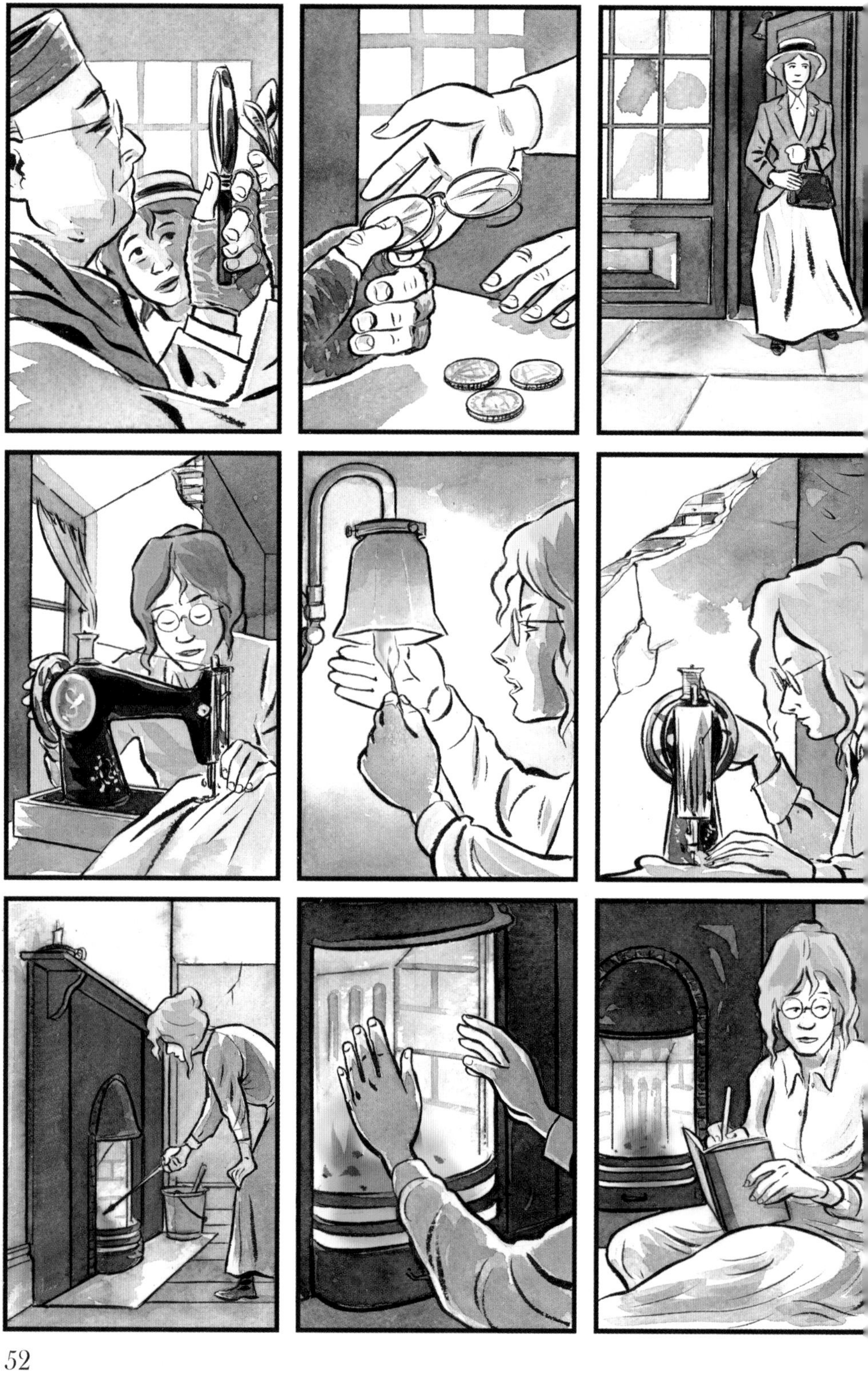

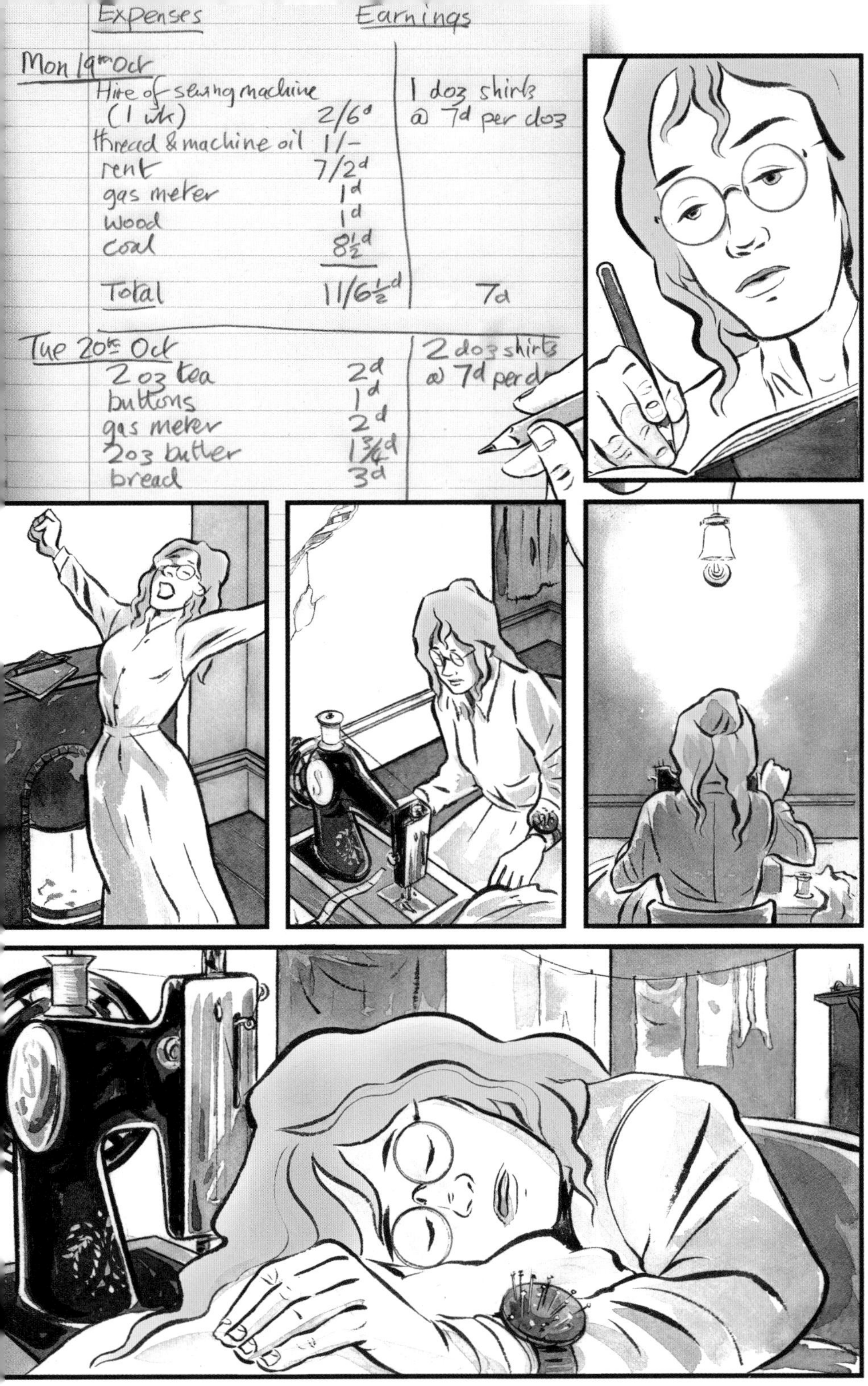
Expenses
Earnings
Mon 19th Oct
Hire of sewing machine (1 wk) 2/6d
thread & machine oil 1/-
rent 7/2d
gas meter 1d
wood 1d
coal 8½d
Total 11/6½d
1 doz shirts @ 7d per doz
7d
Tue 20th Oct
2 oz tea 2d
buttons 1d
gas meter 2d
2oz butter 1¾d
bread 3d
2 doz shirts @ 7d per d

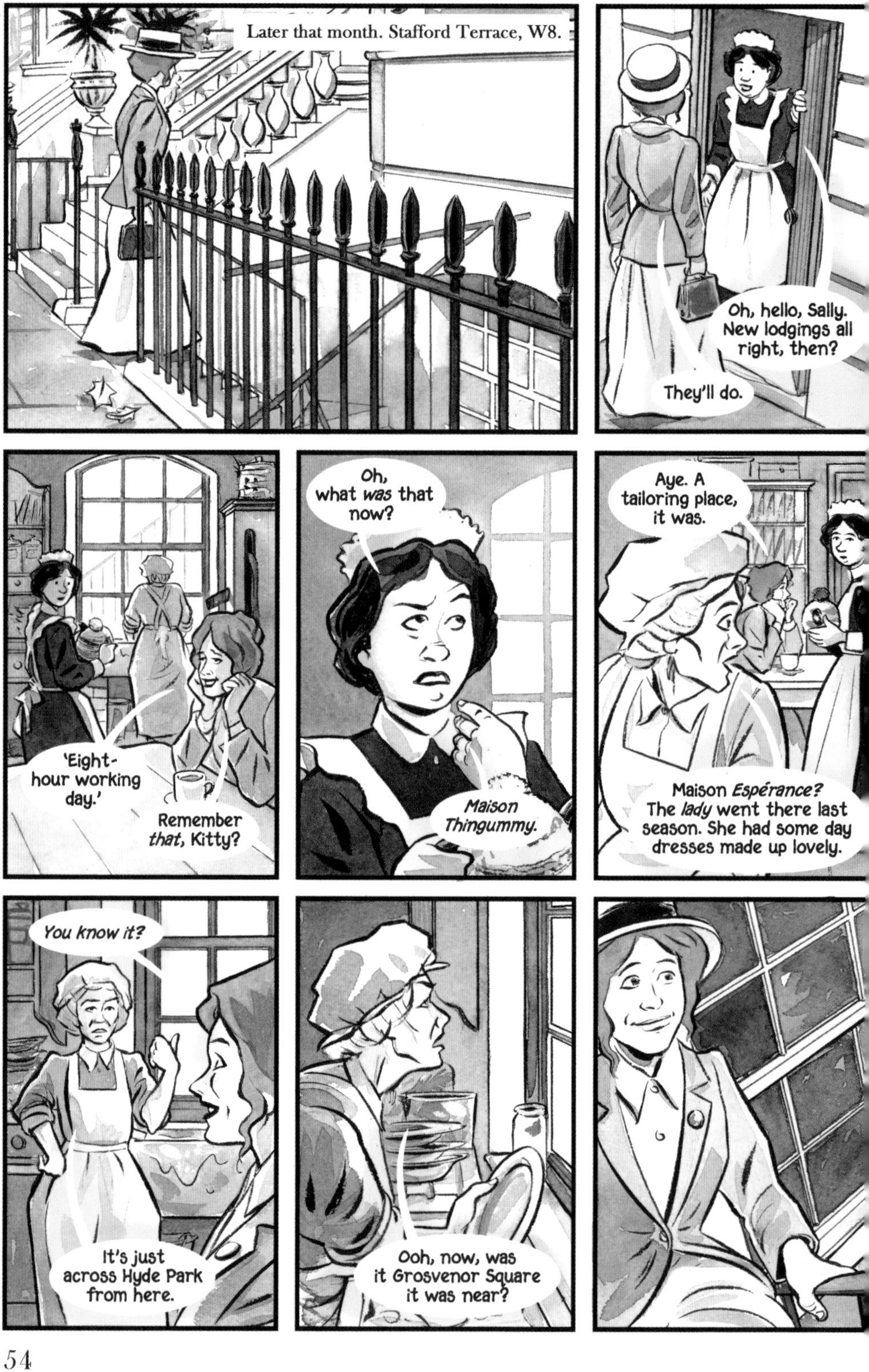
Later that month. Stafford Terrace, W8.
Oh, hello, Sally. New lodgings all right, then?
They'll do.
'Eight-hour working day.'
Remember *that*, Kitty?
Oh, what *was* that now?
Maison Thingummy.
Aye. A tailoring place, it was.
Maison *Espérance?* The *lady* went there last season. She had some day dresses made up lovely.
You know it?
It's just across Hyde Park from here.
Ooh, now, was it Grosvenor Square it was near?

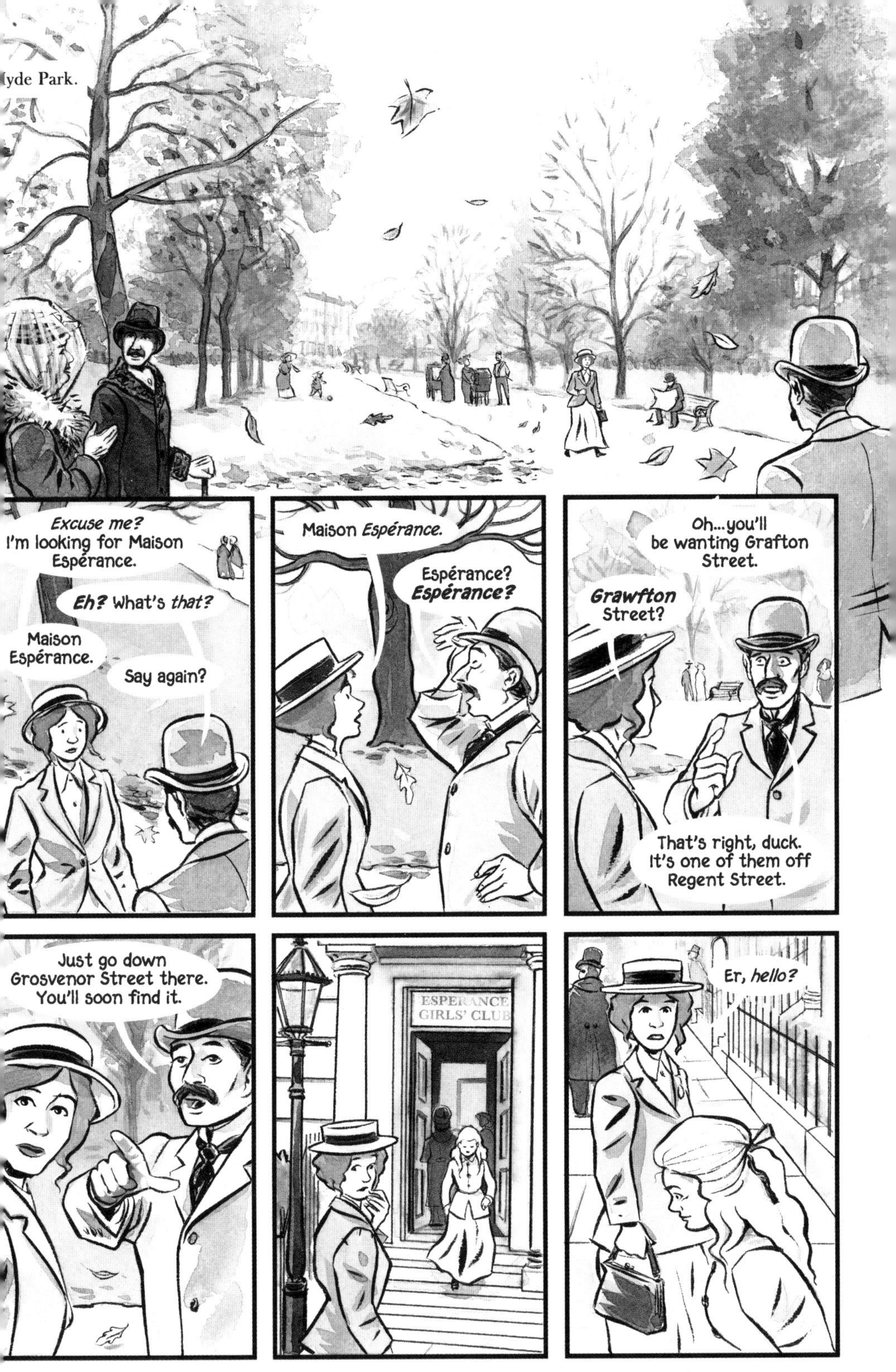

Hyde Park.
Excuse me? I'm looking for Maison Espérance.
Eh? What's that?
Maison Espérance.
Say again?
Maison Espérance.
Espérance? Espérance?
Oh...you'll be wanting Grafton Street.
Grawfton Street?
That's right, duck. It's one of them off Regent Street.
Just go down Grosvenor Street there. You'll soon find it.
ESPERANCE GIRLS' CLUB
Er, hello?

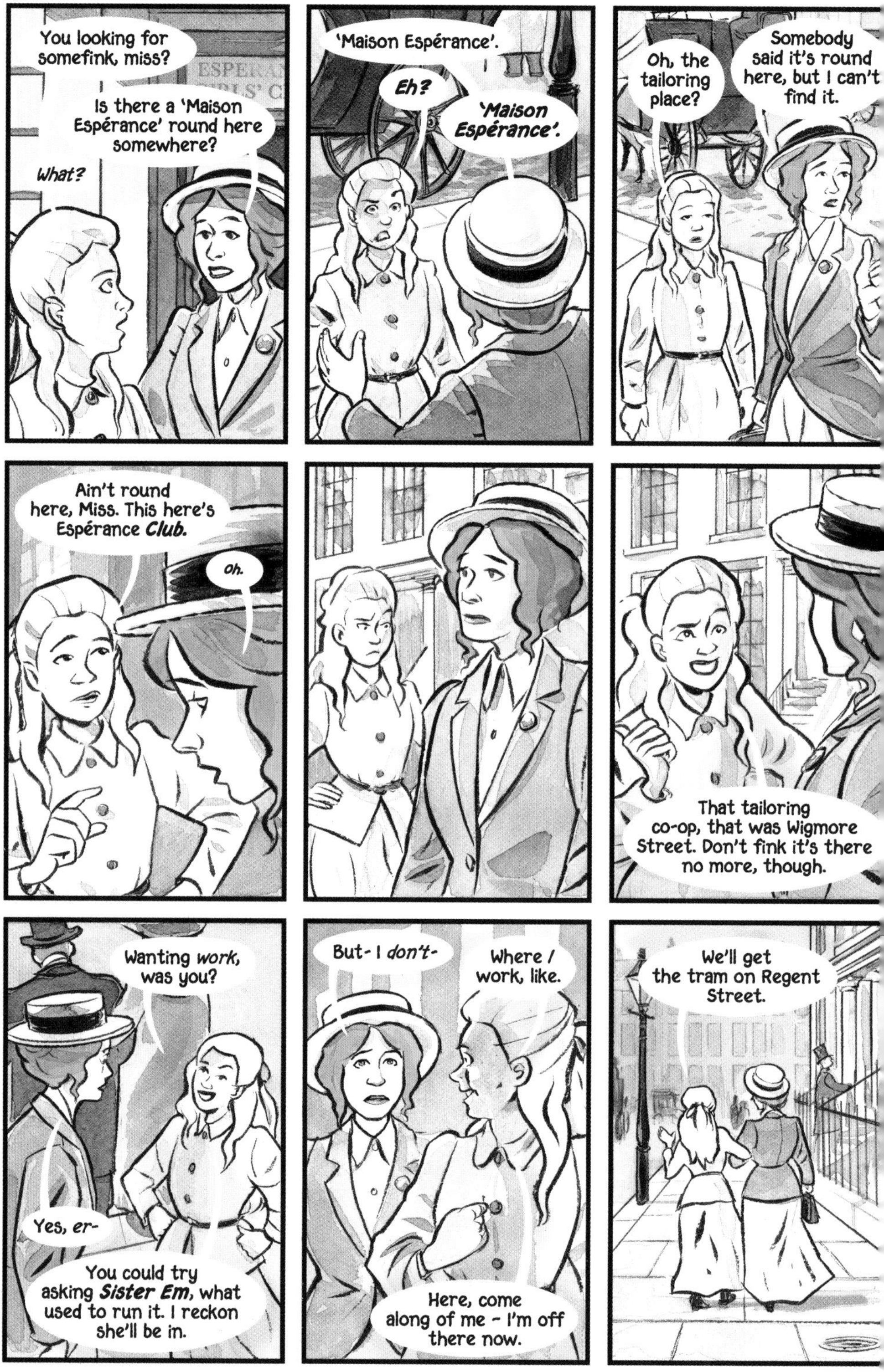
You looking for somefink, miss?
Is there a 'Maison Espérance' round here somewhere?
What?
'Maison Espérance'.
Eh?
'Maison Espérance'.
Oh, the tailoring place?
Somebody said it's round here, but I can't find it.
Ain't round here, Miss. This here's Espérance Club.
Oh.
That tailoring co-op, that was Wigmore Street. Don't fink it's there no more, though.
Wanting work, was you?
Yes, er-
You could try asking Sister Em, what used to run it. I reckon she'll be in.
But- I don't-
Where I work, like.
Here, come along of me - I'm off there now.
We'll get the tram on Regent Street.

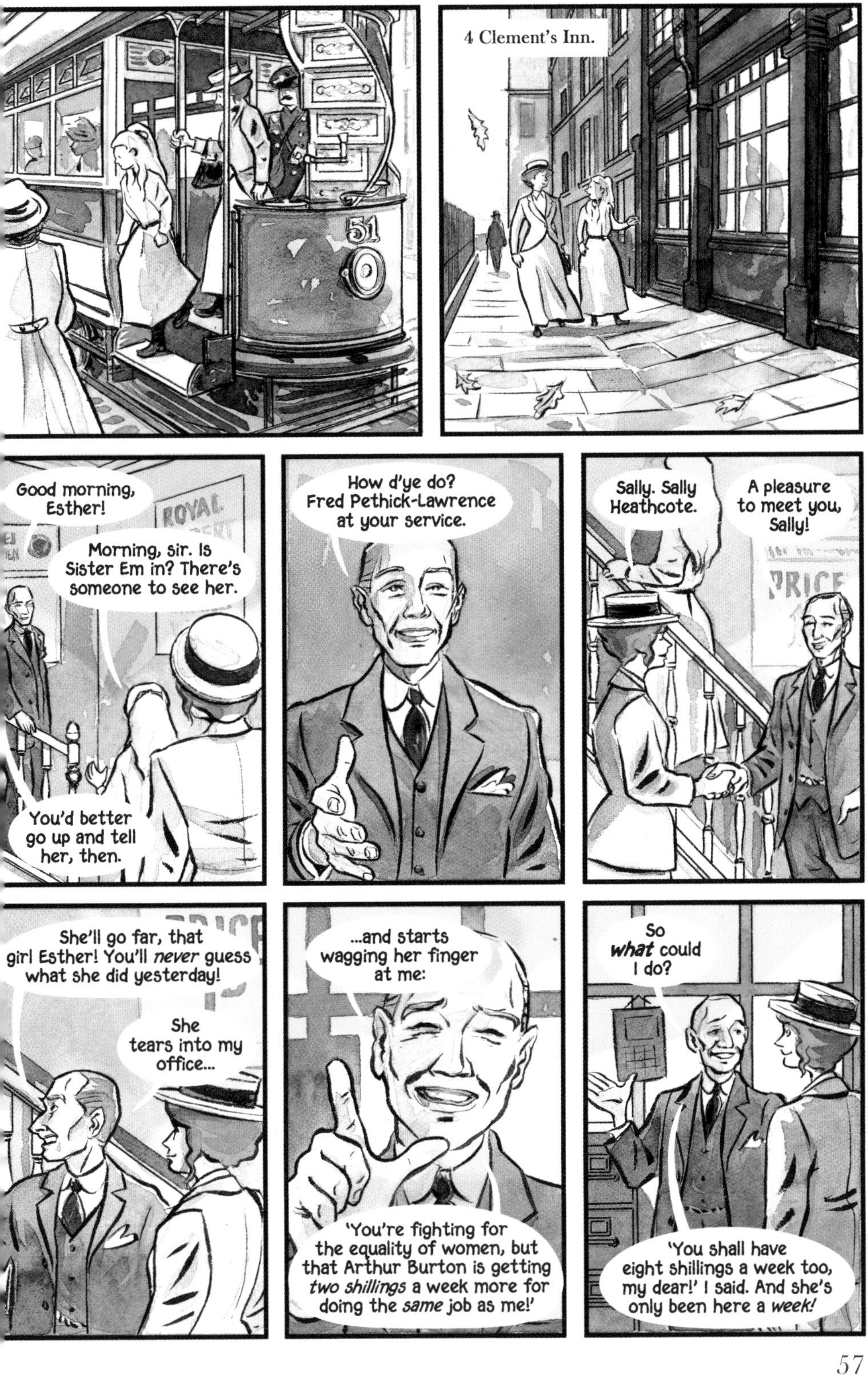
4 Clement's Inn.
Good morning, Esther!
Morning, sir. Is Sister Em in? There's someone to see her.
You'd better go up and tell her, then.
How d'ye do? Fred Pethick-Lawrence at your service.
Sally. Sally Heathcote.
A pleasure to meet you, Sally!
She'll go far, that girl Esther! You'll *never* guess what she did yesterday!
She tears into my office...
...and starts wagging her finger at me:
'You're fighting for the equality of women, but that Arthur Burton is getting *two shillings* a week more for doing the *same* job as me!'
So *what* could I do?
'You shall have eight shillings a week too, my dear!' I said. And she's only been here a *week!*

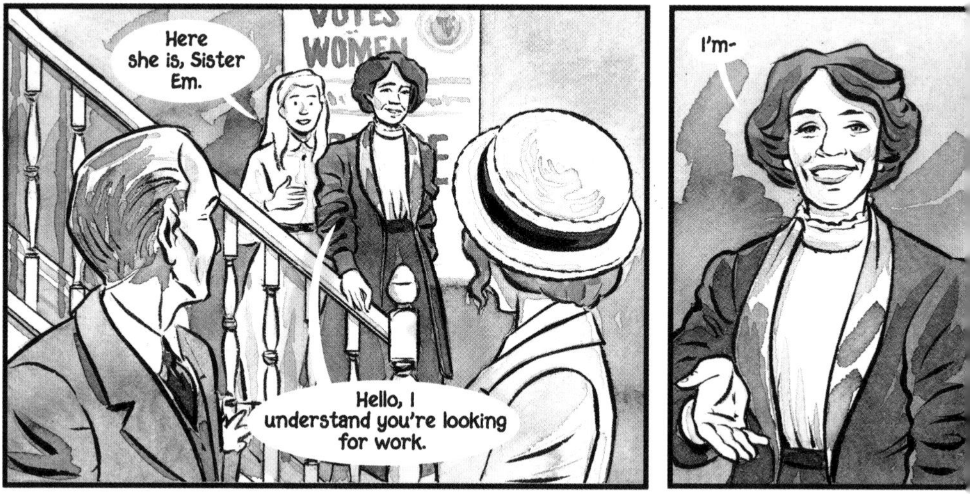
VOTES
WOMEN
Here she is, Sister Em.
Hello, I understand you're looking for work.
I'm-

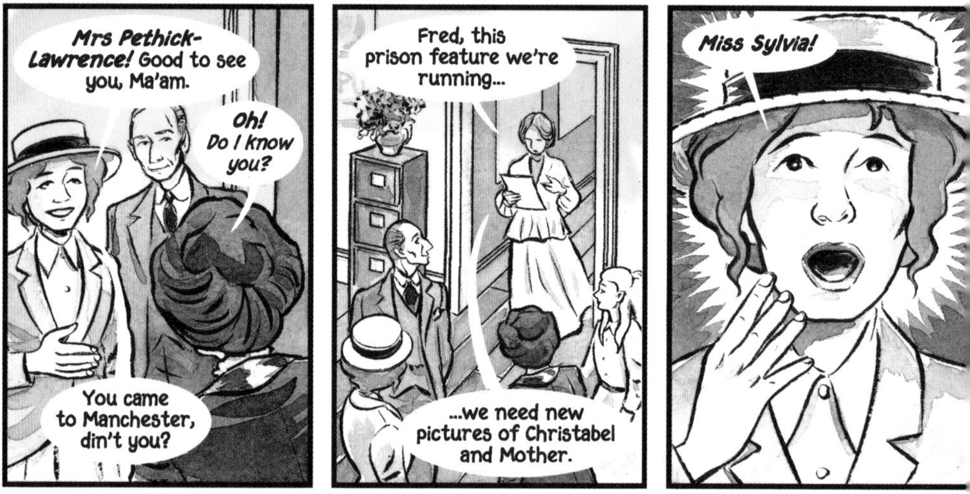
Mrs Pethick-Lawrence! Good to see you, Ma'am.
Oh! Do I know you?
You came to Manchester, din't you?
Fred, this prison feature we're running...
...we need new pictures of Christabel and Mother.
Miss Sylvia!

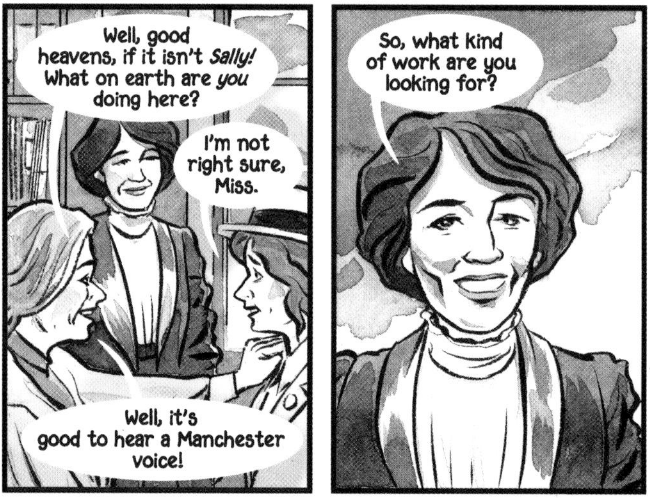
Well, good heavens, if it isn't *Sally!* What on earth are *you* doing here?
I'm not right sure, Miss.
Well, it's good to hear a Manchester voice!
So, what kind of work are you looking for?

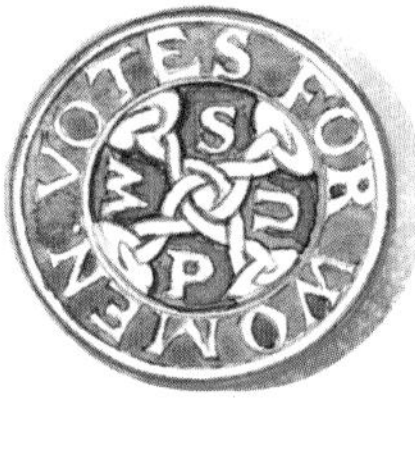
VOTES FOR WOMEN
W S P U

So there it was. They took me in and they helped me with work. I overheard 'Godfather' once saying to his darling Em, 'That Esther expects us to find employment for the whole of London, if not the entire country!' But they never once complained. I never knew a couple with such deep pockets.

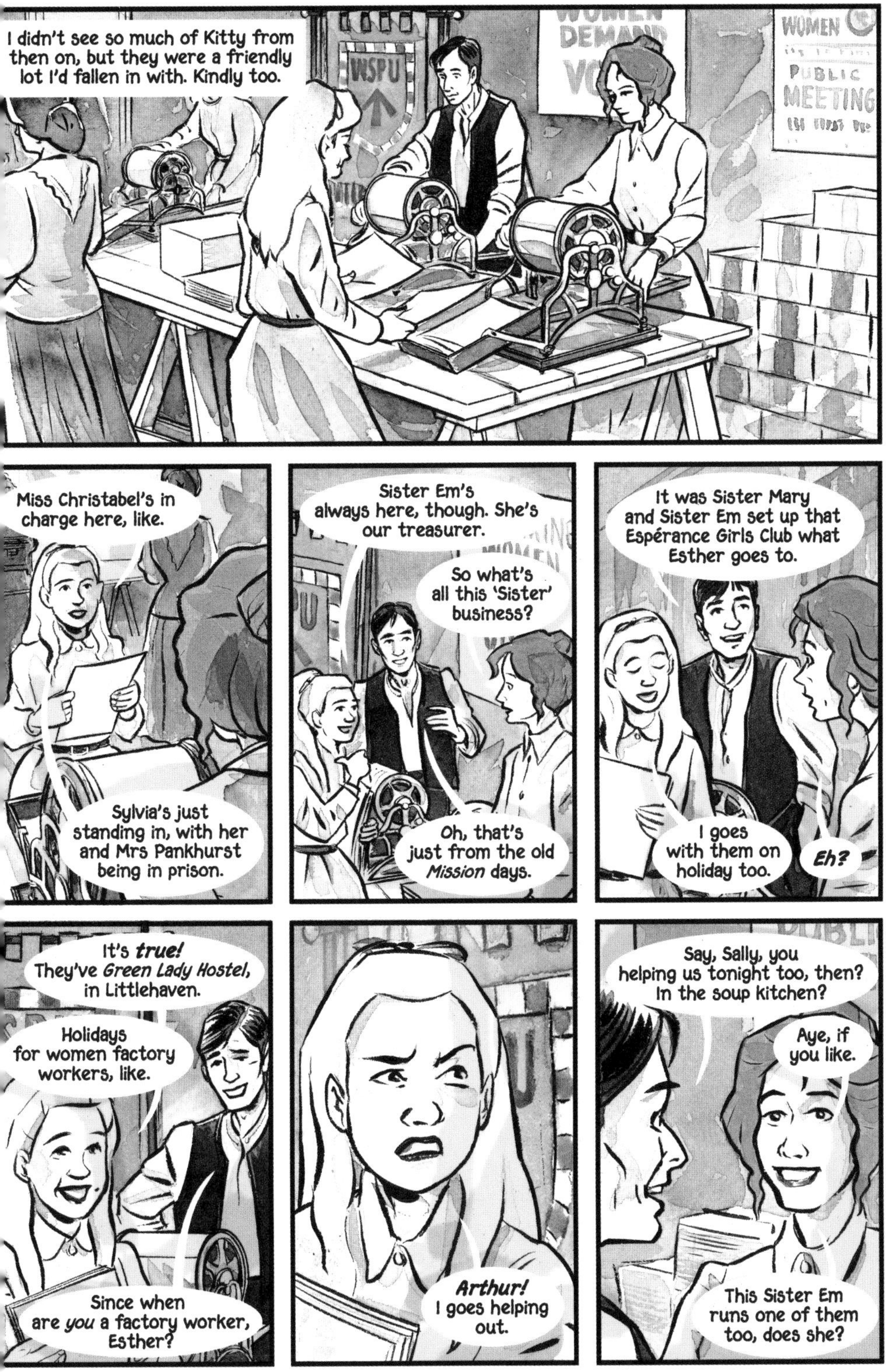
I didn't see so much of Kitty from then on, but they were a friendly lot I'd fallen in with. Kindly too.
WSPU
WOMEN DEMAND VO
WOMEN
PUBLIC MEETING
Miss Christabel's in charge here, like.
Sylvia's just standing in, with her and Mrs Pankhurst being in prison.
Sister Em's always here, though. She's our treasurer.
So what's all this 'Sister' business?
Oh, that's just from the old *Mission* days.
It was Sister Mary and Sister Em set up that Espérance Girls Club what Esther goes to.
I goes with them on holiday too.
Eh?
It's ***true!*** They've *Green Lady Hostel*, in Littlehaven.
Holidays for women factory workers, like.
Since when are *you* a factory worker, Esther?
Arthur! I goes helping out.
Say, Sally, you helping us tonight too, then? In the soup kitchen?
Aye, if you like.
This Sister Em runs one of them too, does she?

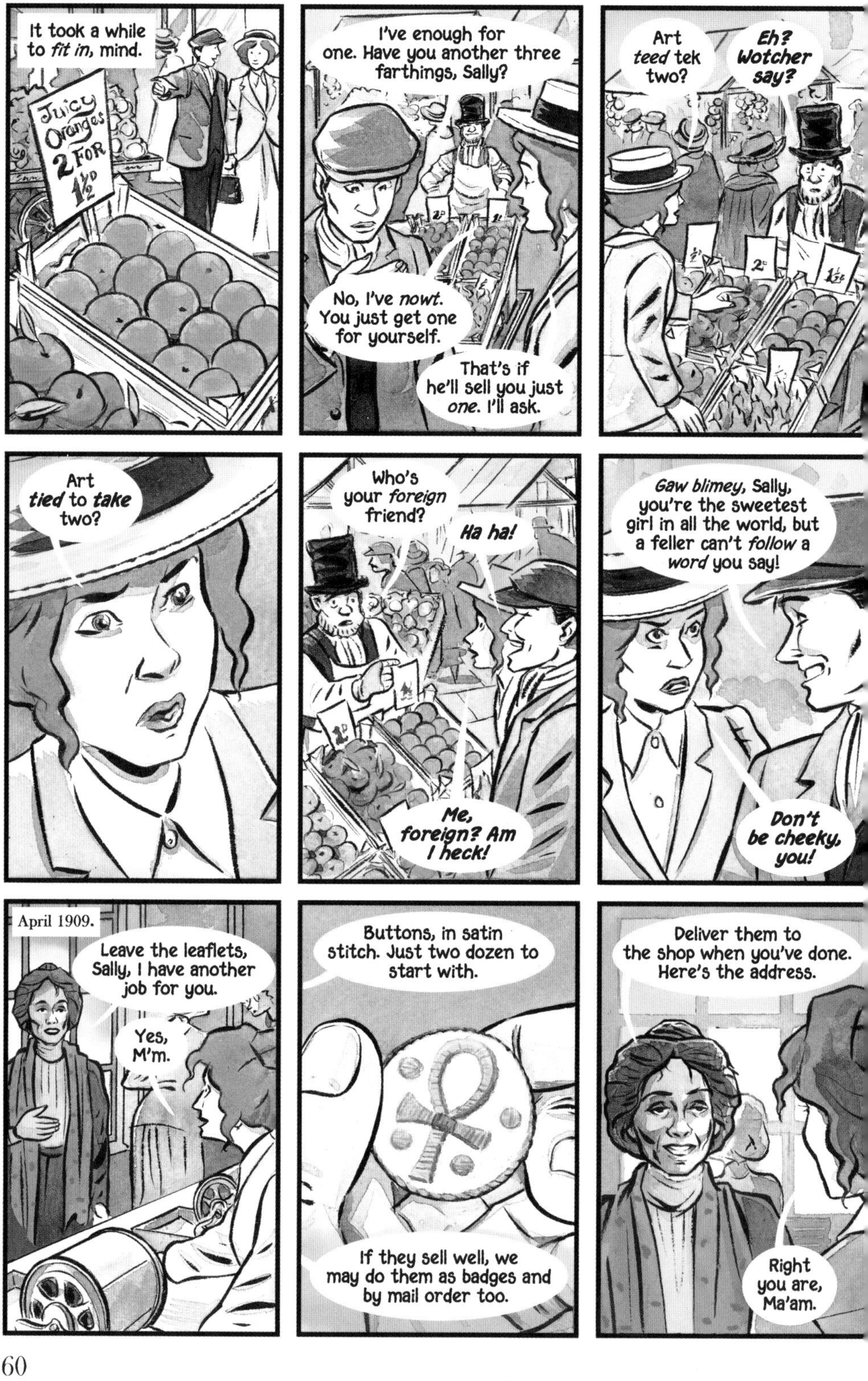
It took a while to *fit in*, mind.
Juicy Oranges 2 FOR 1½D
I've enough for one. Have you another three farthings, Sally?
No, I've *nowt*. You just get one for yourself.
That's if he'll sell you just *one*. I'll ask.
Art *teed* tek two?
Eh? Wotcher say?
Art *tied* to *take* two?
Who's your *foreign* friend?
Ha ha!
Me, foreign? Am I heck!
Gaw blimey, Sally, you're the sweetest girl in all the world, but a feller can't *follow* a *word* you say!
Don't be cheeky, you!
April 1909.
Leave the leaflets, Sally, I have another job for you.
Yes, M'm.
Buttons, in satin stitch. Just two dozen to start with.
If they sell well, we may do them as badges and by mail order too.
Deliver them to the shop when you've done. Here's the address.
Right you are, Ma'am.

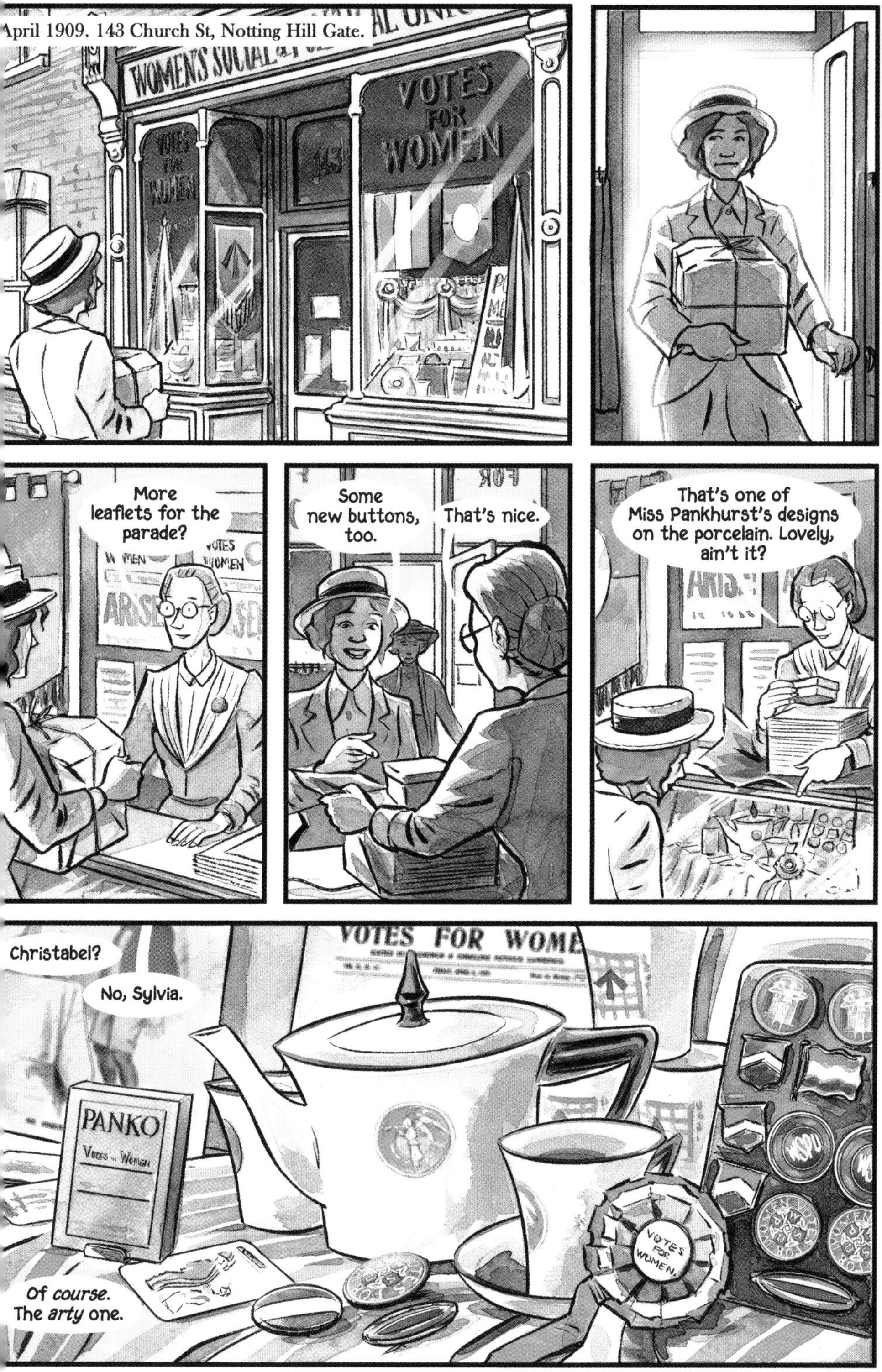
April 1909. 143 Church St, Notting Hill Gate.
WOMEN'S SOCIAL
VOTES FOR WOMEN
143
VOTES FOR WOMEN
More leaflets for the parade?
Some new buttons, too.
That's nice.
That's one of Miss Pankhurst's designs on the porcelain. Lovely, ain't it?
Christabel?
No, Sylvia.
Of course. The *arty* one.
VOTES FOR WOME
PANKO
VOTES FOR WOMEN
WSPU

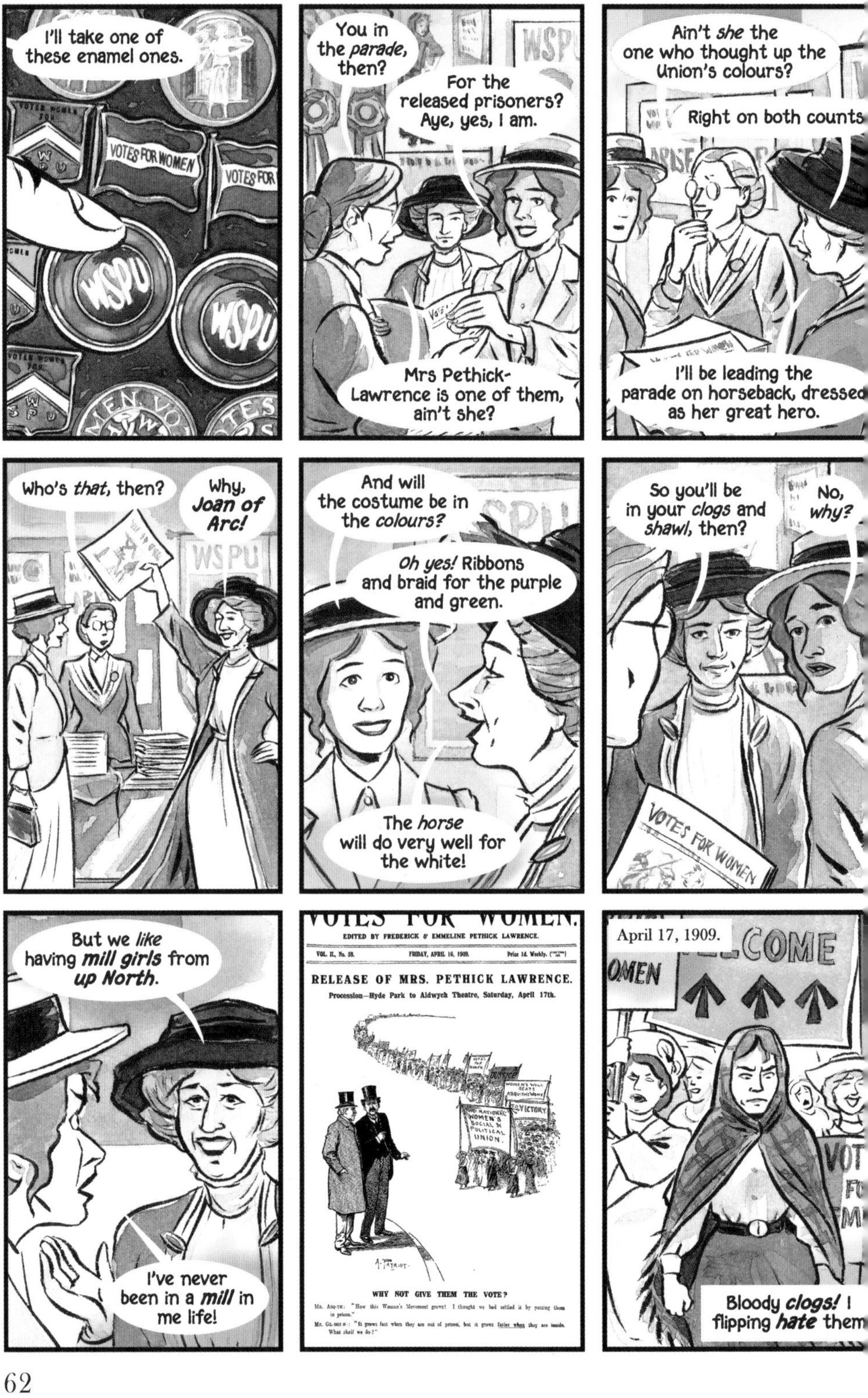
I'll take one of these enamel ones.
VOTES FOR WOMEN
WSPU
You in the *parade*, then?
For the released prisoners? Aye, yes, I am.
Mrs Pethick-Lawrence is one of them, ain't she?
Ain't *she* the one who thought up the Union's colours?
Right on both counts
I'll be leading the parade on horseback, dressed as her great hero.
Who's *that*, then?
Why, ***Joan of Arc!***
WSPU
And will the costume be in the *colours?*
Oh yes! Ribbons and braid for the purple and green.
The *horse* will do very well for the white!
So you'll be in your *clogs* and *shawl*, then?
No, *why?*
VOTES FOR WOMEN
But we *like* having ***mill girls*** from ***up North***.
I've never been in a ***mill*** in me life!
VOTES FOR WOMEN.
EDITED BY FREDERICK & EMMELINE PETHICK LAWRENCE.
VOL. II., No. 58. FRIDAY, APRIL 16, 1909. Price 1d. Weekly.
RELEASE OF MRS. PETHICK LAWRENCE.
Procession—Hyde Park to Aldwych Theatre, Saturday, April 17th.
THE NATIONAL WOMEN'S SOCIAL & POLITICAL UNION.
VICTORY
WHY NOT GIVE THEM THE VOTE?
MR. ASQ-TH: "How this Woman's Movement grows! I thought we had settled it by putting them in prison."
MR. GL-DST-N-: "It grows fast when they are out of prison, but it grows faster when they are inside. What *shall* we do?"
April 17, 1909.
COME
OMEN
Bloody ***clogs!*** I flipping ***hate*** them

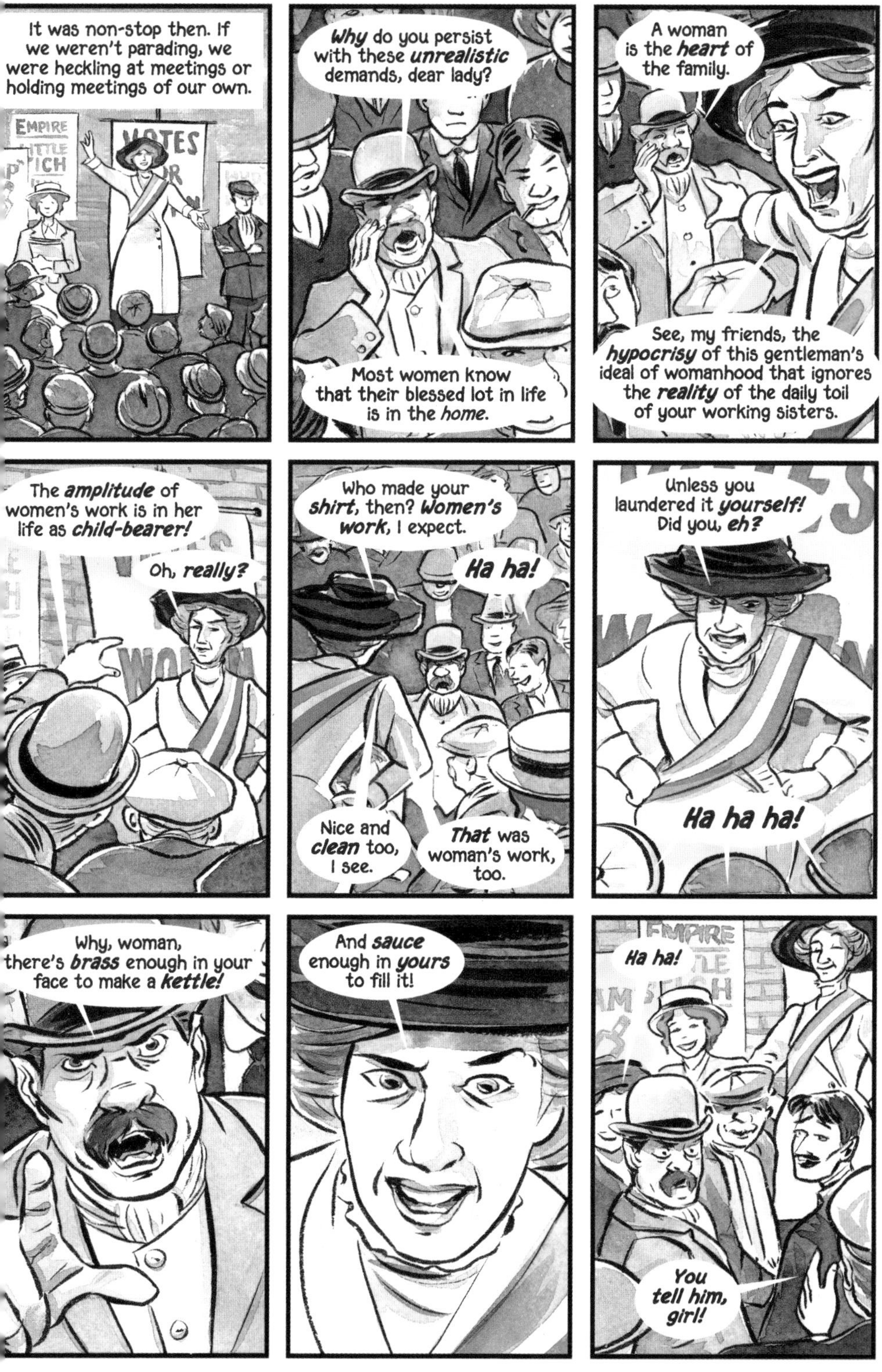
It was non-stop then. If we weren't parading, we were heckling at meetings or holding meetings of our own.
EMPIRE
VOTES
Why do you persist with these unrealistic demands, dear lady?
Most women know that their blessed lot in life is in the home.
A woman is the heart of the family.
See, my friends, the hypocrisy of this gentleman's ideal of womanhood that ignores the reality of the daily toil of your working sisters.
The amplitude of women's work is in her life as child-bearer!
Oh, really?
Who made your shirt, then? Women's work, I expect.
Ha ha!
Nice and clean too, I see.
That was woman's work, too.
Unless you laundered it yourself! Did you, eh?
Ha ha ha!
Why, woman, there's brass enough in your face to make a kettle!
And sauce enough in yours to fill it!
EMPIRE
Ha ha!
You tell him, girl!

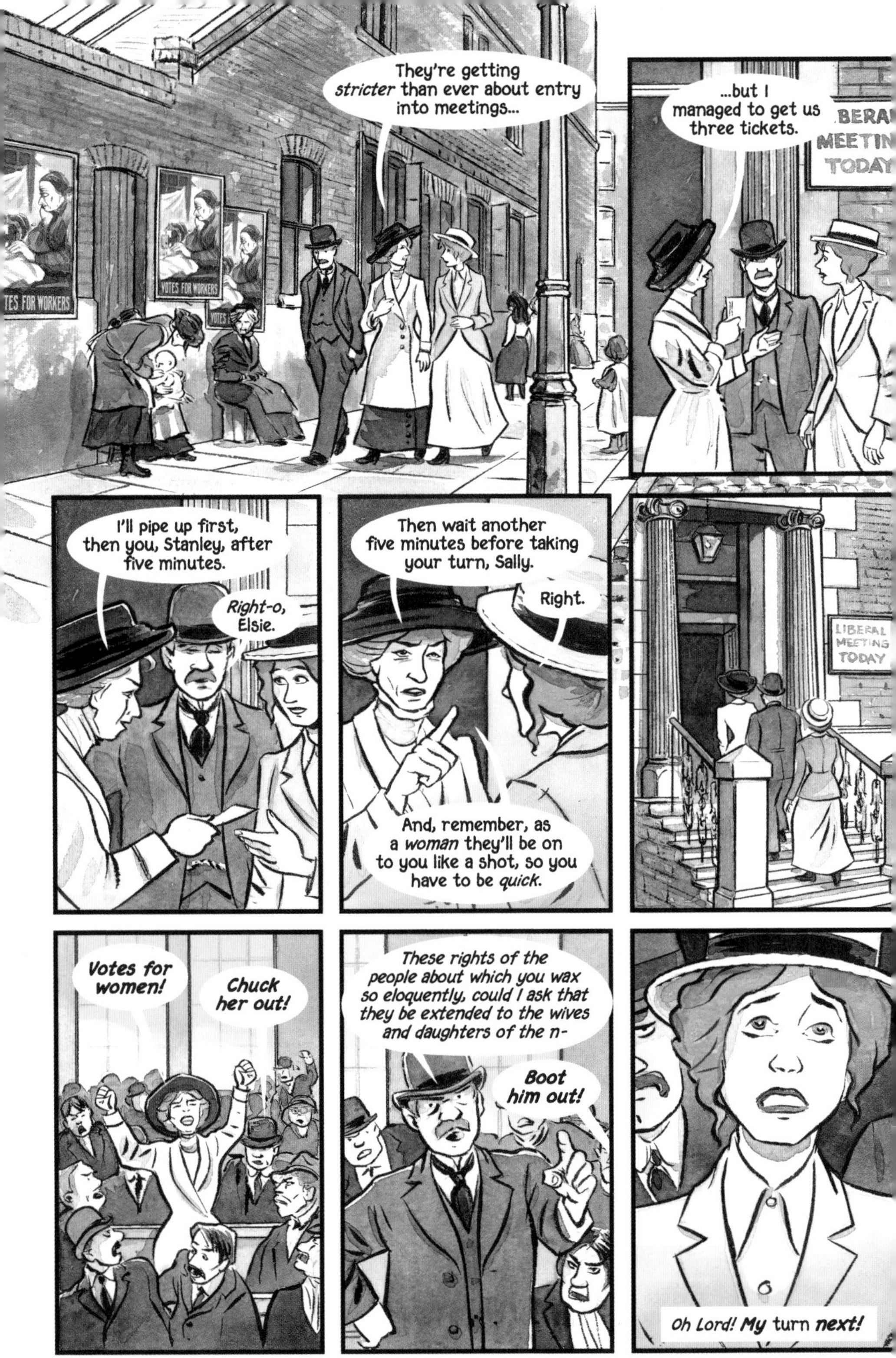
VOTES FOR WORKERS
TES FOR WORKERS
They're getting *stricter* than ever about entry into meetings...
...but I managed to get us three tickets.
BERA MEETIN TODAY
I'll pipe up first, then you, Stanley, after five minutes.
Right-o, Elsie.
Then wait another five minutes before taking your turn, Sally.
Right.
And, remember, as a *woman* they'll be on to you like a shot, so you have to be *quick*.
LIBERAL MEETING TODAY
Votes for women!
Chuck her out!
These rights of the people about which you wax so eloquently, could I ask that they be extended to the wives and daughters of the n-
Boot him out!
Oh Lord! My turn next!

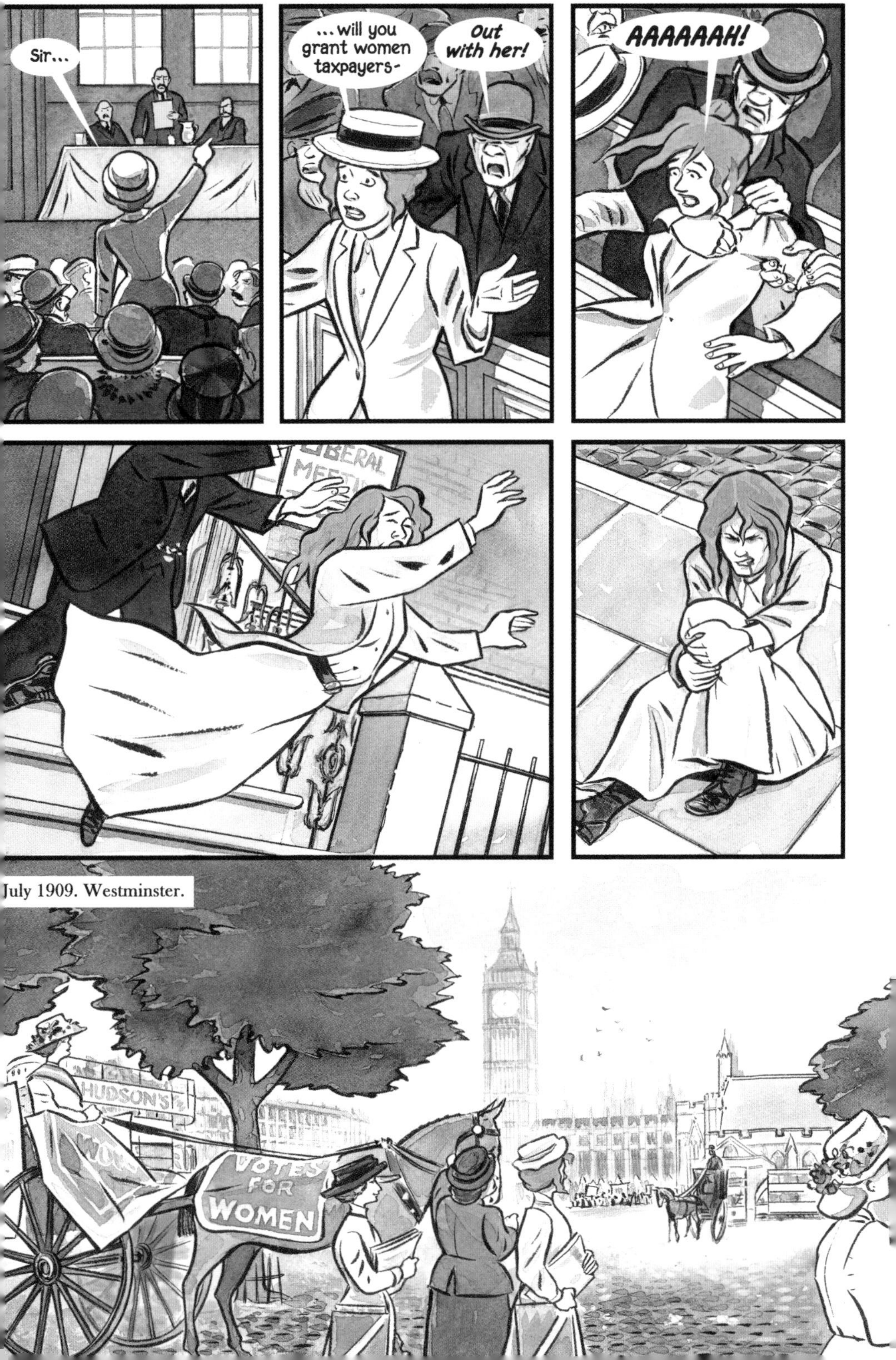
Sir...
...will you grant women taxpayers-
Out with her!
AAAAAAH!
July 1909. Westminster.
HUDSON'S
VOTES FOR WOMEN

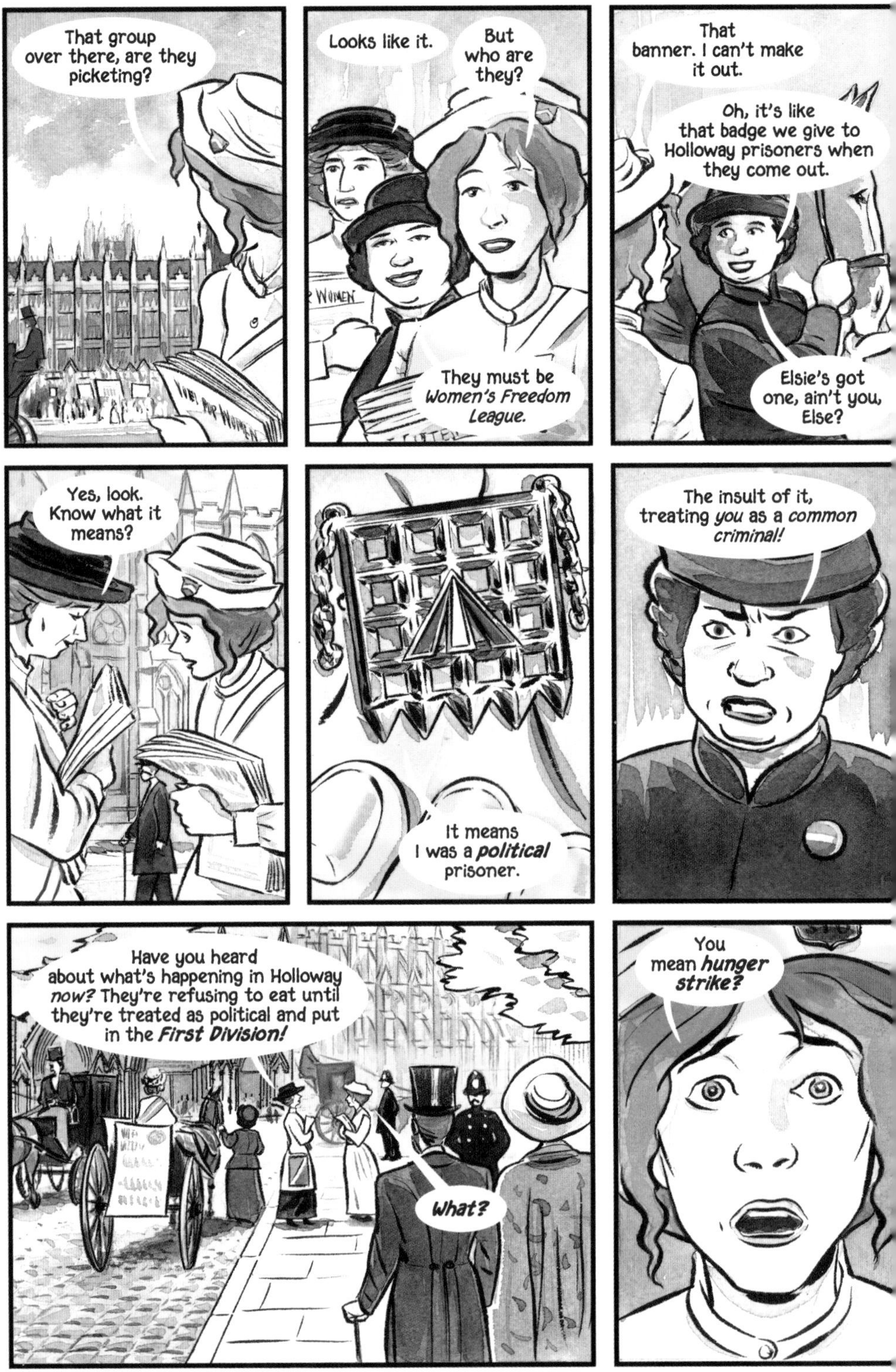

That group over there, are they picketing?
Votes for Women
Looks like it.
But who are they?
r Women
They must be *Women's Freedom League.*
That banner. I can't make it out.
Oh, it's like that badge we give to Holloway prisoners when they come out.
Elsie's got one, ain't you, Else?
Yes, look. Know what it means?
It means I was a ***political*** prisoner.
The insult of it, treating *you* as a *common criminal!*
Have you heard about what's happening in Holloway *now?* They're refusing to eat until they're treated as political and put in the ***First Division!***
What?
You mean ***hunger strike?***

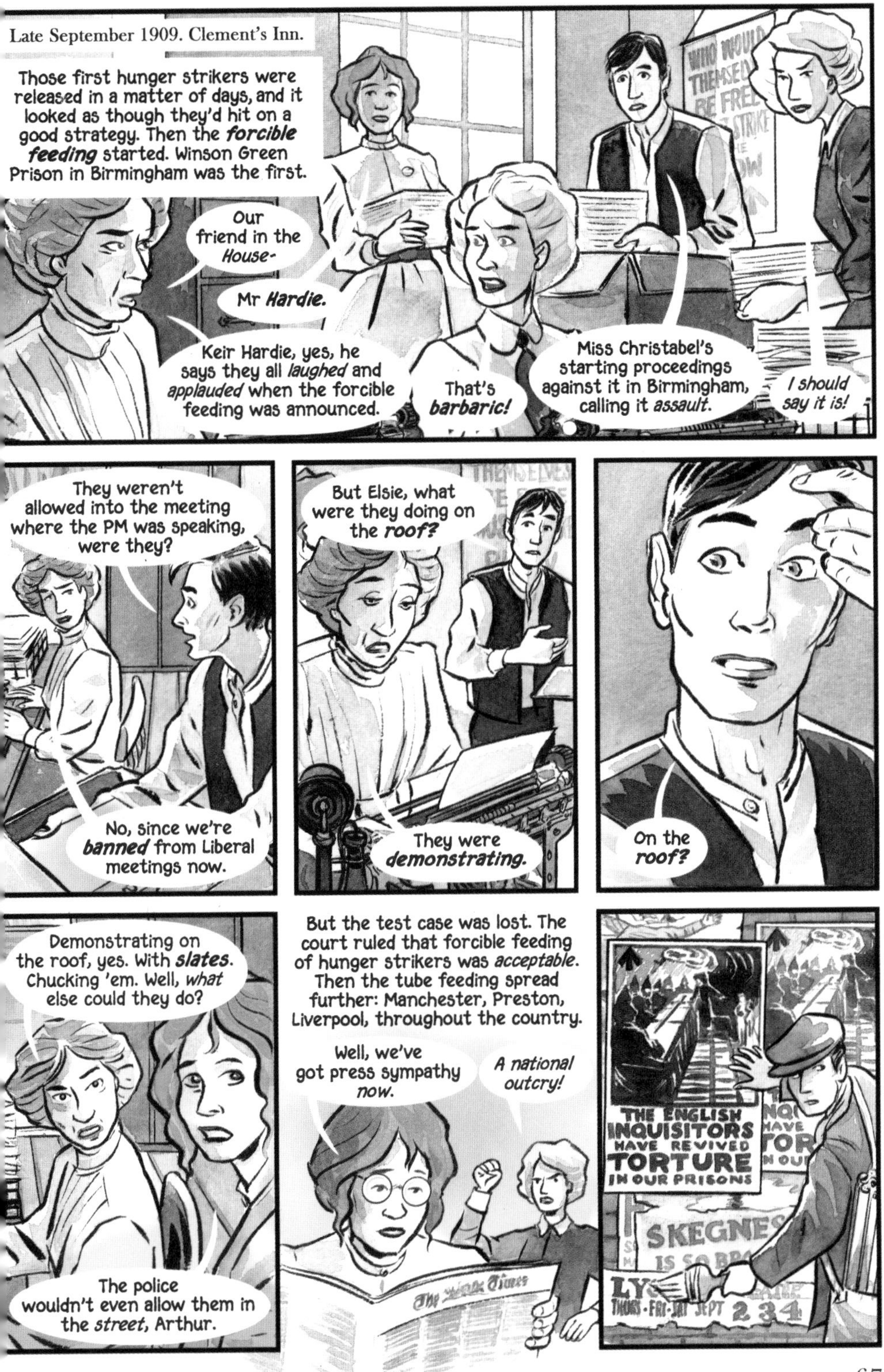

Late September 1909. Clement's Inn.
Those first hunger strikers were released in a matter of days, and it looked as though they'd hit on a good strategy. Then the *forcible feeding* started. Winson Green Prison in Birmingham was the first.
Our friend in the *House*-
Mr ***Hardie.***
Keir Hardie, yes, he says they all *laughed* and *applauded* when the forcible feeding was announced.
That's ***barbaric!***
Miss Christabel's starting proceedings against it in Birmingham, calling it *assault.*
I should say it is!
They weren't allowed into the meeting where the PM was speaking, were they?
No, since we're ***banned*** from Liberal meetings now.
But Elsie, what were they doing on the ***roof?***
They were ***demonstrating.***
On the ***roof?***
Demonstrating on the roof, yes. With ***slates.*** Chucking 'em. Well, *what* else could they do?
The police wouldn't even allow them in the *street,* Arthur.
But the test case was lost. The court ruled that forcible feeding of hunger strikers was *acceptable.* Then the tube feeding spread further: Manchester, Preston, Liverpool, throughout the country.
Well, we've got press sympathy *now.*
A national outcry!
THE ENGLISH INQUISITORS HAVE REVIVED TORTURE IN OUR PRISONS
SKEGNES
THURS · FRI · SAT SEPT 2 3 4

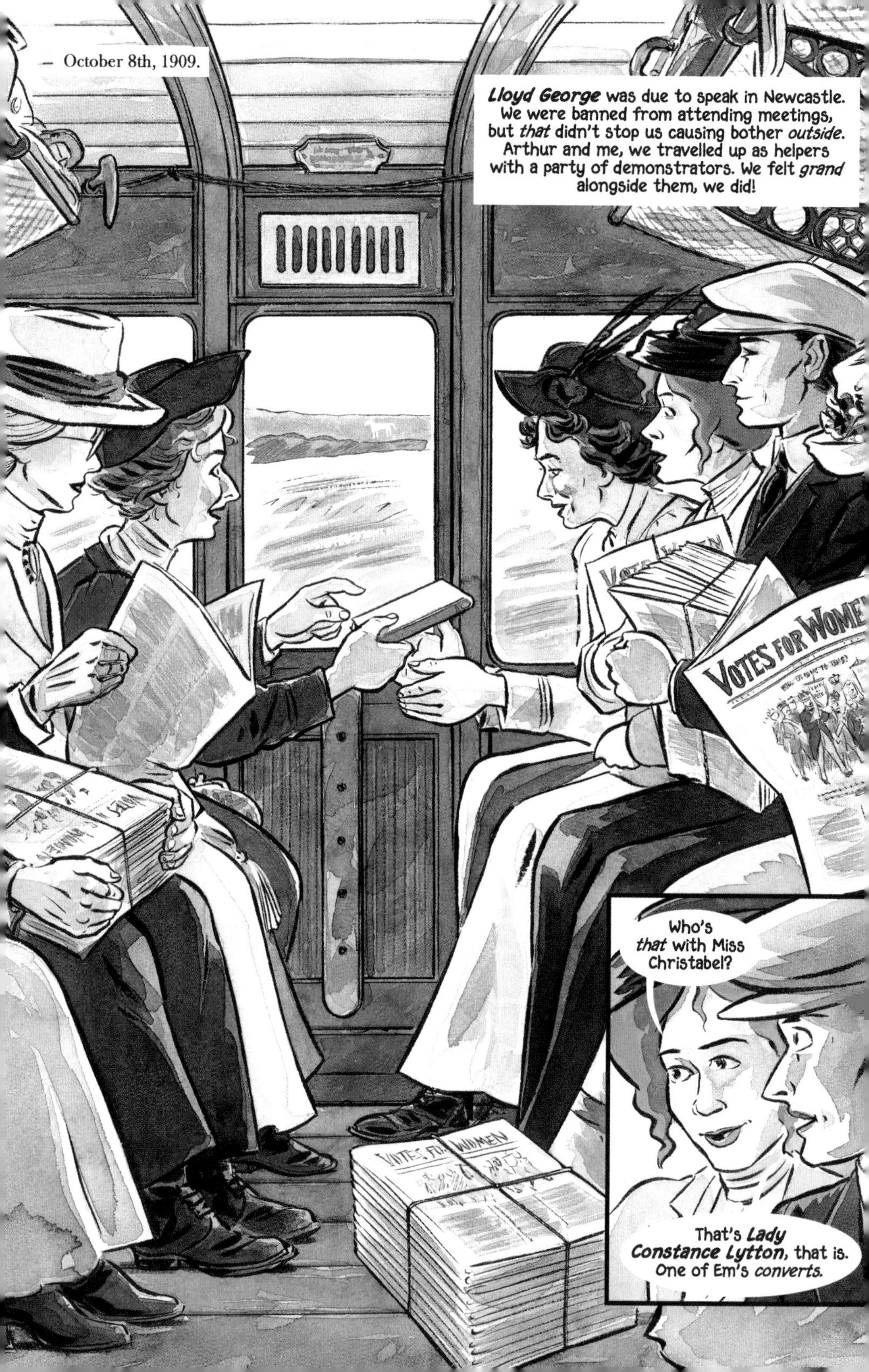
– October 8th, 1909.
Lloyd George was due to speak in Newcastle. We were banned from attending meetings, but that didn't stop us causing bother outside. Arthur and me, we travelled up as helpers with a party of demonstrators. We felt grand alongside them, we did!
VOTES FOR WOMEN
VOTES FOR WOMEN
Who's that with Miss Christabel?
That's Lady Constance Lytton, that is. One of Em's converts.

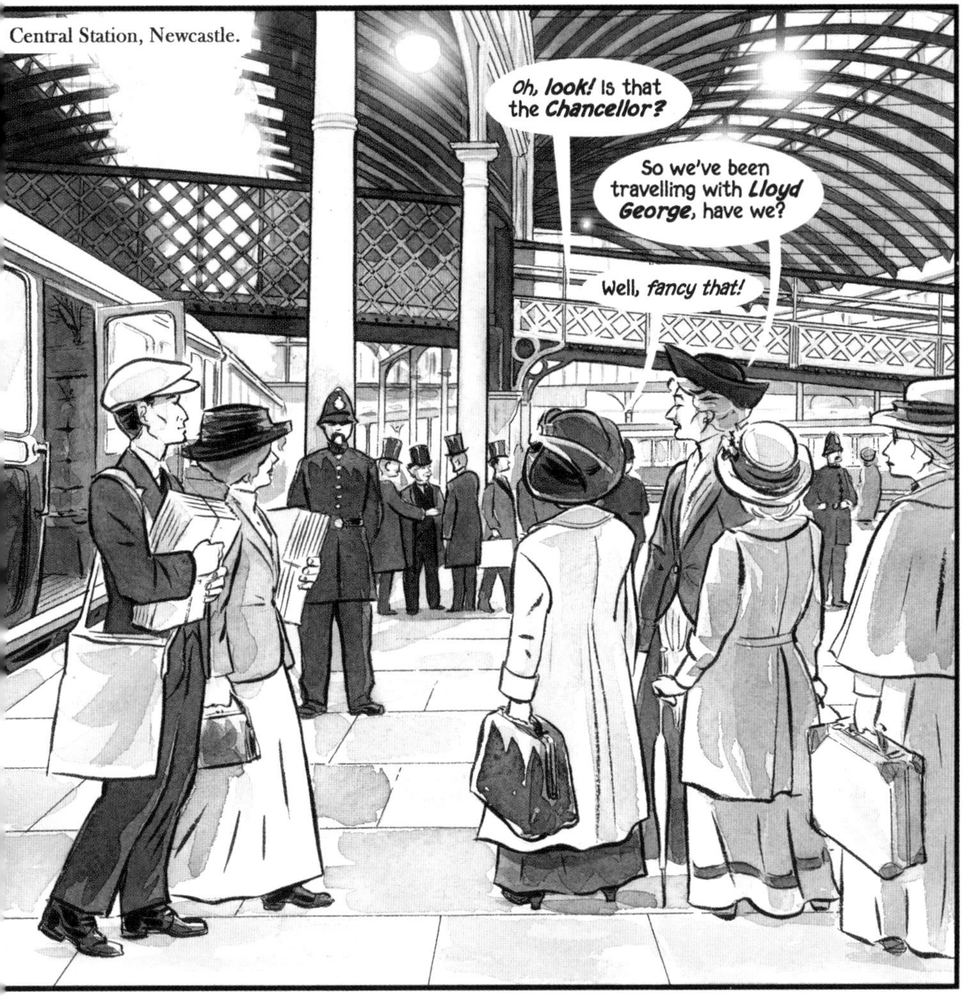
Central Station, Newcastle.
Oh, look! Is that the Chancellor?
So we've been travelling with Lloyd George, have we?
Well, fancy that!

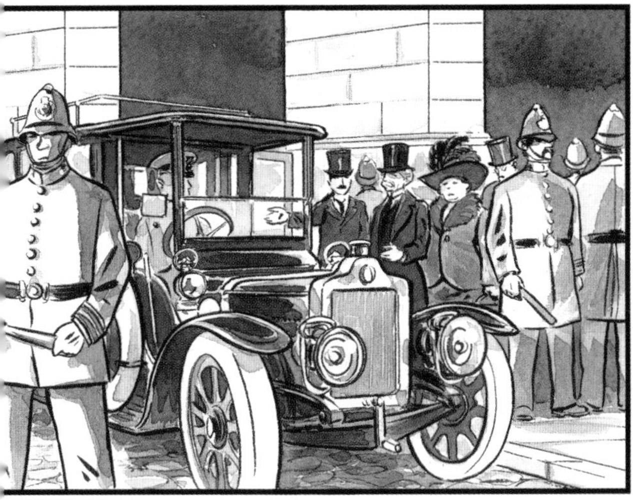

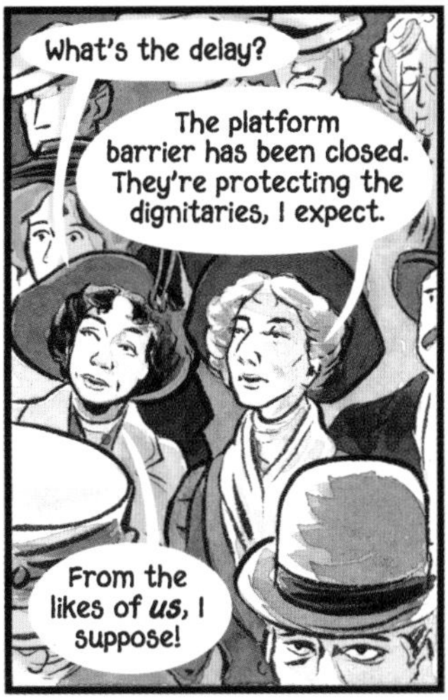
What's the delay?
The platform barrier has been closed. They're protecting the dignitaries, I expect.
From the likes of us, I suppose!

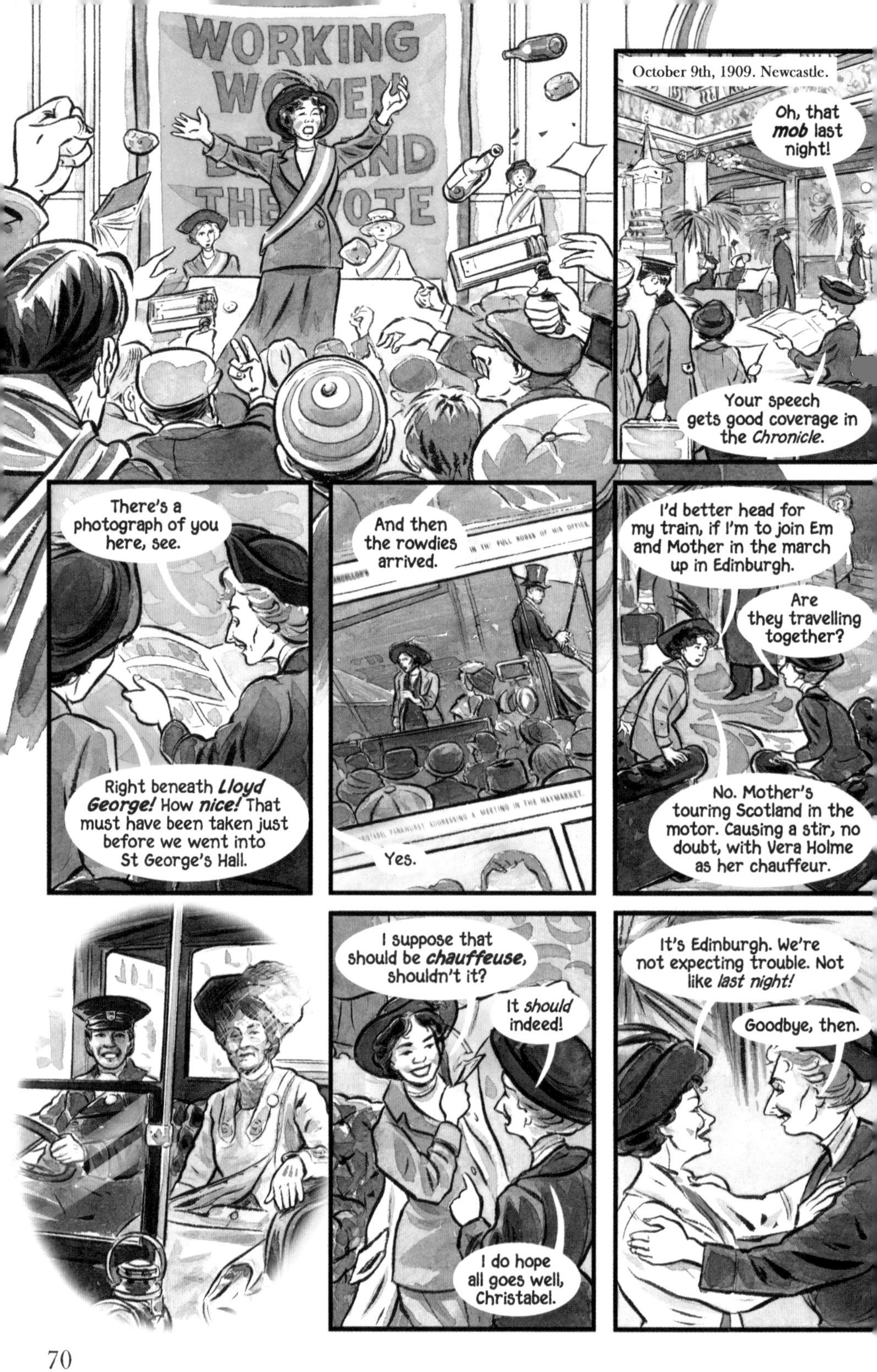
WORKING WOMEN DEMAND THE VOTE
October 9th, 1909. Newcastle.
Oh, that *mob* last night!
Your speech gets good coverage in the *Chronicle*.
There's a photograph of you here, see.
Right beneath *Lloyd George!* How *nice!* That must have been taken just before we went into St George's Hall.
And then the rowdies arrived.
Yes.
I'd better head for my train, if I'm to join Em and Mother in the march up in Edinburgh.
Are they travelling together?
No. Mother's touring Scotland in the motor. Causing a stir, no doubt, with Vera Holme as her chauffeur.
I suppose that should be *chauffeuse*, shouldn't it?
It *should* indeed!
I do hope all goes well, Christabel.
It's Edinburgh. We're not expecting trouble. Not like *last night!*
Goodbye, then.

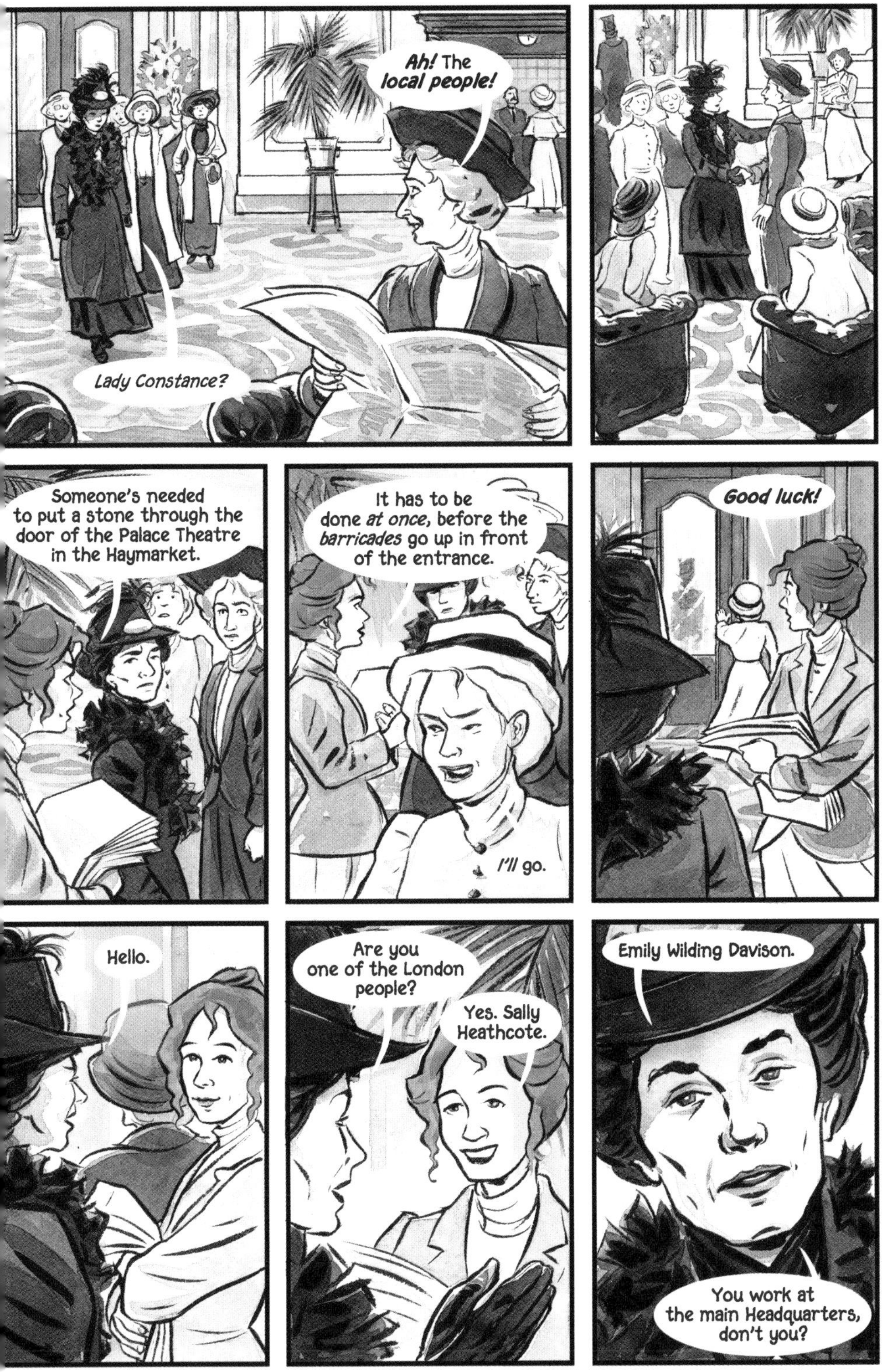

Ah! The *local people!*
Lady Constance?
Someone's needed to put a stone through the door of the Palace Theatre in the Haymarket.
It has to be done *at once*, before the *barricades* go up in front of the entrance.
I'll go.
Good luck!
Hello.
Are you one of the London people?
Yes. Sally Heathcote.
Emily Wilding Davison.
You work at the main Headquarters, don't you?

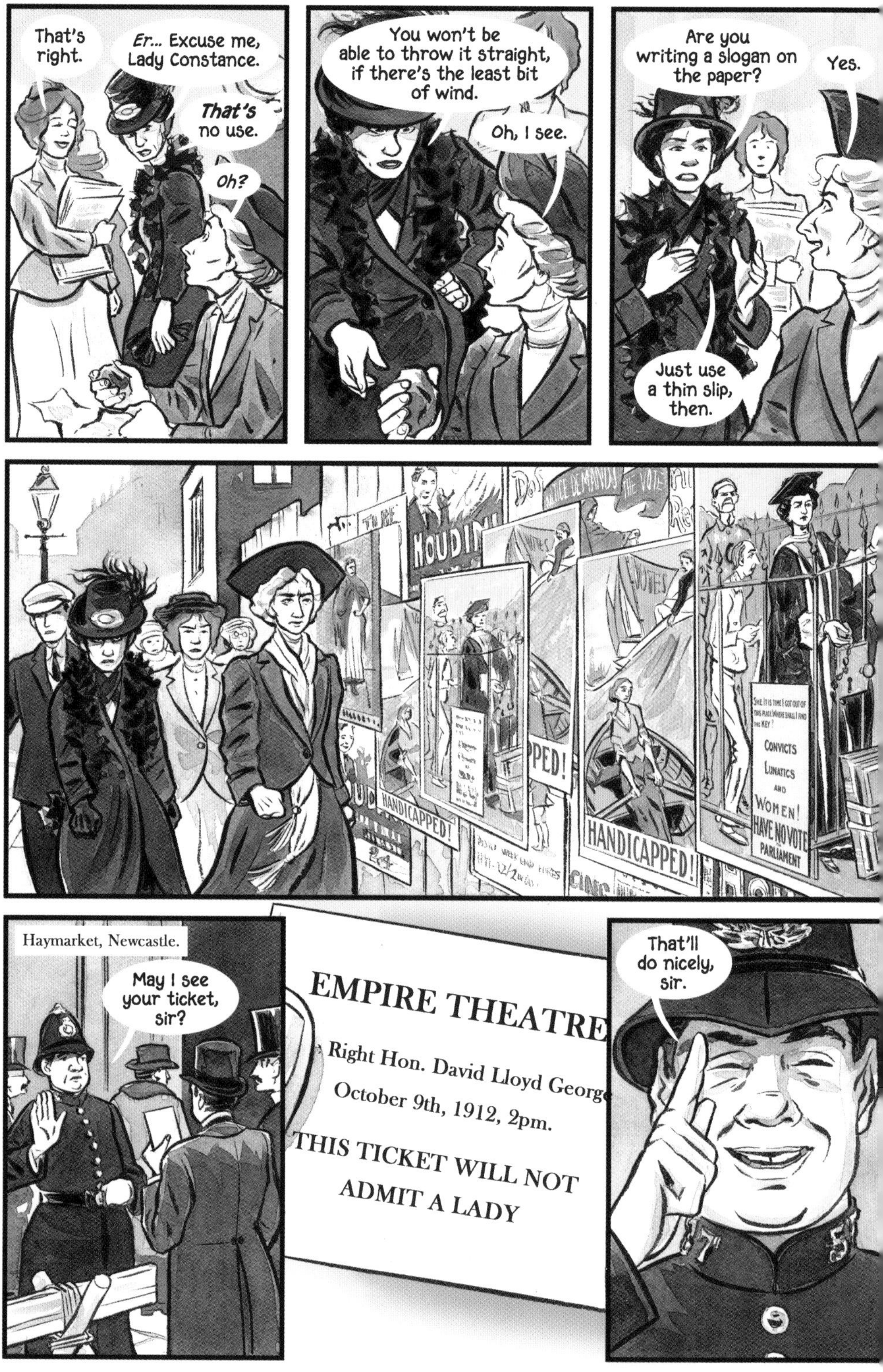

That's right.
Er... Excuse me, Lady Constance.
That's no use.
Oh?
You won't be able to throw it straight, if there's the least bit of wind.
Oh, I see.
Are you writing a slogan on the paper?
Yes.
Just use a thin slip, then.
HANDICAPPED!
HANDICAPPED!
CONVICTS
LUNATICS
AND
WOMEN!
HAVE NO VOTE
PARLIAMENT
Haymarket, Newcastle.
May I see your ticket, sir?
EMPIRE THEATRE
Right Hon. David Lloyd George
October 9th, 1912, 2pm.
THIS TICKET WILL NOT ADMIT A LADY
That'll do nicely, sir.

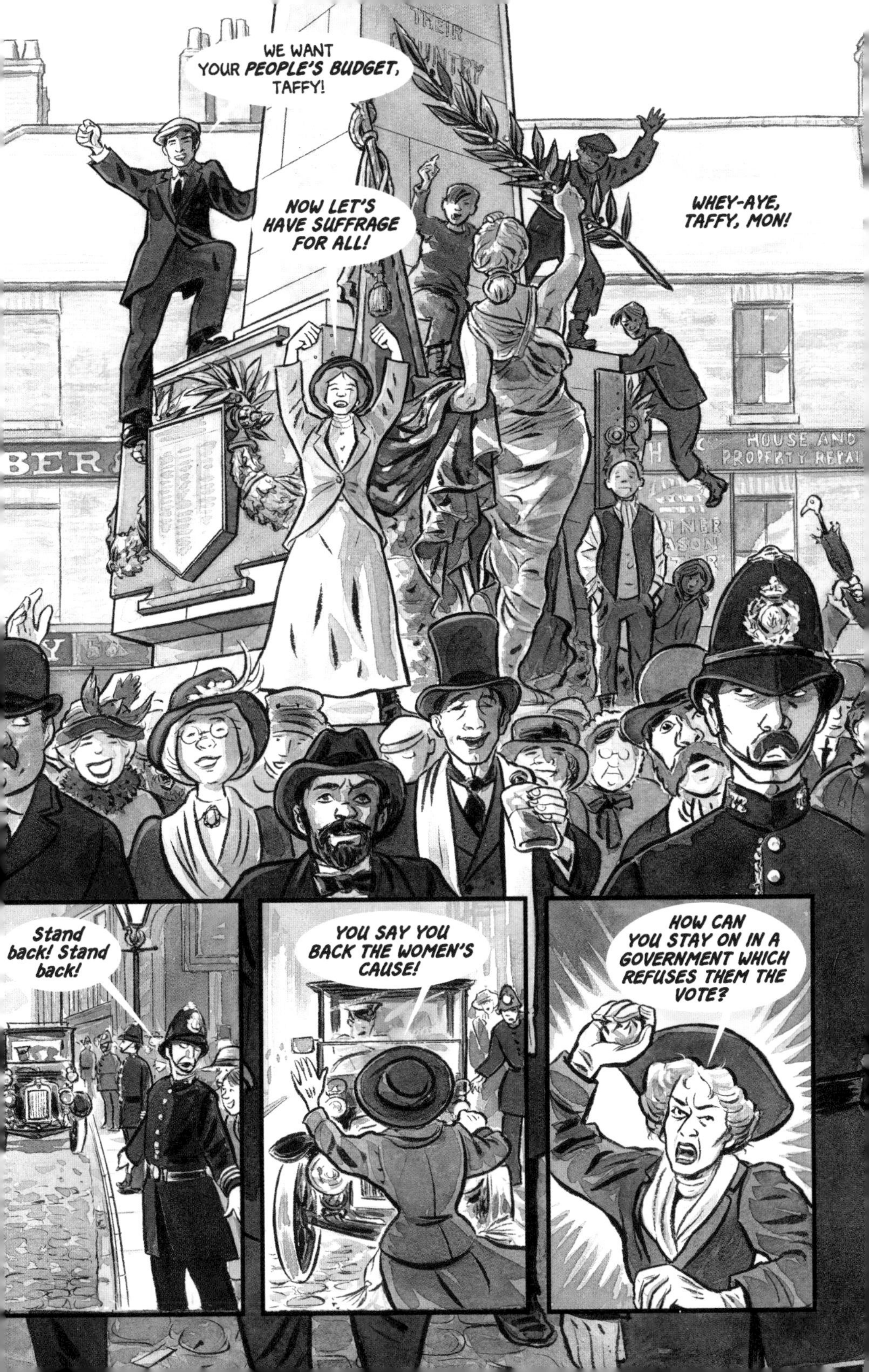
THEIR
COUNTRY
WE WANT YOUR PEOPLE'S BUDGET, TAFFY!
NOW LET'S HAVE SUFFRAGE FOR ALL!
WHEY-AYE, TAFFY, MON!
HOUSE AND PROPERTY REPAI
Stand back! Stand back!
YOU SAY YOU BACK THE WOMEN'S CAUSE!
HOW CAN YOU STAY ON IN A GOVERNMENT WHICH REFUSES THEM THE VOTE?

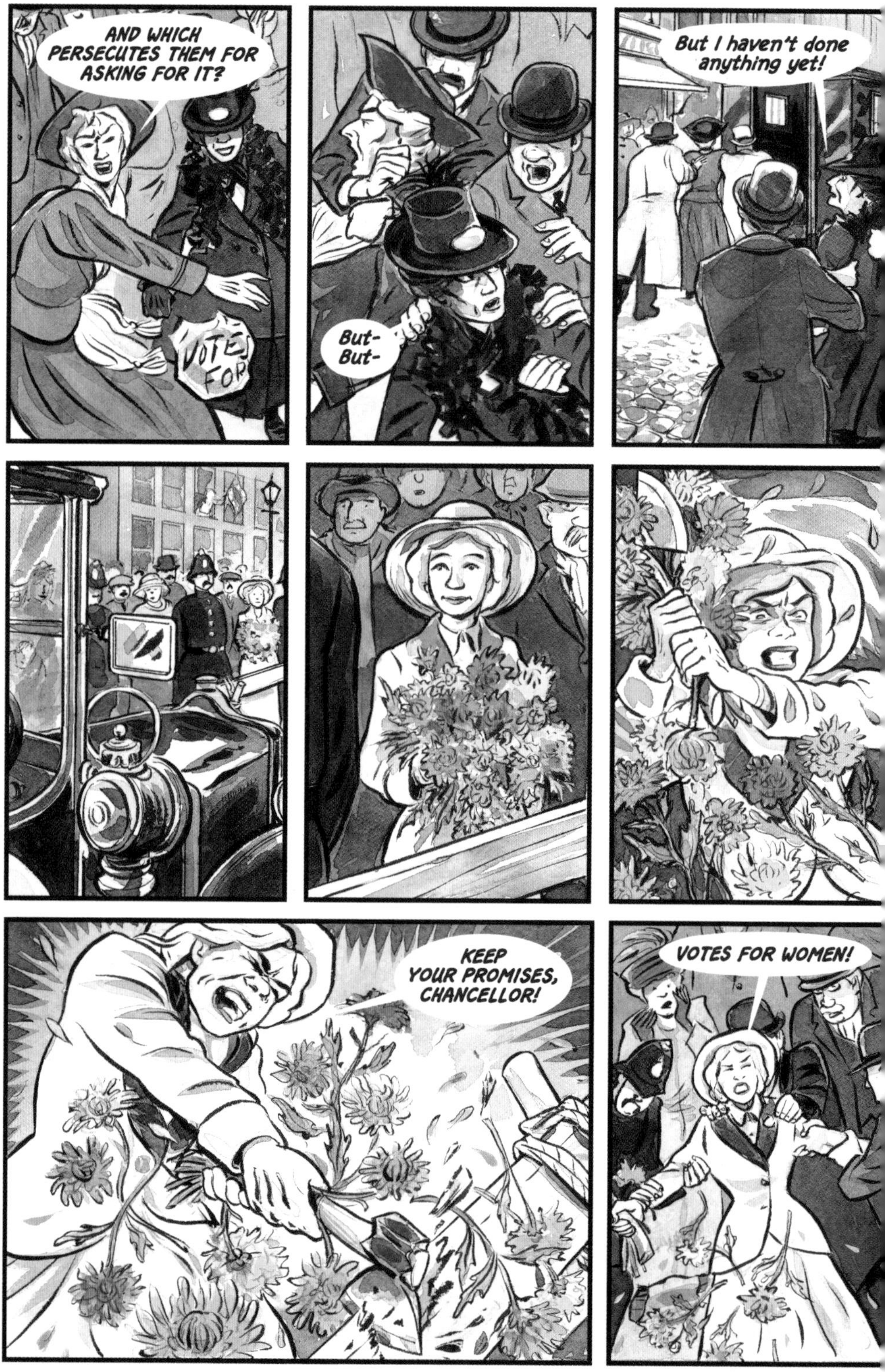

AND WHICH PERSECUTES THEM FOR ASKING FOR IT?
VOTES FOR
But- But-
But I haven't done anything yet!
KEEP YOUR PROMISES, CHANCELLOR!
VOTES FOR WOMEN!

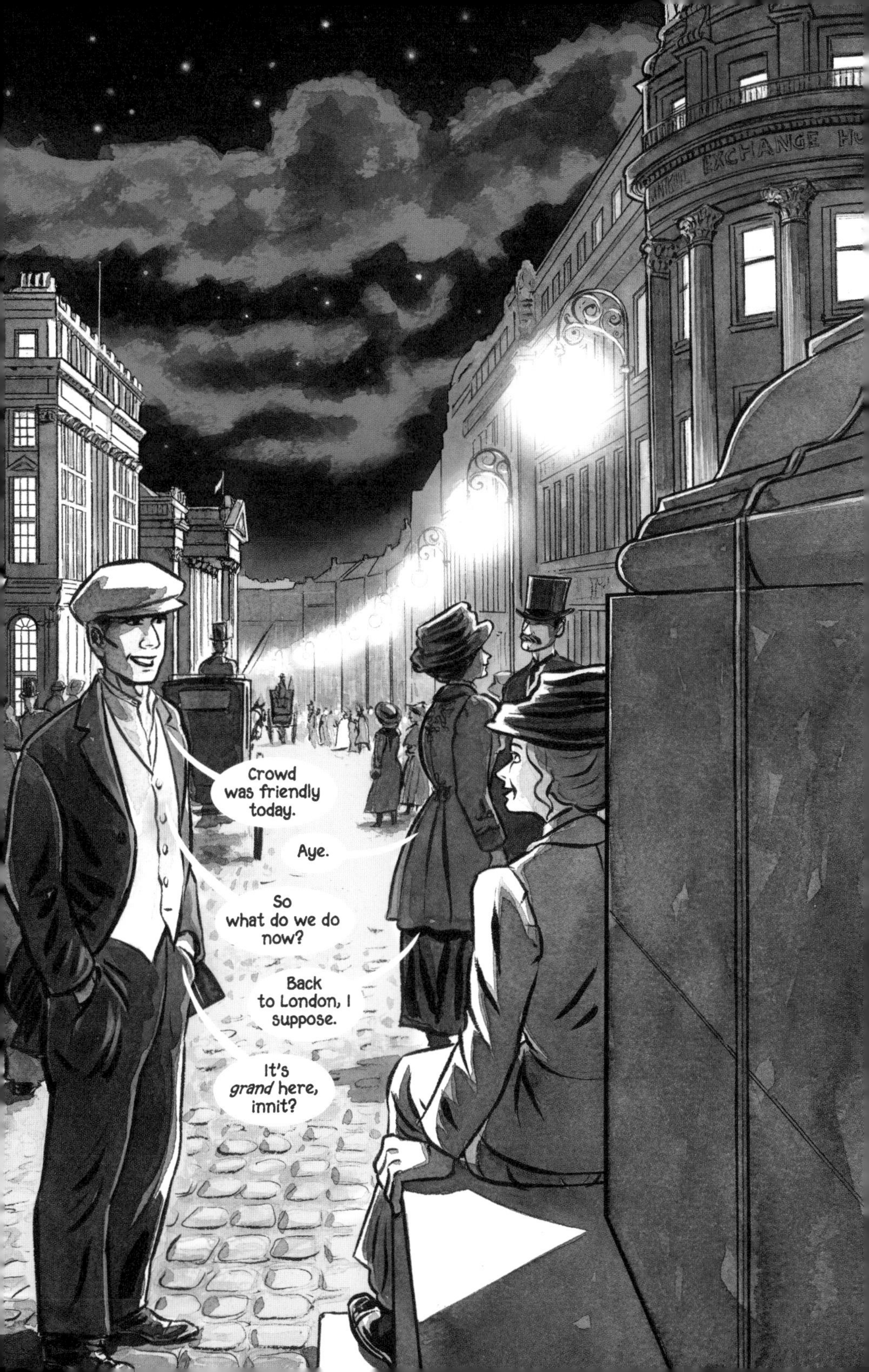
EXCHANGE
Crowd was friendly today.
Aye.
So what do we do now?
Back to London, I suppose.
It's *grand* here, innit?

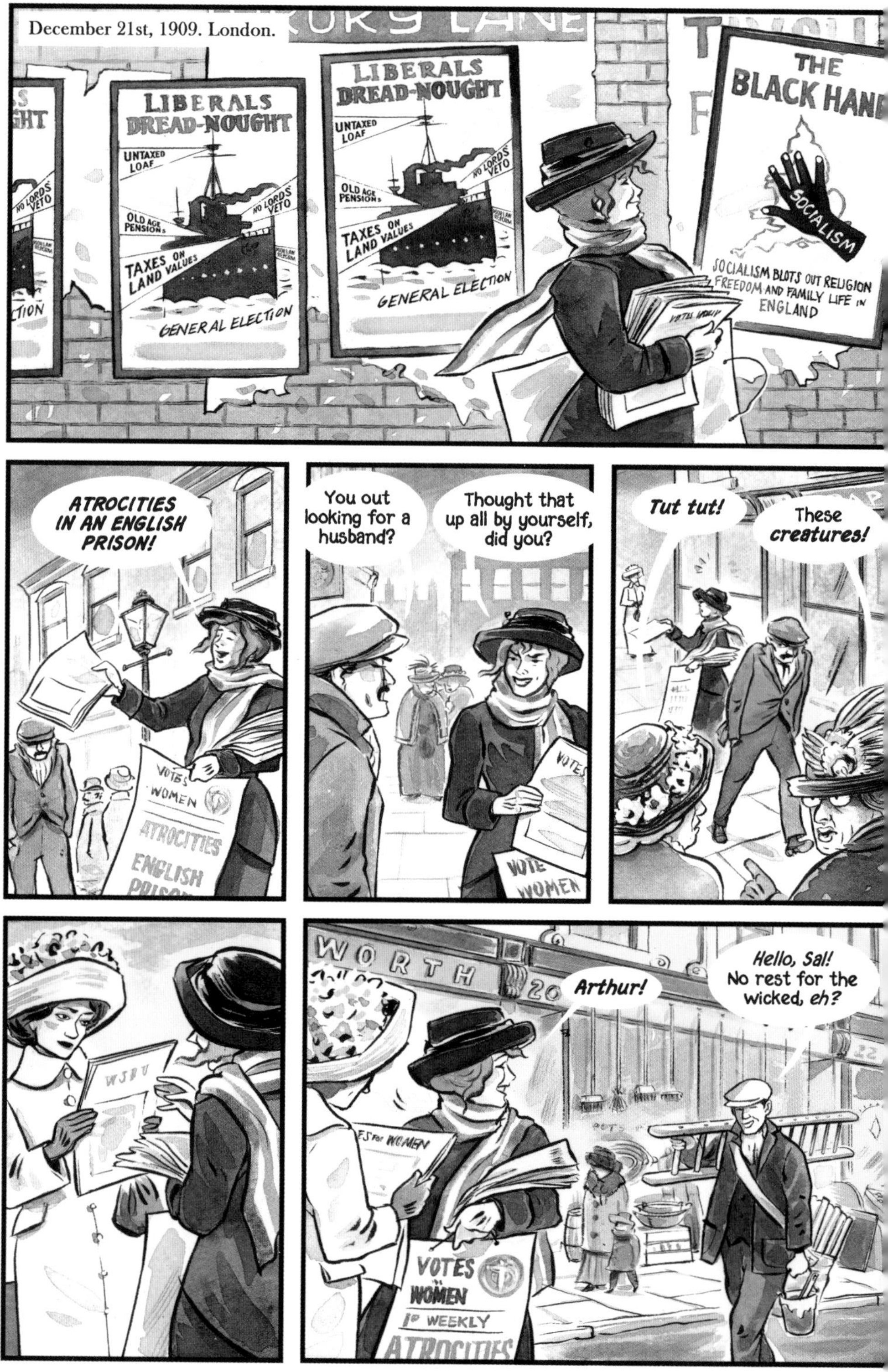
December 21st, 1909. London.
LIBERALS DREAD-NOUGHT
UNTAXED LOAF
OLD AGE PENSIONS
TAXES ON LAND VALUES
NO LORDS VETO
GENERAL ELECTION
THE BLACK HAND
SOCIALISM
SOCIALISM BLOTS OUT RELIGION FREEDOM AND FAMILY LIFE IN ENGLAND
ATROCITIES IN AN ENGLISH PRISON!
VOTES WOMEN
ATROCITIES
ENGLISH
You out looking for a husband?
Thought that up all by yourself, did you?
VOTE WOMEN
Tut tut!
These creatures!
WSPU
WORTH
Arthur!
Hello, Sal! No rest for the wicked, eh?
VOTES FOR WOMEN
VOTES WOMEN
1d WEEKLY

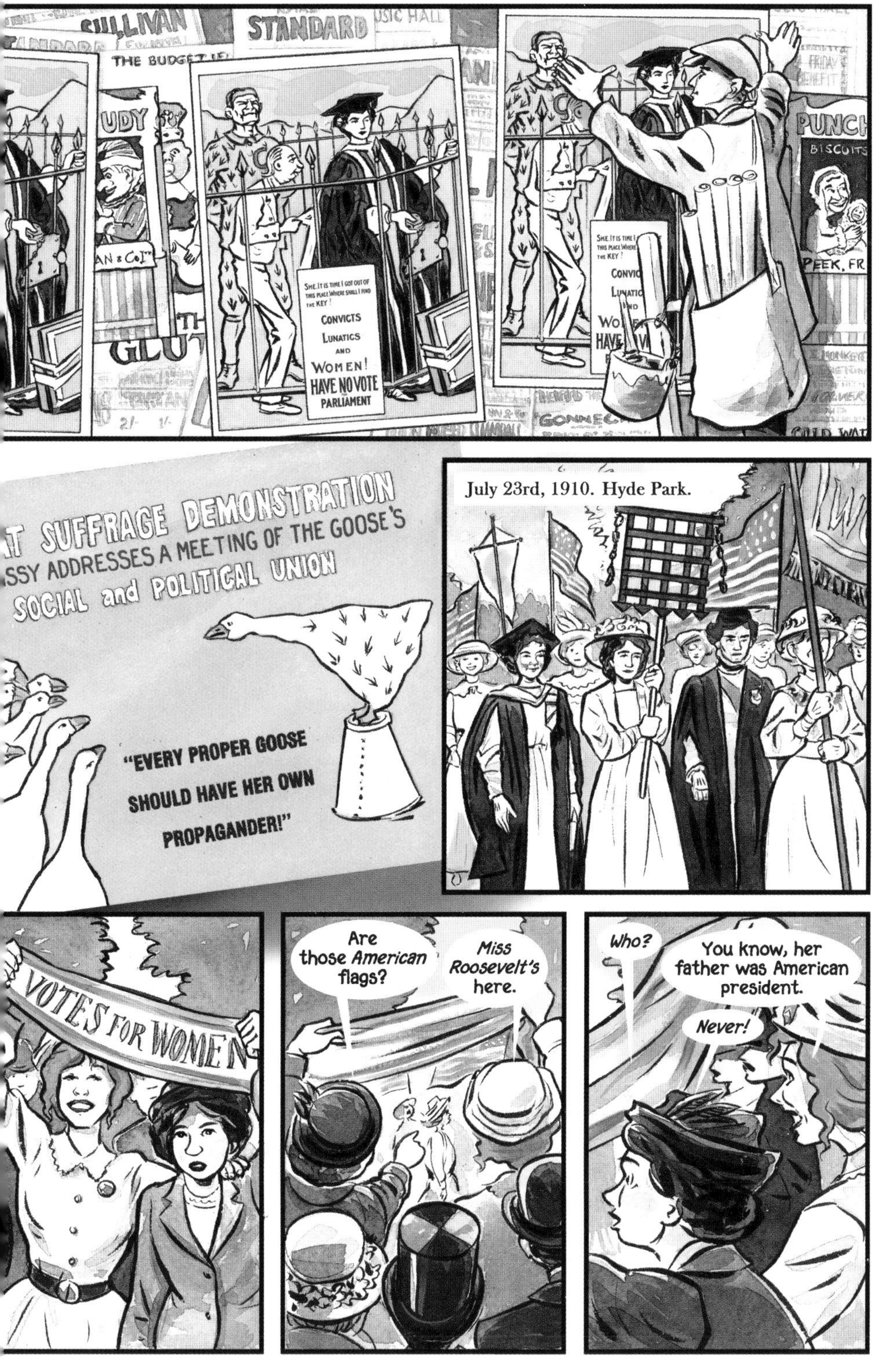
SULLIVAN
STANDARD
THE BUDGET
SHE. IT IS TIME I GOT OUT OF THIS PLACE. WHERE SHALL I FIND THE KEY!
CONVICTS
LUNATICS
AND
WOMEN!
HAVE NO VOTE
PARLIAMENT
PUNCH
BISCUITS
T SUFFRAGE DEMONSTRATION
SSY ADDRESSES A MEETING OF THE GOOSE'S
SOCIAL and POLITICAL UNION
"EVERY PROPER GOOSE SHOULD HAVE HER OWN PROPAGANDER!"
July 23rd, 1910. Hyde Park.
VOTES FOR WOMEN
Are those *American* flags?
Miss Roosevelt's here.
Who?
You know, her father was American president.
Never!

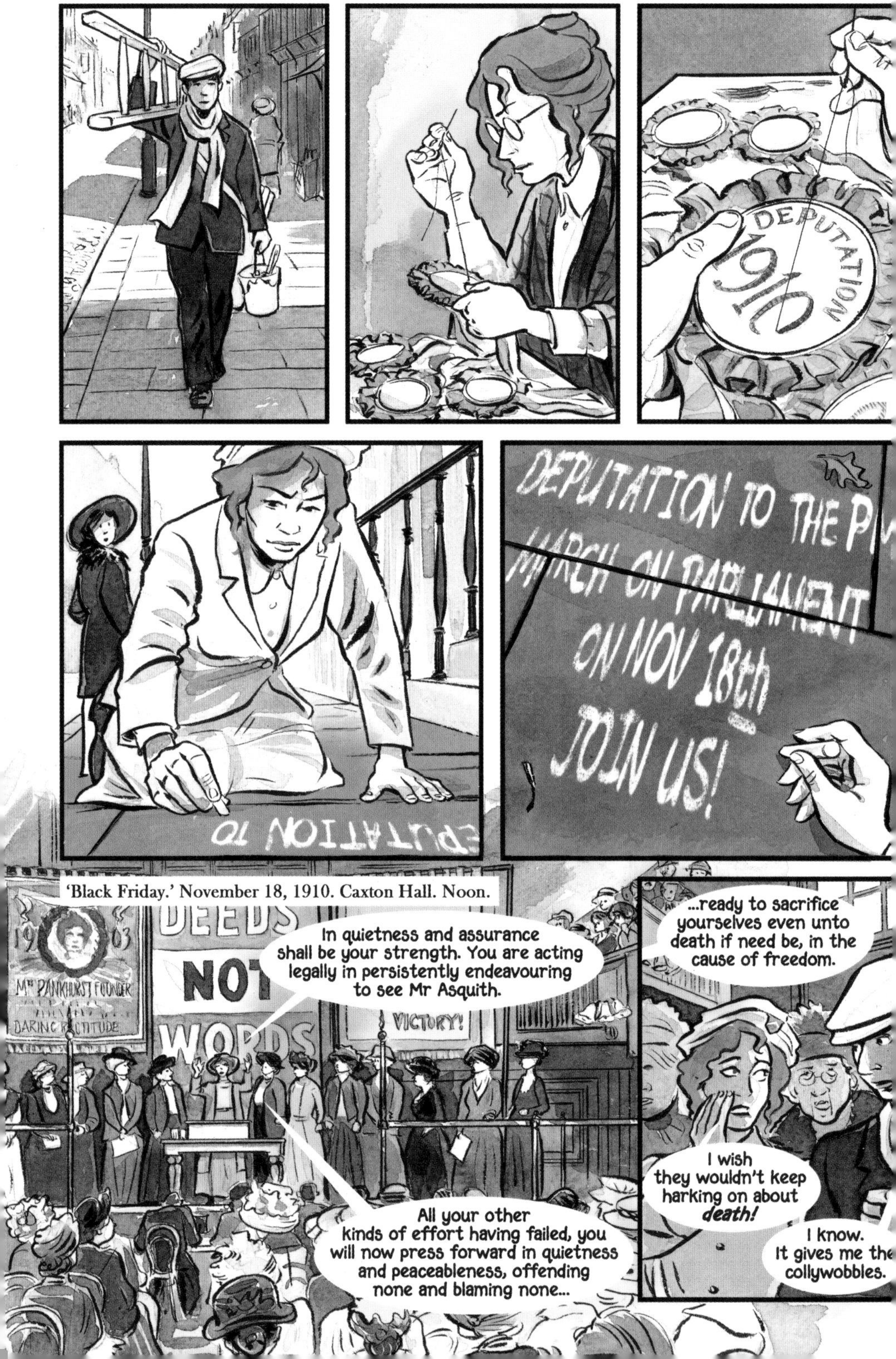
DEPUTATION
1910
DEPUTATION TO
DEPUTATION TO THE P
MARCH ON PARLIAMENT
ON NOV 18th
JOIN US!
'Black Friday.' November 18, 1910. Caxton Hall. Noon.
DEEDS NOT WORDS
19 03
MRS PANKHURST FOUNDER
DARING RECTITUDE
VICTORY!
In quietness and assurance shall be your strength. You are acting legally in persistently endeavouring to see Mr Asquith.
All your other kinds of effort having failed, you will now press forward in quietness and peaceableness, offending none and blaming none...
...ready to sacrifice yourselves even unto death if need be, in the cause of freedom.
I wish they wouldn't keep harking on about *death!*
I know. It gives me the collywobbles.

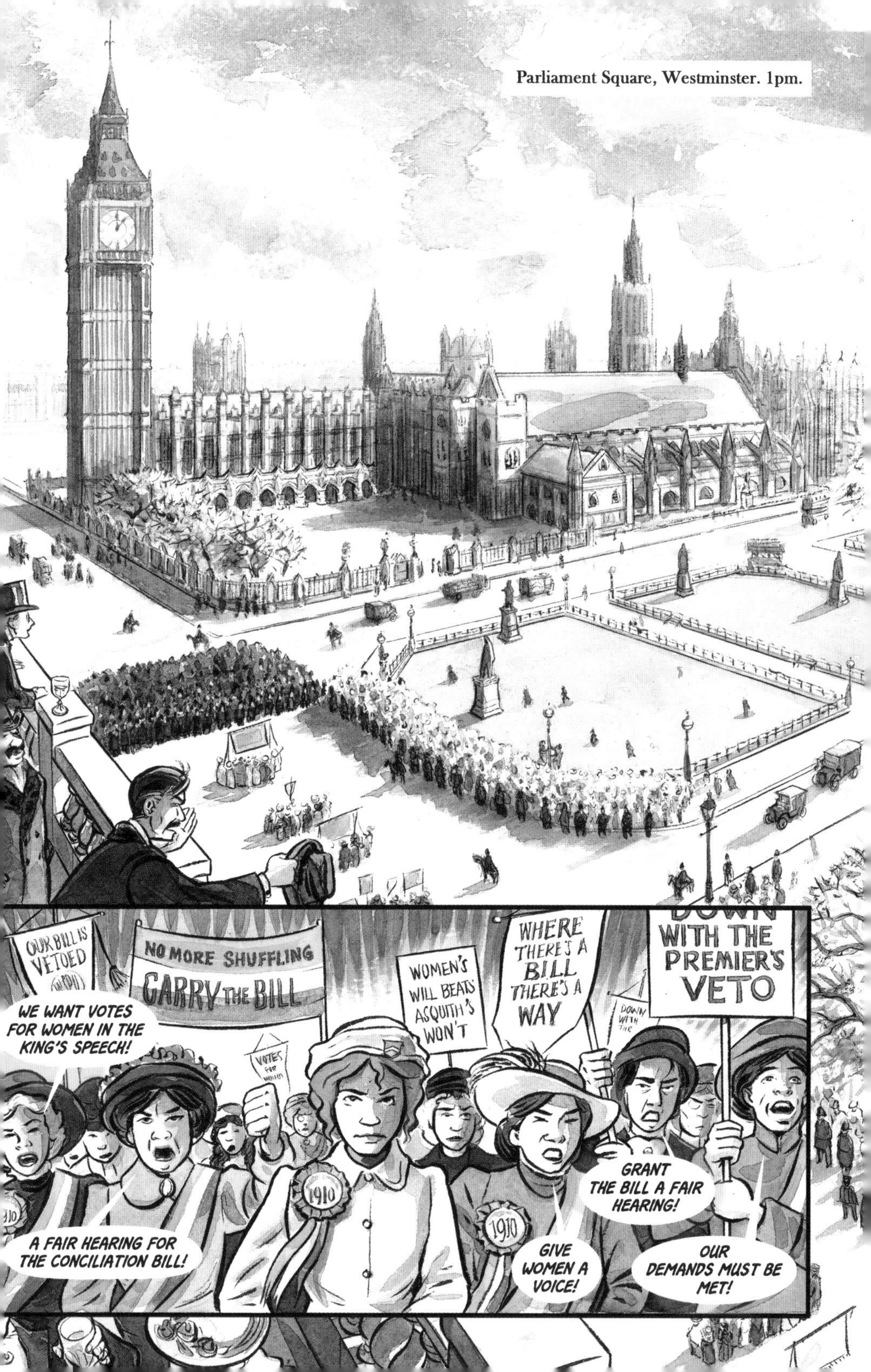
Parliament Square, Westminster. 1pm.
OUR BILL IS VETOED
NO MORE SHUFFLING CARRY THE BILL
WOMEN'S WILL BEATS ASQUITH'S WON'T
WHERE THERE'S A BILL THERE'S A WAY
DOWN WITH THE
WITH THE PREMIER'S VETO
WE WANT VOTES FOR WOMEN IN THE KING'S SPEECH!
A FAIR HEARING FOR THE CONCILIATION BILL!
GRANT THE BILL A FAIR HEARING!
GIVE WOMEN A VOICE!
OUR DEMANDS MUST BE MET!

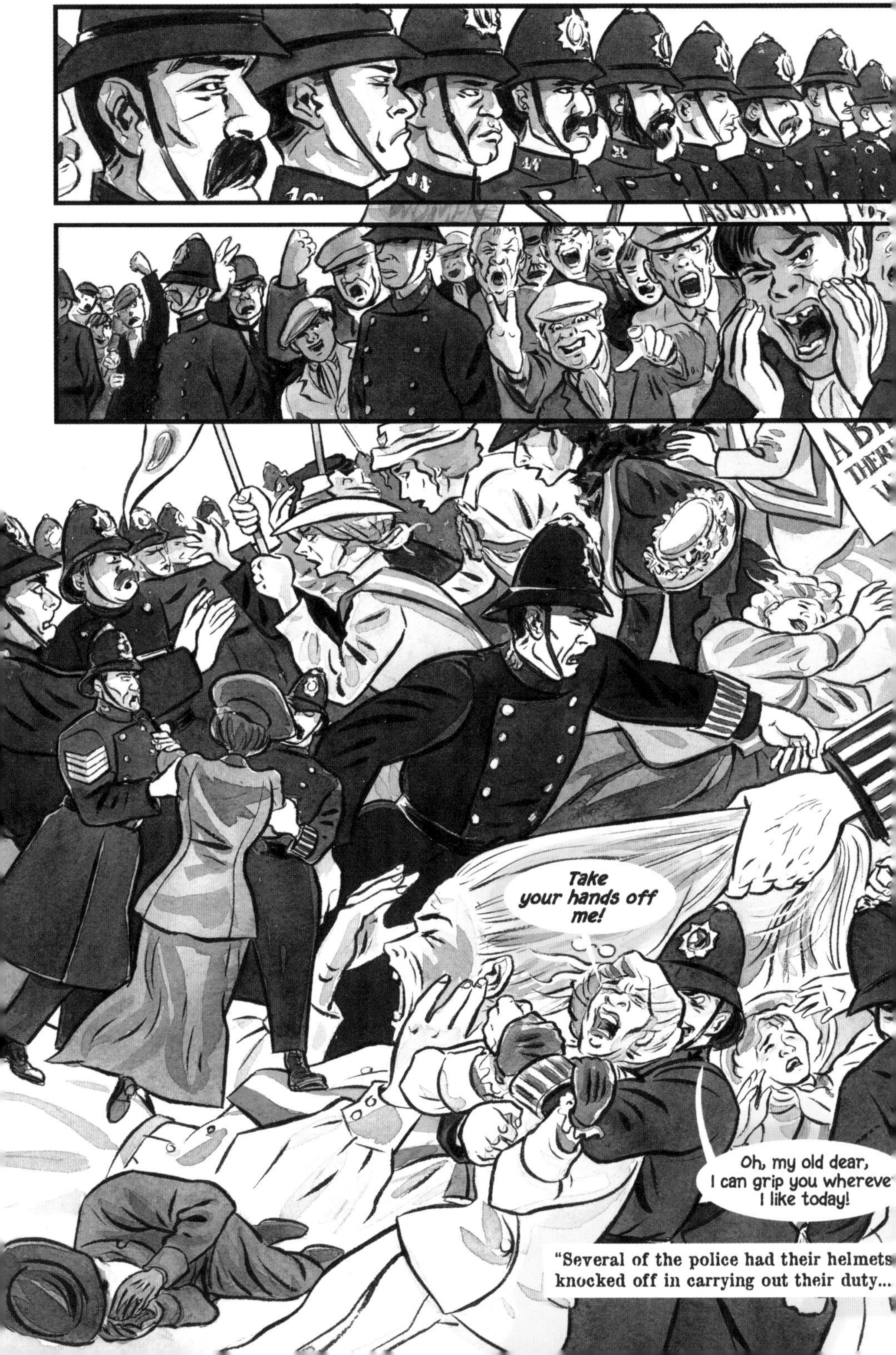
Take your hands off me!
Oh, my old dear, I can grip you whereve I like today!
“Several of the police had their helmets knocked off in carrying out their duty...

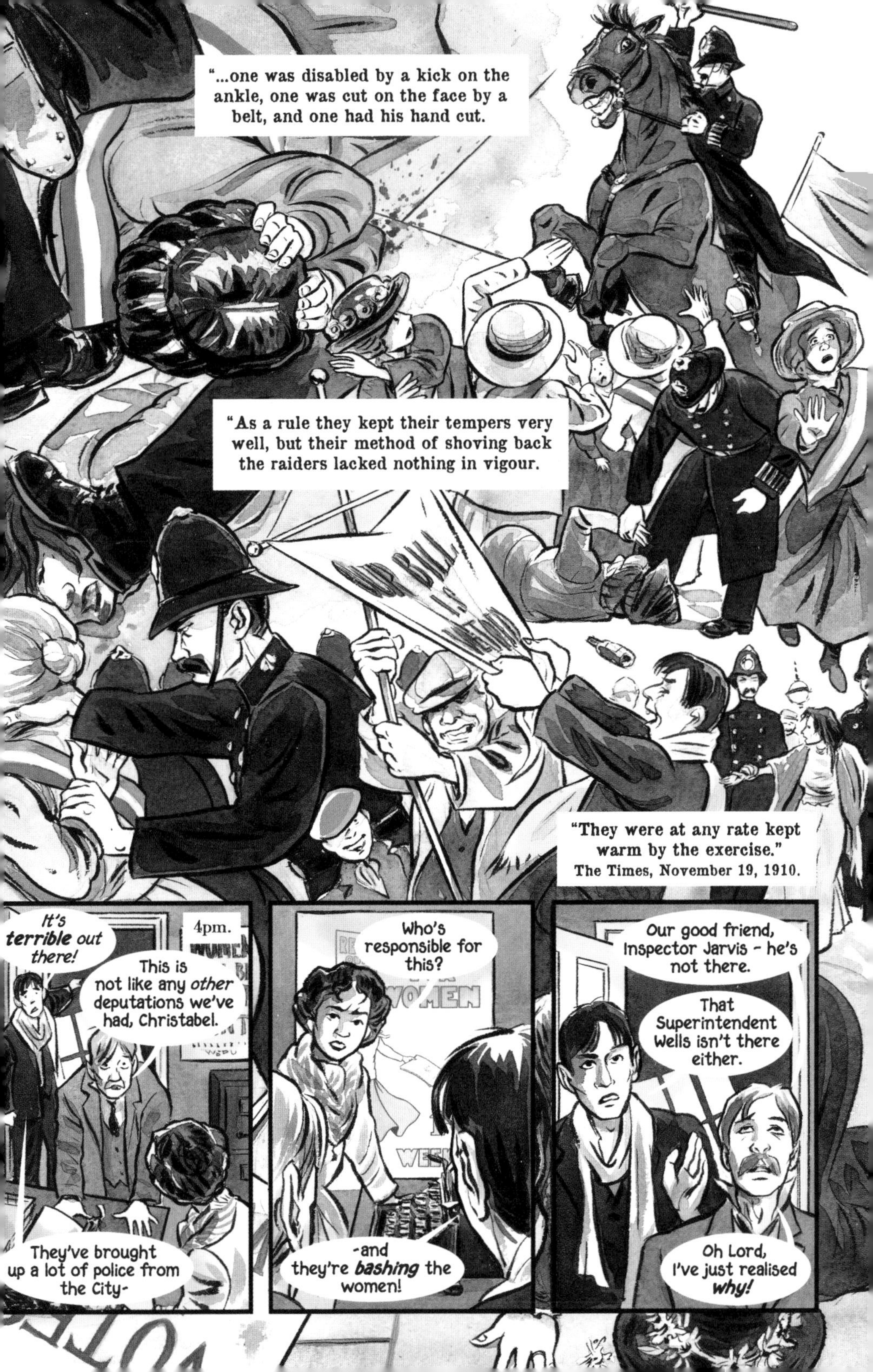
"...one was disabled by a kick on the ankle, one was cut on the face by a belt, and one had his hand cut.
"As a rule they kept their tempers very well, but their method of shoving back the raiders lacked nothing in vigour.
"They were at any rate kept warm by the exercise."
The Times, November 19, 1910.
4pm.
It's terrible out there!
This is not like any other deputations we've had, Christabel.
They've brought up a lot of police from the City-
Who's responsible for this?
-and they're bashing the women!
Our good friend, Inspector Jarvis - he's not there.
That Superintendent Wells isn't there either.
Oh Lord, I've just realised why!

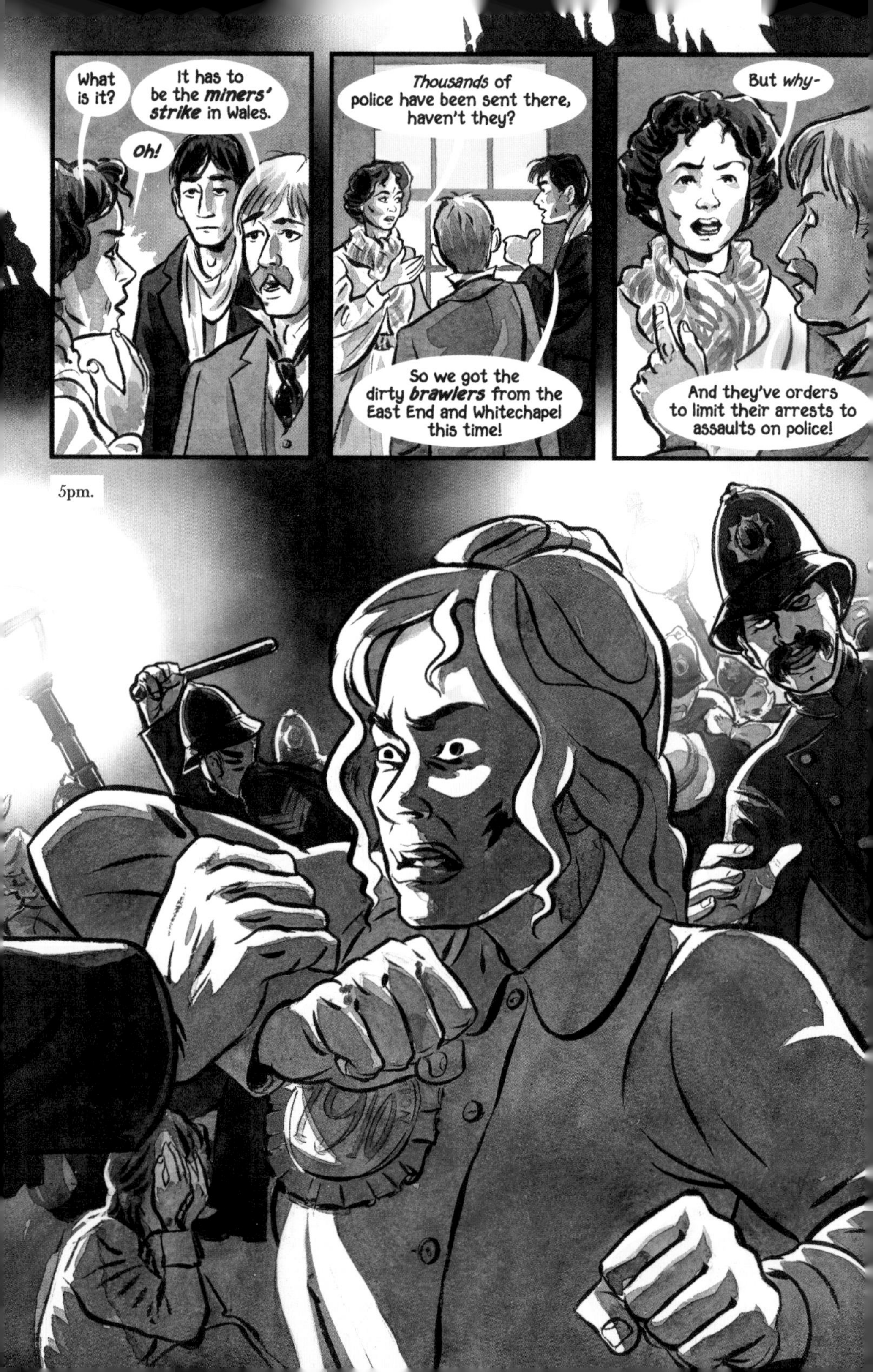
What is it?
It has to be the *miners' strike* in Wales.
Oh!
Thousands of police have been sent there, haven't they?
So we got the dirty *brawlers* from the East End and Whitechapel this time!
But *why-*
And they've orders to limit their arrests to assaults on police!
5pm.
1910

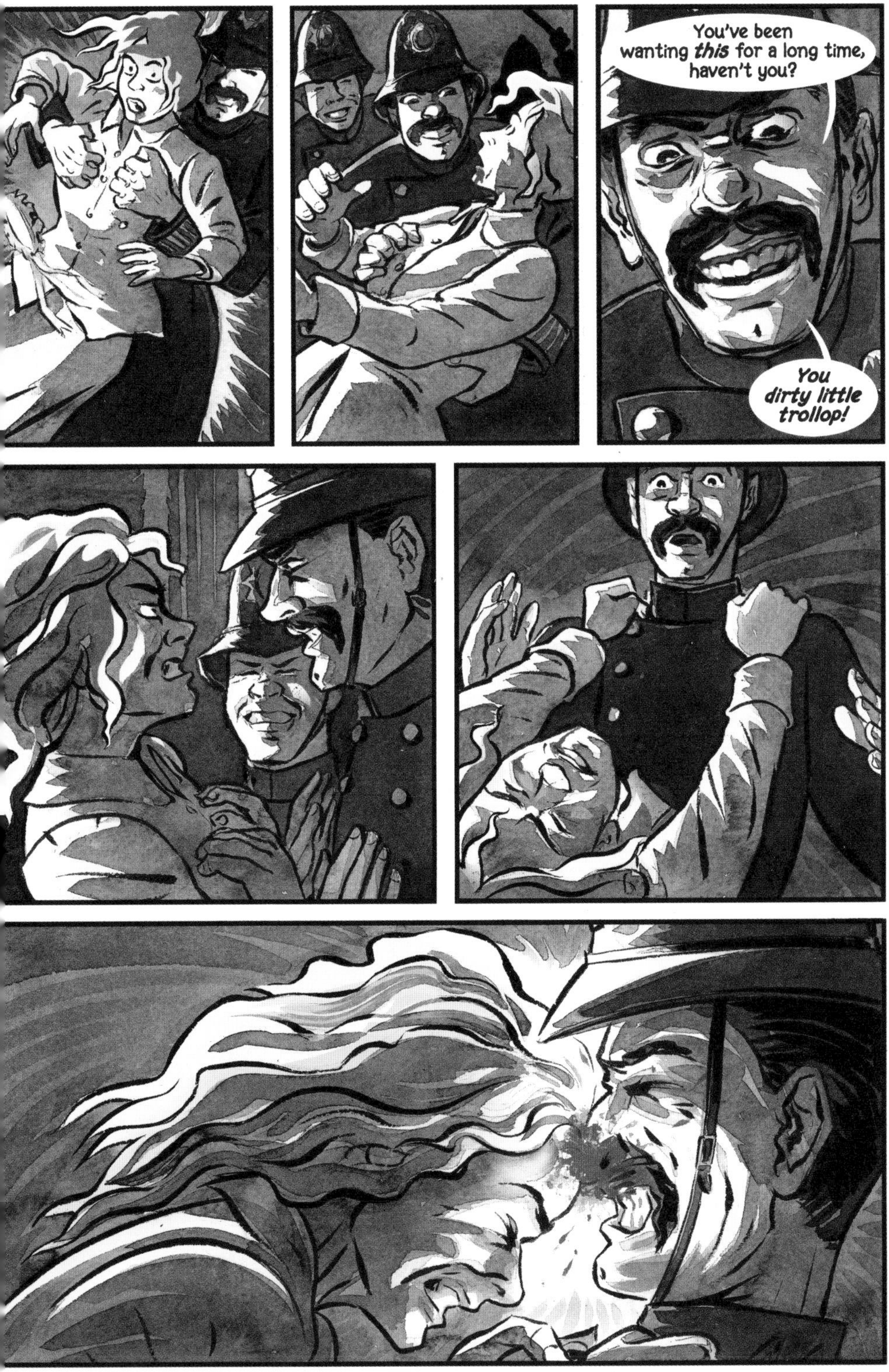
You've been wanting *this* for a long time, haven't you?
You dirty little trollop!

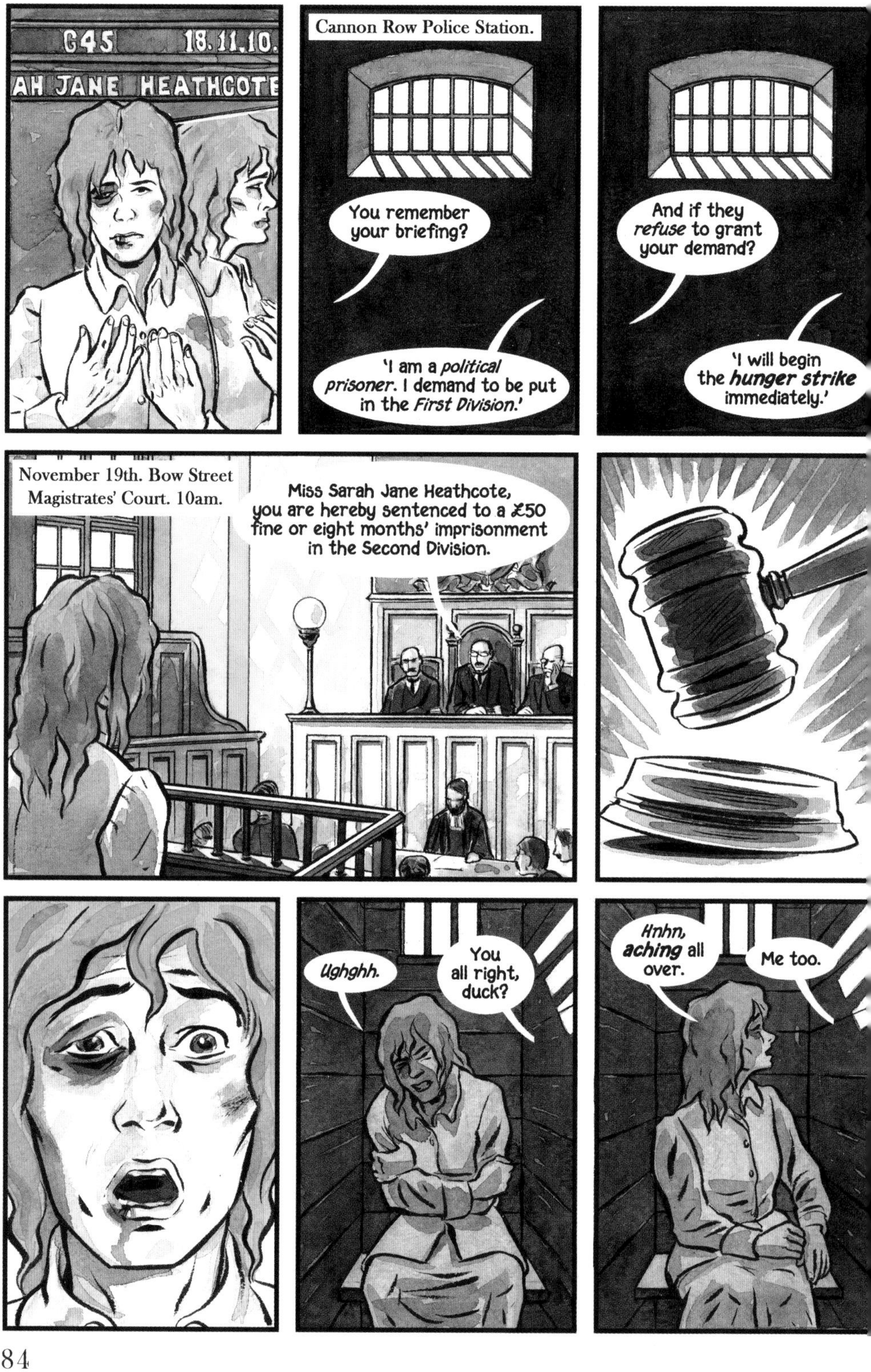
G45 18.11.10.
AH JANE HEATHCOTE
Cannon Row Police Station.
You remember your briefing?
'I am a *political prisoner*. I demand to be put in the *First Division*.'
And if they *refuse* to grant your demand?
'I will begin the ***hunger strike*** immediately.'
November 19th. Bow Street Magistrates' Court. 10am.
Miss Sarah Jane Heathcote, you are hereby sentenced to a £50 fine or eight months' imprisonment in the Second Division.
Ughghh.
You all right, duck?
Hnhn, ***aching*** all over.
Me too.

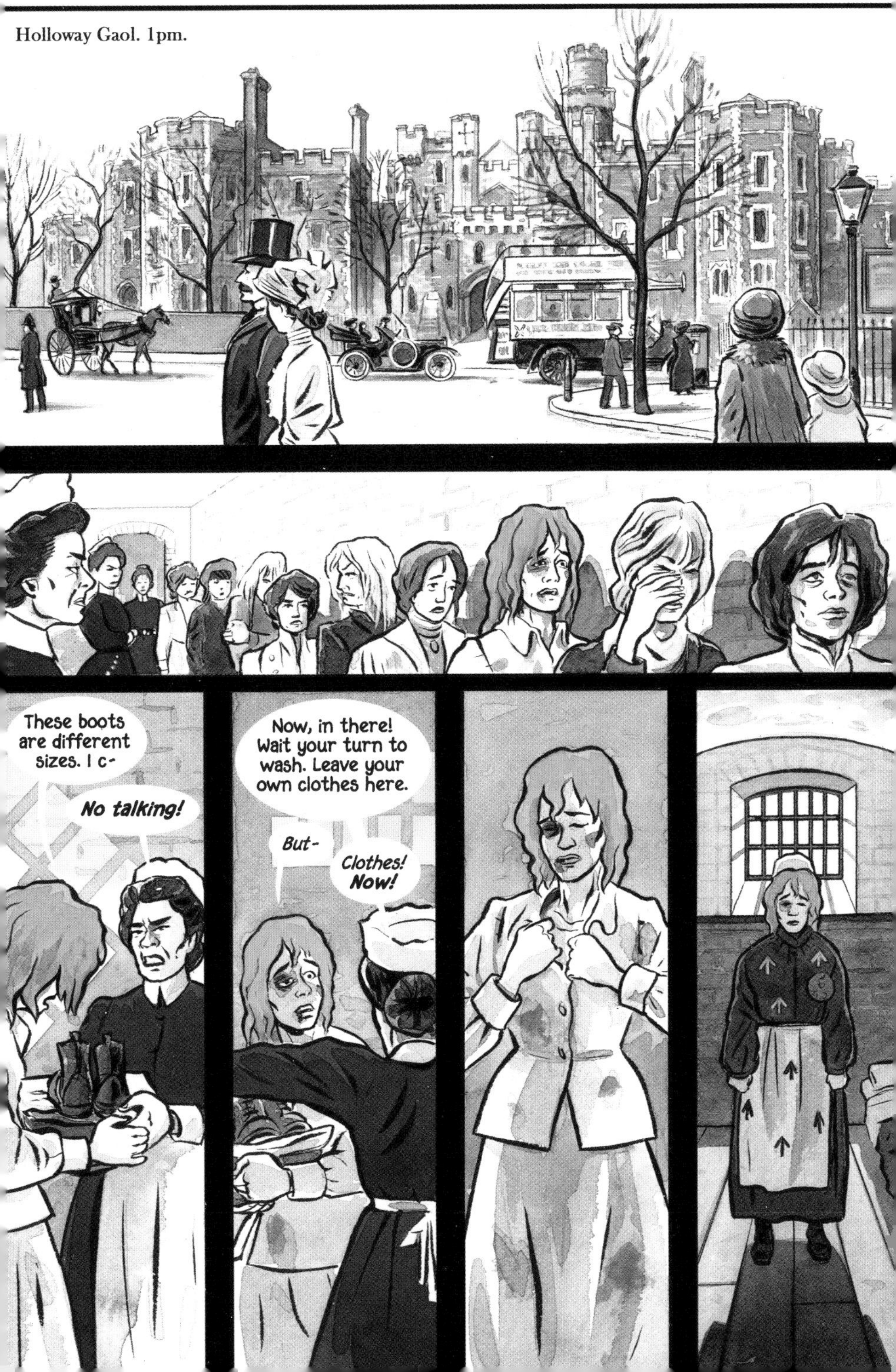
Holloway Gaol. 1pm.
These boots are different sizes. I c-
No talking!
Now, in there! Wait your turn to wash. Leave your own clothes here.
But-
Clothes! Now!

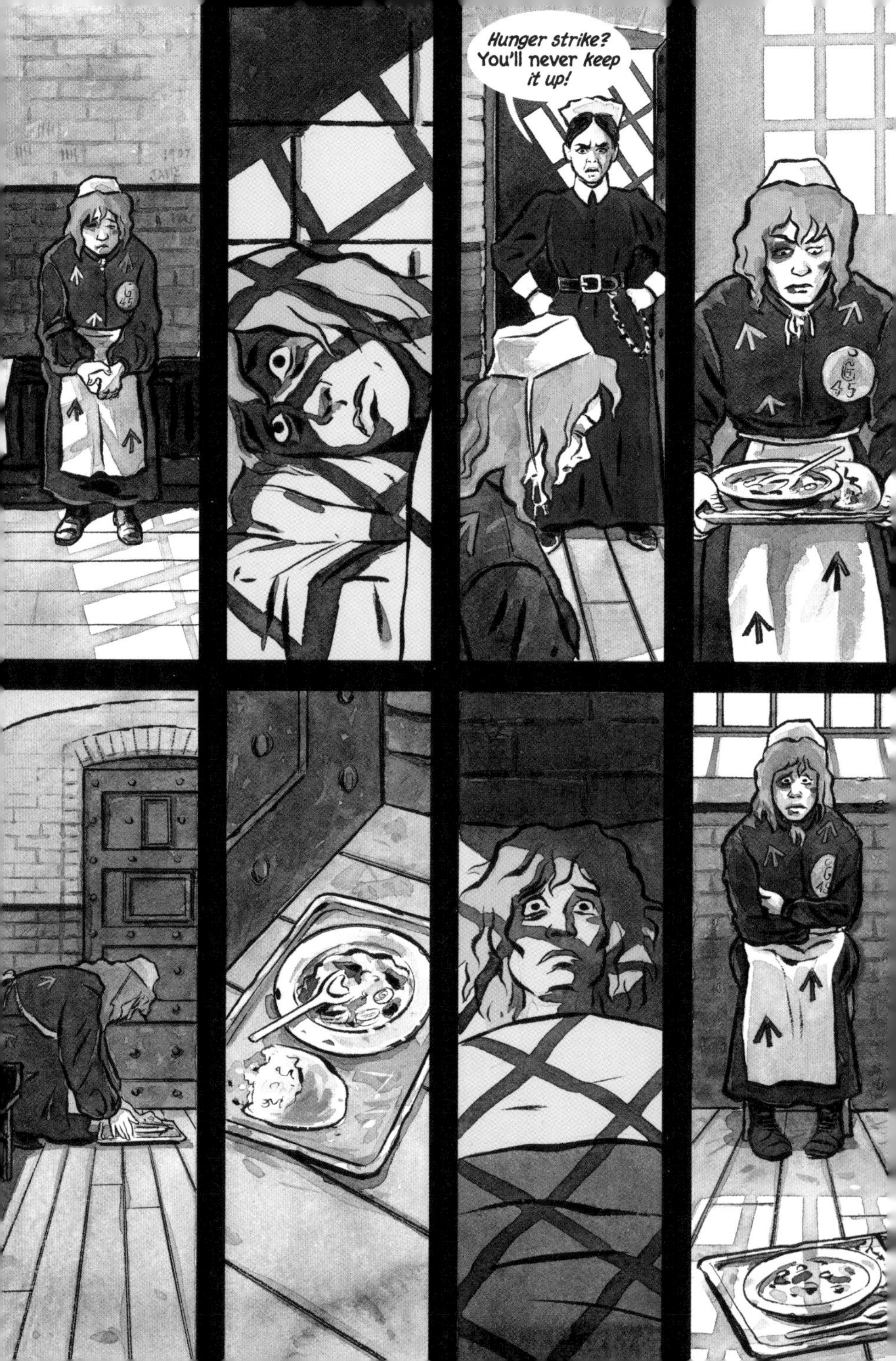
Hunger strike? You'll never keep it up!

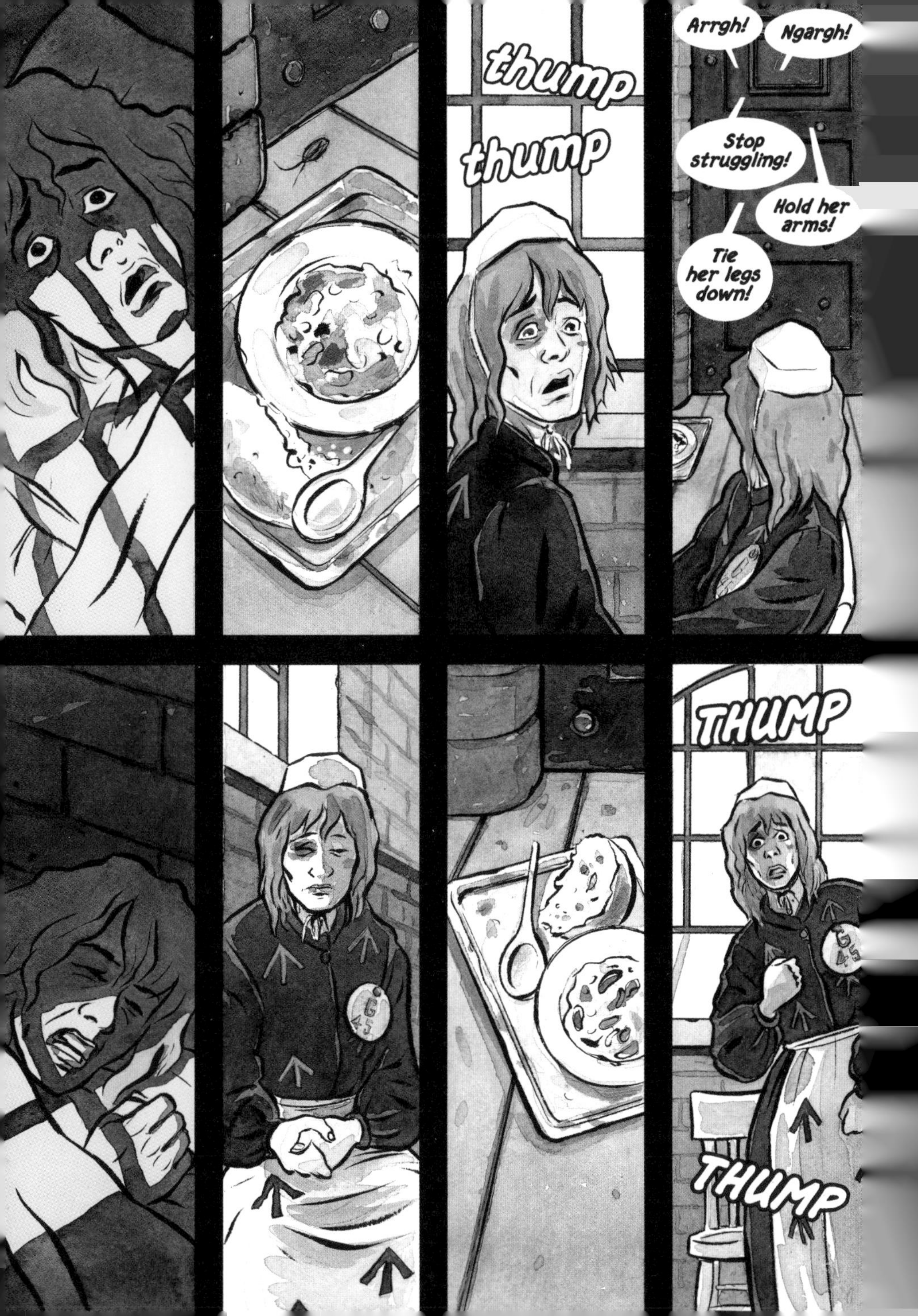
thump
thump
Arrgh!
Ngargh!
Stop struggling!
Hold her arms!
Tie her legs down!
G 45
G 45
THUMP
THUMP

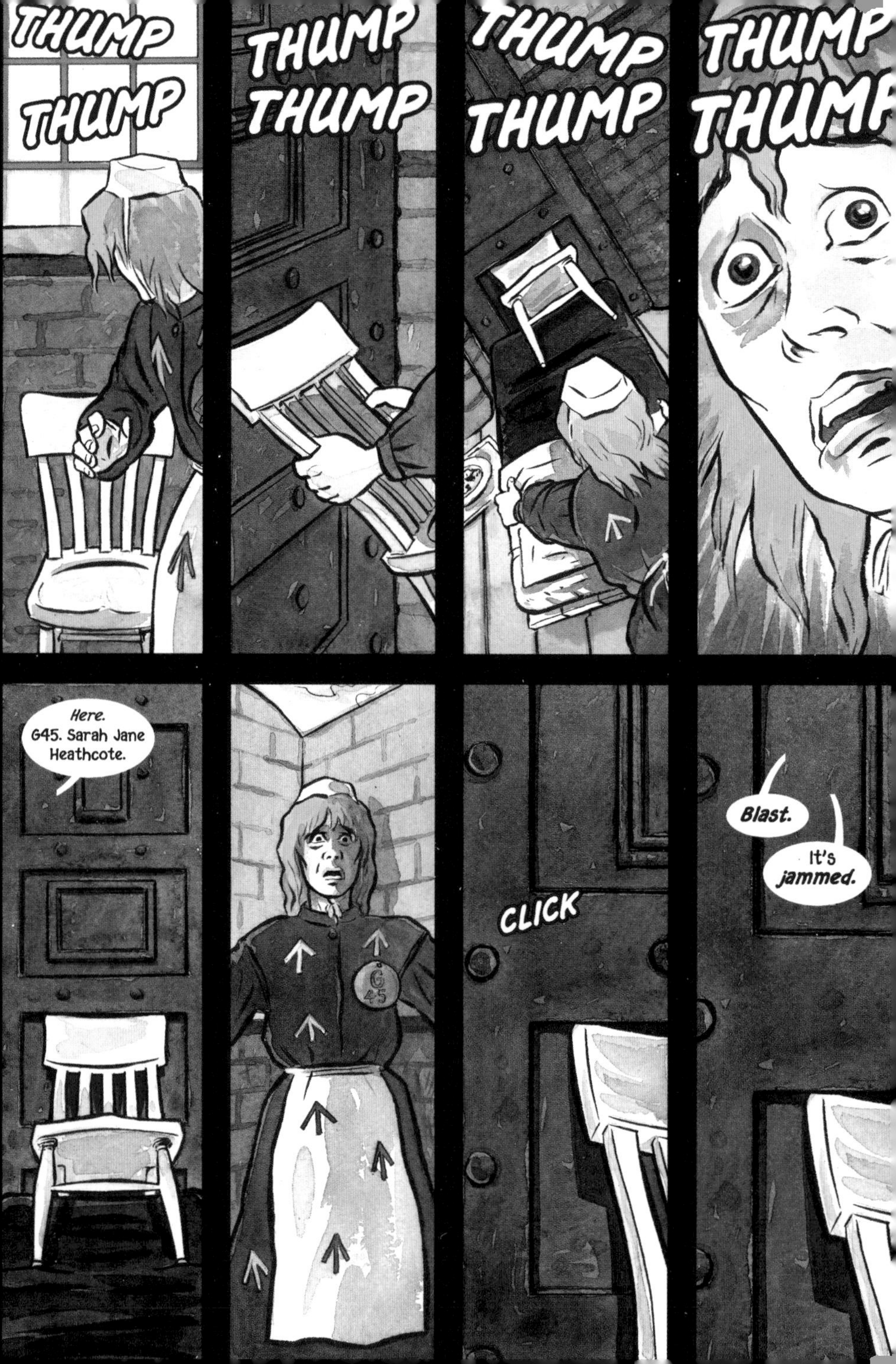
THUMP
THUMP
THUMP
THUMP
THUMP
THUMP
THUMP
THUMP
Here. G45. Sarah Jane Heathcote.
CLICK
Blast.
It's jammed.

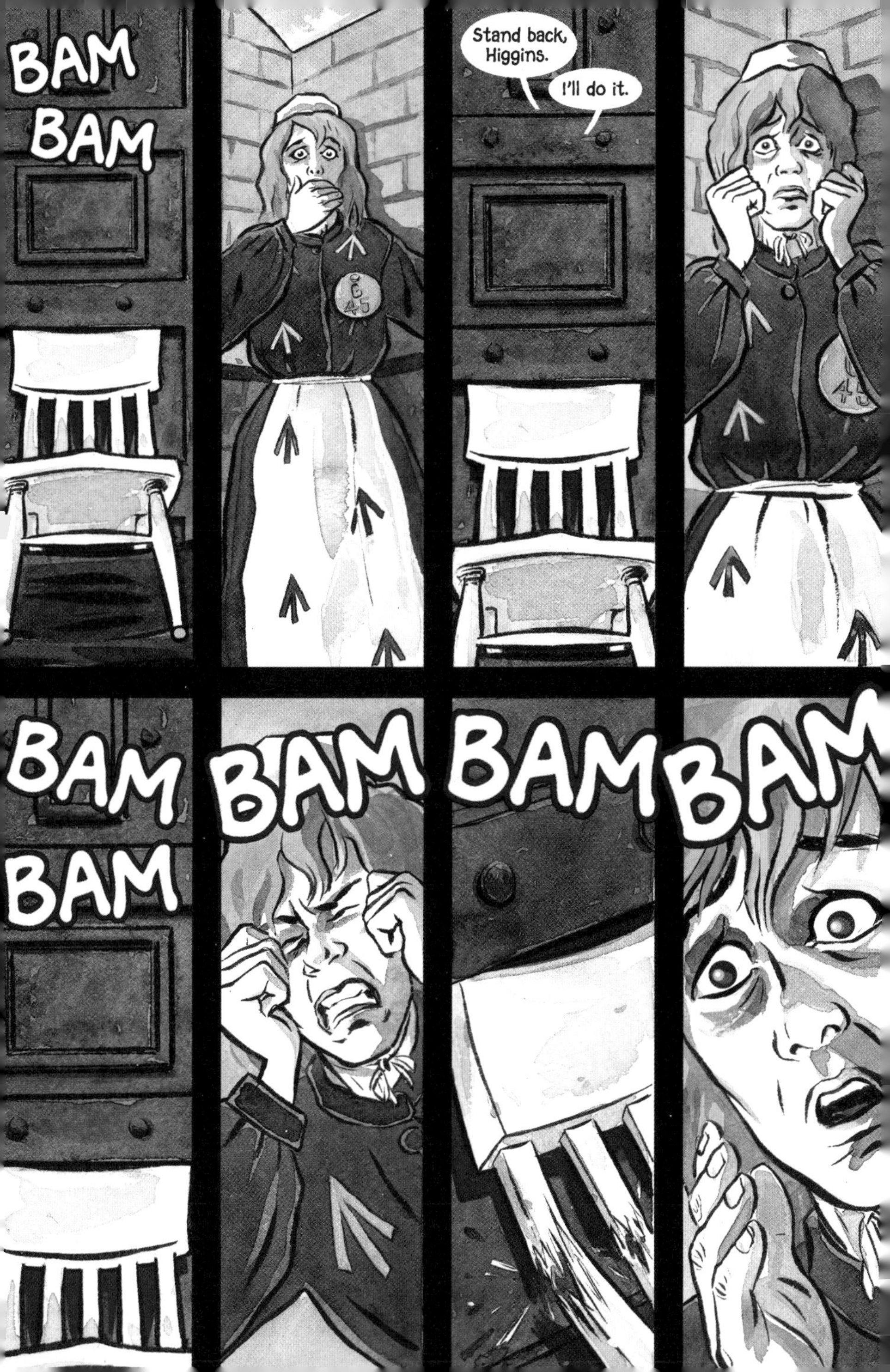
BAM
BAM
Stand back, Higgins.
I'll do it.
BAM
BAM
BAM
BAM
BAM

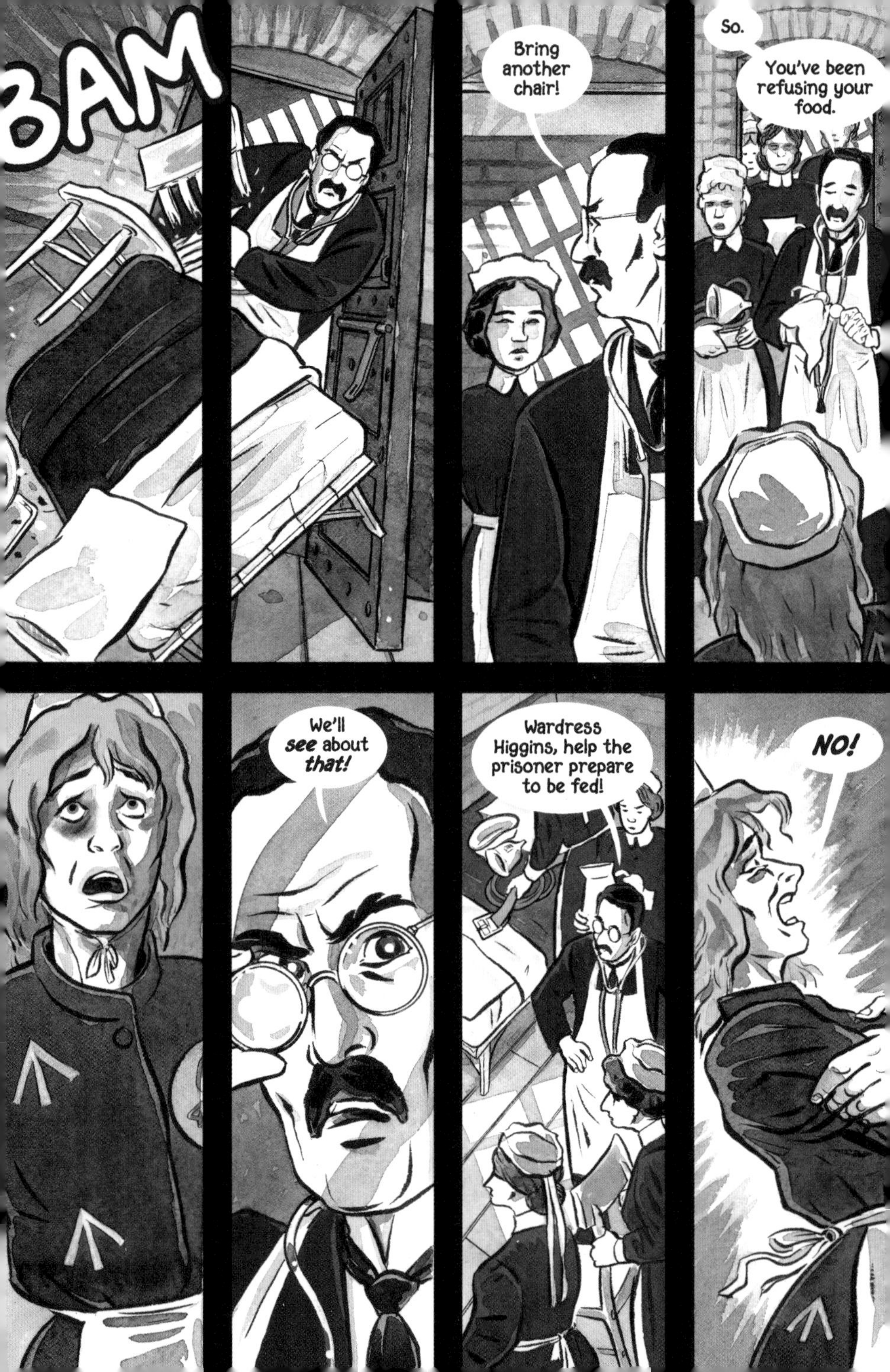
BAM
Bring another chair!
So.
You've been refusing your food.
We'll *see* about *that!*
Wardress Higgins, help the prisoner prepare to be fed!
NO!

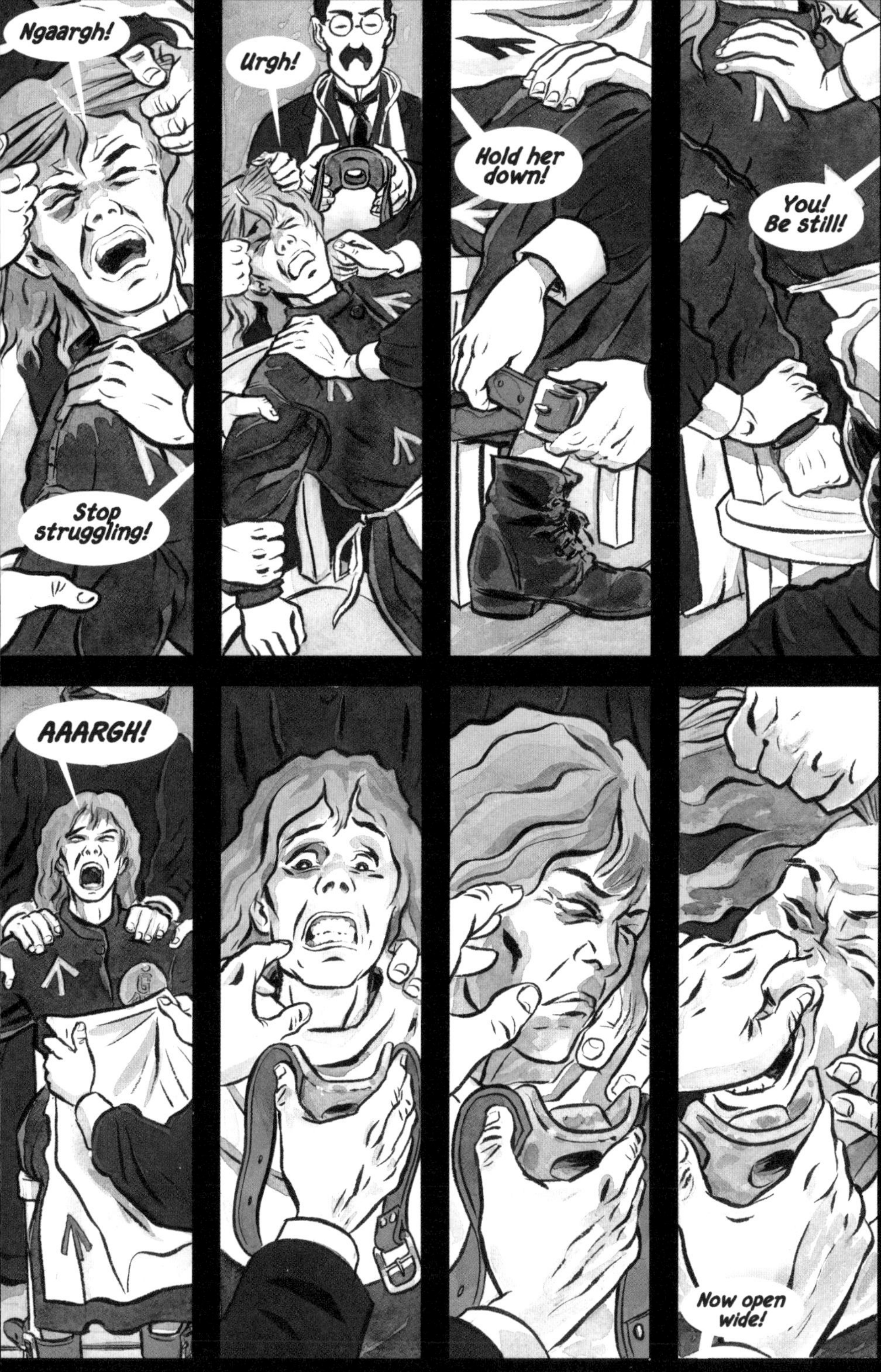
Ngaargh!
Stop struggling!
Urgh!
Hold her down!
You! Be still!
AAARGH!
Now open wide!

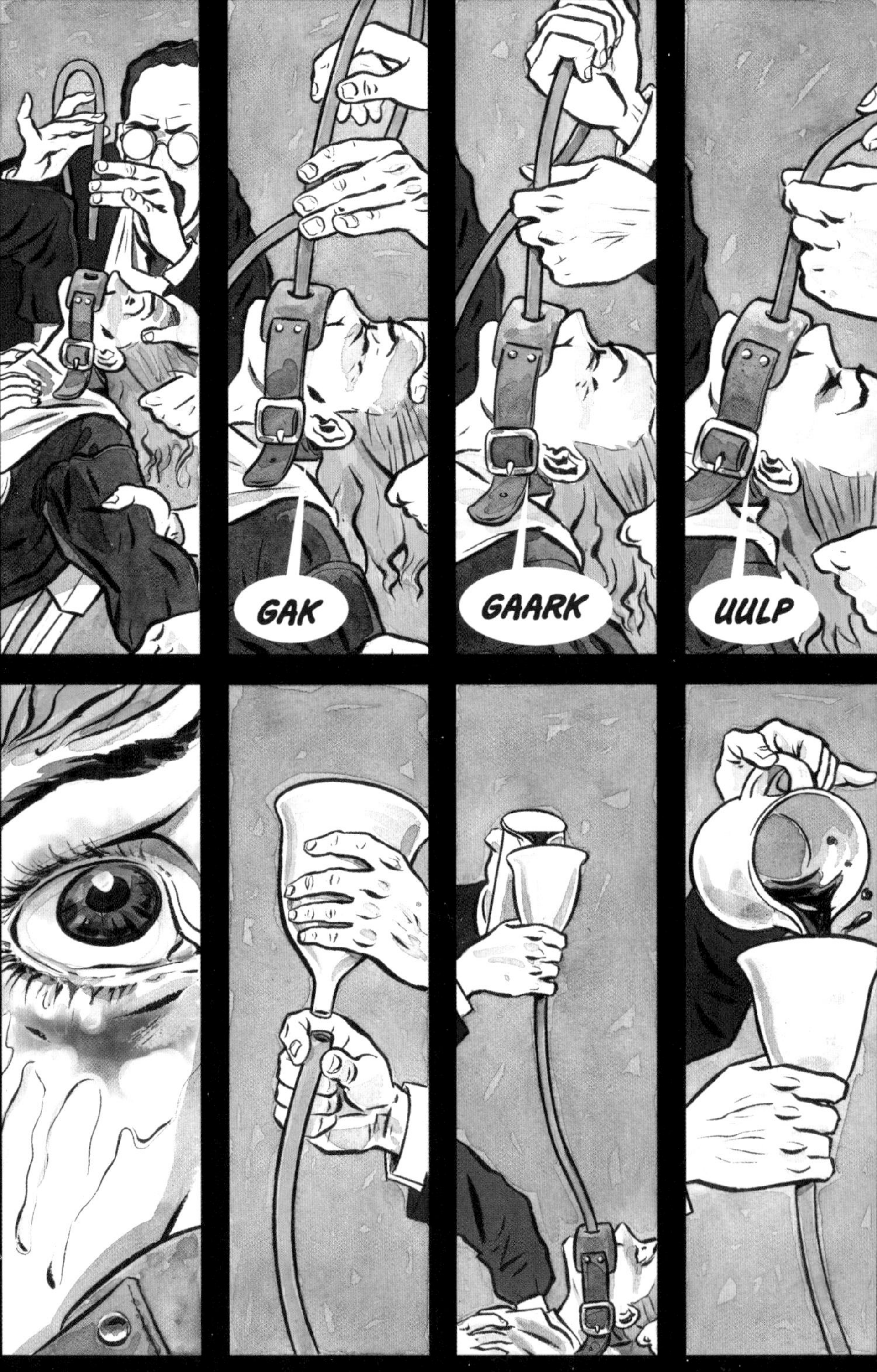
GAK
GAARK
UULP

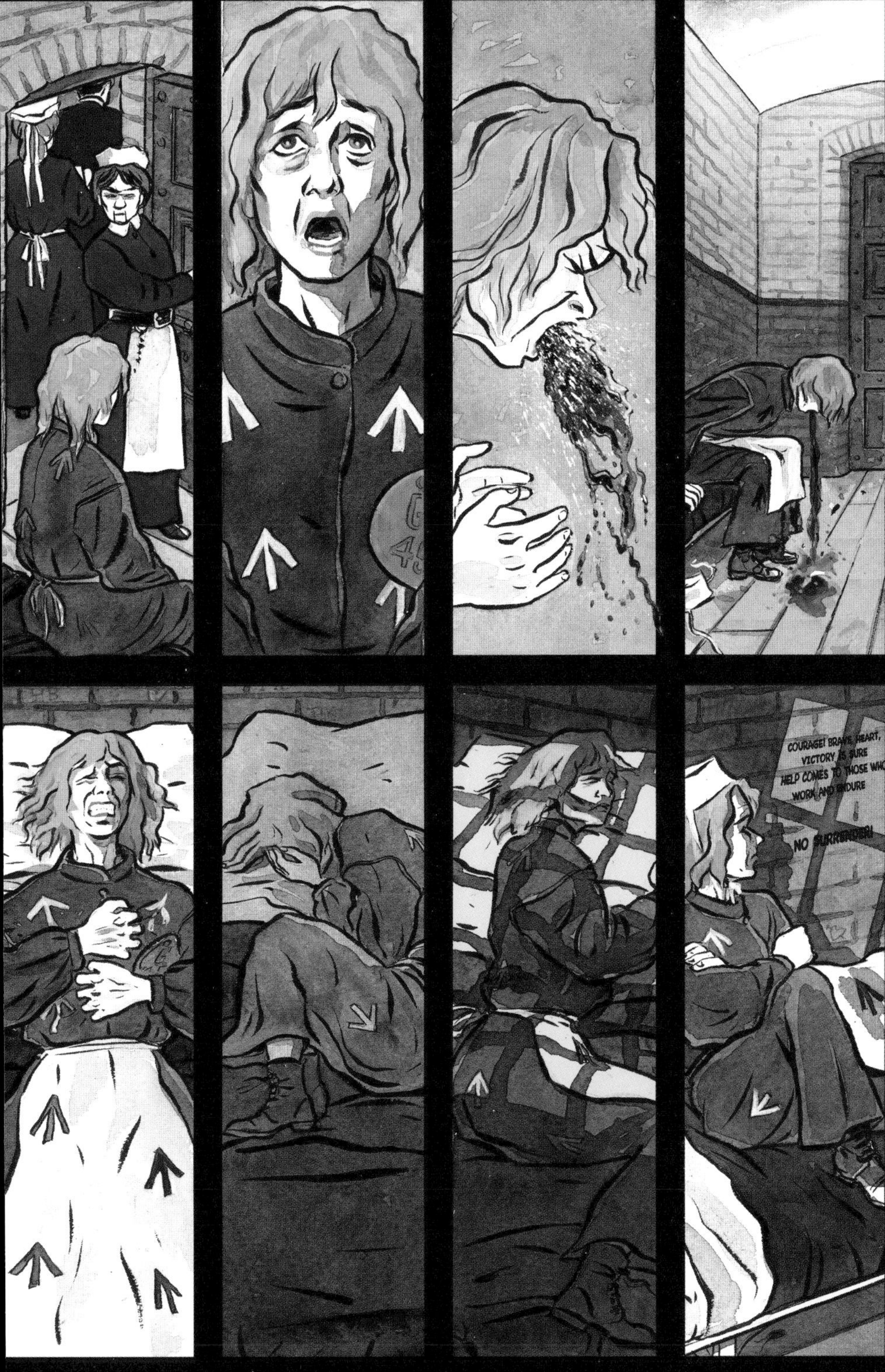
COURAGE! BRAVE HEART,
VICTORY IS SURE
HELP COMES TO THOSE WHO
WORK AND ENDURE
NO SURRENDER!

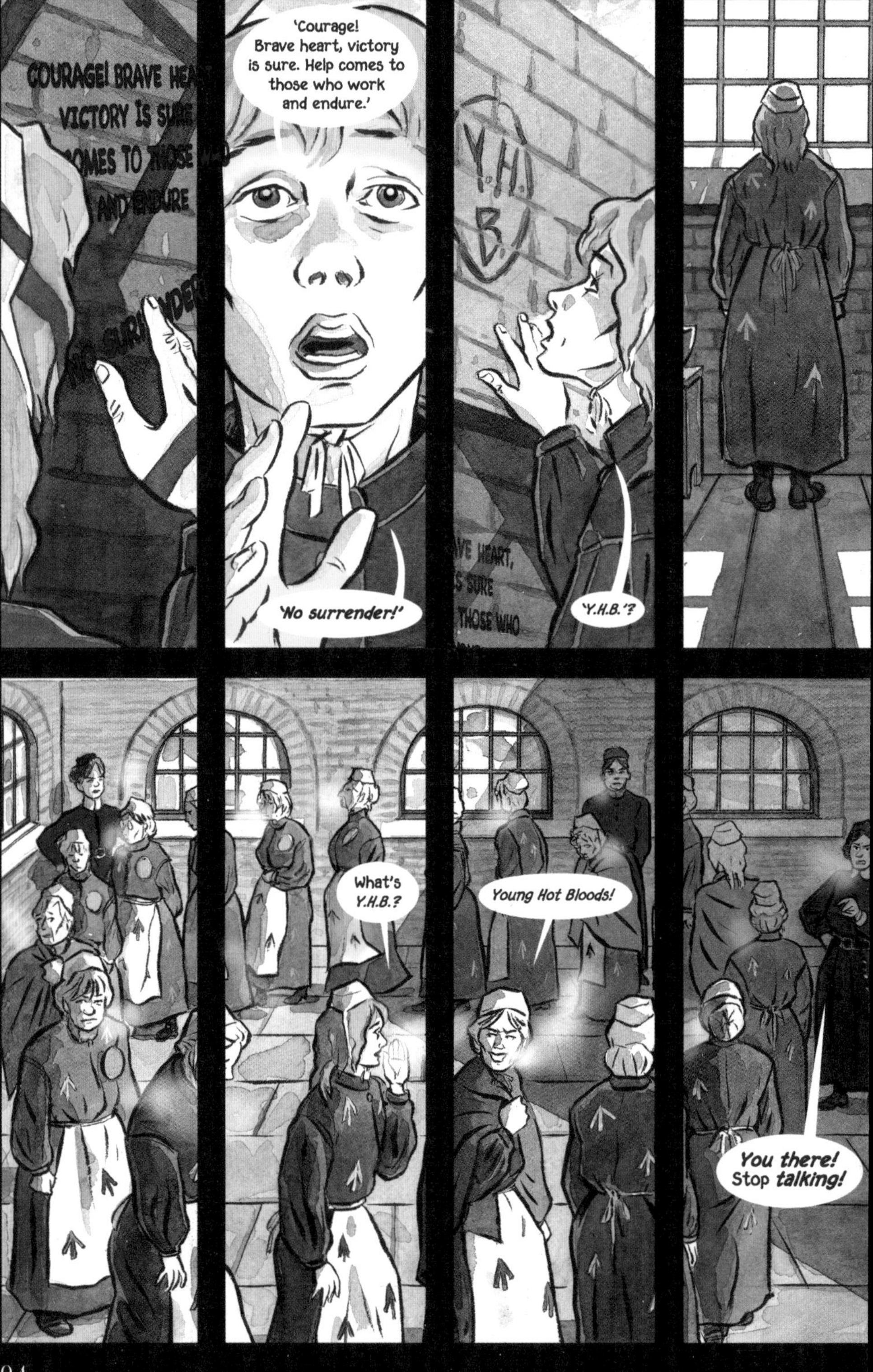
COURAGE! BRAVE HEA
VICTORY IS SURE
OMES TO THOSE WH
AND ENDURE
NO SURR NDER
'Courage! Brave heart, victory is sure. Help comes to those who work and endure.'
'No surrender!'
Y.H. B.
'Y.H.B.'?
What's Y.H.B.?
Young Hot Bloods!
You there! Stop talking!

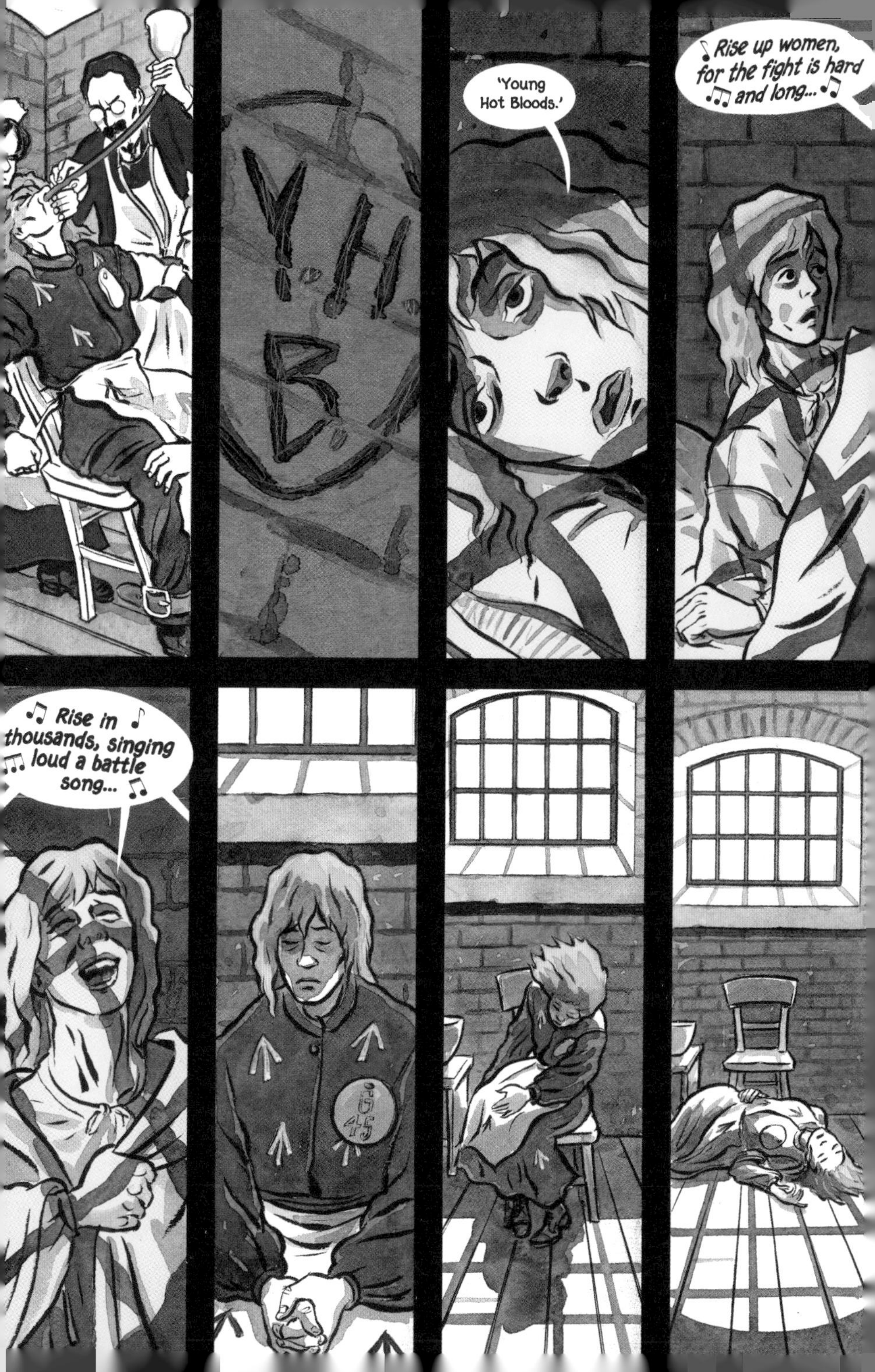
Y.H.B.
'Young Hot Bloods.'
Rise up women, for the fight is hard and long...
Rise in thousands, singing loud a battle song...
G 45

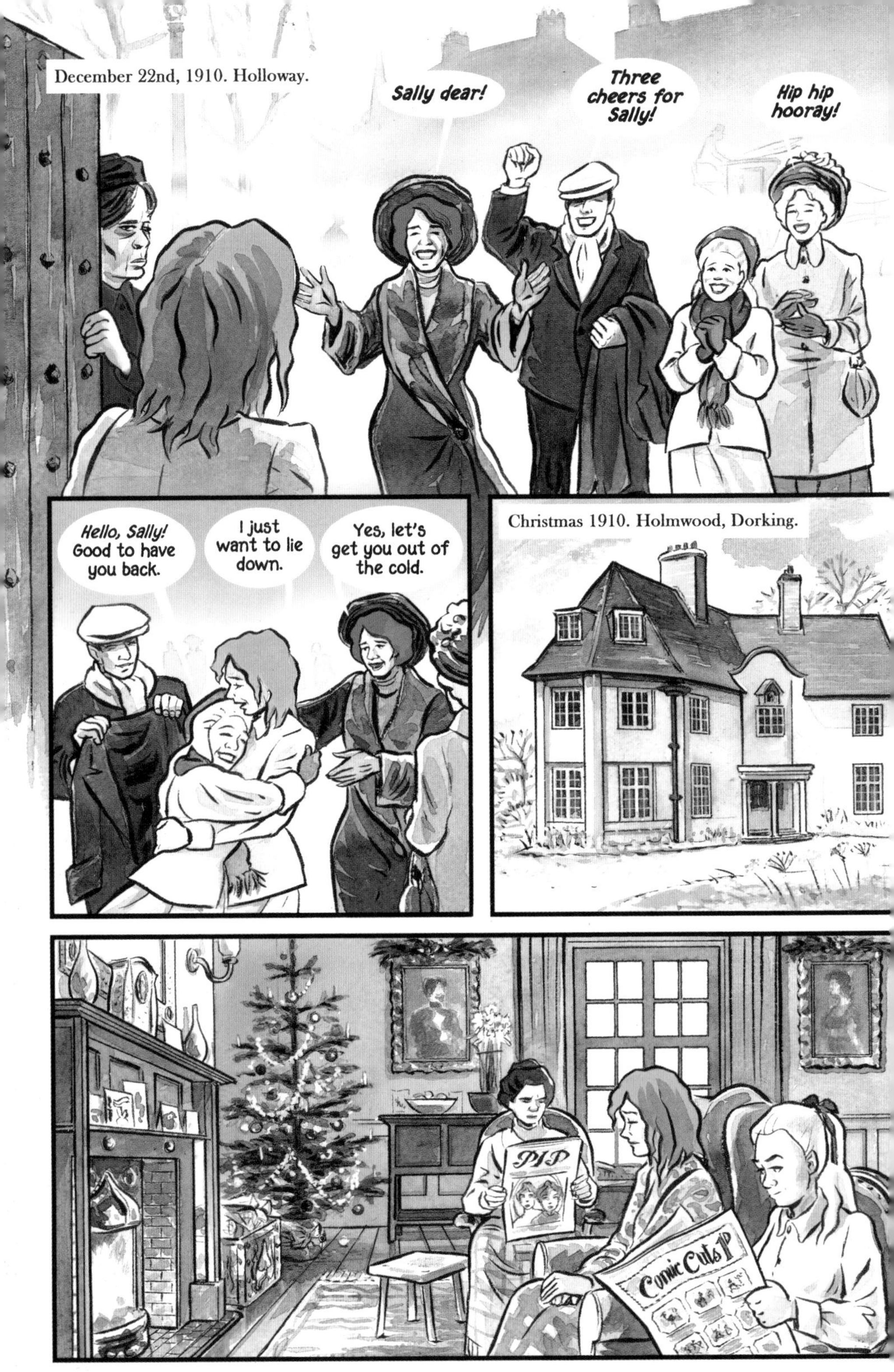

December 22nd, 1910. Holloway.
Sally dear!
Three cheers for Sally!
Hip hip hooray!
Hello, Sally! Good to have you back.
I just want to lie down.
Yes, let's get you out of the cold.
Christmas 1910. Holmwood, Dorking.
PIP
Comic Cuts

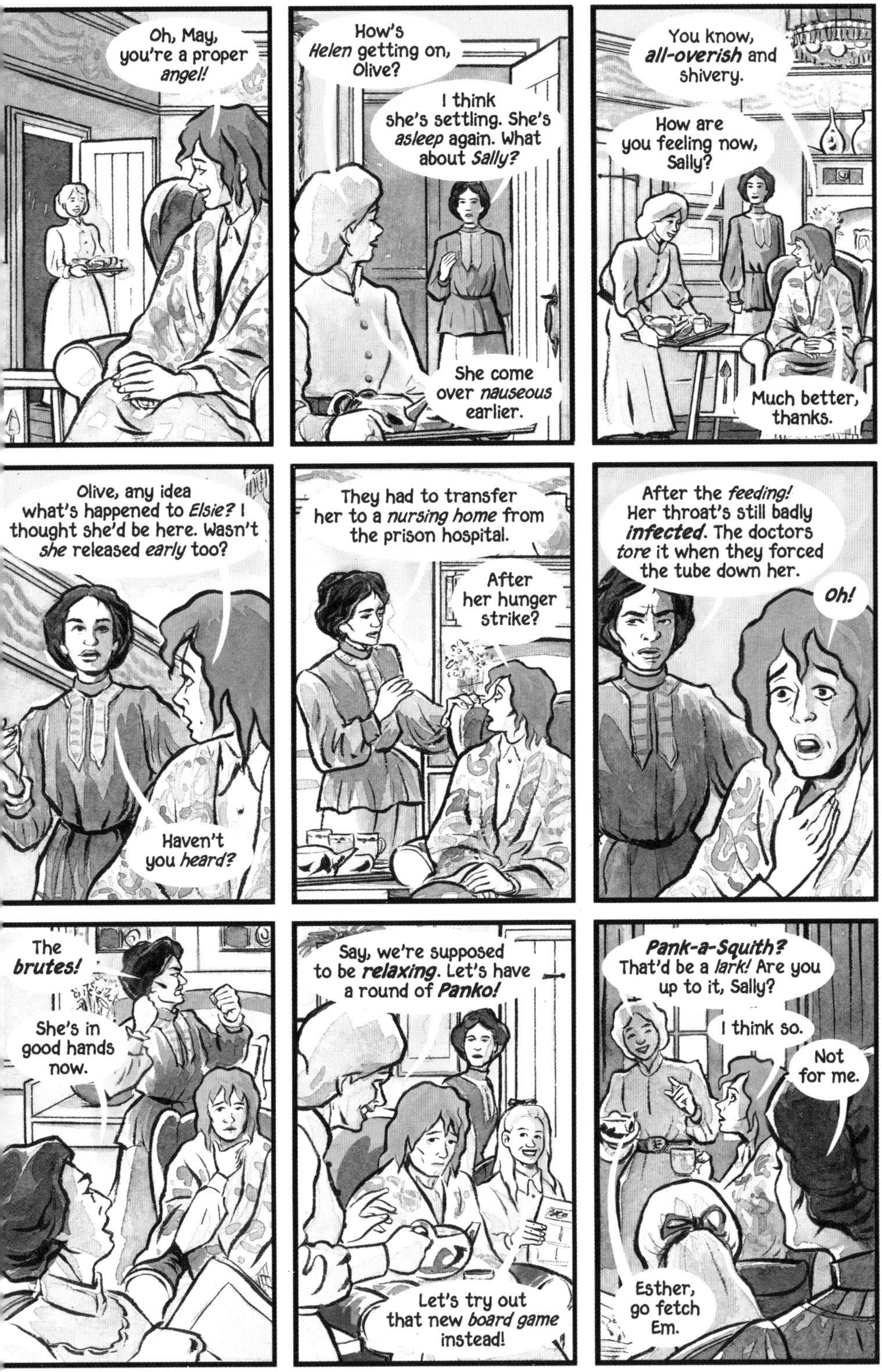
Oh, May, you're a proper *angel!*
How's *Helen* getting on, Olive?
I think she's settling. She's *asleep* again. What about *Sally?*
She come over *nauseous* earlier.
You know, **all-overish** and shivery.
How are you feeling now, Sally?
Much better, thanks.
Olive, any idea what's happened to *Elsie?* I thought she'd be here. Wasn't *she* released *early* too?
Haven't you *heard?*
They had to transfer her to a *nursing home* from the prison hospital.
After her hunger strike?
After the *feeding!* Her throat's still badly **infected**. The doctors *tore* it when they forced the tube down her.
Oh!
The **brutes!**
She's in good hands now.
Say, we're supposed to be **relaxing**. Let's have a round of **Panko!**
Let's try out that new *board game* instead!
Pank-a-Squith? That'd be a *lark!* Are you up to it, Sally?
I think so.
Not for me.
Esther, go fetch Em.

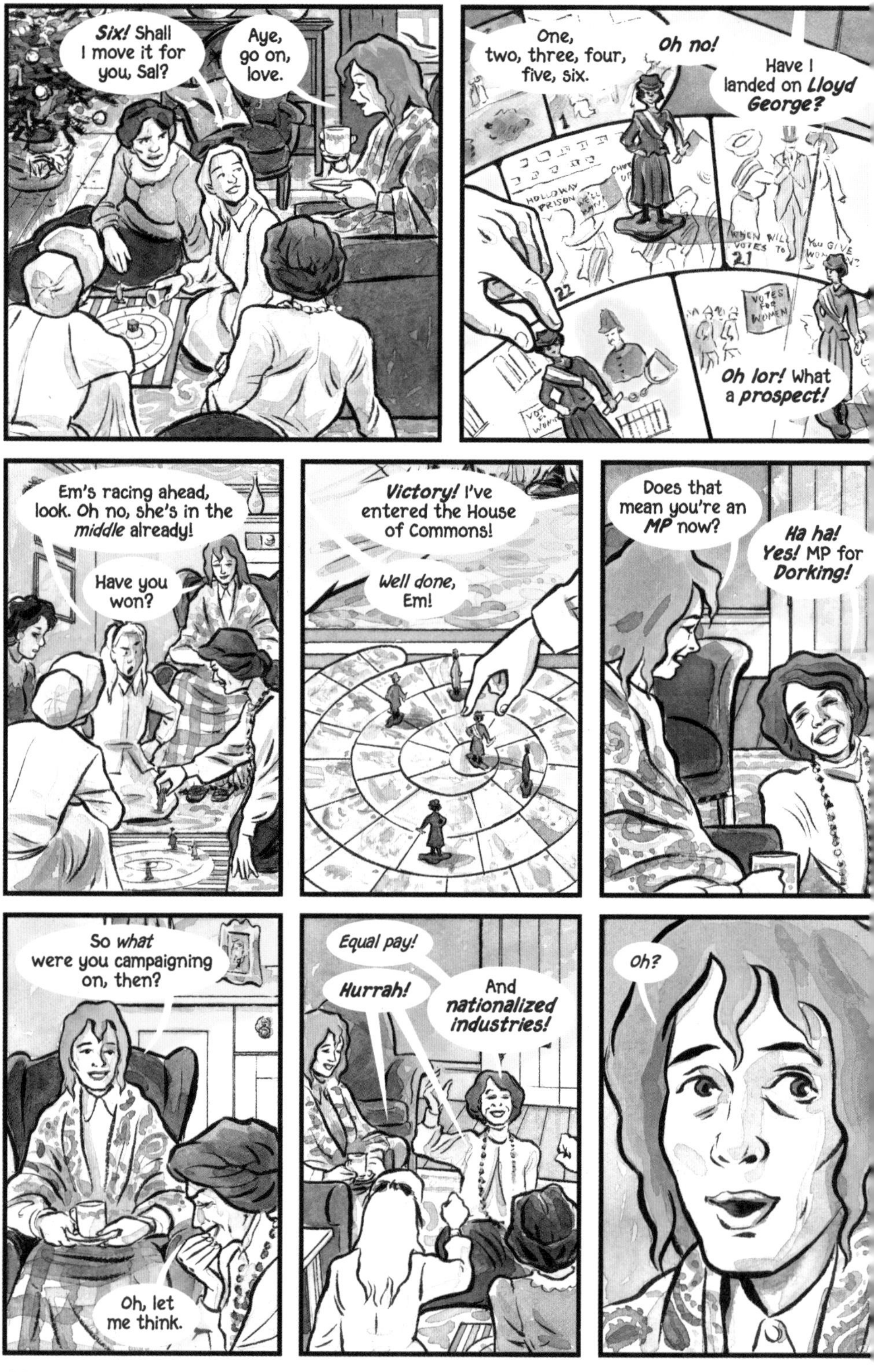

Six! Shall I move it for you, Sal?
Aye, go on, love.
One, two, three, four, five, six.
Oh no!
Have I landed on Lloyd George?
HOLLOWAY PRISON
21
22
VOTES FOR WOMEN
Oh lor! What a prospect!
Em's racing ahead, look. Oh no, she's in the middle already!
Have you won?
Victory! I've entered the House of Commons!
Well done, Em!
Does that mean you're an MP now?
Ha ha! Yes! MP for Dorking!
So what were you campaigning on, then?
Oh, let me think.
Equal pay!
Hurrah!
And nationalized industries!
Oh?

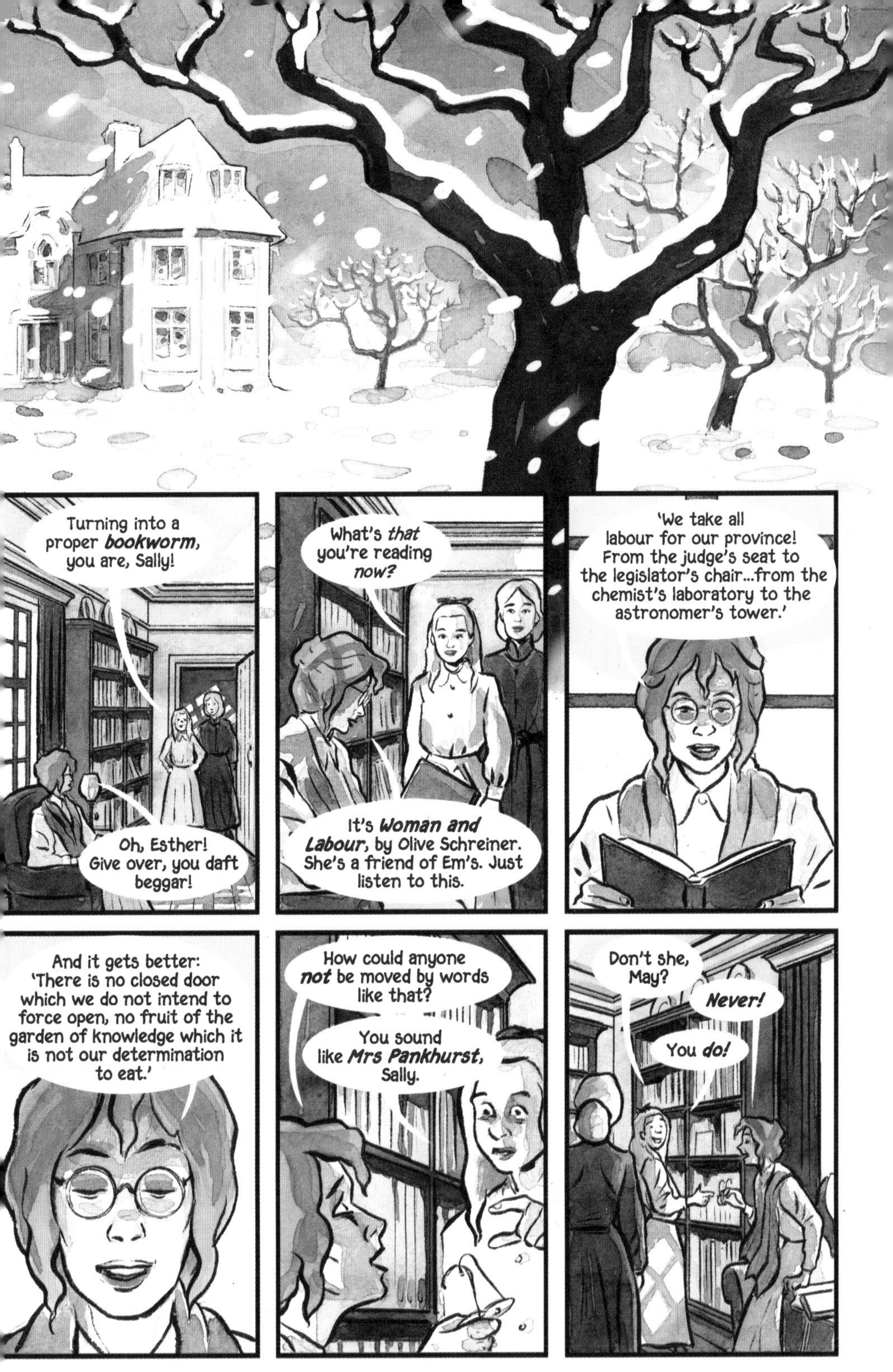
Turning into a proper ***bookworm***, you are, Sally!
Oh, Esther! Give over, you daft beggar!
What's *that* you're reading *now?*
It's ***Woman and Labour***, by Olive Schreiner. She's a friend of Em's. Just listen to this.
'We take all labour for our province! From the judge's seat to the legislator's chair...from the chemist's laboratory to the astronomer's tower.'
And it gets better: 'There is no closed door which we do not intend to force open, no fruit of the garden of knowledge which it is not our determination to eat.'
How could anyone ***not*** be moved by words like that?
You sound like ***Mrs Pankhurst***, Sally.
Don't she, May?
Never!
You ***do!***

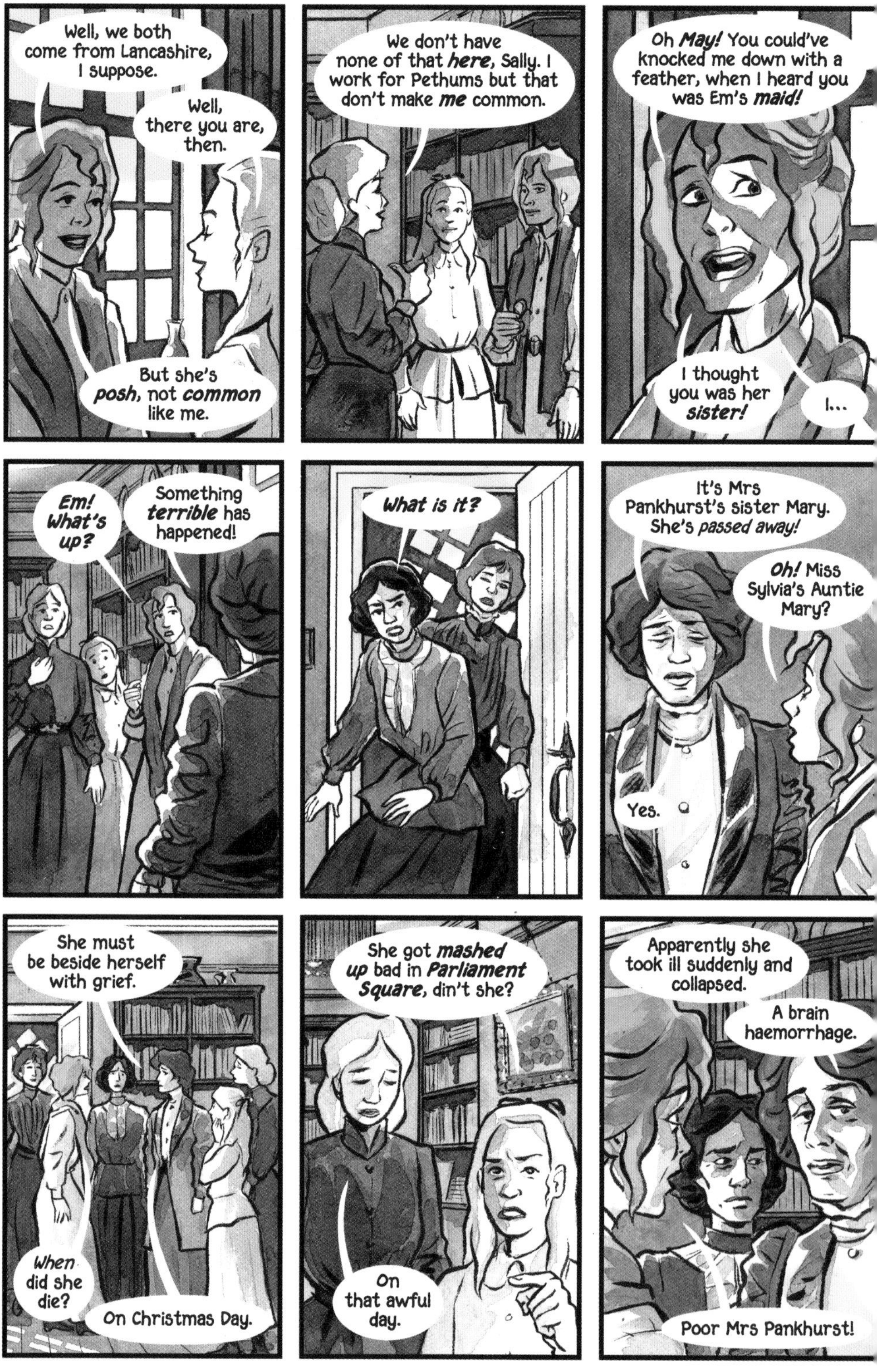
Well, we both come from Lancashire, I suppose.
Well, there you are, then.
But she's *posh*, not *common* like me.
We don't have none of that *here*, Sally. I work for Pethums but that don't make *me* common.
Oh *May!* You could've knocked me down with a feather, when I heard you was Em's *maid!*
I thought you was her *sister!*
I...
Em! What's up?
Something *terrible* has happened!
What is it?
It's Mrs Pankhurst's sister Mary. She's *passed away!*
Oh! Miss Sylvia's Auntie Mary?
Yes.
She must be beside herself with grief.
When did she die?
On Christmas Day.
She got *mashed up* bad in *Parliament Square*, din't she?
On that awful day.
Apparently she took ill suddenly and collapsed.
A brain haemorrhage.
Poor Mrs Pankhurst!

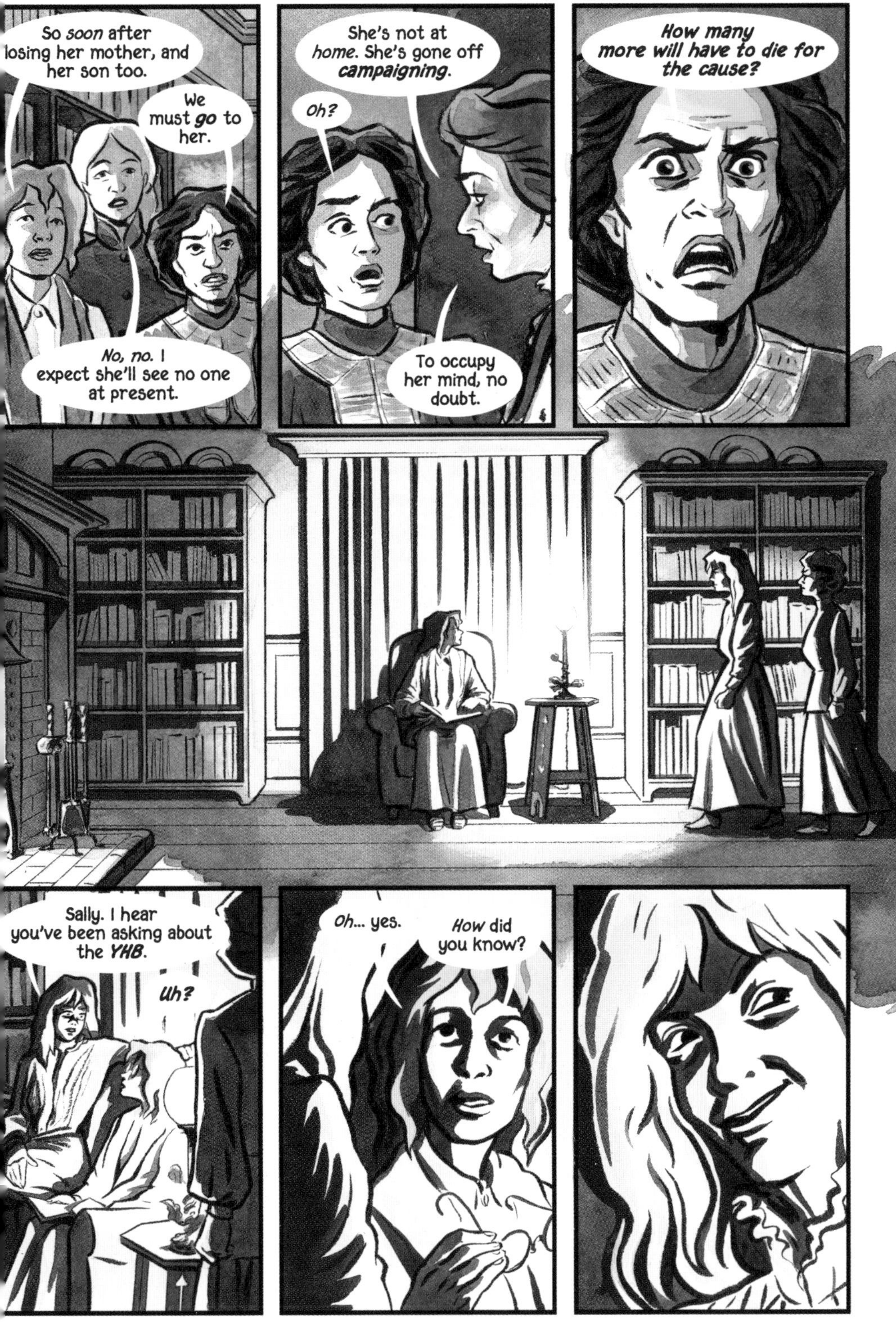

So soon after losing her mother, and her son too.
We must go to her.
No, no. I expect she'll see no one at present.
She's not at home. She's gone off campaigning.
Oh?
To occupy her mind, no doubt.
How many more will have to die for the cause?
Sally. I hear you've been asking about the YHB.
Uh?
Oh... yes.
How did you know?

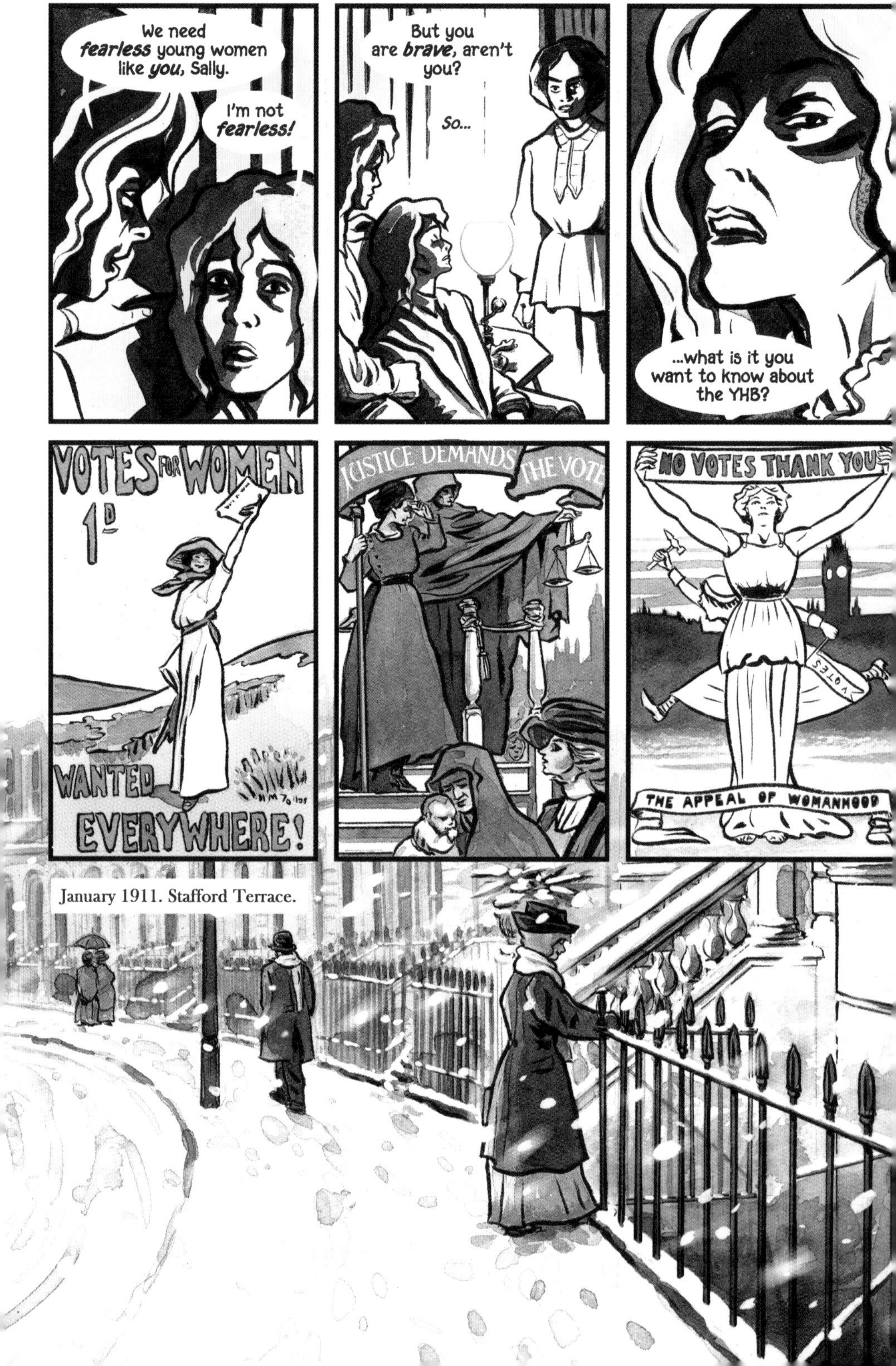

We need *fearless* young women like *you*, Sally.
I'm not *fearless!*
But you are *brave*, aren't you?
So...
...what is it you want to know about the YHB?
VOTES FOR WOMEN
1D
WANTED
EVERYWHERE!
JUSTICE DEMANDS THE VOTE
NO VOTES THANK YOU
VOTES
THE APPEAL OF WOMANHOOD
January 1911. Stafford Terrace.

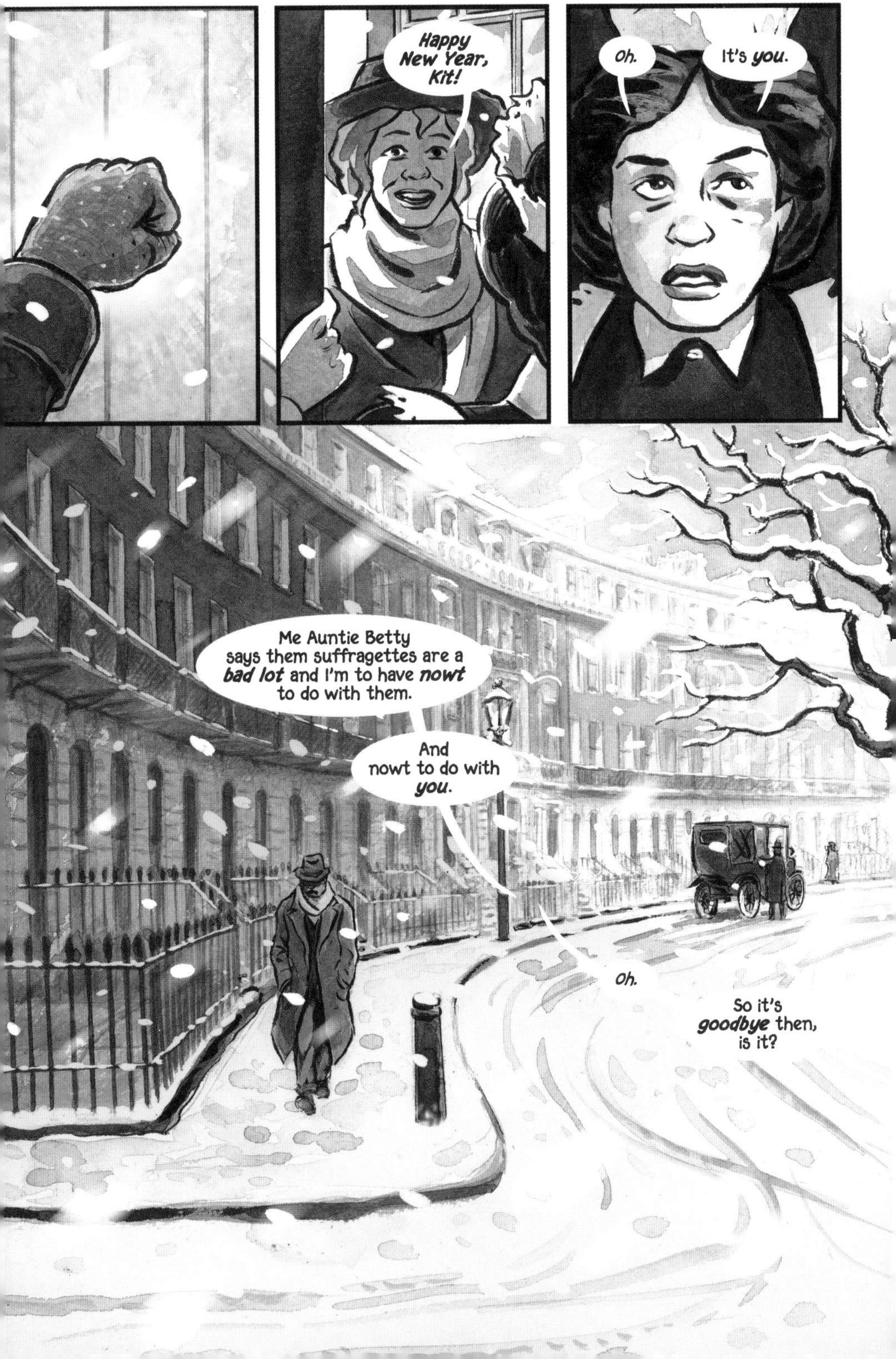
Happy New Year, Kit!
Oh.
It's *you*.
Me Auntie Betty says them suffragettes are a *bad lot* and I'm to have *nowt* to do with them.
And nowt to do with *you*.
Oh.
So it's *goodbye* then, is it?

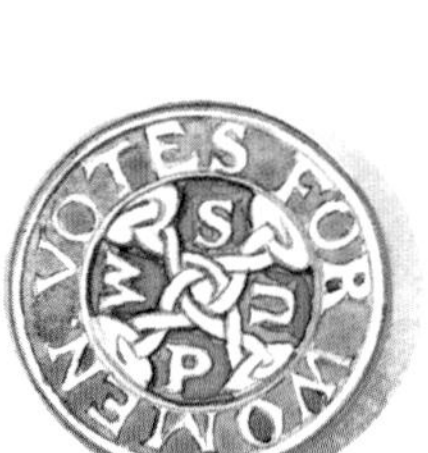
VOTES FOR WOMEN
W S P U

PART THREE

NO SURRENDER!

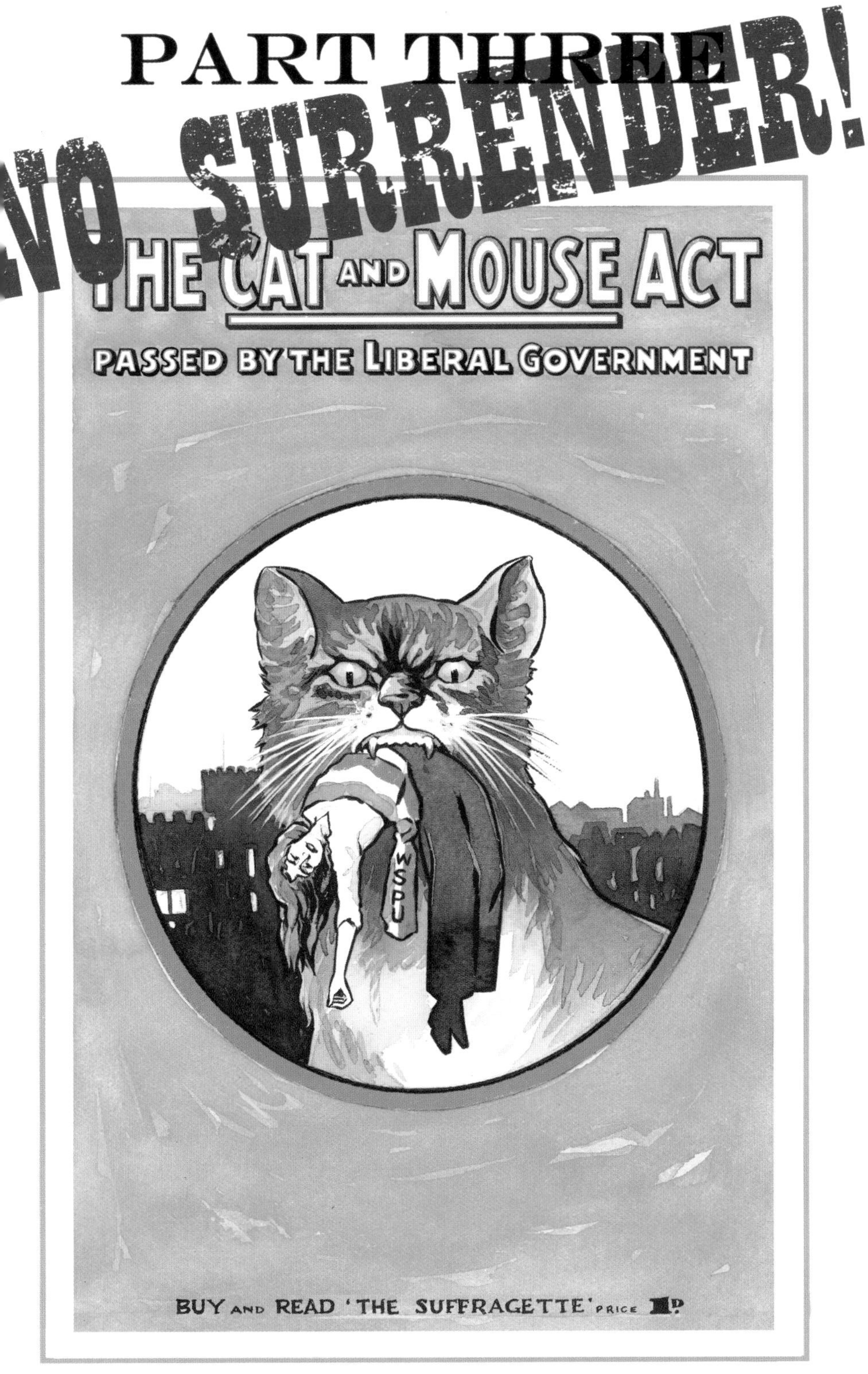
THE CAT AND MOUSE ACT
PASSED BY THE LIBERAL GOVERNMENT
WSPU
BUY AND READ 'THE SUFFRAGETTE' PRICE 1D.

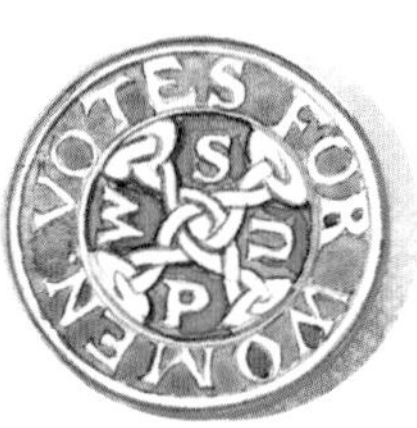
VOTES FOR WOMEN
W S P U

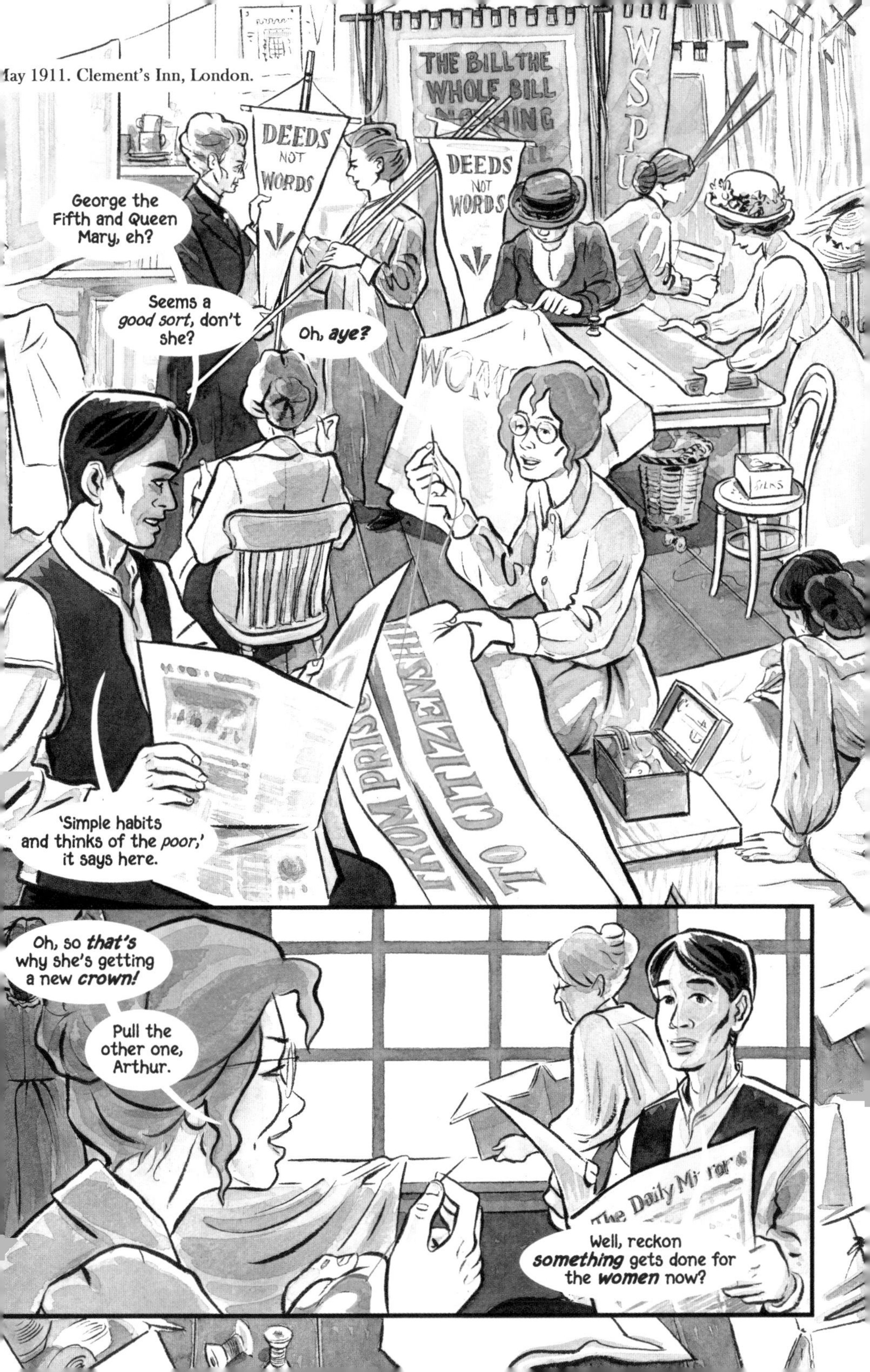

ay 1911. Clement's Inn, London.
THE BILL THE WHOLE BILL
WSPU
DEEDS NOT WORDS
DEEDS NOT WORDS
George the Fifth and Queen Mary, eh?
Seems a *good sort*, don't she?
Oh, ***aye?***
SILKS
FROM PRISO
TO CITIZENSHI
'Simple habits and thinks of the *poor*,' it says here.
Oh, so ***that's*** why she's getting a new ***crown!***
Pull the other one, Arthur.
The Daily Mirror
Well, reckon ***something*** gets done for the ***women*** now?

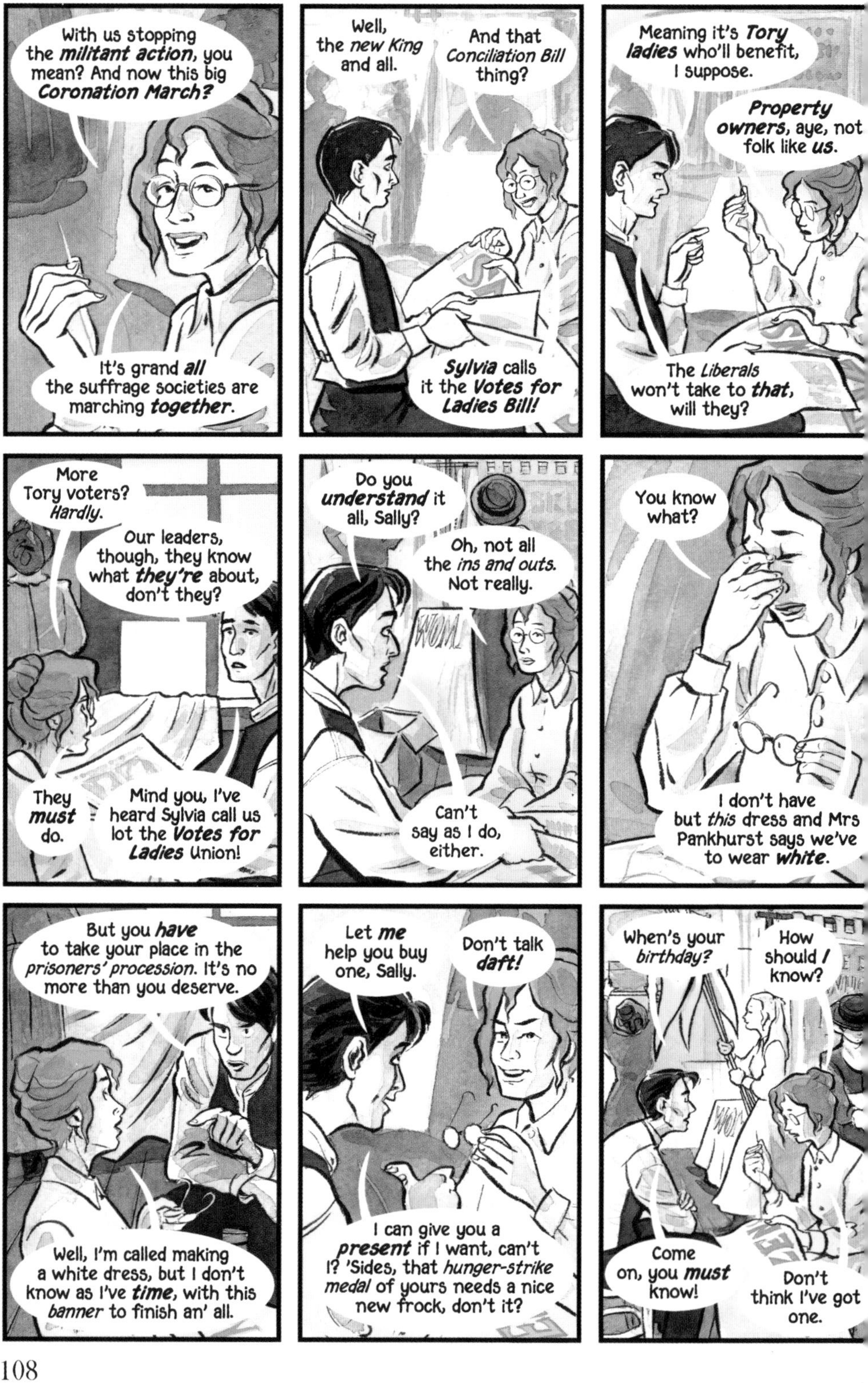

With us stopping the *militant action*, you mean? And now this big *Coronation March?*
It's grand *all* the suffrage societies are marching *together*.
Well, the *new King* and all.
And that *Conciliation Bill* thing?
Sylvia calls it the *Votes for Ladies Bill!*
Meaning it's *Tory ladies* who'll benefit, I suppose.
Property owners, aye, not folk like *us*.
The *Liberals* won't take to *that*, will they?
More Tory voters? *Hardly*.
Our leaders, though, they know what *they're* about, don't they?
They *must* do.
Mind you, I've heard Sylvia call us lot the *Votes for Ladies* Union!
Do you *understand* it all, Sally?
Oh, not all the *ins and outs*. Not really.
Can't say as I do, either.
You know what?
I don't have but *this* dress and Mrs Pankhurst says we've to wear *white*.
But you *have* to take your place in the *prisoners' procession*. It's no more than you deserve.
Well, I'm called making a white dress, but I don't know as I've *time*, with this *banner* to finish an' all.
Let *me* help you buy one, Sally.
Don't talk *daft!*
I can give you a *present* if I want, can't I? 'Sides, that *hunger-strike medal* of yours needs a nice new frock, don't it?
When's your *birthday?*
How should *I* know?
Come on, you *must* know!
Don't think I've got one.

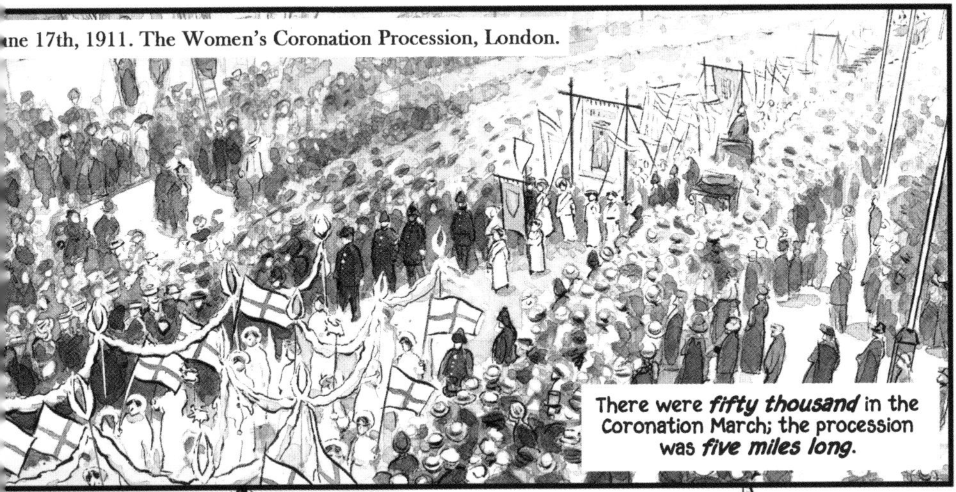
une 17th, 1911. The Women's Coronation Procession, London.
There were *fifty thousand* in the Coronation March; the procession was *five miles long*.

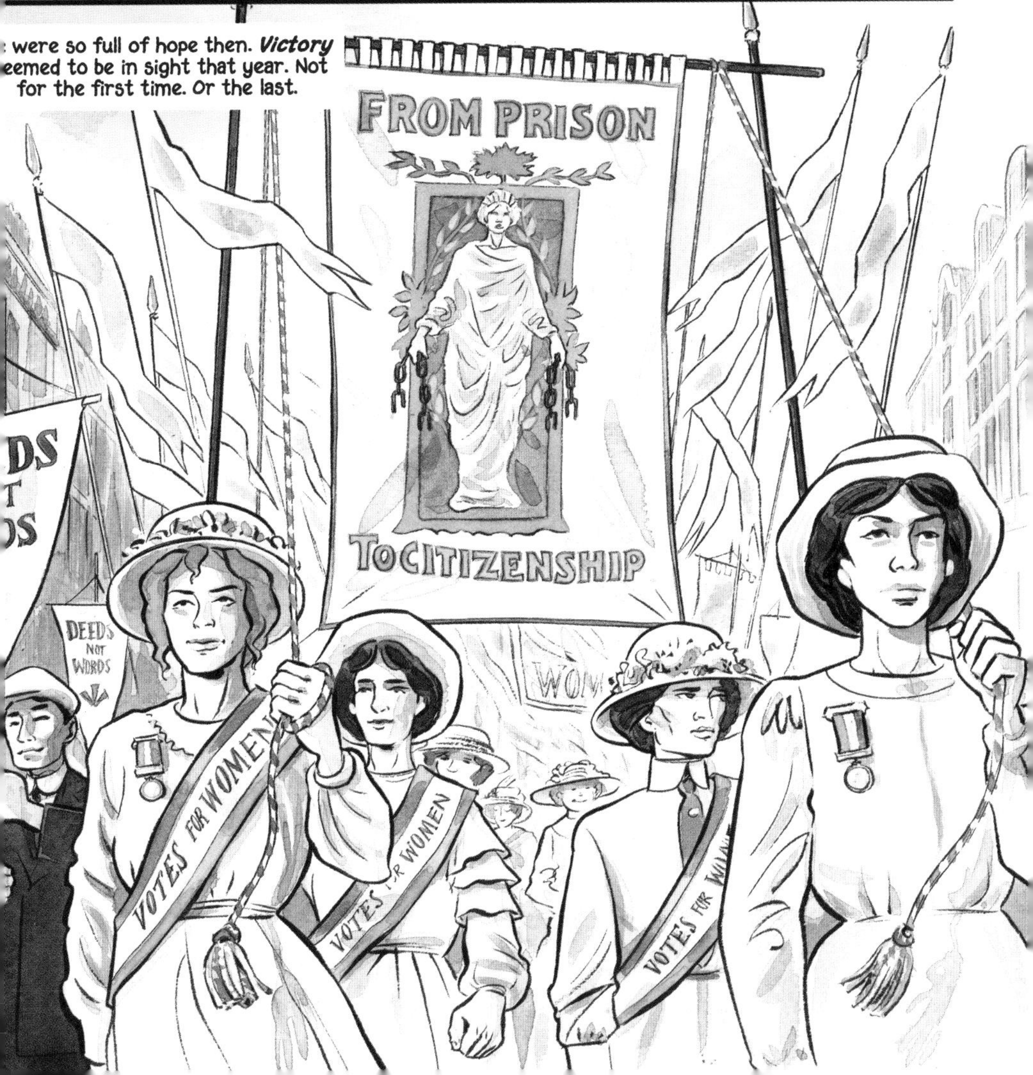
were so full of hope then. *Victory* eemed to be in sight that year. Not for the first time. Or the last.
FROM PRISON
TO CITIZENSHIP
DEEDS NOT WORDS
VOTES FOR WOMEN
VOTES FOR WOMEN

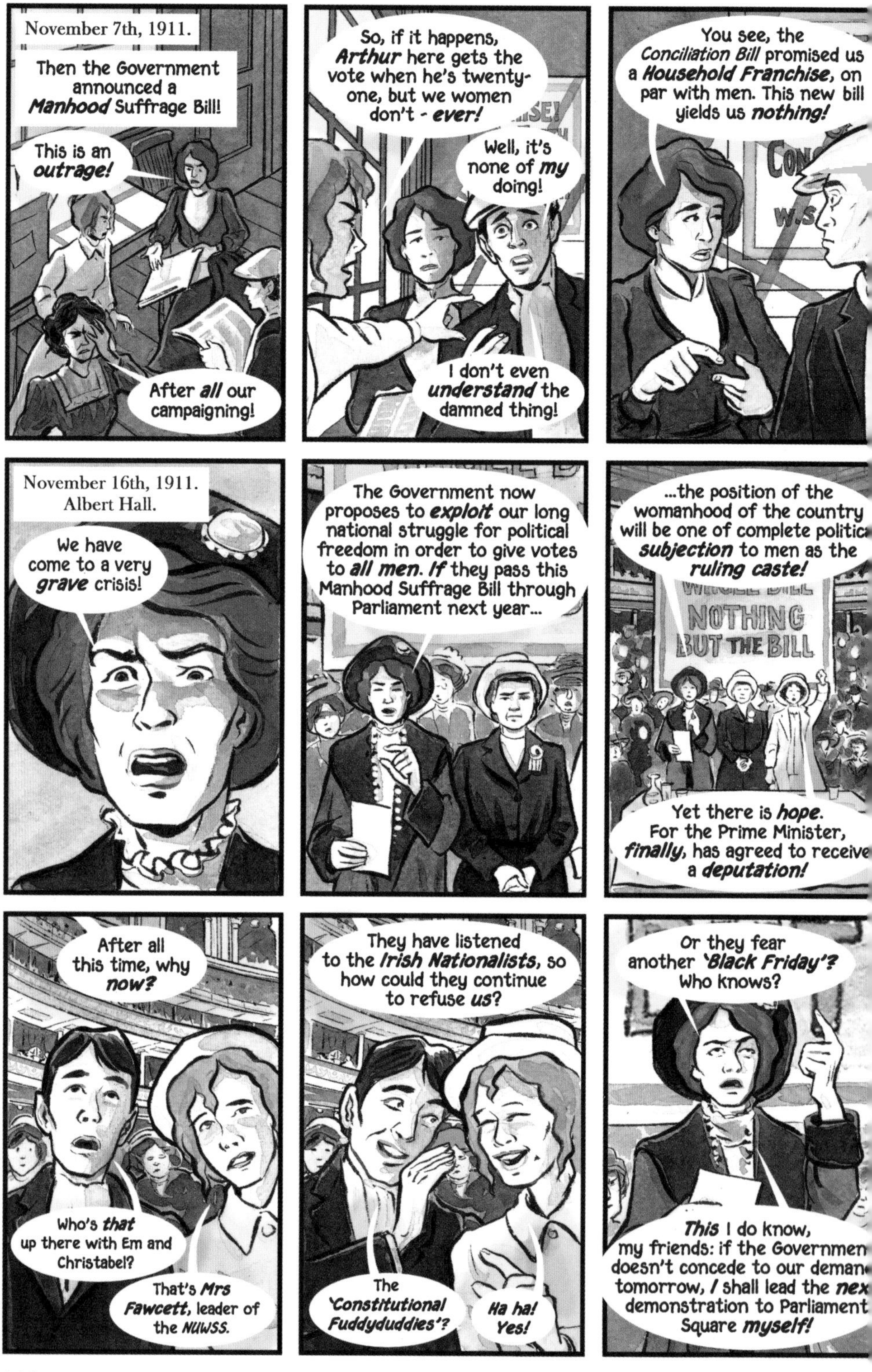

November 7th, 1911.
Then the Government announced a Manhood Suffrage Bill!
This is an outrage!
After all our campaigning!
So, if it happens, Arthur here gets the vote when he's twenty-one, but we women don't - ever!
Well, it's none of my doing!
I don't even understand the damned thing!
You see, the Conciliation Bill promised us a Household Franchise, on par with men. This new bill yields us nothing!
November 16th, 1911. Albert Hall.
We have come to a very grave crisis!
The Government now proposes to exploit our long national struggle for political freedom in order to give votes to all men. If they pass this Manhood Suffrage Bill through Parliament next year...
...the position of the womanhood of the country will be one of complete politic subjection to men as the ruling caste!
NOTHING BUT THE BILL
Yet there is hope. For the Prime Minister, finally, has agreed to receive a deputation!
After all this time, why now?
Who's that up there with Em and Christabel?
That's Mrs Fawcett, leader of the NUWSS.
They have listened to the Irish Nationalists, so how could they continue to refuse us?
The 'Constitutional Fuddyduddies'?
Ha ha! Yes!
Or they fear another 'Black Friday'? Who knows?
This I do know, my friends: if the Governmen doesn't concede to our deman tomorrow, I shall lead the nex demonstration to Parliament Square myself!

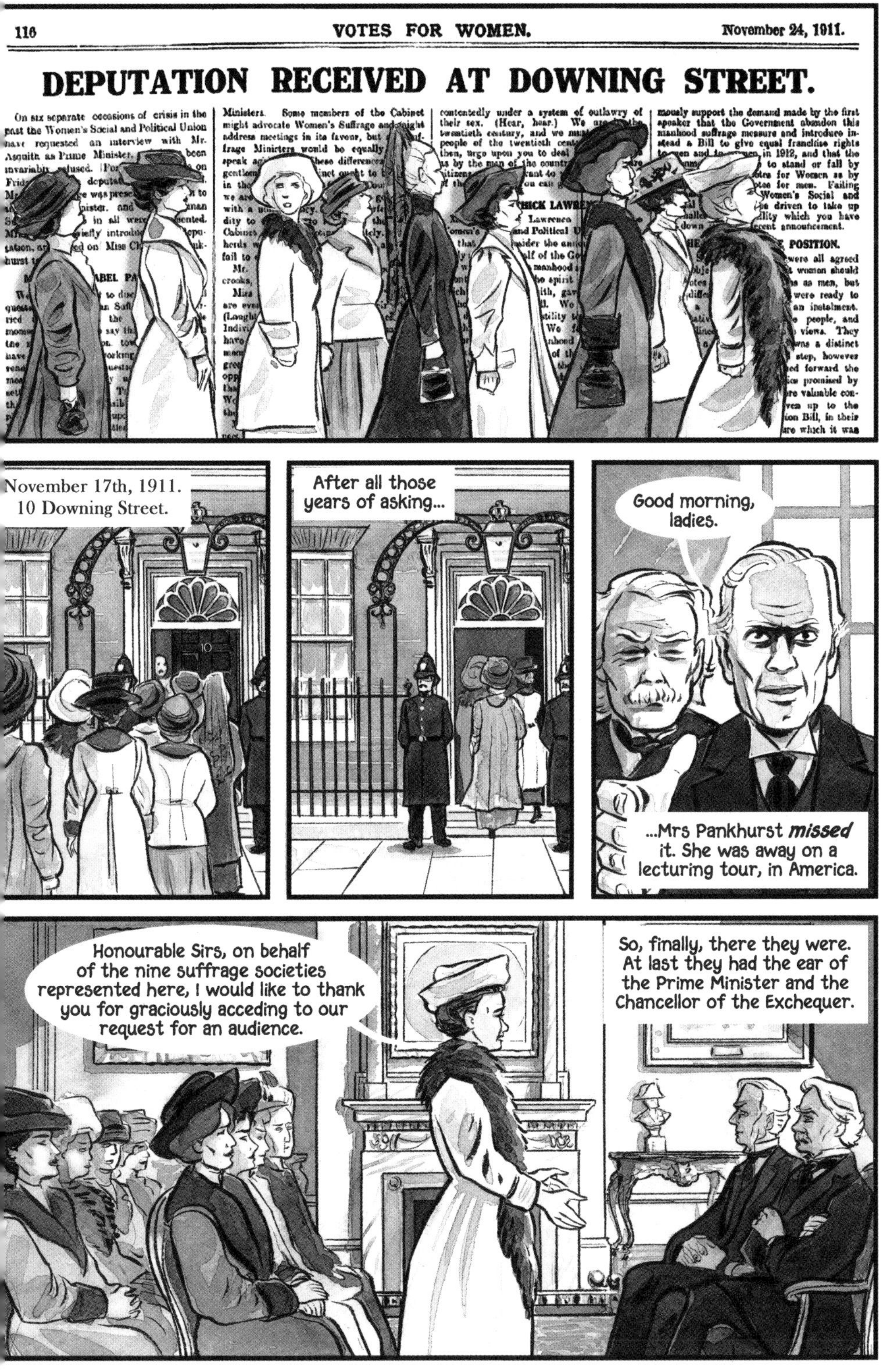
116 VOTES FOR WOMEN. November 24, 1911.
DEPUTATION RECEIVED AT DOWNING STREET.
November 17th, 1911. 10 Downing Street.
After all those years of asking...
Good morning, ladies.
...Mrs Pankhurst *missed* it. She was away on a lecturing tour, in America.
Honourable Sirs, on behalf of the nine suffrage societies represented here, I would like to thank you for graciously acceding to our request for an audience.
So, finally, there they were. At last they had the ear of the Prime Minister and the Chancellor of the Exchequer.

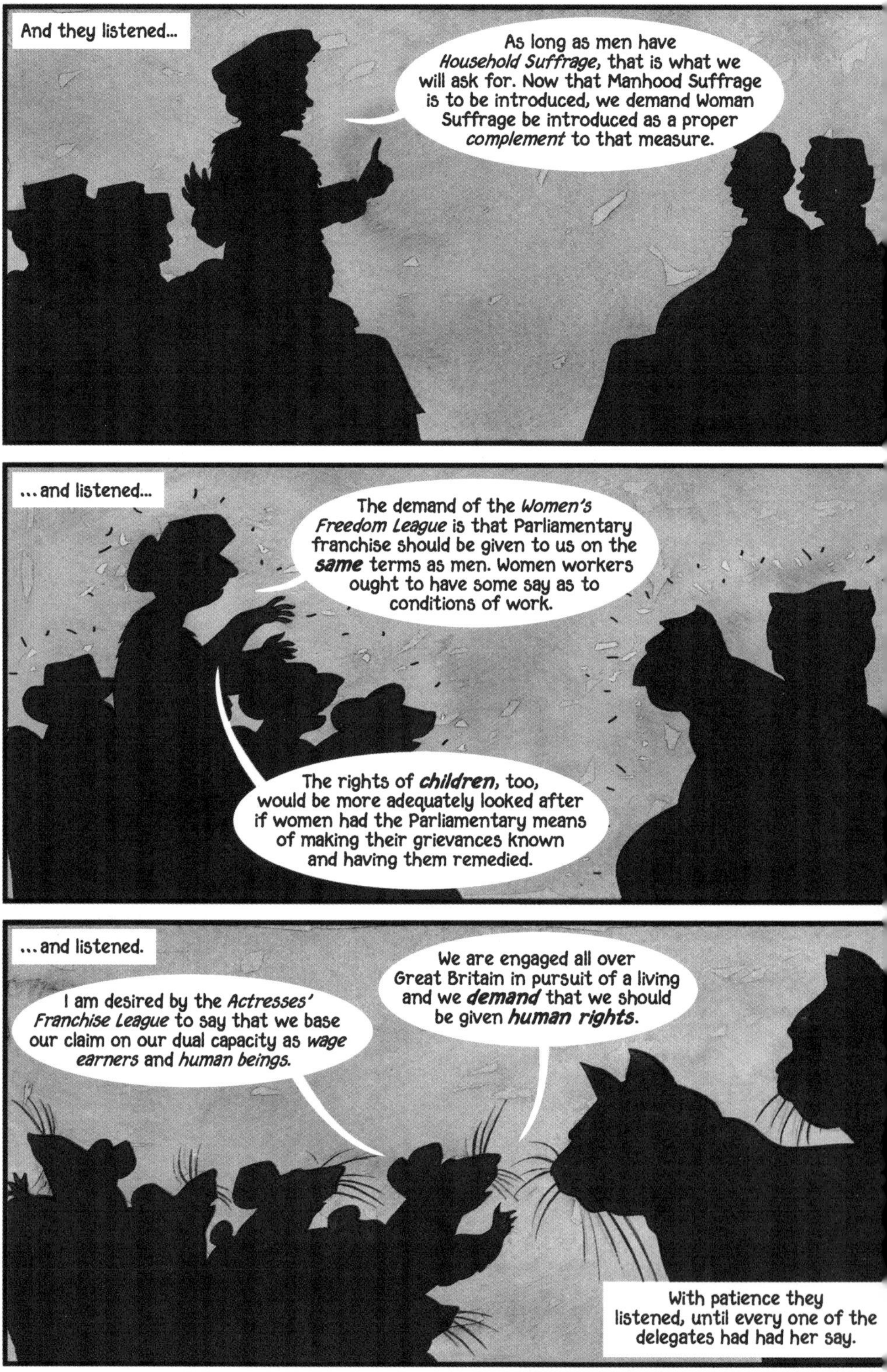
And they listened...
As long as men have *Household Suffrage*, that is what we will ask for. Now that Manhood Suffrage is to be introduced, we demand Woman Suffrage be introduced as a proper *complement* to that measure.
...and listened...
The demand of the *Women's Freedom League* is that Parliamentary franchise should be given to us on the ***same*** terms as men. Women workers ought to have some say as to conditions of work.
The rights of ***children***, too, would be more adequately looked after if women had the Parliamentary means of making their grievances known and having them remedied.
...and listened.
I am desired by the *Actresses' Franchise League* to say that we base our claim on our dual capacity as *wage earners* and *human beings*.
We are engaged all over Great Britain in pursuit of a living and we ***demand*** that we should be given ***human rights***.
With patience they listened, until every one of the delegates had had her say.

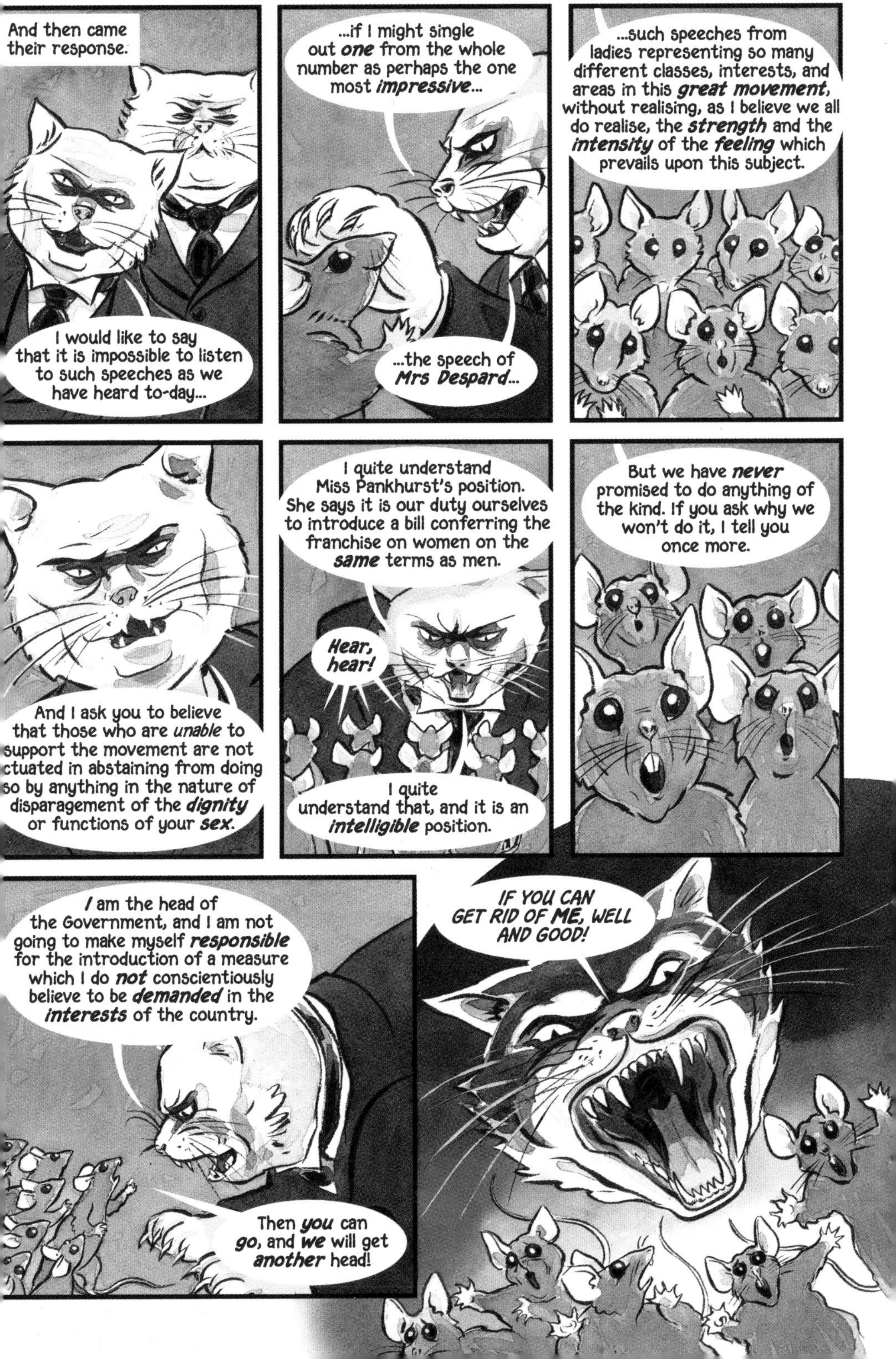
And then came their response.
I would like to say that it is impossible to listen to such speeches as we have heard to-day...
...if I might single out *one* from the whole number as perhaps the one most *impressive*...
...the speech of *Mrs Despard*...
...such speeches from ladies representing so many different classes, interests, and areas in this *great movement*, without realising, as I believe we all do realise, the *strength* and the *intensity* of the *feeling* which prevails upon this subject.
And I ask you to believe that those who are *unable* to support the movement are not ctuated in abstaining from doing so by anything in the nature of disparagement of the *dignity* or functions of your *sex*.
I quite understand Miss Pankhurst's position. She says it is our duty ourselves to introduce a bill conferring the franchise on women on the *same* terms as men.
Hear, hear!
I quite understand that, and it is an *intelligible* position.
But we have *never* promised to do anything of the kind. If you ask why we won't do it, I tell you once more.
I am the head of the Government, and I am not going to make myself *responsible* for the introduction of a measure which I do *not* conscientiously believe to be *demanded* in the *interests* of the country.
Then *you* can *go*, and *we* will get *another* head!
IF YOU CAN GET RID OF *ME*, WELL AND GOOD!

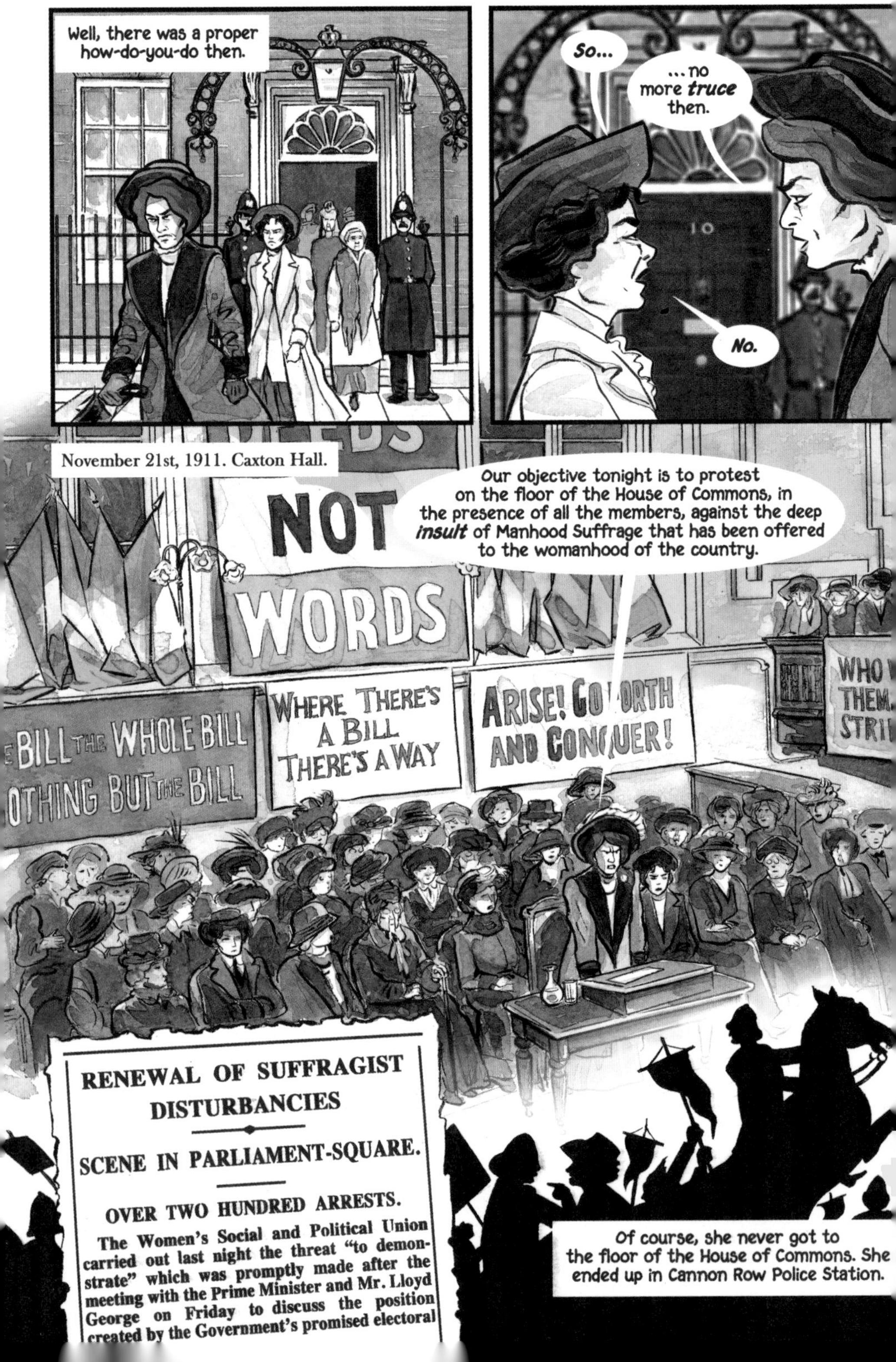
Well, there was a proper how-do-you-do then.
So...
...no more *truce* then.
No.
November 21st, 1911. Caxton Hall.
NOT WORDS
WHERE THERE'S A BILL THERE'S A WAY
Our objective tonight is to protest on the floor of the House of Commons, in the presence of all the members, against the deep *insult* of Manhood Suffrage that has been offered to the womanhood of the country.
RENEWAL OF SUFFRAGIST DISTURBANCIES
SCENE IN PARLIAMENT-SQUARE.
OVER TWO HUNDRED ARRESTS.
The Women's Social and Political Union carried out last night the threat "to demonstrate" which was promptly made after the meeting with the Prime Minister and Mr. Lloyd George on Friday to discuss the position created by the Government's promised electoral
Of course, she never got to the floor of the House of Commons. She ended up in Cannon Row Police Station.

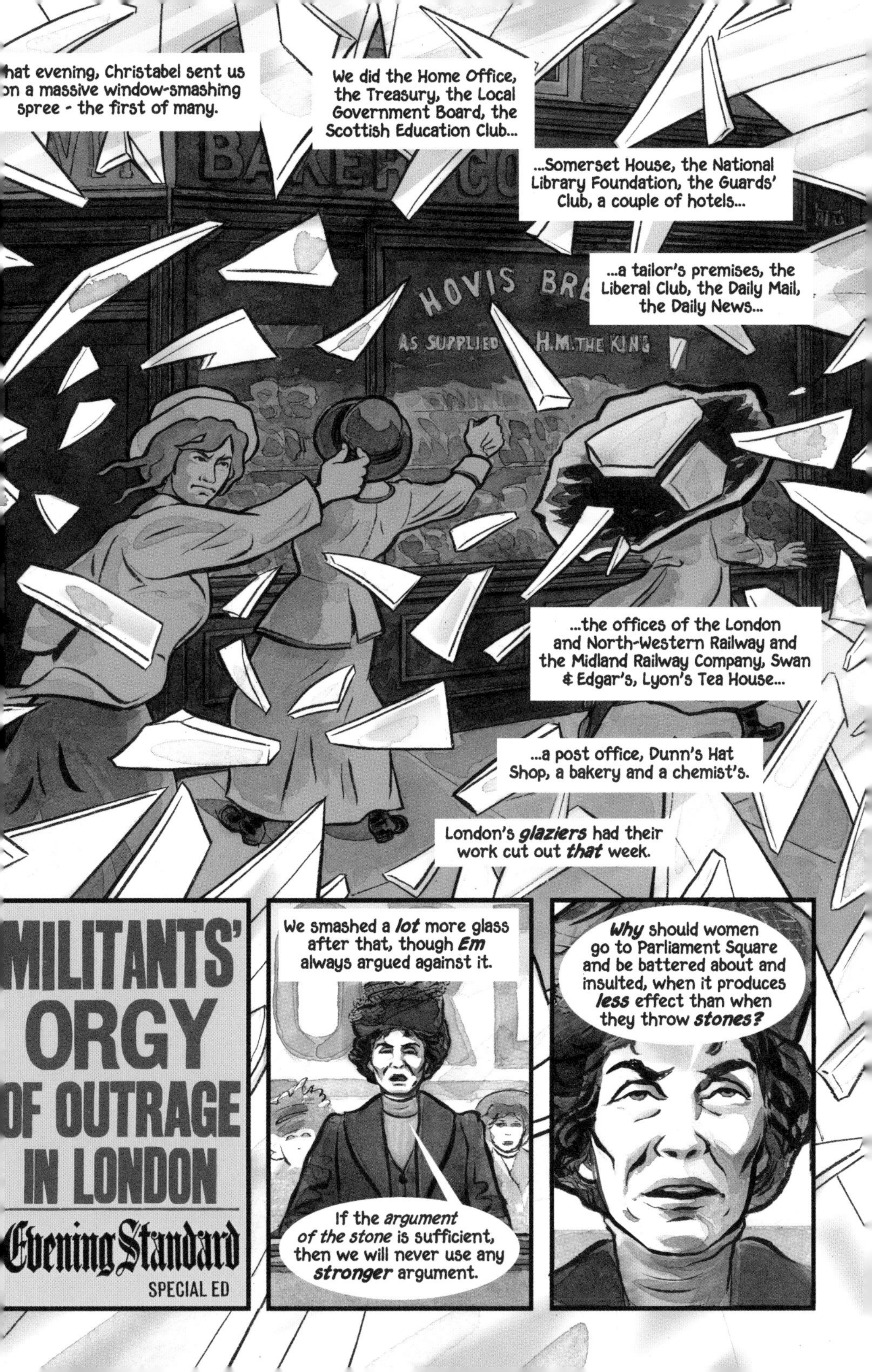
hat evening, Christabel sent us on a massive window-smashing spree - the first of many.
We did the Home Office, the Treasury, the Local Government Board, the Scottish Education Club...
...Somerset House, the National Library Foundation, the Guards' Club, a couple of hotels...
...a tailor's premises, the Liberal Club, the Daily Mail, the Daily News...
HOVIS BRE
AS SUPPLIED H.M. THE KING
...the offices of the London and North-Western Railway and the Midland Railway Company, Swan & Edgar's, Lyon's Tea House...
...a post office, Dunn's Hat Shop, a bakery and a chemist's.
London's *glaziers* had their work cut out *that* week.
MILITANTS' ORGY OF OUTRAGE IN LONDON
Evening Standard
SPECIAL ED
We smashed a *lot* more glass after that, though *Em* always argued against it.
If the *argument of the stone* is sufficient, then we will never use any *stronger* argument.
Why should women go to Parliament Square and be battered about and insulted, when it produces *less* effect than when they throw *stones?*

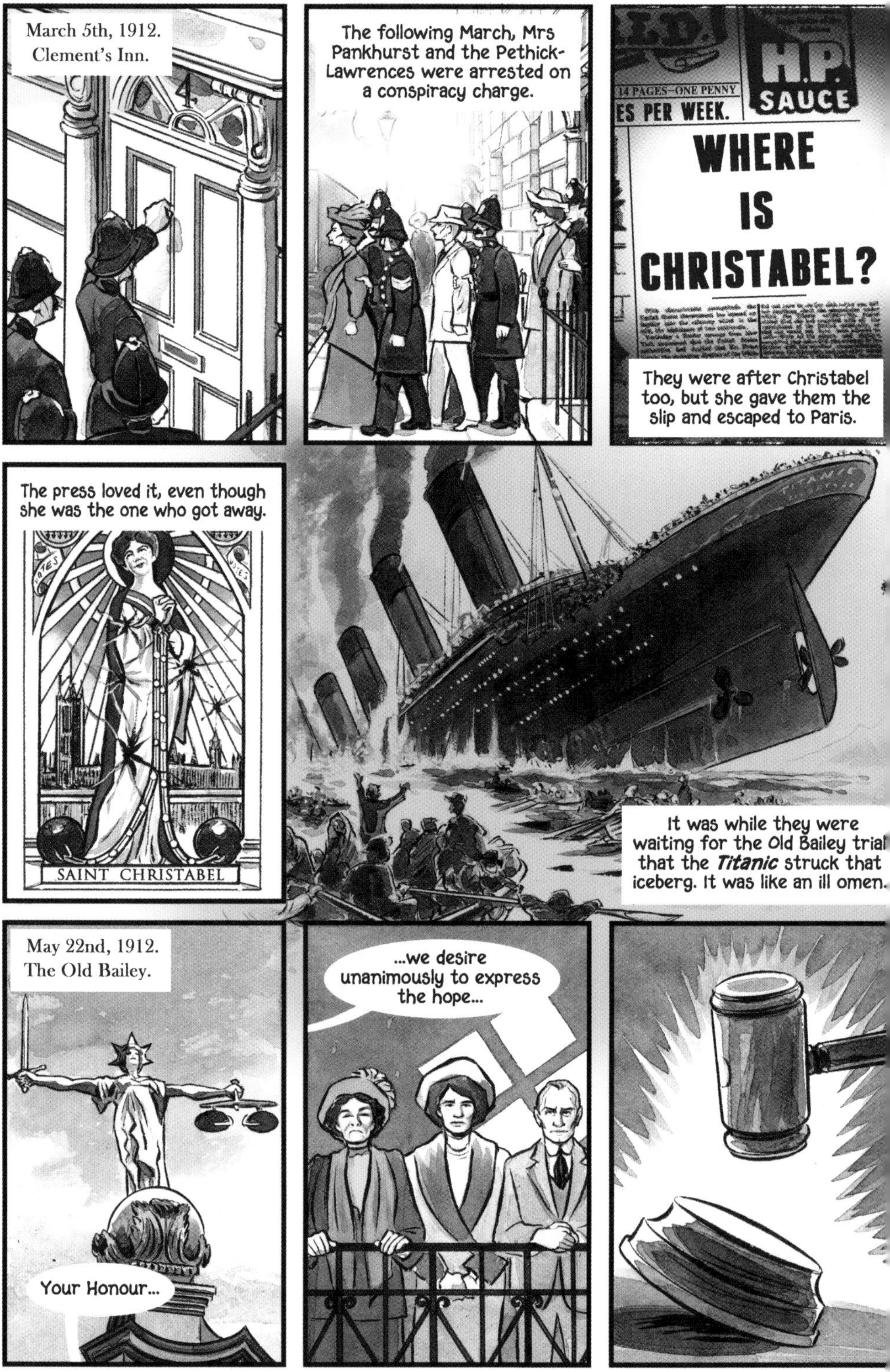
March 5th, 1912.
Clement's Inn.
The following March, Mrs Pankhurst and the Pethick-Lawrences were arrested on a conspiracy charge.
14 PAGES—ONE PENNY
ES PER WEEK.
H.P. SAUCE
WHERE IS CHRISTABEL?
They were after Christabel too, but she gave them the slip and escaped to Paris.
The press loved it, even though she was the one who got away.
SAINT CHRISTABEL
It was while they were waiting for the Old Bailey trial that the *Titanic* struck that iceberg. It was like an ill omen.
May 22nd, 1912.
The Old Bailey.
Your Honour...
...we desire unanimously to express the hope...

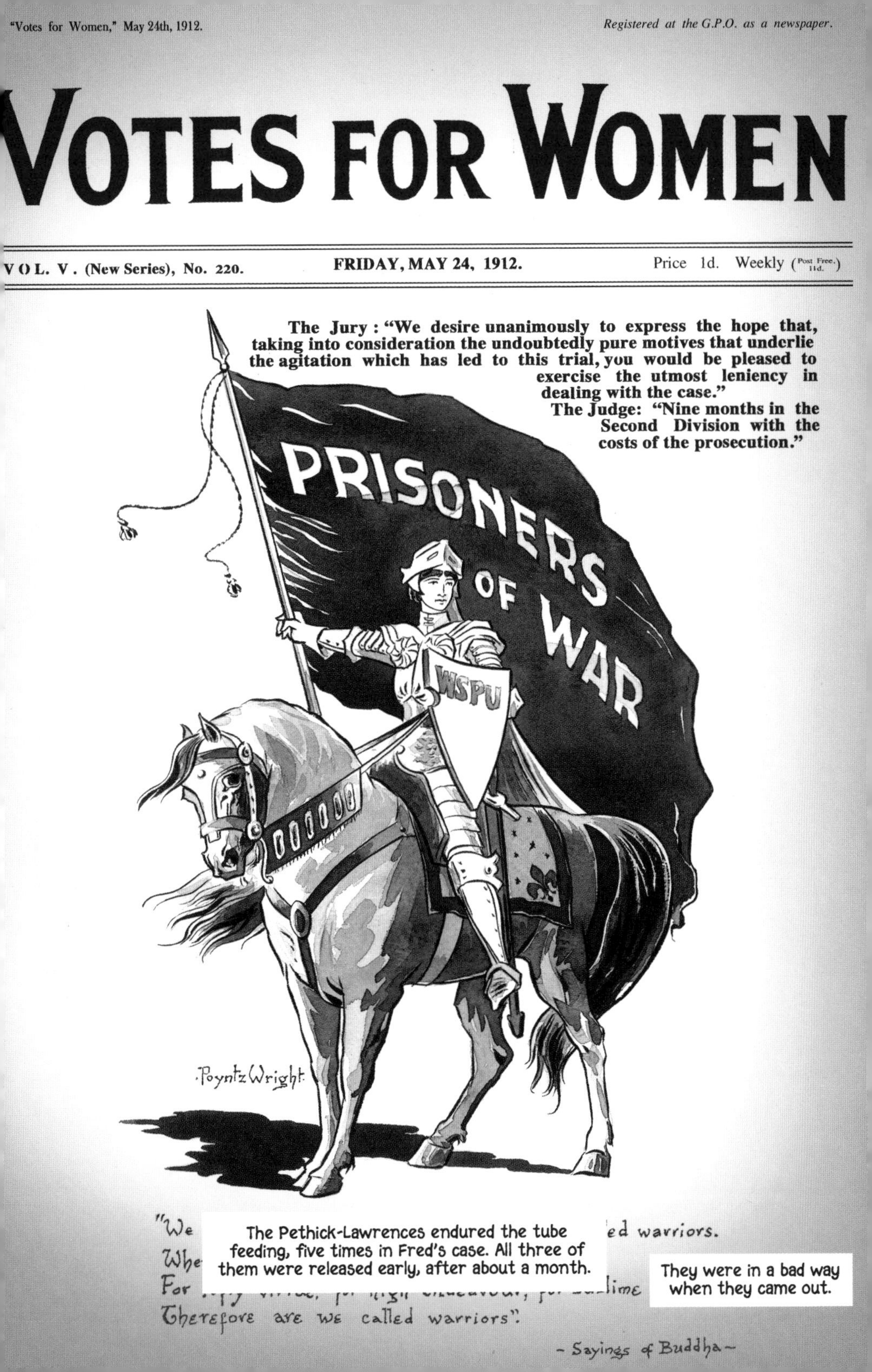
"Votes for Women," May 24th, 1912. Registered at the G.P.O. as a newspaper.

VOTES FOR WOMEN

VOL. V. (New Series), No. 220. FRIDAY, MAY 24, 1912. Price 1d. Weekly (Post Free, 1½d.)

The Jury: "We desire unanimously to express the hope that, taking into consideration the undoubtedly pure motives that underlie the agitation which has led to this trial, you would be pleased to exercise the utmost leniency in dealing with the case."

The Judge: "Nine months in the Second Division with the costs of the prosecution."

PRISONERS OF WAR
WSPU
·Poyntz Wright·
"We ... ed warriors.
Whe...
For ... lime
Therefore are we called warriors".
– Sayings of Buddha –
The Pethick-Lawrences endured the tube feeding, five times in Fred's case. All three of them were released early, after about a month.
They were in a bad way when they came out.

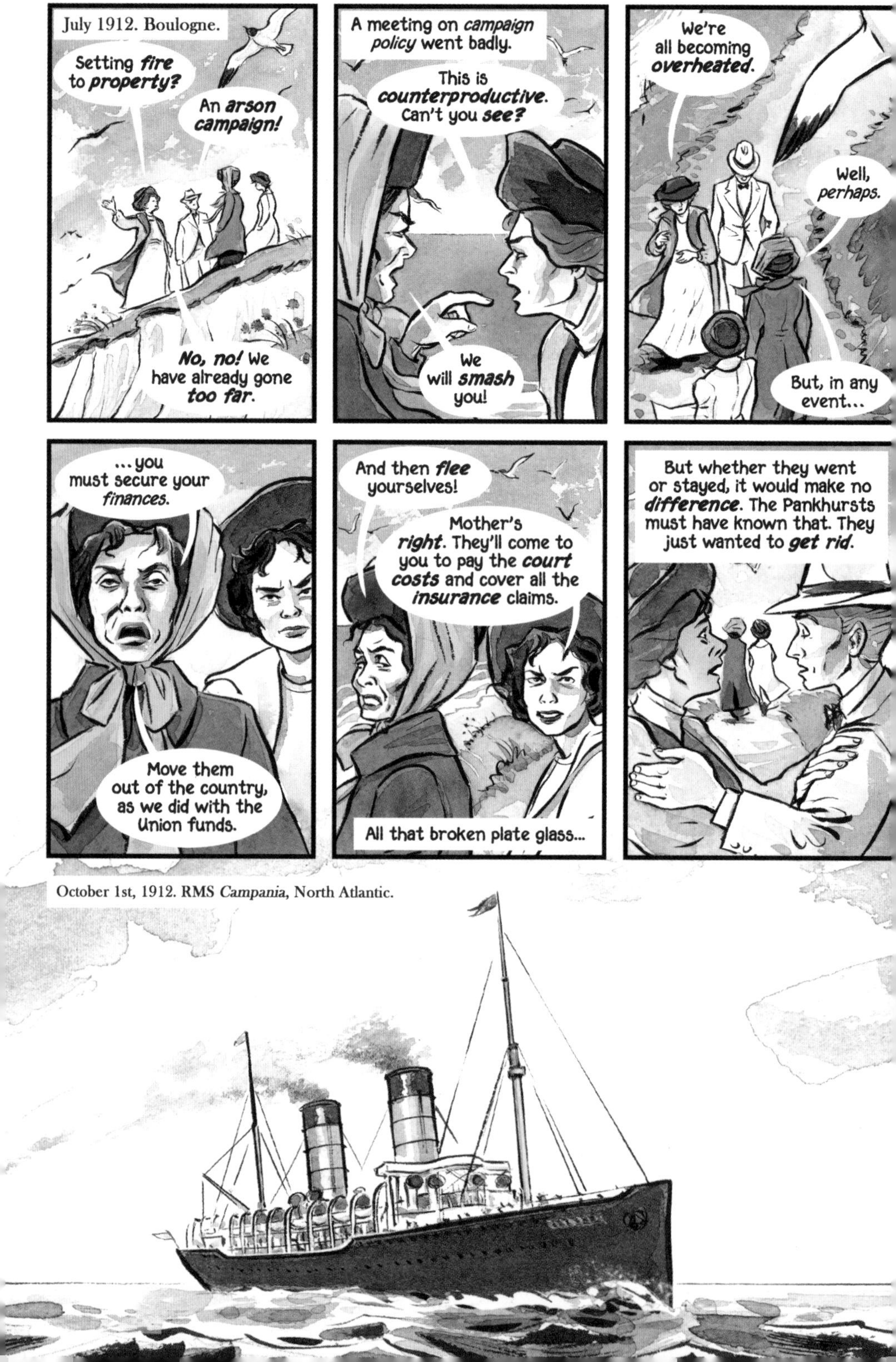

July 1912. Boulogne.
Setting *fire* to *property?*
An *arson campaign!*
No, no! We have already gone *too far*.
A meeting on *campaign policy* went badly.
This is *counterproductive*. Can't you *see?*
We will *smash* you!
We're all becoming *overheated*.
Well, *perhaps*.
But, in any event...
...you must secure your *finances*.
Move them out of the country, as we did with the Union funds.
And then *flee* yourselves!
Mother's *right*. They'll come to you to pay the *court costs* and cover all the *insurance* claims.
All that broken plate glass...
But whether they went or stayed, it would make no *difference*. The Pankhursts must have known that. They just wanted to *get rid*.
October 1st, 1912. RMS *Campania*, North Atlantic.

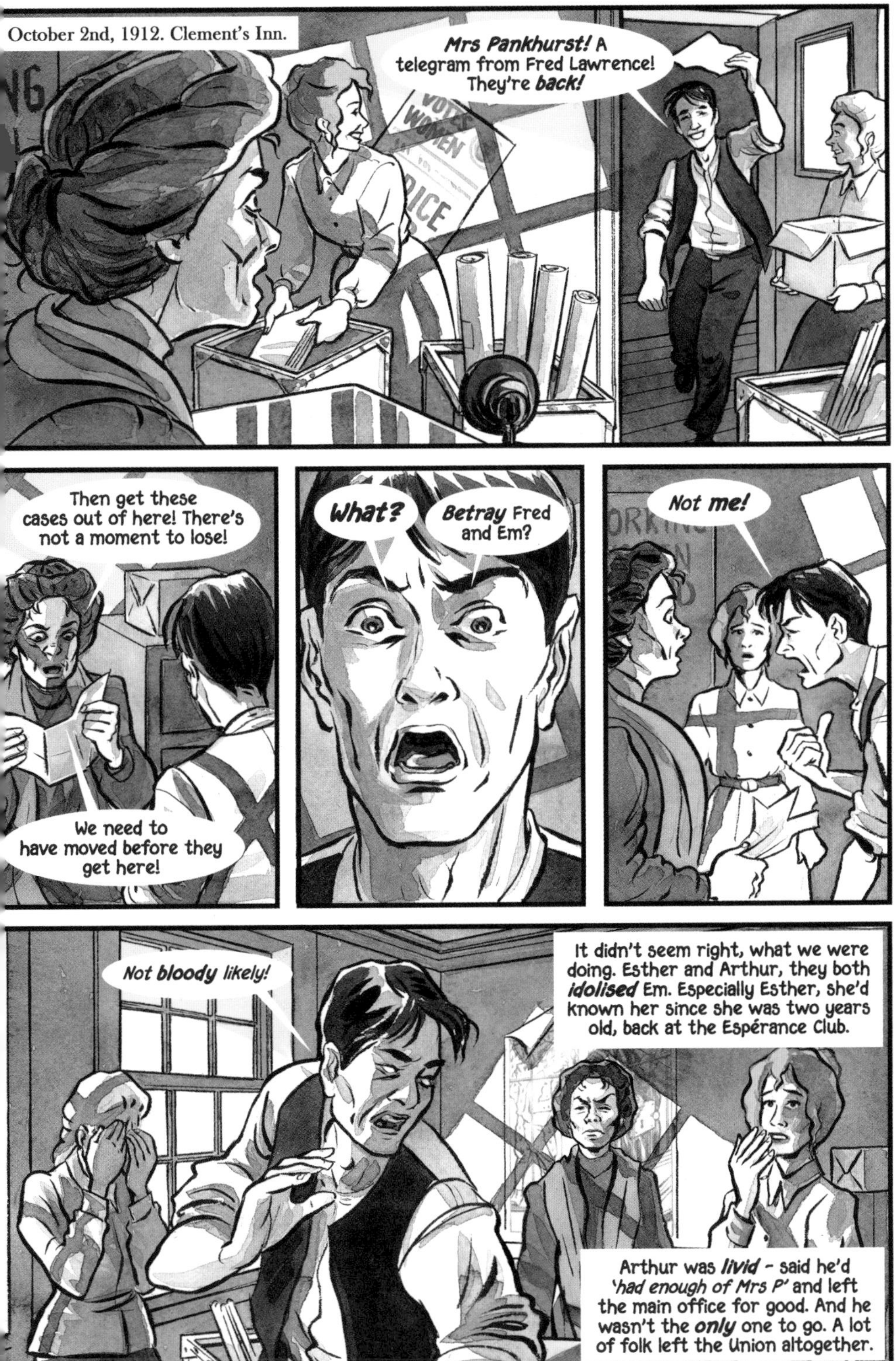

October 2nd, 1912. Clement's Inn.
Mrs Pankhurst! A telegram from Fred Lawrence! They're back!
Then get these cases out of here! There's not a moment to lose!
We need to have moved before they get here!
What?
Betray Fred and Em?
Not me!
Not bloody likely!
It didn't seem right, what we were doing. Esther and Arthur, they both idolised Em. Especially Esther, she'd known her since she was two years old, back at the Espérance Club.
Arthur was livid - said he'd 'had enough of Mrs P' and left the main office for good. And he wasn't the only one to go. A lot of folk left the Union altogether.

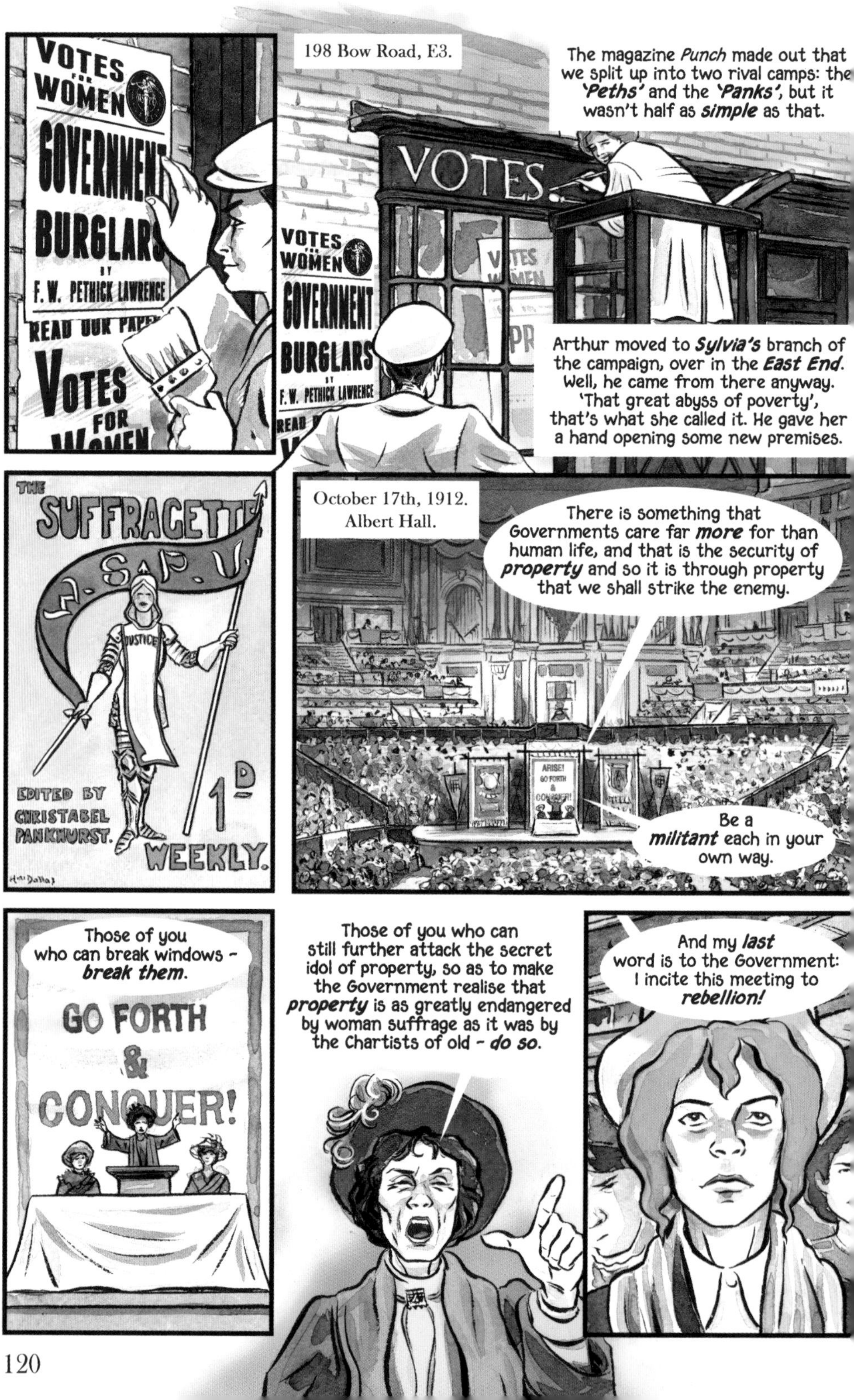
VOTES FOR WOMEN
GOVERNMENT BURGLARS BY F.W. PETHICK LAWRENCE
READ OUR PAPER
VOTES FOR WOMEN
198 Bow Road, E3.
The magazine *Punch* made out that we split up into two rival camps: the ***'Peths'*** and the ***'Panks'***, but it wasn't half as ***simple*** as that.
VOTES
VOTES FOR WOMEN
GOVERNMENT BURGLARS BY F.W. PETHICK LAWRENCE
Arthur moved to ***Sylvia's*** branch of the campaign, over in the ***East End***. Well, he came from there anyway. 'That great abyss of poverty', that's what she called it. He gave her a hand opening some new premises.
THE SUFFRAGETTE
W.S.P.U.
JUSTICE
EDITED BY CHRISTABEL PANKHURST.
1D WEEKLY.
October 17th, 1912. Albert Hall.
There is something that Governments care far ***more*** for than human life, and that is the security of ***property*** and so it is through property that we shall strike the enemy.
ARISE! GO FORTH & CONQUER!
Be a ***militant*** each in your own way.
Those of you who can break windows - ***break them***.
GO FORTH & CONQUER!
Those of you who can still further attack the secret idol of property, so as to make the Government realise that ***property*** is as greatly endangered by woman suffrage as it was by the Chartists of old - ***do so***.
And my ***last*** word is to the Government: I incite this meeting to ***rebellion!***

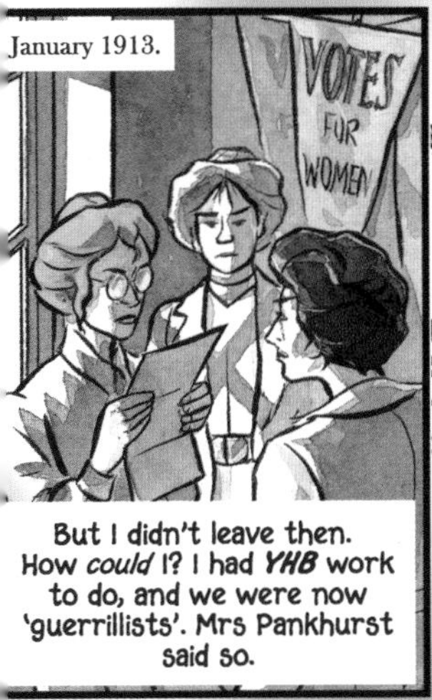
January 1913.
VOTES FOR WOMEN
But I didn't leave then. How *could* I? I had *YHB* work to do, and we were now 'guerrillists'. Mrs Pankhurst said so.

VOTES FOR WOMEN.

The Women's Social and Political Union.

OFFICE: LINCOLN'S INN HOUSE, KINGSWAY, W.C.

Private and Confidential.   January 10th, 1913

Dear Friend,

The Prime Minister has announced that in the week beginning January 20th the Women's Amendments to the Manhood Suffrage Bill will be discussed and voted upon. This means that within a few short days the fate of these Amendments will be finally decided.

The W.S.P.U. has, from the first declined, to call any truce on the strength of the Prime Minister's so-called pledge, and has refused to depend upon the Amendments in question, because the Government have not accepted the responsibility of getting them carried.

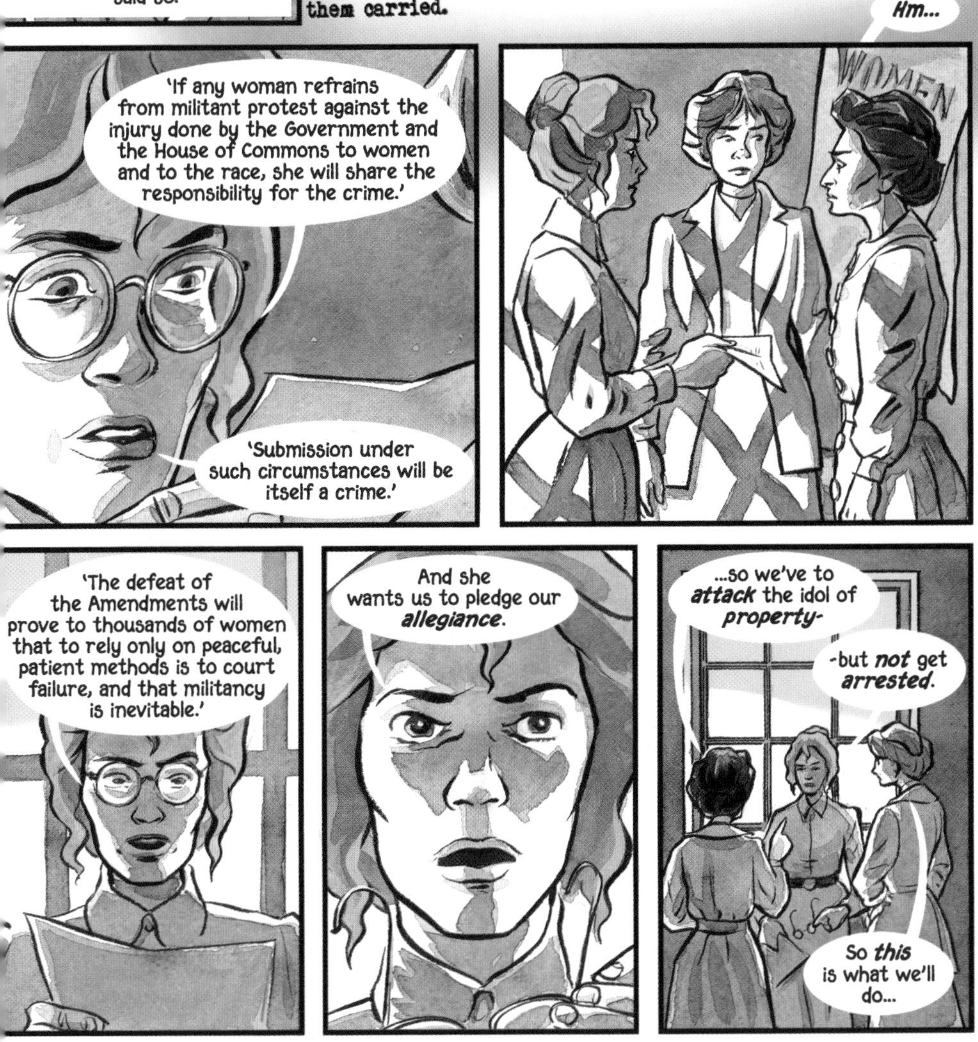
Hm...
'If any woman refrains from militant protest against the injury done by the Government and the House of Commons to women and to the race, she will share the responsibility for the crime.'
'Submission under such circumstances will be itself a crime.'
WOMEN
'The defeat of the Amendments will prove to thousands of women that to rely only on peaceful, patient methods is to court failure, and that militancy is inevitable.'
And she wants us to pledge our *allegiance*.
...so we've to *attack* the idol of *property*-
-but *not* get *arrested*.
So *this* is what we'll do...

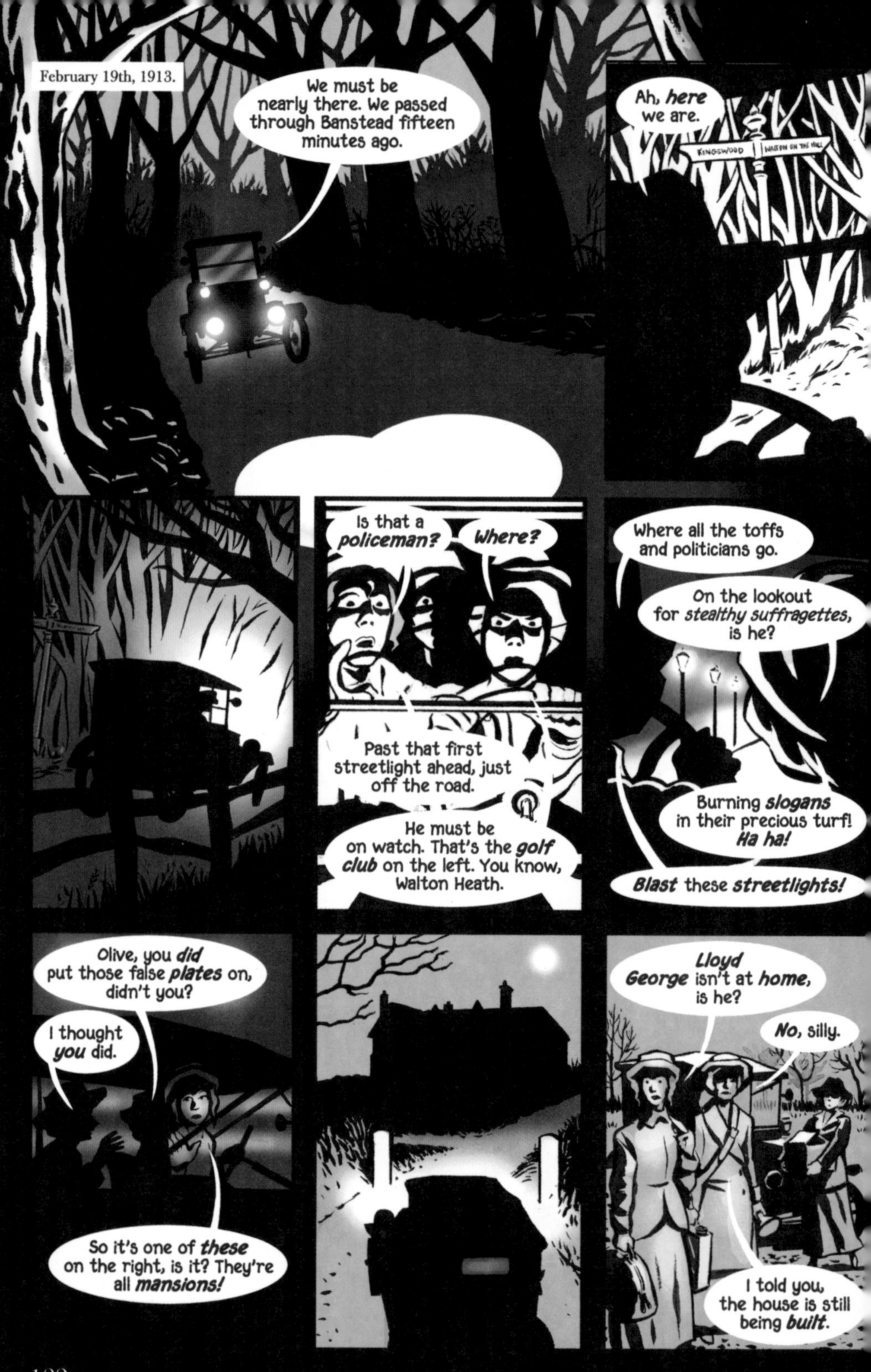
February 19th, 1913.
We must be nearly there. We passed through Banstead fifteen minutes ago.
Ah, *here* we are.
KINGSWOOD
WALTON ON THE HILL
Is that a *policeman?*
Where?
Past that first streetlight ahead, just off the road.
He must be on watch. That's the *golf club* on the left. You know, Walton Heath.
Where all the toffs and politicians go.
On the lookout for *stealthy suffragettes,* is he?
Burning *slogans* in their precious turf! *Ha ha!*
Blast these *streetlights!*
Olive, you *did* put those false *plates* on, didn't you?
I thought *you* did.
So it's one of *these* on the right, is it? They're all *mansions!*
Lloyd George isn't at *home,* is he?
No, silly.
I told you, the house is still being *built.*

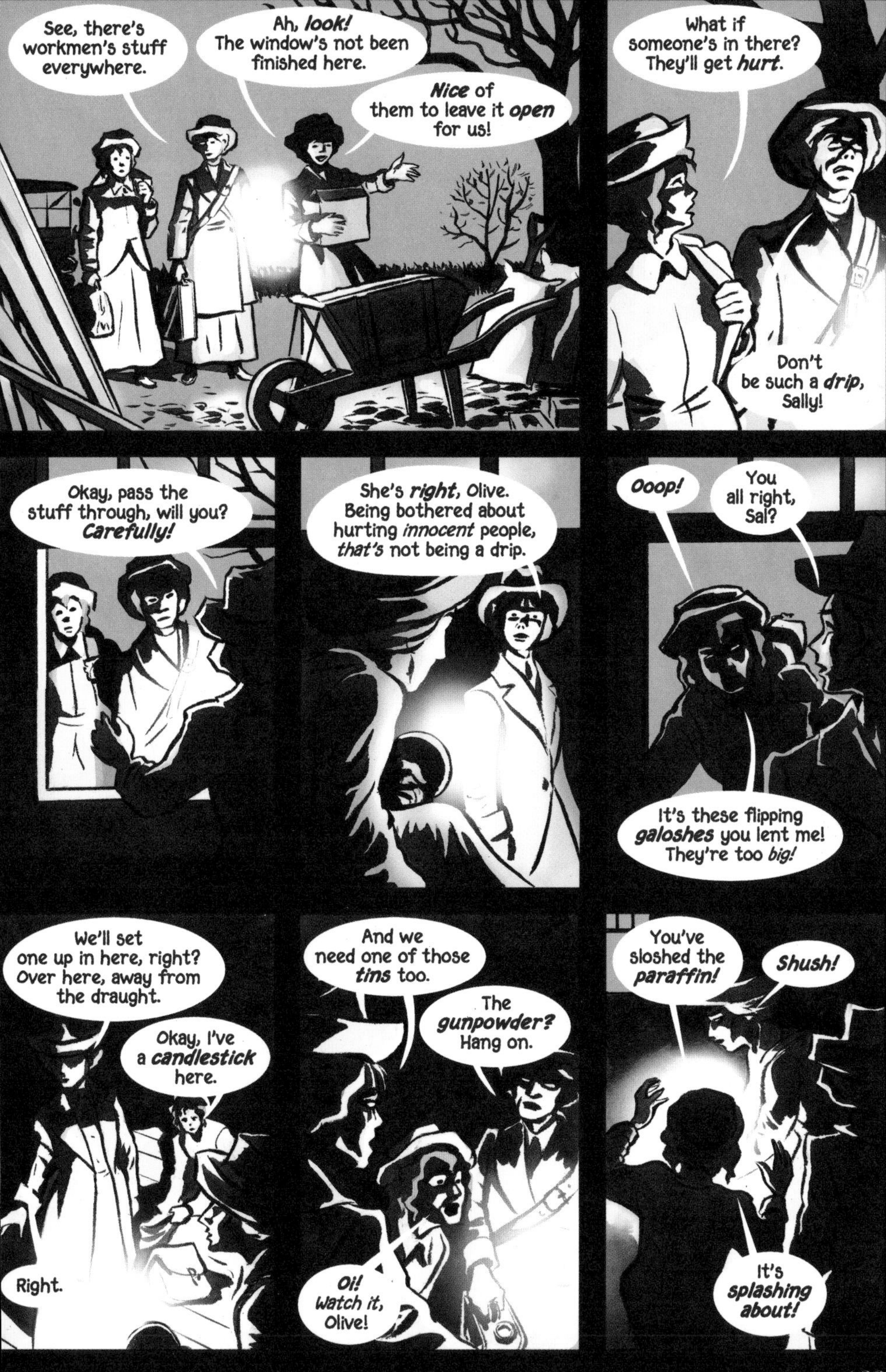
See, there's workmen's stuff everywhere.
Ah, look! The window's not been finished here.
Nice of them to leave it open for us!
What if someone's in there? They'll get hurt.
Don't be such a drip, Sally!
Okay, pass the stuff through, will you? Carefully!
She's right, Olive. Being bothered about hurting innocent people, that's not being a drip.
Ooop!
You all right, Sal?
It's these flipping galoshes you lent me! They're too big!
We'll set one up in here, right? Over here, away from the draught.
Okay, I've a candlestick here.
Right.
And we need one of those tins too.
The gunpowder? Hang on.
Oi! Watch it, Olive!
You've sloshed the paraffin!
Shush!
It's splashing about!

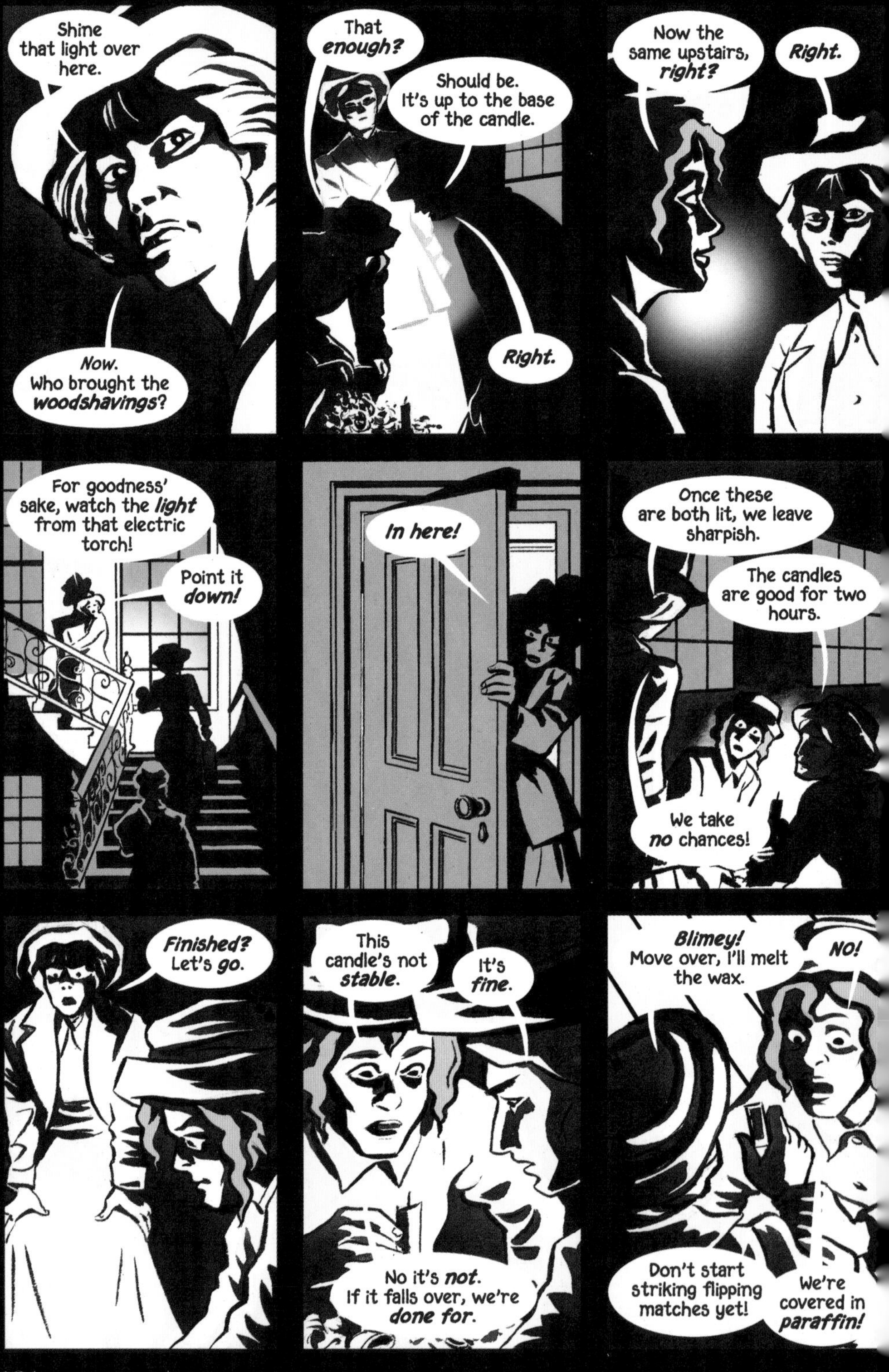
Shine that light over here.
Now. Who brought the woodshavings?
That enough?
Should be. It's up to the base of the candle.
Right.
Now the same upstairs, right?
Right.
For goodness' sake, watch the light from that electric torch!
Point it down!
In here!
Once these are both lit, we leave sharpish.
The candles are good for two hours.
We take no chances!
Finished? Let's go.
This candle's not stable.
It's fine.
No it's not. If it falls over, we're done for.
Blimey! Move over, I'll melt the wax.
NO!
Don't start striking flipping matches yet!
We're covered in paraffin!

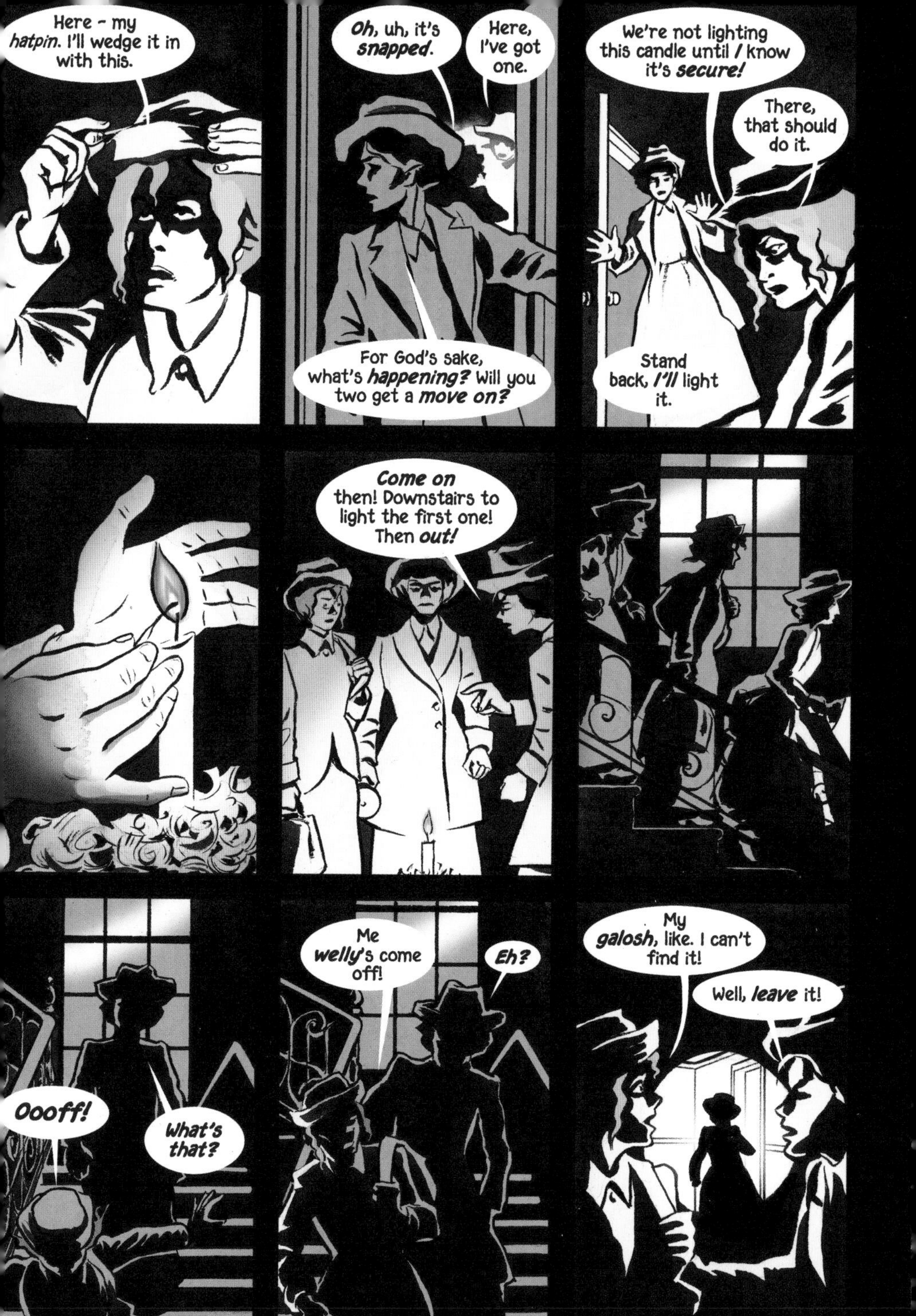
Here - my hatpin. I'll wedge it in with this.
Oh, uh, it's snapped.
Here, I've got one.
For God's sake, what's happening? Will you two get a move on?
We're not lighting this candle until I know it's secure!
There, that should do it.
Stand back, I'll light it.
Come on then! Downstairs to light the first one! Then out!
Oooff!
What's that?
Me welly's come off!
Eh?
My galosh, like. I can't find it!
Well, leave it!

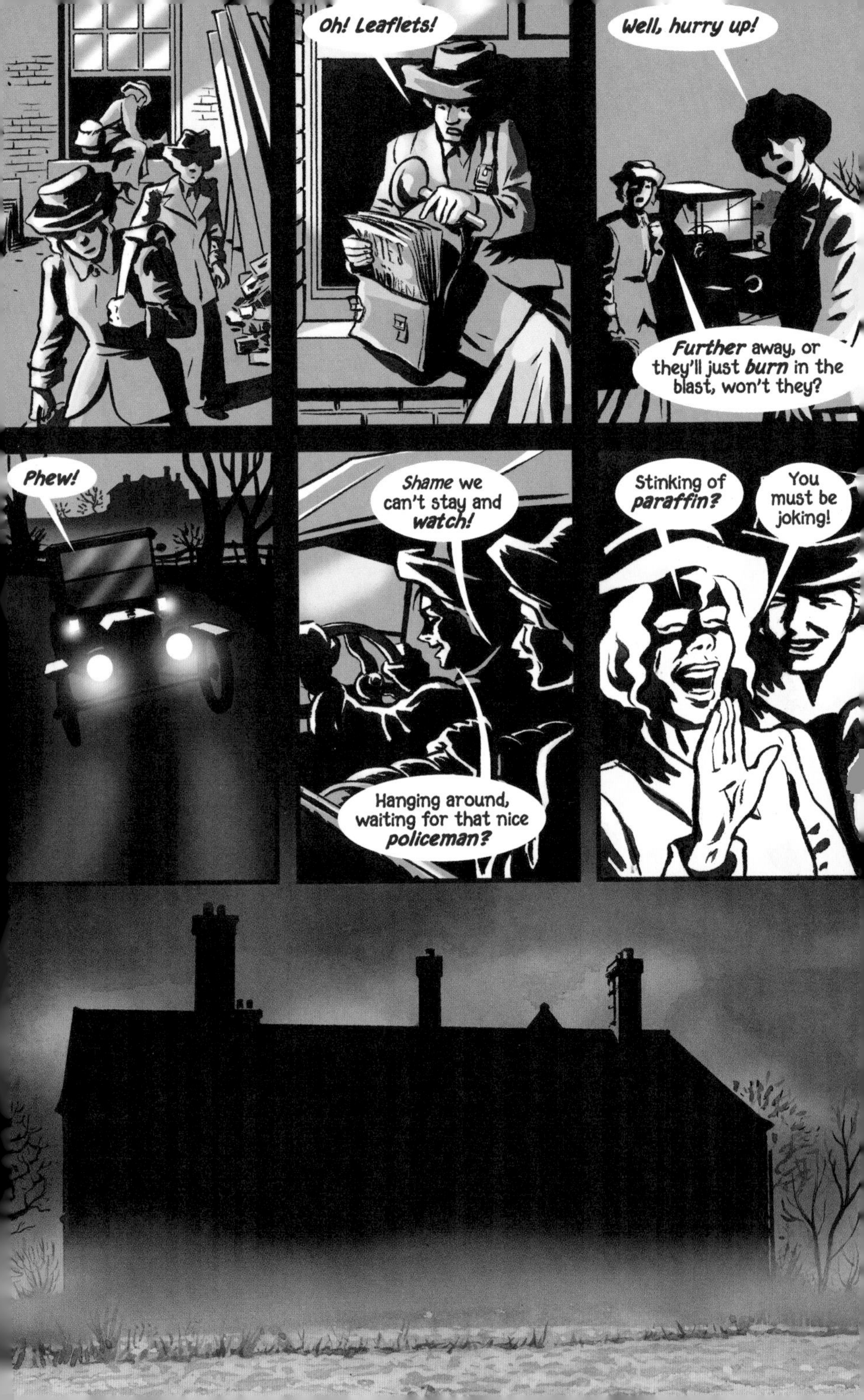
Oh! Leaflets!
Well, hurry up!
Further away, or they'll just burn in the blast, won't they?
Phew!
Shame we can't stay and watch!
Hanging around, waiting for that nice policeman?
Stinking of paraffin?
You must be joking!

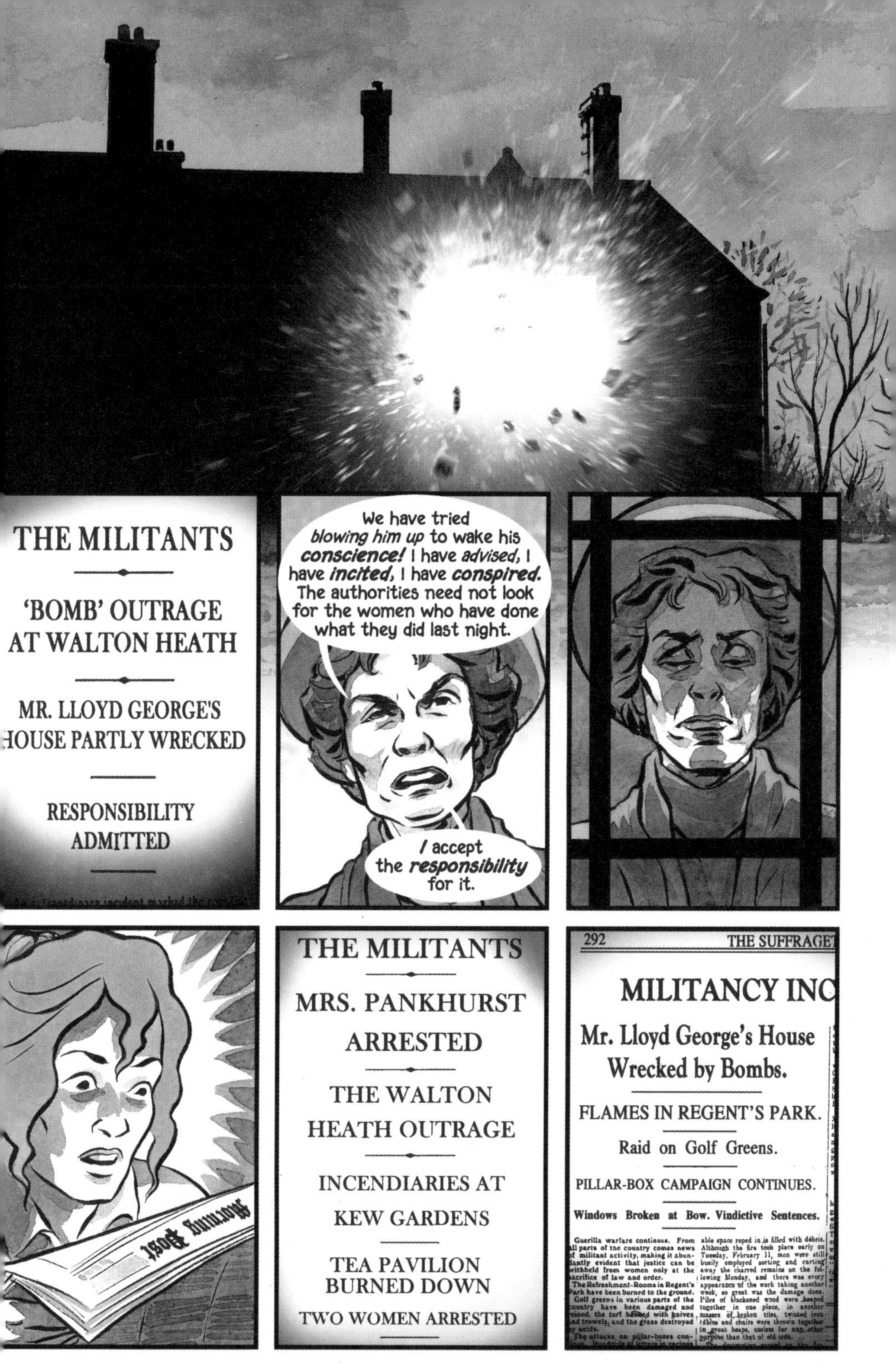
THE MILITANTS
'BOMB' OUTRAGE AT WALTON HEATH
MR. LLOYD GEORGE'S HOUSE PARTLY WRECKED
RESPONSIBILITY ADMITTED
We have tried *blowing him up* to wake his ***conscience!*** I have *advised,* I have ***incited,*** I have ***conspired.*** The authorities need not look for the women who have done what they did last night.
I accept the ***responsibility*** for it.
THE MILITANTS
MRS. PANKHURST ARRESTED
THE WALTON HEATH OUTRAGE
INCENDIARIES AT KEW GARDENS
TEA PAVILION BURNED DOWN
TWO WOMEN ARRESTED
292
MILITANCY INC
Mr. Lloyd George's House Wrecked by Bombs.
FLAMES IN REGENT'S PARK.
Raid on Golf Greens.
PILLAR-BOX CAMPAIGN CONTINUES.
Windows Broken at Bow. Vindictive Sentences.

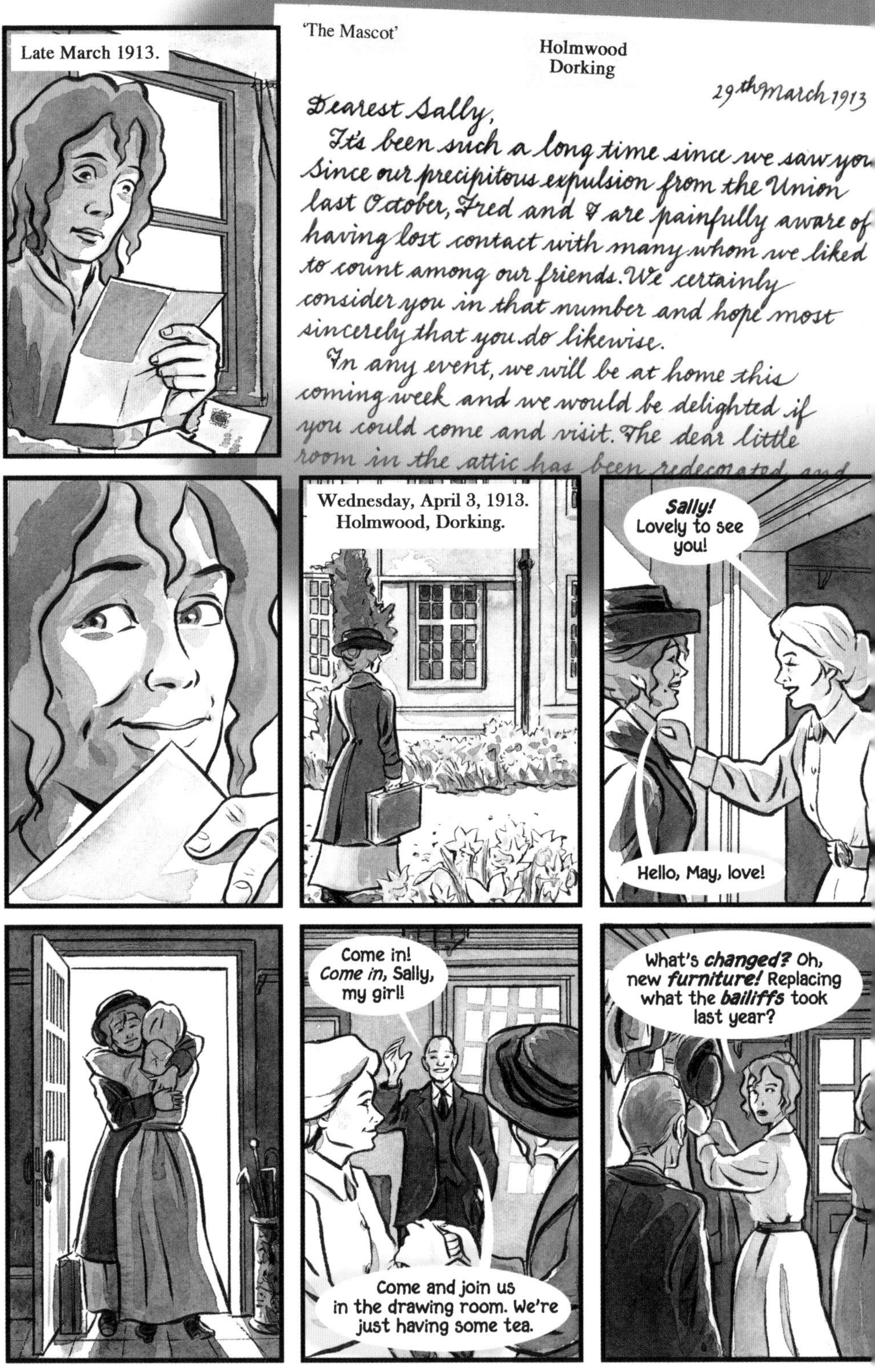

Late March 1913.
'The Mascot'
Holmwood
Dorking
29th March 1913
Dearest Sally,
It's been such a long time since we saw you. Since our precipitous expulsion from the Union last October, Fred and I are painfully aware of having lost contact with many whom we liked to count among our friends. We certainly consider you in that number and hope most sincerely that you do likewise.
In any event, we will be at home this coming week and we would be delighted if you could come and visit. The dear little room in the attic has been redecorated and
Wednesday, April 3, 1913.
Holmwood, Dorking.
Sally!
Lovely to see you!
Hello, May, love!
Come in!
Come in, Sally, my girl!
Come and join us in the drawing room. We're just having some tea.
What's changed? Oh, new furniture! Replacing what the bailiffs took last year?

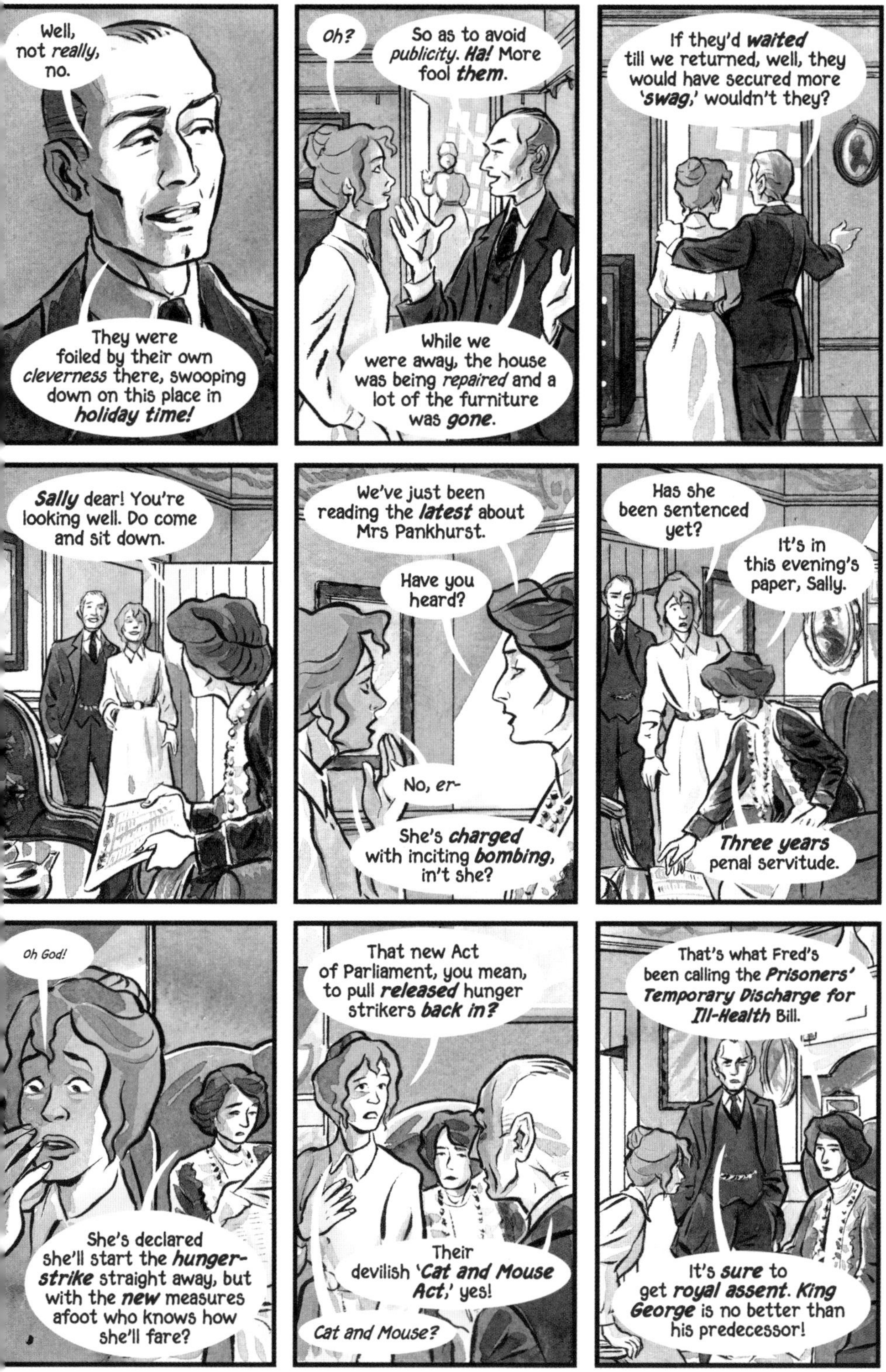
Well, not *really*, no.
They were foiled by their own *cleverness* there, swooping down on this place in **holiday time!**
Oh?
So as to avoid *publicity*. ***Ha!*** More fool **them**.
While we were away, the house was being *repaired* and a lot of the furniture was **gone**.
If they'd **waited** till we returned, well, they would have secured more '**swag**,' wouldn't they?
Sally dear! You're looking well. Do come and sit down.
We've just been reading the ***latest*** about Mrs Pankhurst.
Have you heard?
No, *er-*
She's ***charged*** with inciting ***bombing***, in't she?
Has she been sentenced yet?
It's in this evening's paper, Sally.
Three years penal servitude.
Oh God!
She's declared she'll start the ***hunger-strike*** straight away, but with the ***new*** measures afoot who knows how she'll fare?
That new Act of Parliament, you mean, to pull ***released*** hunger strikers ***back in?***
Their devilish '***Cat and Mouse Act***,' yes!
Cat and Mouse?
That's what Fred's been calling the ***Prisoners' Temporary Discharge for Ill-Health*** Bill.
It's ***sure*** to get ***royal assent***. ***King George*** is no better than his predecessor!

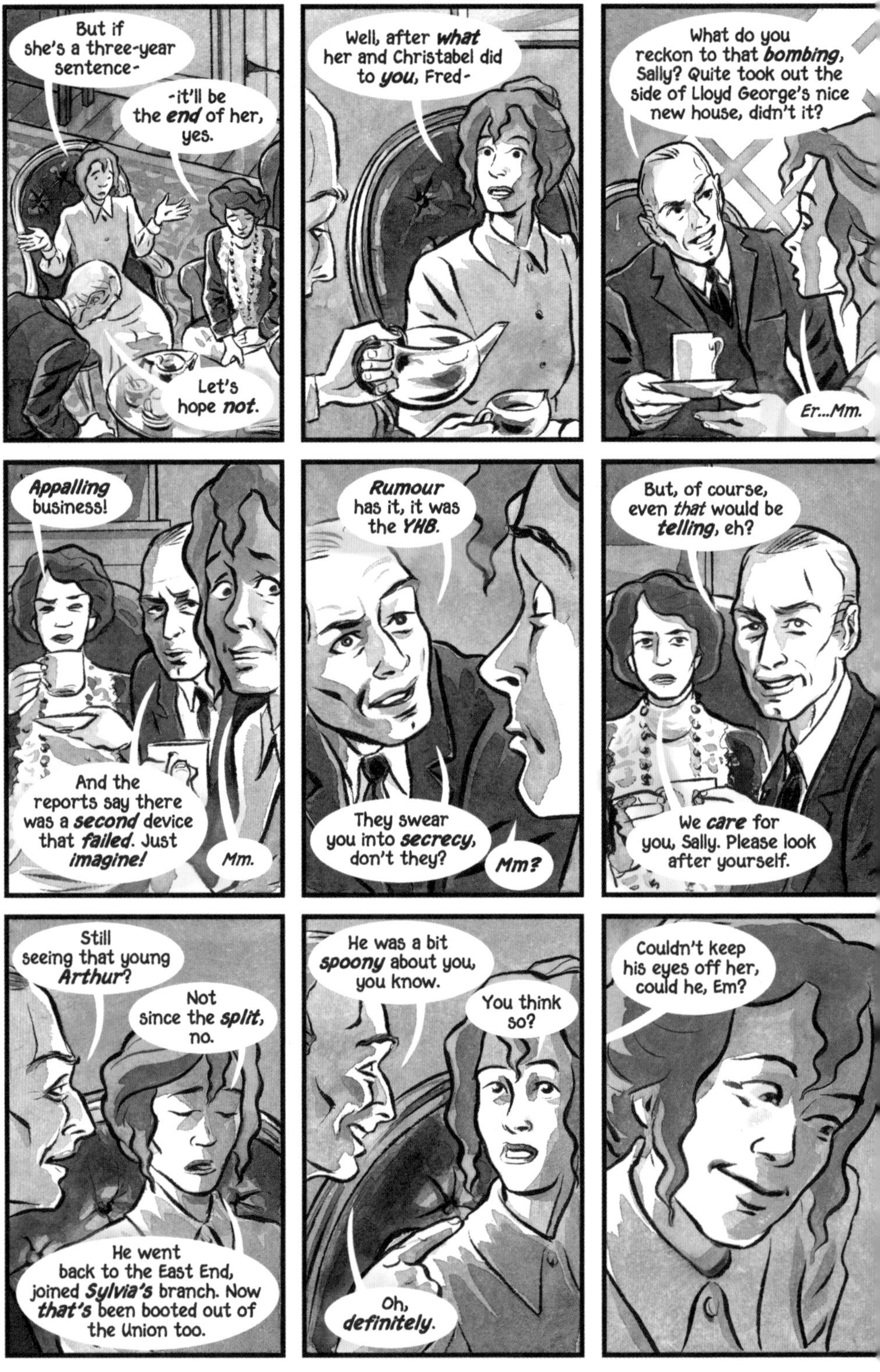
But if she's a three-year sentence-
-it'll be the end of her, yes.
Let's hope not.
Well, after what her and Christabel did to you, Fred-
What do you reckon to that bombing, Sally? Quite took out the side of Lloyd George's nice new house, didn't it?
Er...Mm.
Appalling business!
And the reports say there was a second device that failed. Just imagine!
Mm.
Rumour has it, it was the YHB.
They swear you into secrecy, don't they?
Mm?
But, of course, even that would be telling, eh?
We care for you, Sally. Please look after yourself.
Still seeing that young Arthur?
Not since the split, no.
He went back to the East End, joined Sylvia's branch. Now that's been booted out of the Union too.
He was a bit spoony about you, you know.
You think so?
Oh, definitely.
Couldn't keep his eyes off her, could he, Em?

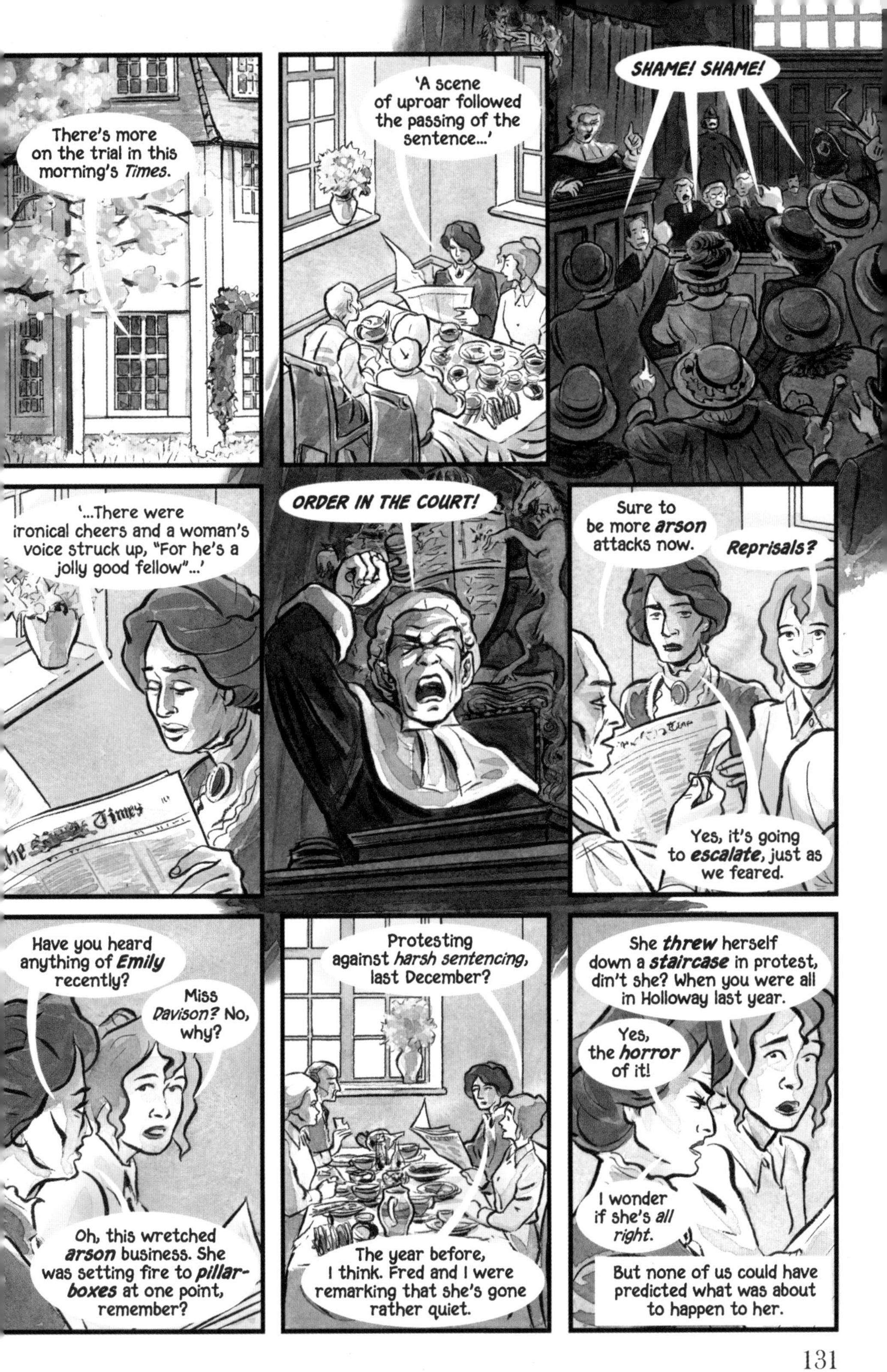

There's more on the trial in this morning's *Times*.
'A scene of uproar followed the passing of the sentence...'
SHAME! SHAME!
'...There were ironical cheers and a woman's voice struck up, "For he's a jolly good fellow"...'
ORDER IN THE COURT!
Sure to be more *arson* attacks now.
Reprisals?
Yes, it's going to *escalate*, just as we feared.
Have you heard anything of *Emily* recently?
Miss *Davison?* No, why?
Oh, this wretched *arson* business. She was setting fire to *pillar-boxes* at one point, remember?
Protesting against *harsh sentencing*, last December?
The year before, I think. Fred and I were remarking that she's gone rather quiet.
She *threw* herself down a *staircase* in protest, din't she? When you were all in Holloway last year.
Yes, the *horror* of it!
I wonder if she's *all right*.
But none of us could have predicted what was about to happen to her.

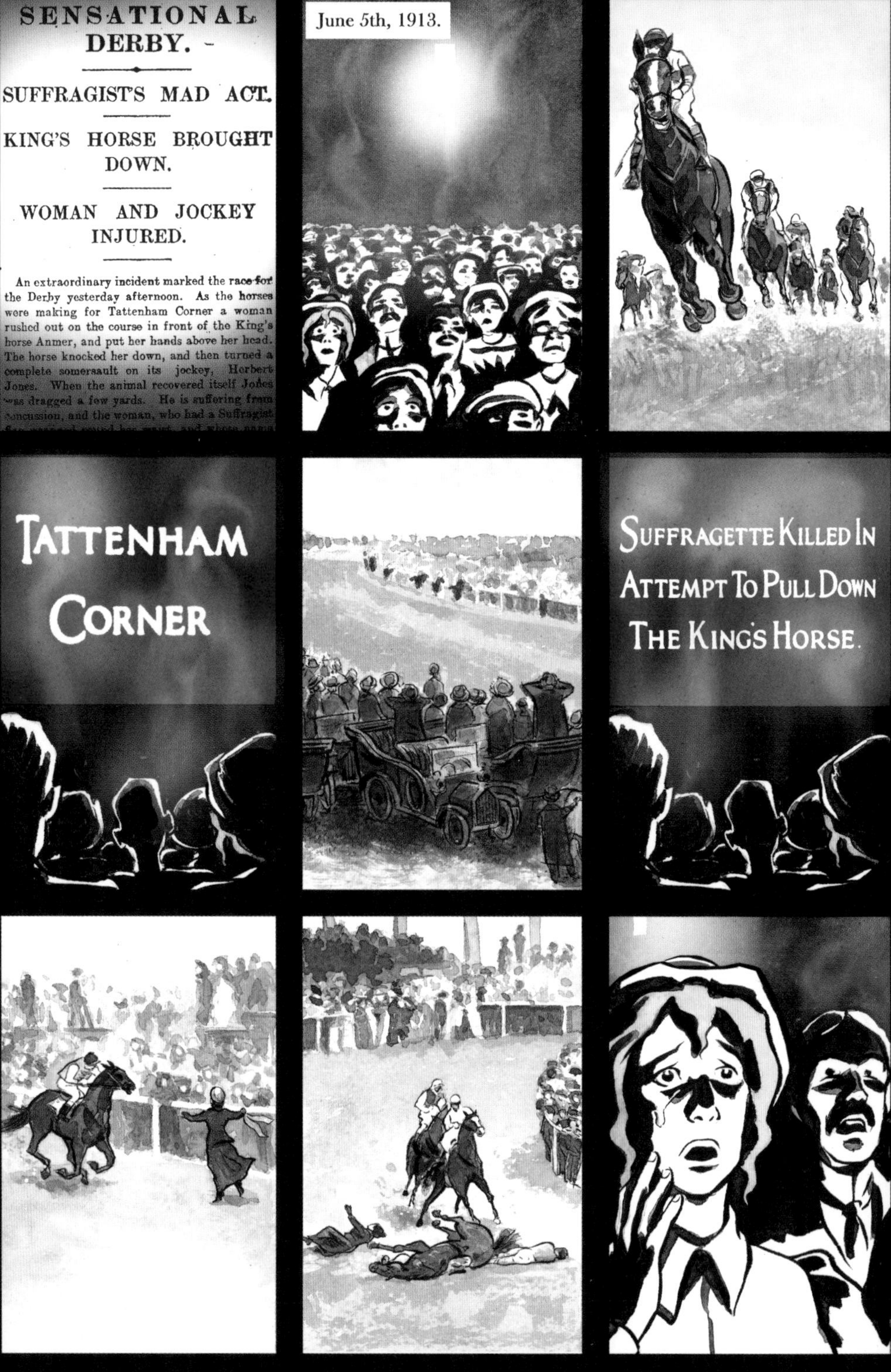
SENSATIONAL DERBY.
SUFFRAGIST'S MAD ACT.
KING'S HORSE BROUGHT DOWN.
WOMAN AND JOCKEY INJURED.
An extraordinary incident marked the race for the Derby yesterday afternoon. As the horses were making for Tattenham Corner a woman rushed out on the course in front of the King's horse Anmer, and put her hands above her head. The horse knocked her down, and then turned a complete somersault on its jockey, Herbert Jones. When the animal recovered itself Jones was dragged a few yards. He is suffering from oncussion, and the woman, who had a Suffragist
June 5th, 1913.
TATTENHAM CORNER
SUFFRAGETTE KILLED IN ATTEMPT TO PULL DOWN THE KING'S HORSE.

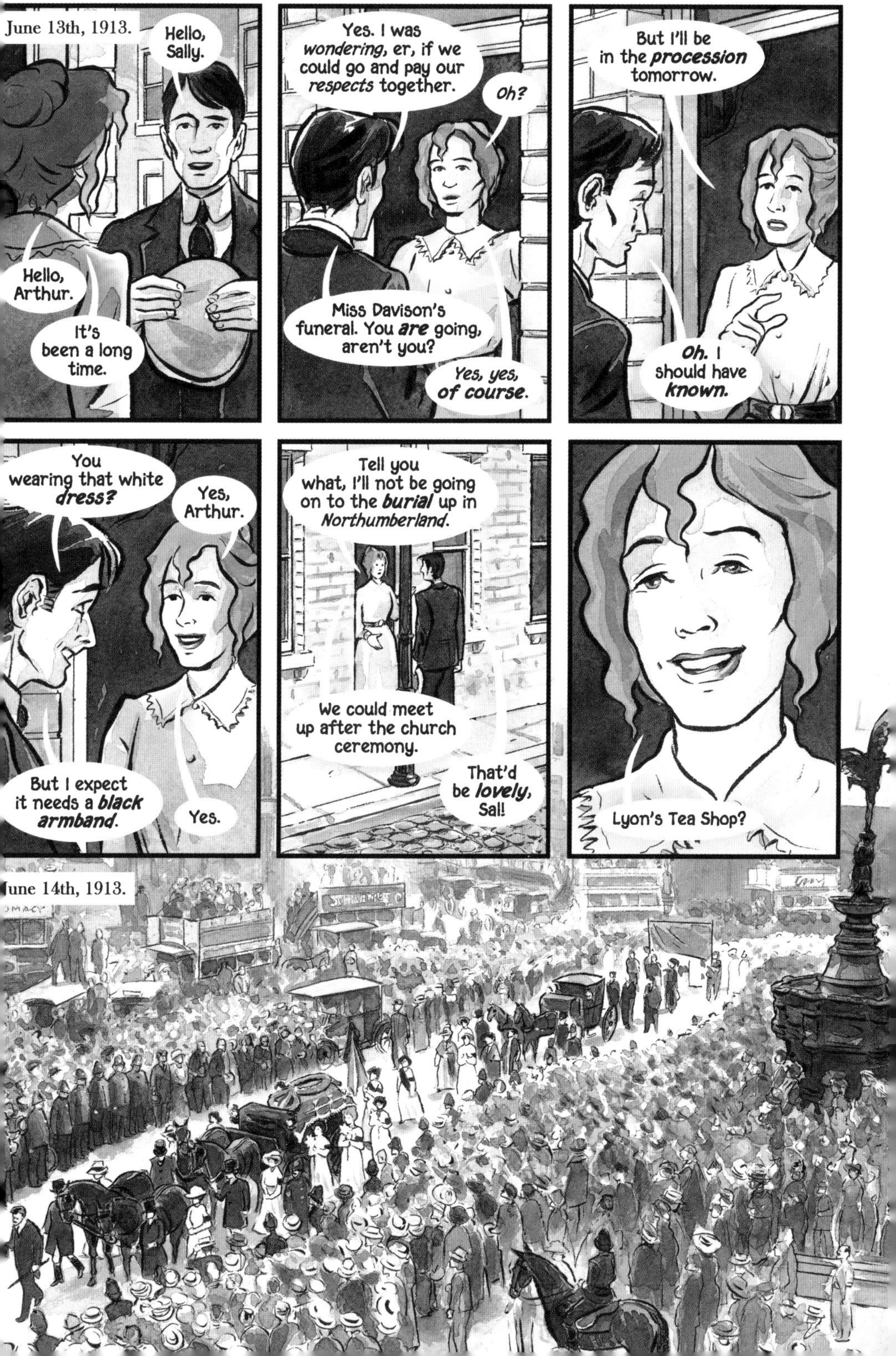
June 13th, 1913.
Hello, Sally.
Hello, Arthur.
It's been a long time.
Yes. I was wondering, er, if we could go and pay our respects together.
Oh?
Miss Davison's funeral. You are going, aren't you?
Yes, yes, of course.
But I'll be in the procession tomorrow.
Oh. I should have known.
You wearing that white dress?
Yes, Arthur.
But I expect it needs a black armband.
Yes.
Tell you what, I'll not be going on to the burial up in Northumberland.
We could meet up after the church ceremony.
That'd be lovely, Sal!
Lyon's Tea Shop?
June 14th, 1913.

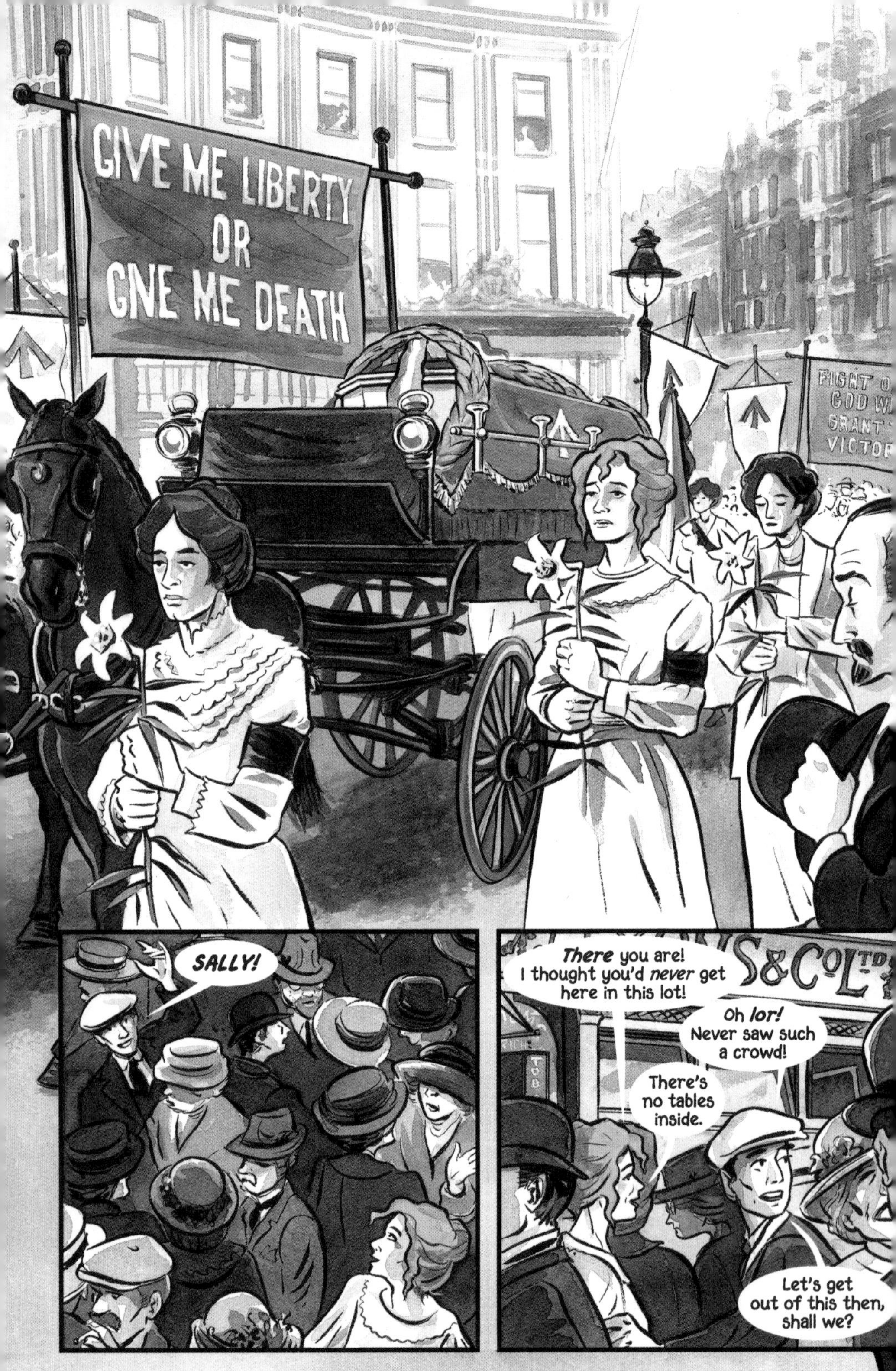
GIVE ME LIBERTY OR GIVE ME DEATH
SALLY!
There you are! I thought you'd *never* get here in this lot!
Oh *lor!* Never saw such a crowd!
There's no tables inside.
Let's get out of this then, shall we?

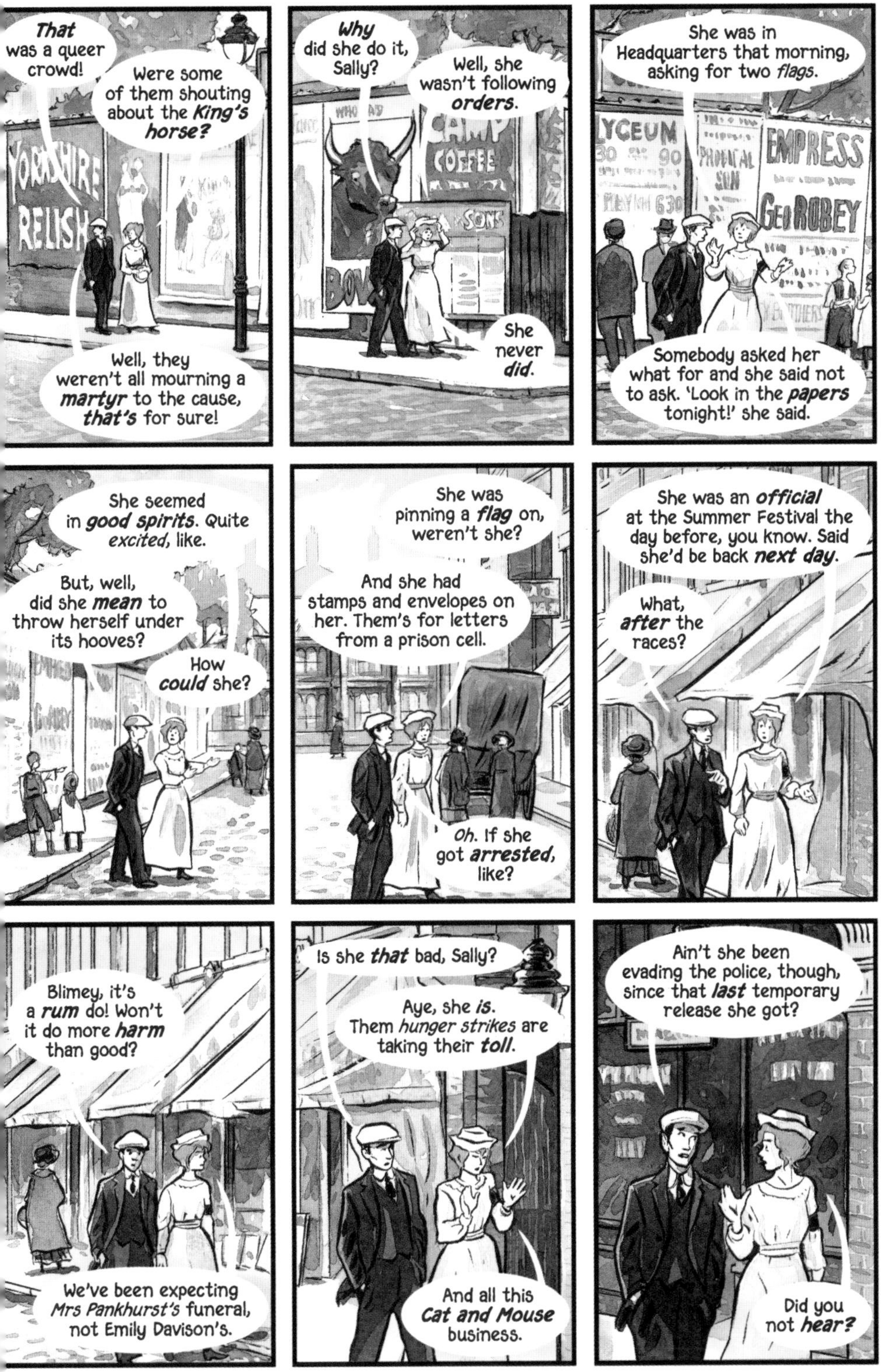
That was a queer crowd!
Were some of them shouting about the King's horse?
YORKSHIRE RELISH
Well, they weren't all mourning a martyr to the cause, that's for sure!
Why did she do it, Sally?
Well, she wasn't following orders.
COFFEE
She never did.
She was in Headquarters that morning, asking for two flags.
LYCEUM
EMPRESS
GEO ROBEY
PRODIGAL SON
Somebody asked her what for and she said not to ask. 'Look in the papers tonight!' she said.
She seemed in good spirits. Quite excited, like.
But, well, did she mean to throw herself under its hooves?
How could she?
She was pinning a flag on, weren't she?
And she had stamps and envelopes on her. Them's for letters from a prison cell.
Oh. If she got arrested, like?
She was an official at the Summer Festival the day before, you know. Said she'd be back next day.
What, after the races?
Blimey, it's a rum do! Won't it do more harm than good?
We've been expecting Mrs Pankhurst's funeral, not Emily Davison's.
Is she that bad, Sally?
Aye, she is. Them hunger strikes are taking their toll.
And all this Cat and Mouse business.
Ain't she been evading the police, though, since that last temporary release she got?
Did you not hear?

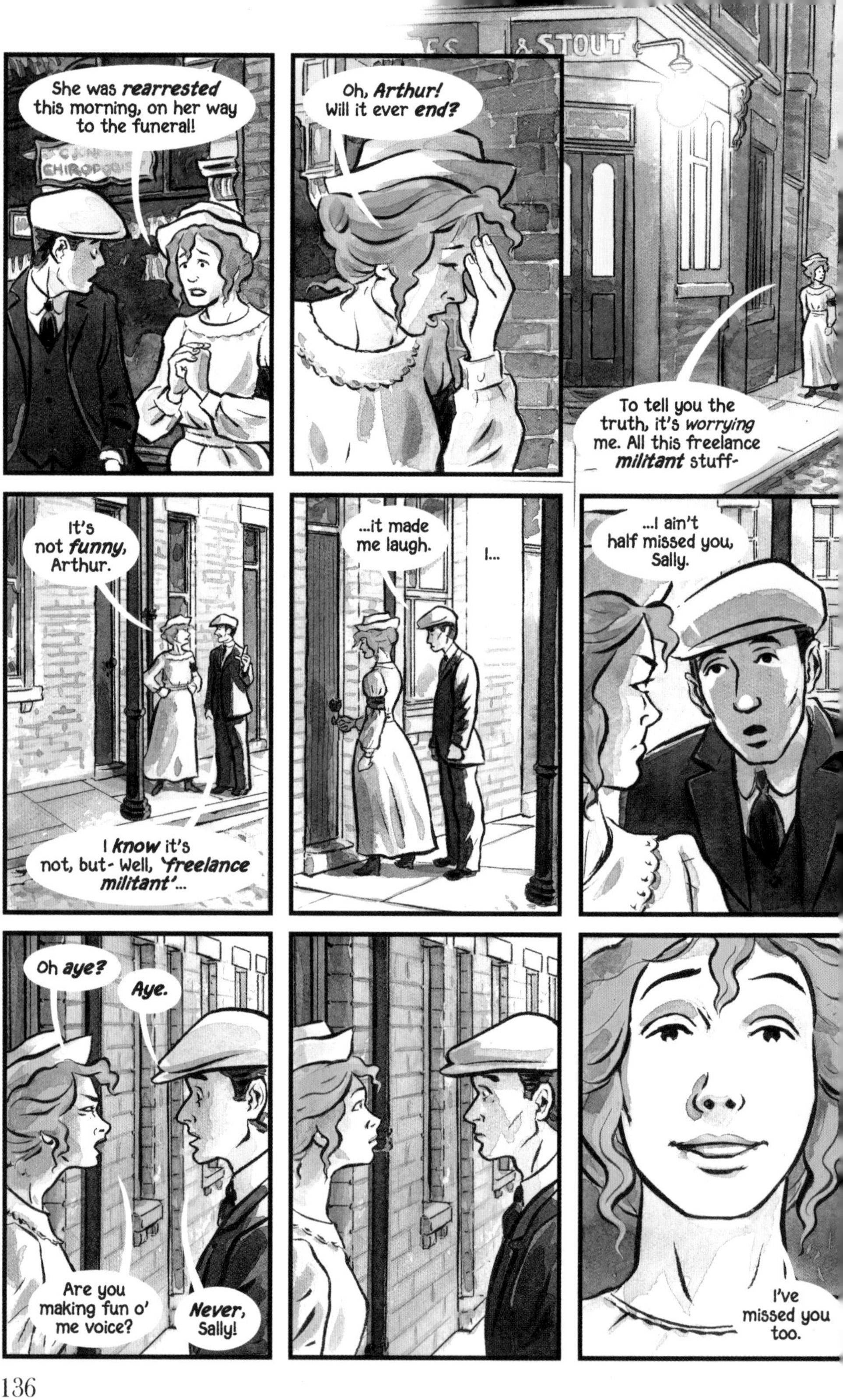
She was *rearrested* this morning, on her way to the funeral!
Oh, *Arthur!* Will it ever *end?*
&STOUT
To tell you the truth, it's *worrying* me. All this freelance *militant* stuff-
It's not *funny,* Arthur.
I *know* it's not, but- Well, *'freelance militant'*...
...it made me laugh.
I...
...I ain't half missed you, Sally.
Oh *aye?*
Aye.
Are you making fun o' me voice?
Never, Sally!
I've missed you too.

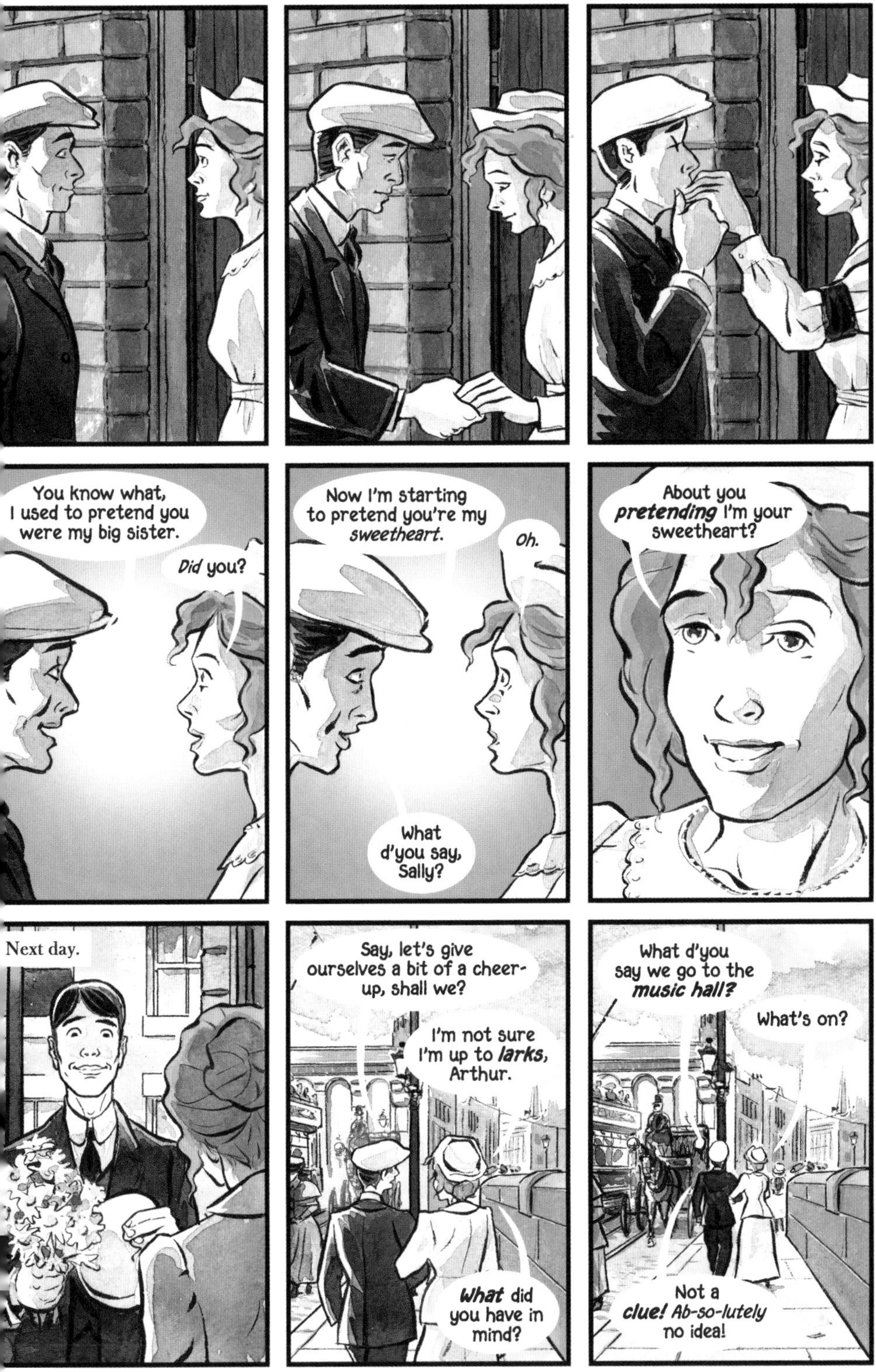

You know what, I used to pretend you were my big sister.
Did you?
Now I'm starting to pretend you're my *sweetheart*.
Oh.
What d'you say, Sally?
About you ***pretending*** I'm your sweetheart?
Next day.
Say, let's give ourselves a bit of a cheer-up, shall we?
I'm not sure I'm up to ***larks***, Arthur.
What did you have in mind?
What d'you say we go to the ***music hall?***
What's on?
Not a ***clue!*** *Ab-so-lutely* no idea!

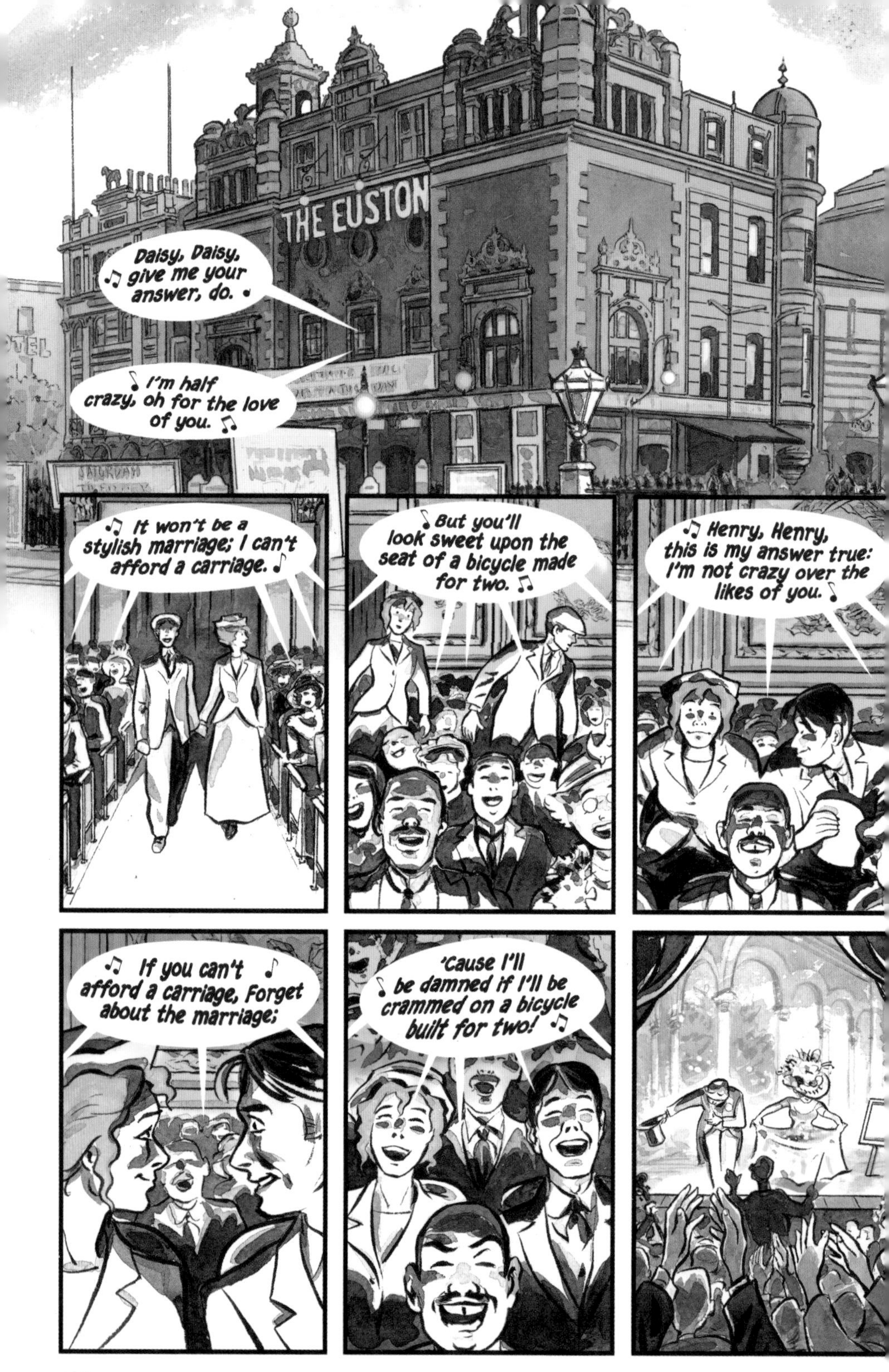
THE EUSTON
Daisy, Daisy, give me your answer, do.
I'm half crazy, oh for the love of you.
It won't be a stylish marriage; I can't afford a carriage.
But you'll look sweet upon the seat of a bicycle made for two.
Henry, Henry, this is my answer true: I'm not crazy over the likes of you.
If you can't afford a carriage, Forget about the marriage;
'Cause I'll be damned if I'll be crammed on a bicycle built for two!

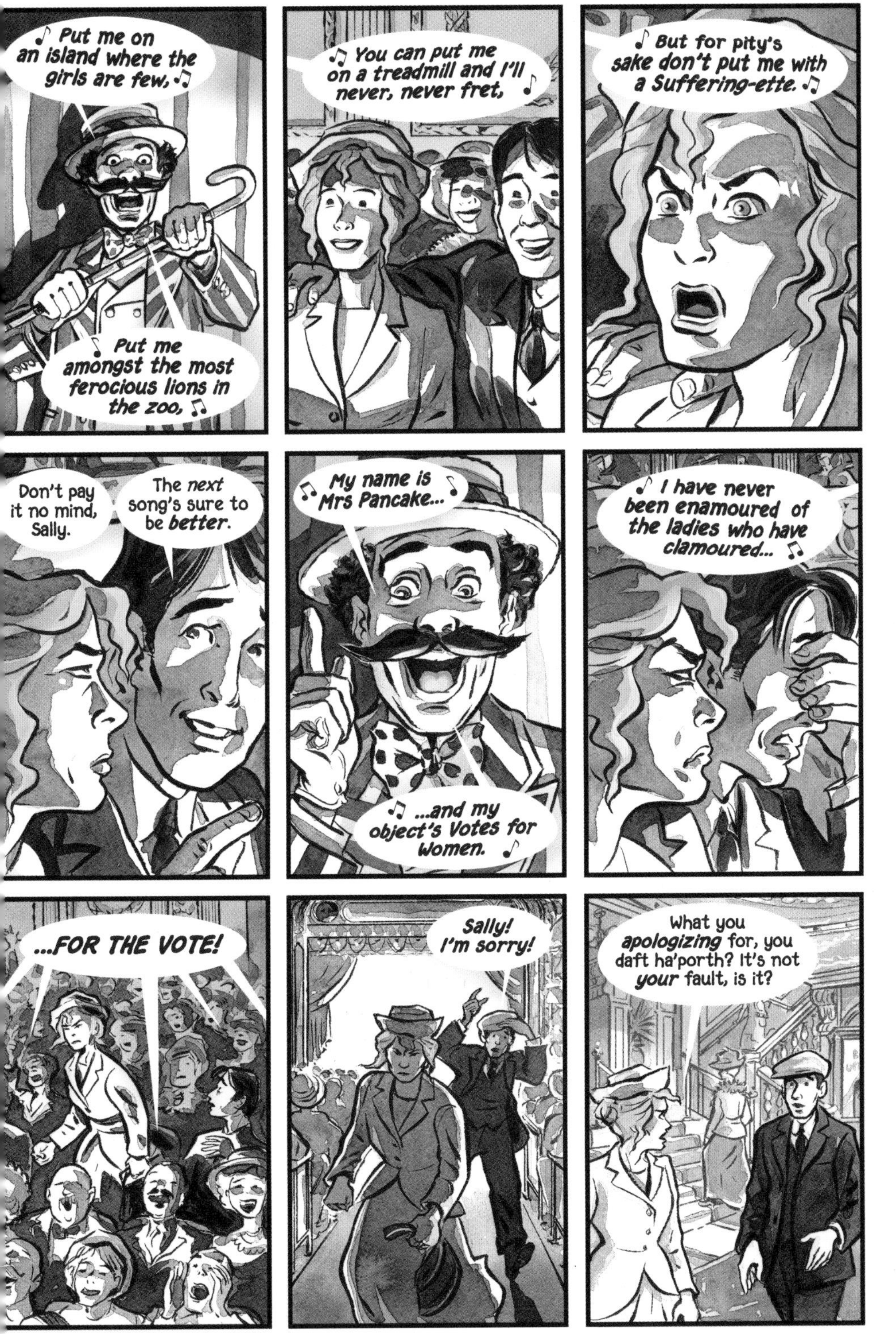
♪ Put me on an island where the girls are few, ♫
♪ Put me amongst the most ferocious lions in the zoo, ♫
♫ You can put me on a treadmill and I'll never, never fret, ♪
♪ But for pity's sake don't put me with a Suffering-ette. ♫
Don't pay it no mind, Sally.
The *next* song's sure to be *better*.
♫ My name is Mrs Pancake... ♪
♫ ...and my object's Votes for Women. ♪
♪ I have never been enamoured of the ladies who have clamoured... ♫
...FOR THE VOTE!
Sally! I'm sorry!
What you *apologizing* for, you daft ha'porth? It's not *your* fault, is it?

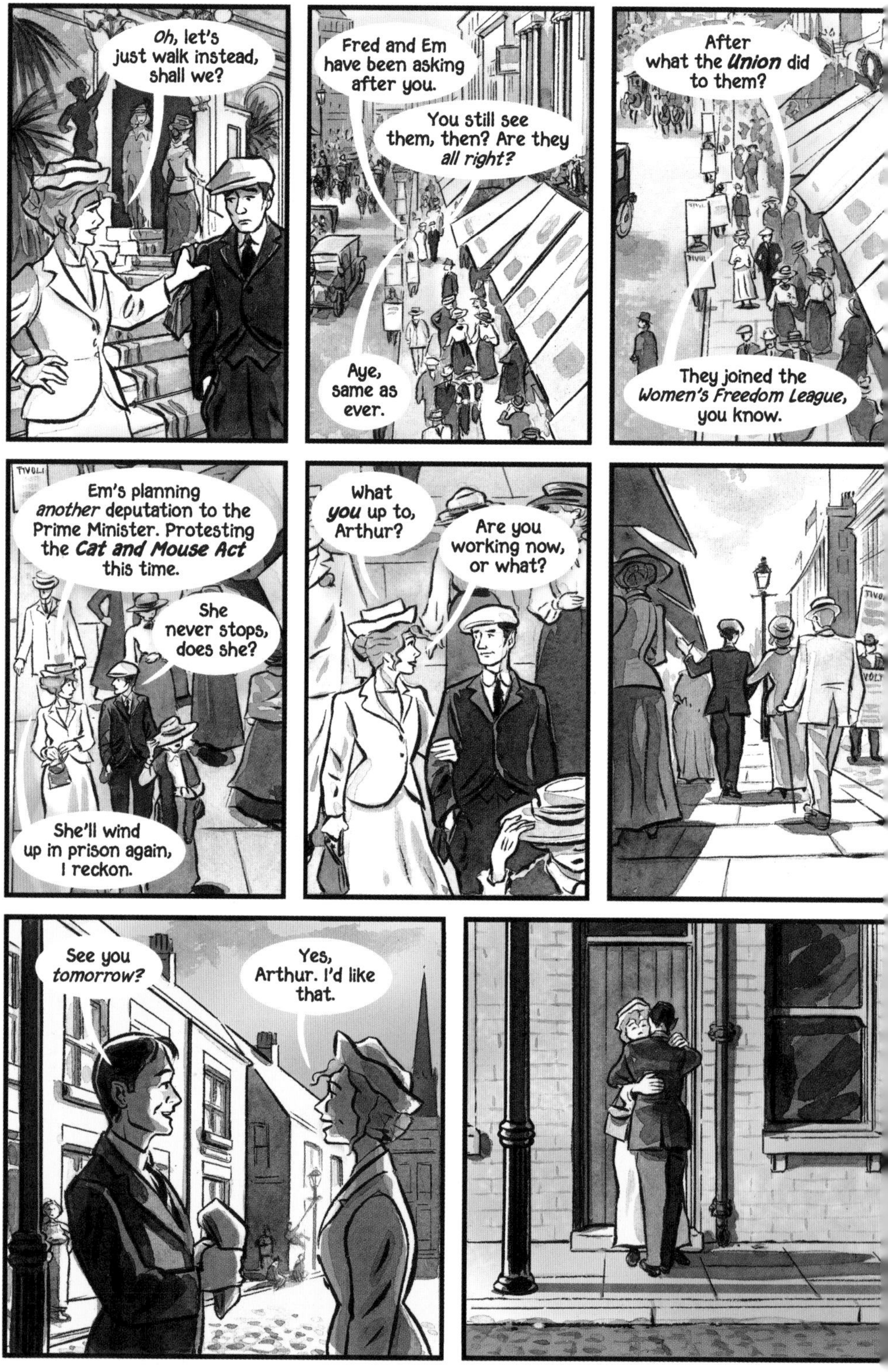

Oh, let's just walk instead, shall we?
Fred and Em have been asking after you.
You still see them, then? Are they *all right?*
Aye, same as ever.
After what the ***Union*** did to them?
They joined the *Women's Freedom League*, you know.
TIVOLI
Em's planning *another* deputation to the Prime Minister. Protesting the ***Cat and Mouse Act*** this time.
She never stops, does she?
She'll wind up in prison again, I reckon.
What ***you*** up to, Arthur?
Are you working now, or what?
See you *tomorrow?*
Yes, Arthur. I'd like that.

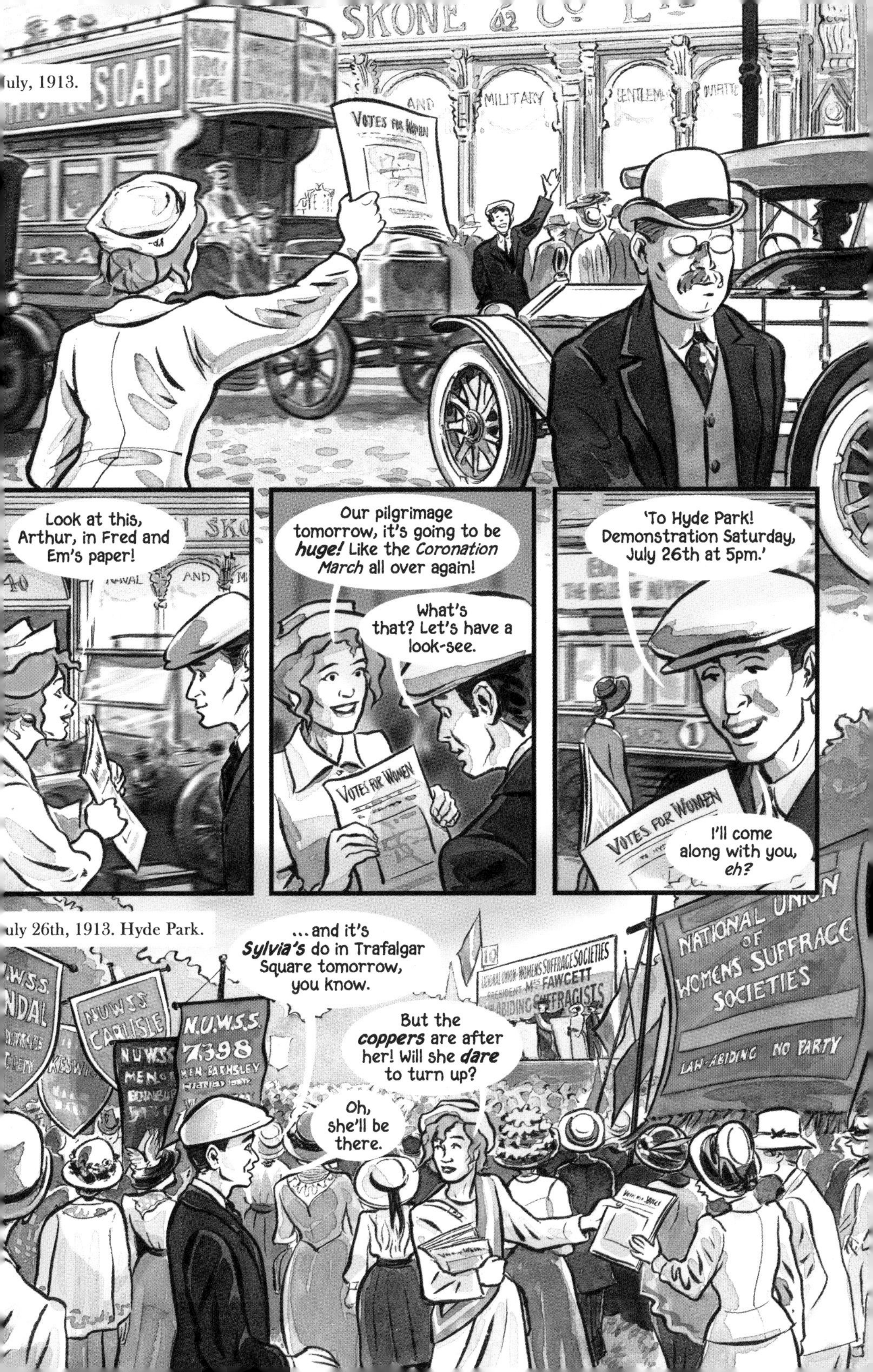
uly, 1913.
SKONE & Co
SOAP
VOTES FOR WOMEN
MILITARY
Look at this, Arthur, in Fred and Em's paper!
Our pilgrimage tomorrow, it's going to be **huge!** Like the *Coronation March* all over again!
What's that? Let's have a look-see.
VOTES FOR WOMEN
'To Hyde Park! Demonstration Saturday, July 26th at 5pm.'
VOTES FOR WOMEN
I'll come along with you, *eh?*
uly 26th, 1913. Hyde Park.
...and it's ***Sylvia's*** do in Trafalgar Square tomorrow, you know.
But the ***coppers*** are after her! Will she ***dare*** to turn up?
Oh, she'll be there.
NATIONAL UNION OF WOMENS SUFFRAGE SOCIETIES
LAW-ABIDING NO PARTY
NATIONAL UNION WOMENS SUFFRAGE SOCIETIES
PRESIDENT Mrs FAWCETT
N.U.W.S.S. CARLISLE
N.U.W.S.S.

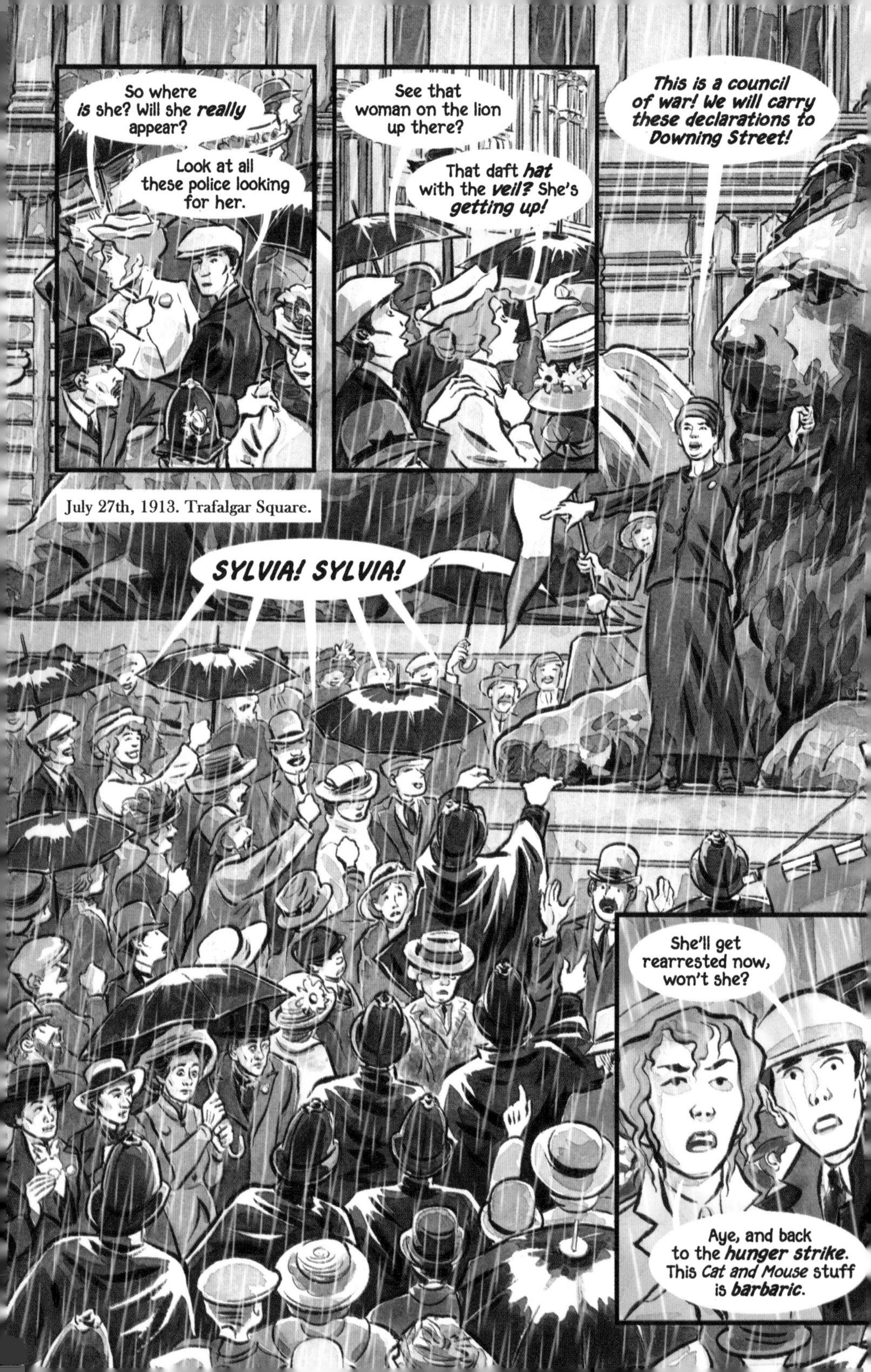

So where *is* she? Will she *really* appear?
Look at all these police looking for her.
See that woman on the lion up there?
That daft *hat* with the *veil?* She's *getting up!*
This is a council of war! We will carry these declarations to Downing Street!
July 27th, 1913. Trafalgar Square.
SYLVIA! SYLVIA!
She'll get rearrested now, won't she?
Aye, and back to the *hunger strike*. This *Cat and Mouse* stuff is *barbaric*.

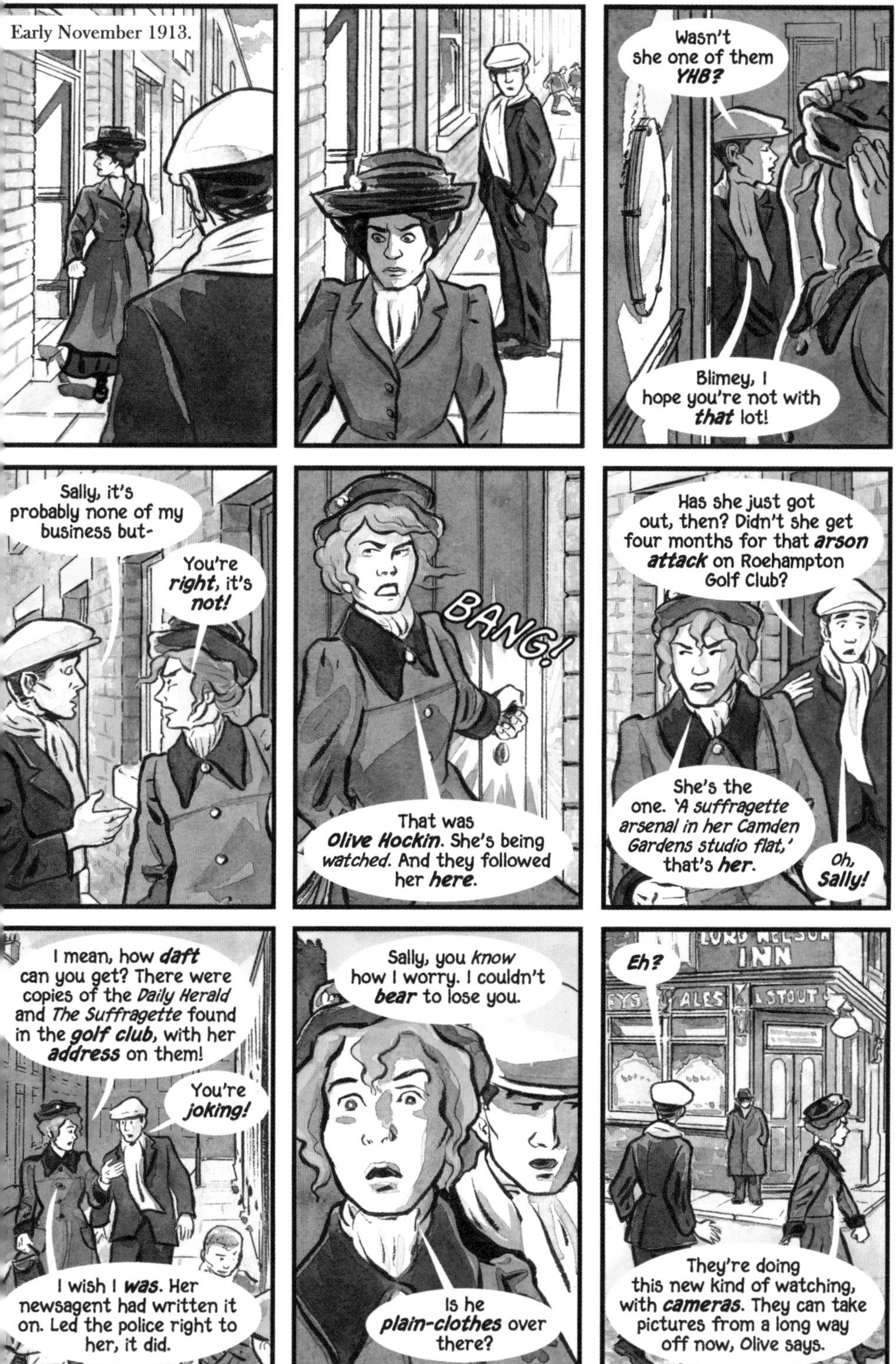

Early November 1913.
Wasn't she one of them YHB?
Blimey, I hope you're not with that lot!
Sally, it's probably none of my business but-
You're right, it's not!
BANG!
That was Olive Hockin. She's being watched. And they followed her here.
Has she just got out, then? Didn't she get four months for that arson attack on Roehampton Golf Club?
She's the one. 'A suffragette arsenal in her Camden Gardens studio flat,' that's her.
Oh, Sally!
I mean, how daft can you get? There were copies of the Daily Herald and The Suffragette found in the golf club, with her address on them!
You're joking!
I wish I was. Her newsagent had written it on. Led the police right to her, it did.
Sally, you know how I worry. I couldn't bear to lose you.
Is he plain-clothes over there?
LORD NELSON INN
ALES
STOUT
Eh?
They're doing this new kind of watching, with cameras. They can take pictures from a long way off now, Olive says.

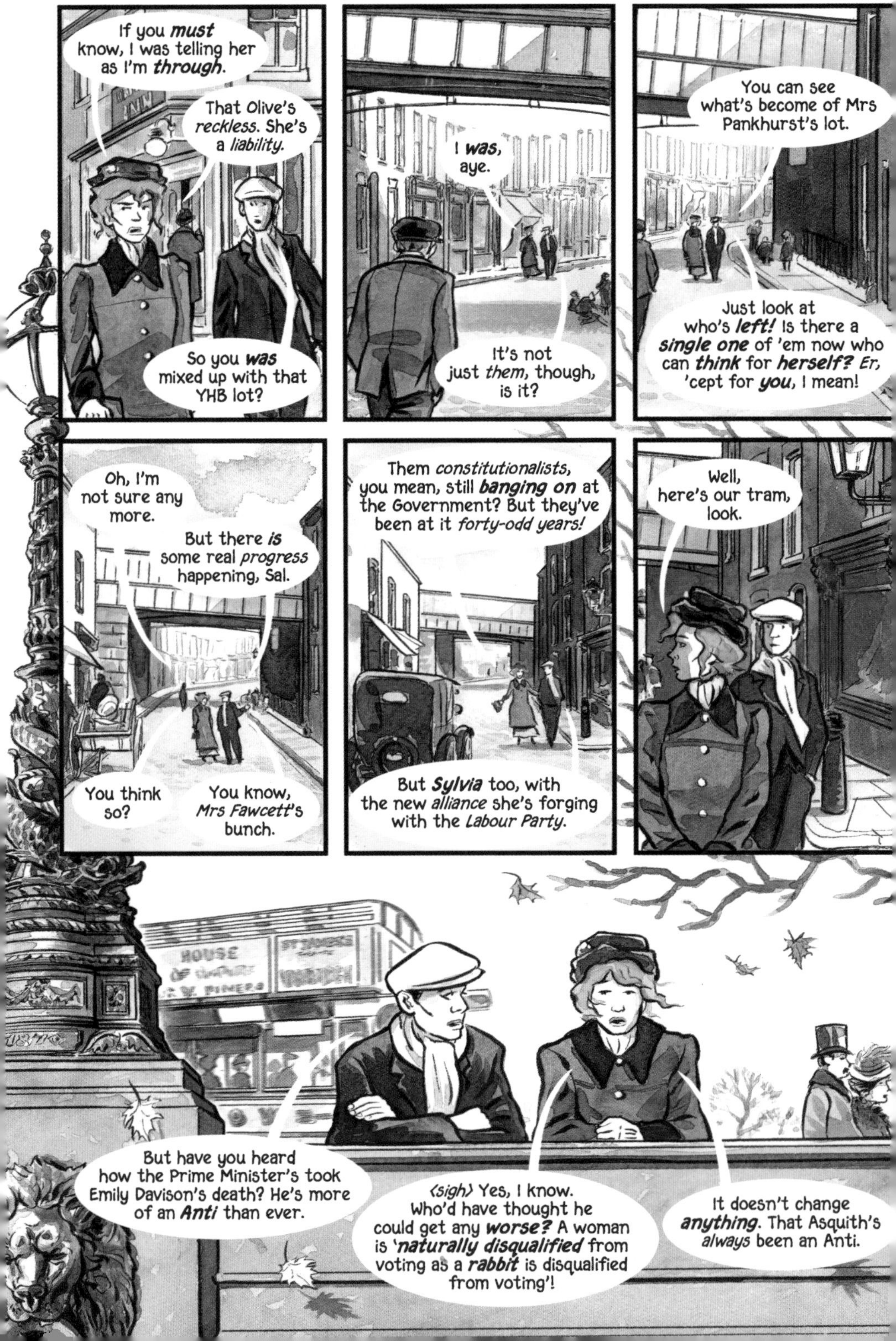

If you must know, I was telling her as I'm through.
That Olive's reckless. She's a liability.
So you was mixed up with that YHB lot?
I was, aye.
It's not just them, though, is it?
You can see what's become of Mrs Pankhurst's lot.
Just look at who's left! Is there a single one of 'em now who can think for herself? Er, 'cept for you, I mean!
Oh, I'm not sure any more.
But there is some real progress happening, Sal.
You think so?
You know, Mrs Fawcett's bunch.
Them constitutionalists, you mean, still banging on at the Government? But they've been at it forty-odd years!
But Sylvia too, with the new alliance she's forging with the Labour Party.
Well, here's our tram, look.
But have you heard how the Prime Minister's took Emily Davison's death? He's more of an Anti than ever.
<sigh> Yes, I know. Who'd have thought he could get any worse? A woman is 'naturally disqualified from voting as a rabbit is disqualified from voting'!
It doesn't change anything. That Asquith's always been an Anti.

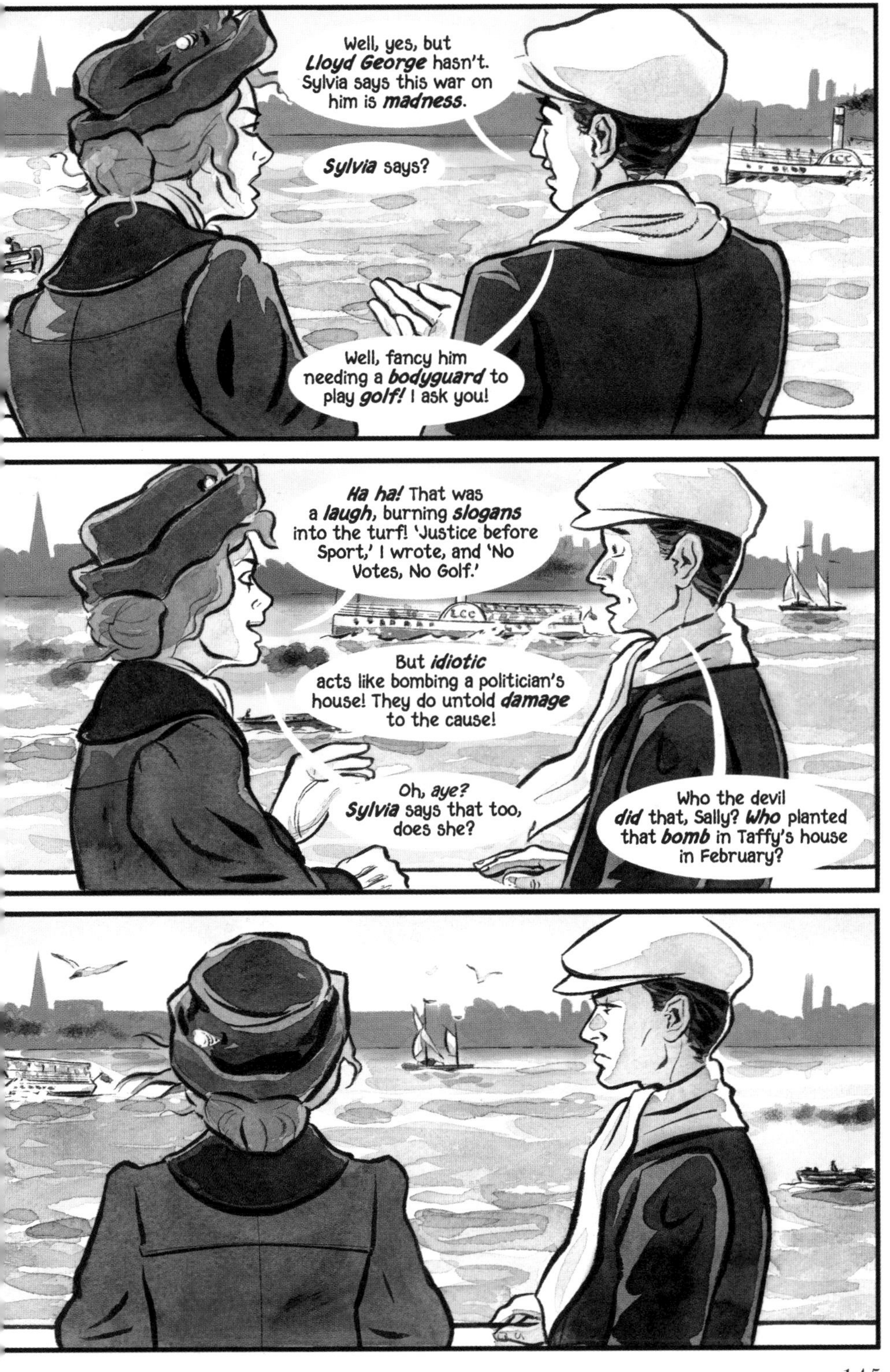
Well, yes, but *Lloyd George* hasn't. Sylvia says this war on him is *madness*.
Sylvia says?
Well, fancy him needing a *bodyguard* to play *golf!* I ask you!
Ha ha! That was a *laugh*, burning *slogans* into the turf! 'Justice before Sport,' I wrote, and 'No Votes, No Golf.'
But *idiotic* acts like bombing a politician's house! They do untold *damage* to the cause!
Oh, *aye?* *Sylvia* says that too, does she?
Who the devil *did* that, Sally? *Who* planted that *bomb* in Taffy's house in February?

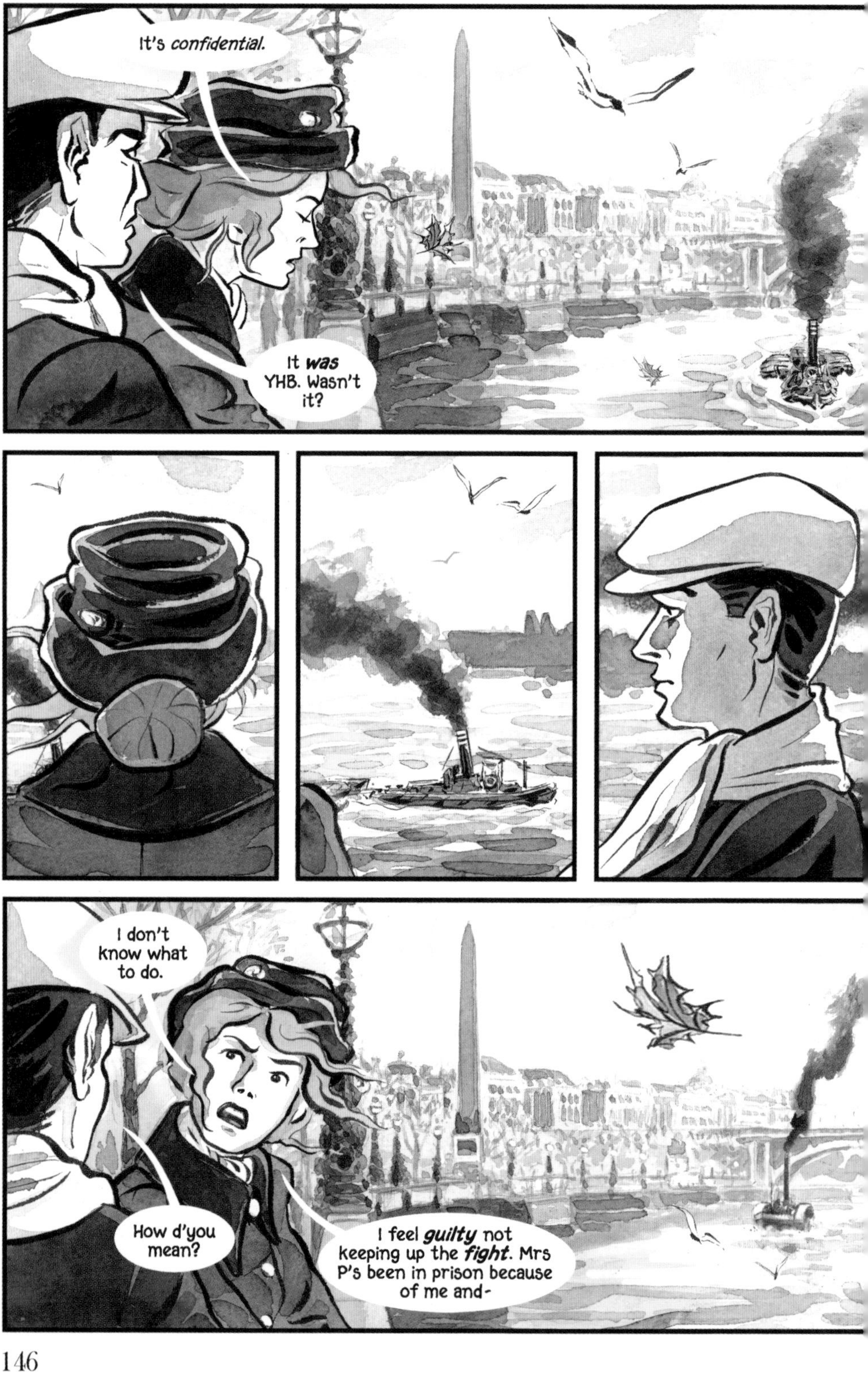
It's *confidential.*
It ***was*** YHB. Wasn't it?
I don't know what to do.
How d'you mean?
I feel ***guilty*** not keeping up the ***fight***. Mrs P's been in prison because of me and-

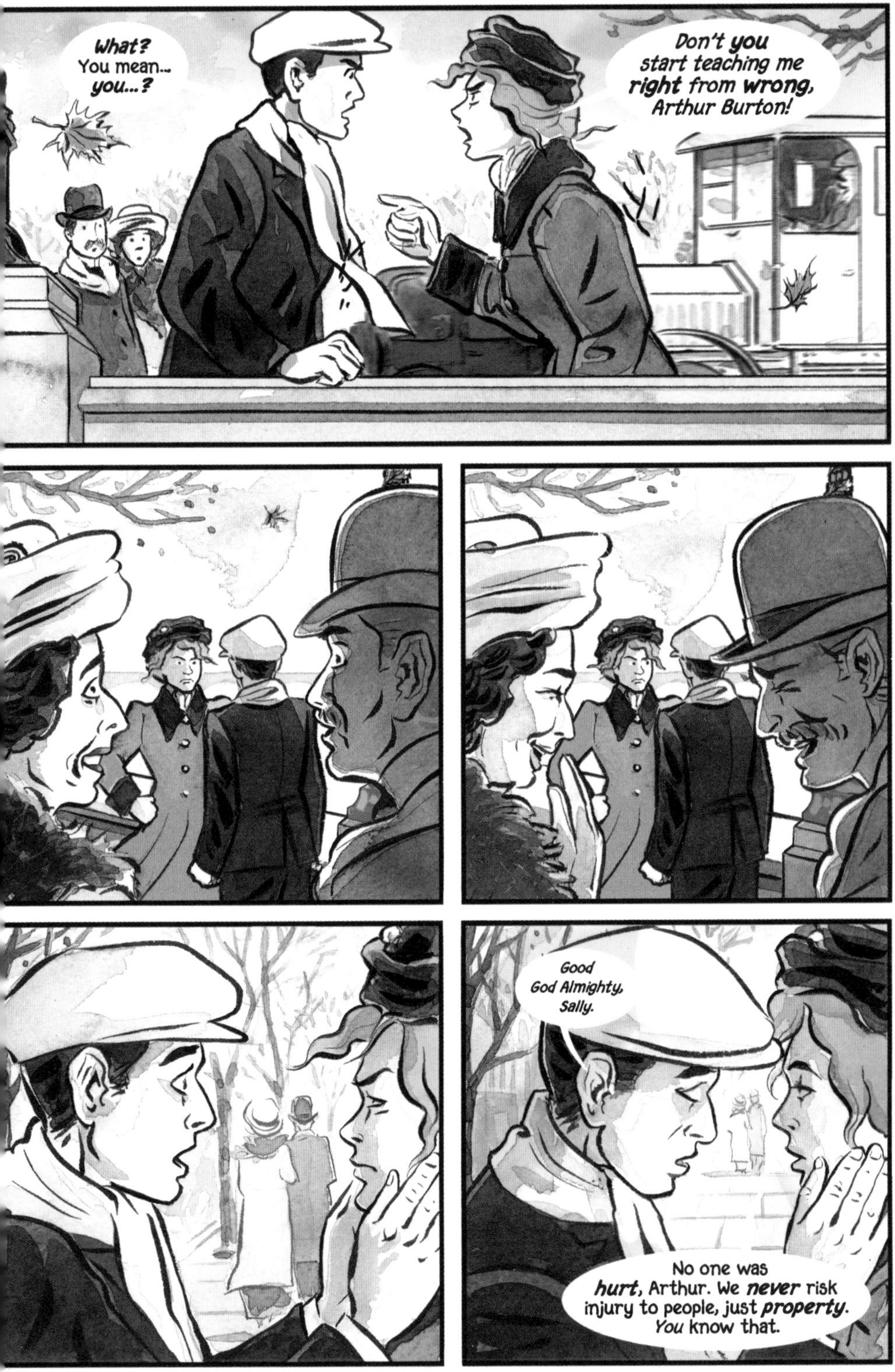
What? You mean... you...?
Don't you start teaching me right from wrong, Arthur Burton!
Good God Almighty, Sally.
No one was hurt, Arthur. We never risk injury to people, just property. You know that.

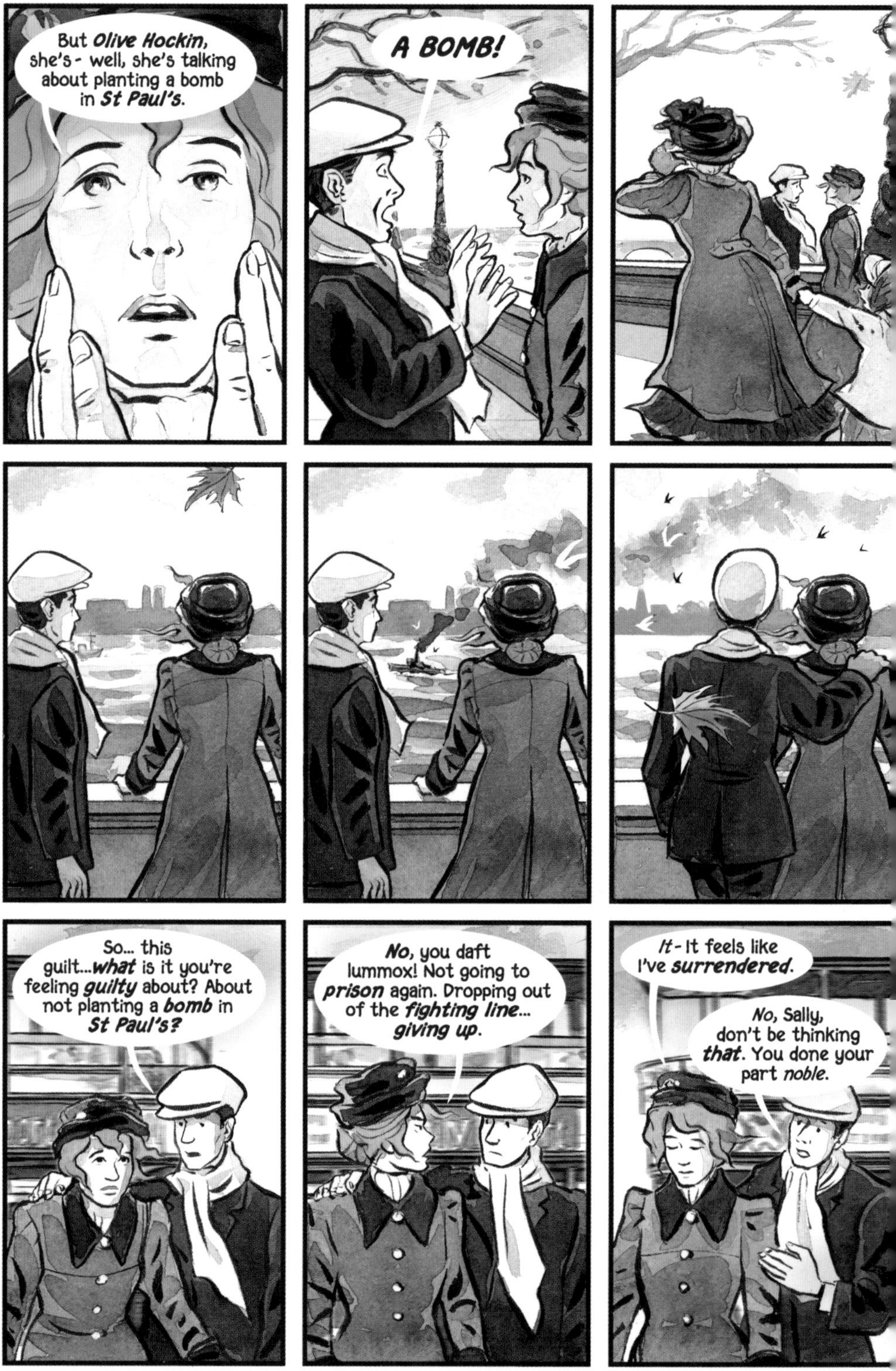
But Olive Hockin, she's - well, she's talking about planting a bomb in St Paul's.
A BOMB!
So... this guilt...what is it you're feeling guilty about? About not planting a bomb in St Paul's?
No, you daft lummox! Not going to prison again. Dropping out of the fighting line... giving up.
It - It feels like I've surrendered.
No, Sally, don't be thinking that. You done your part noble.

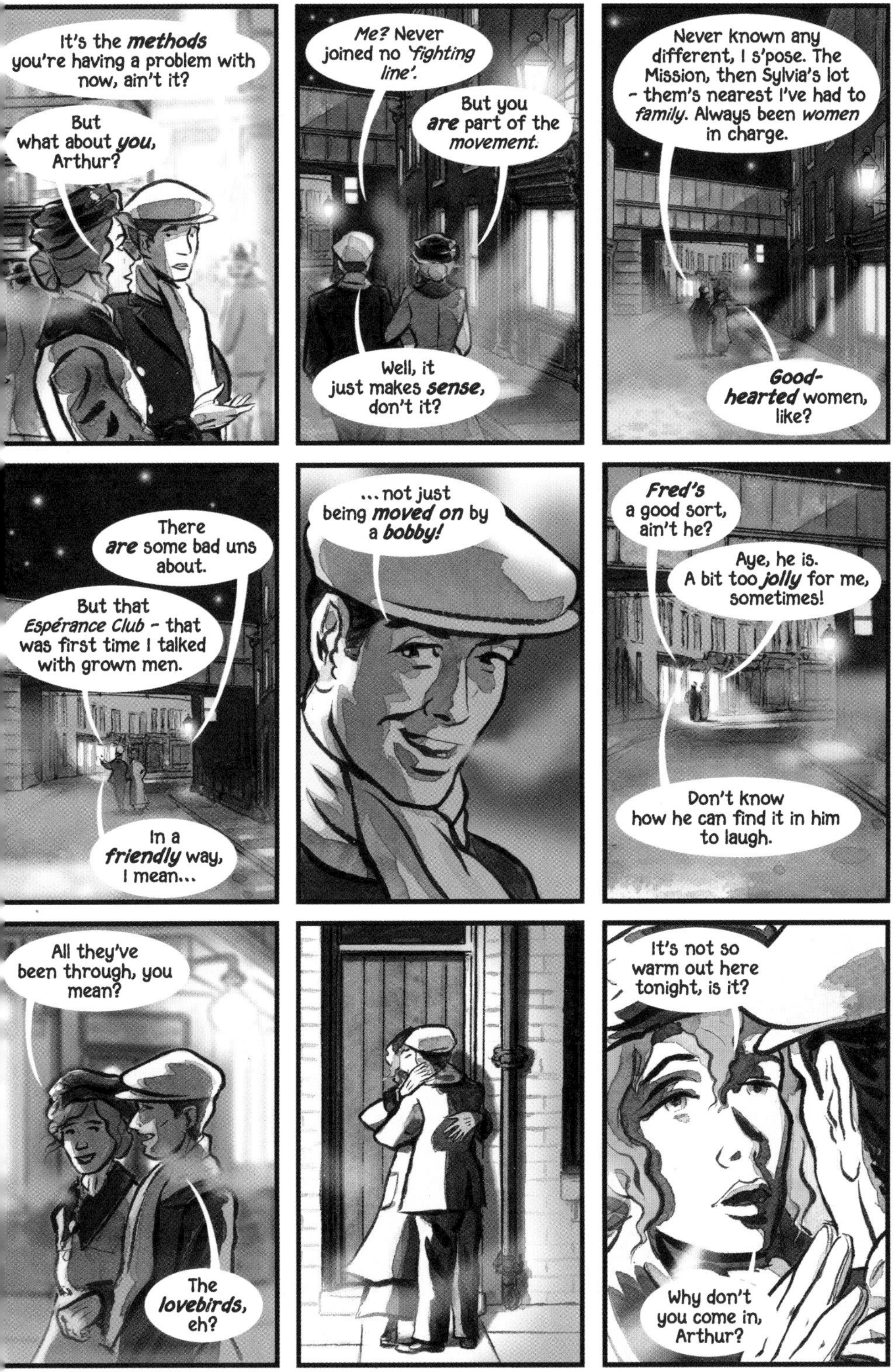
It's the *methods* you're having a problem with now, ain't it?
But what about *you*, Arthur?
Me? Never joined no *'fighting line'*.
But you *are* part of the *movement*.
Well, it just makes *sense*, don't it?
Never known any different, I s'pose. The Mission, then Sylvia's lot - them's nearest I've had to *family*. Always been *women* in charge.
Good-hearted women, like?
There *are* some bad uns about.
But that *Espérance Club* - that was first time I talked with grown men.
In a *friendly* way, I mean...
...not just being *moved on* by a *bobby!*
Fred's a good sort, ain't he?
Aye, he is. A bit too *jolly* for me, sometimes!
Don't know how he can find it in him to laugh.
All they've been through, you mean?
The *lovebirds*, eh?
It's not so warm out here tonight, is it?
Why don't you come in, Arthur?

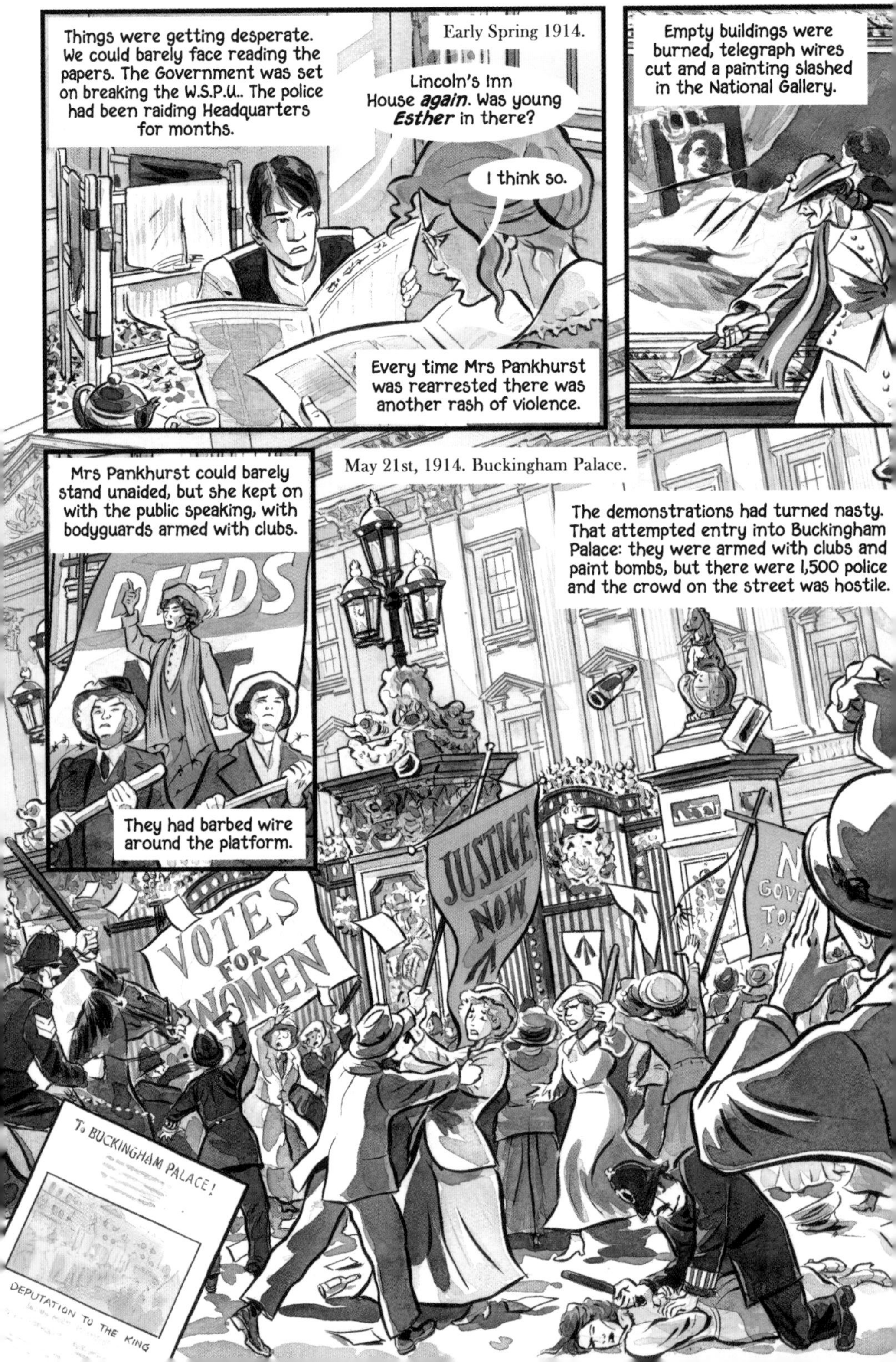

Things were getting desperate. We could barely face reading the papers. The Government was set on breaking the W.S.P.U.. The police had been raiding Headquarters for months.
Early Spring 1914.
Lincoln's Inn House ***again***. Was young ***Esther*** in there?
I think so.
Every time Mrs Pankhurst was rearrested there was another rash of violence.
Empty buildings were burned, telegraph wires cut and a painting slashed in the National Gallery.
Mrs Pankhurst could barely stand unaided, but she kept on with the public speaking, with bodyguards armed with clubs.
DEEDS
They had barbed wire around the platform.
May 21st, 1914. Buckingham Palace.
The demonstrations had turned nasty. That attempted entry into Buckingham Palace: they were armed with clubs and paint bombs, but there were 1,500 police and the crowd on the street was hostile.
JUSTICE NOW
VOTES FOR WOMEN
To BUCKINGHAM PALACE!
DEPUTATION TO THE KING

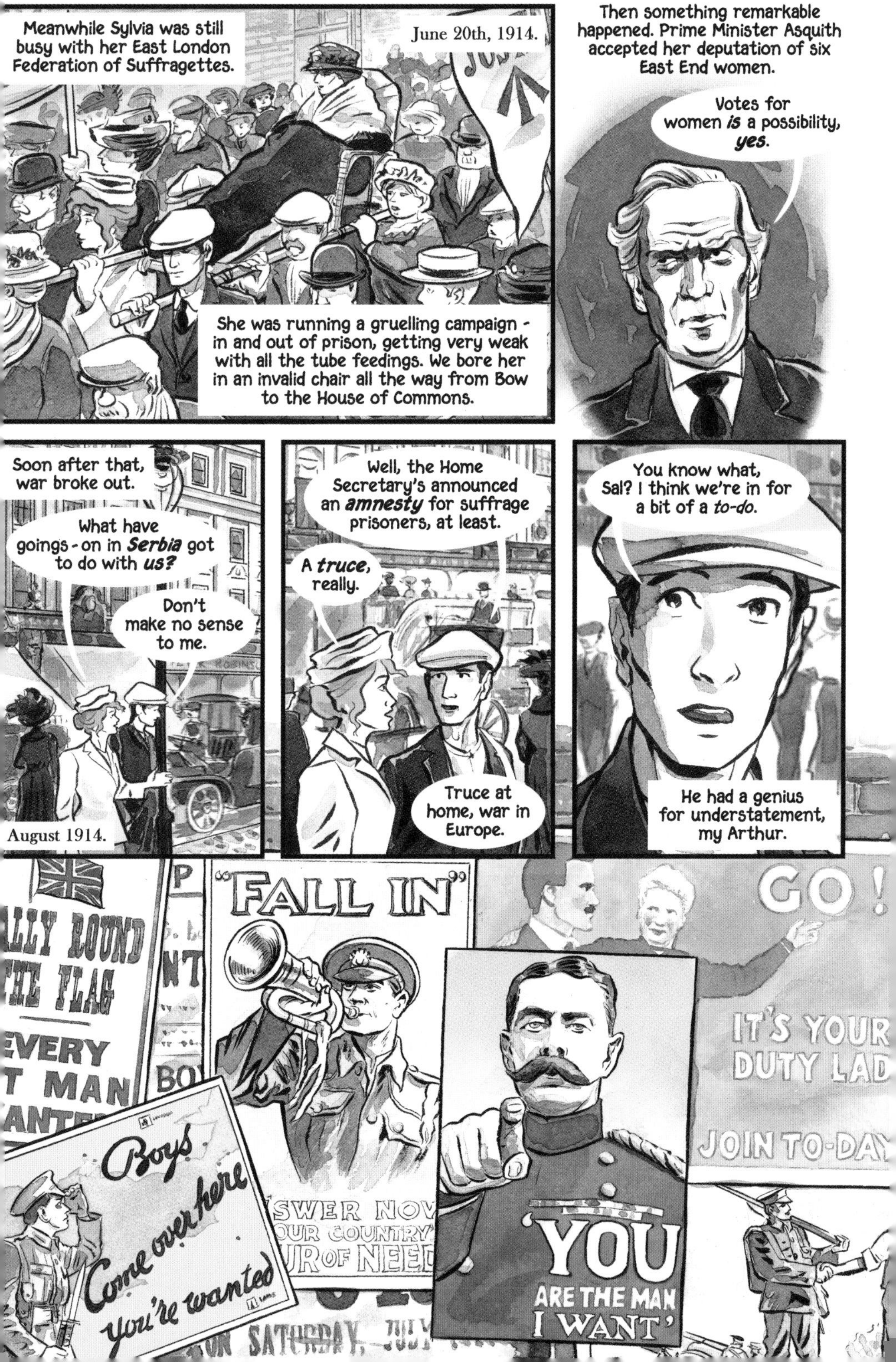
Meanwhile Sylvia was still busy with her East London Federation of Suffragettes.
June 20th, 1914.
She was running a gruelling campaign - in and out of prison, getting very weak with all the tube feedings. We bore her in an invalid chair all the way from Bow to the House of Commons.
Then something remarkable happened. Prime Minister Asquith accepted her deputation of six East End women.
Votes for women *is* a possibility, ***yes***.
Soon after that, war broke out.
What have goings - on in ***Serbia*** got to do with ***us?***
Don't make no sense to me.
August 1914.
Well, the Home Secretary's announced an ***amnesty*** for suffrage prisoners, at least.
A ***truce***, really.
Truce at home, war in Europe.
You know what, Sal? I think we're in for a bit of a *to-do*.
He had a genius for understatement, my Arthur.
"FALL IN"
GO!
IT'S YOUR DUTY LAD
JOIN TO-DAY
Boys
Come over here
you're wanted
YOU
ARE THE MAN
I WANT'

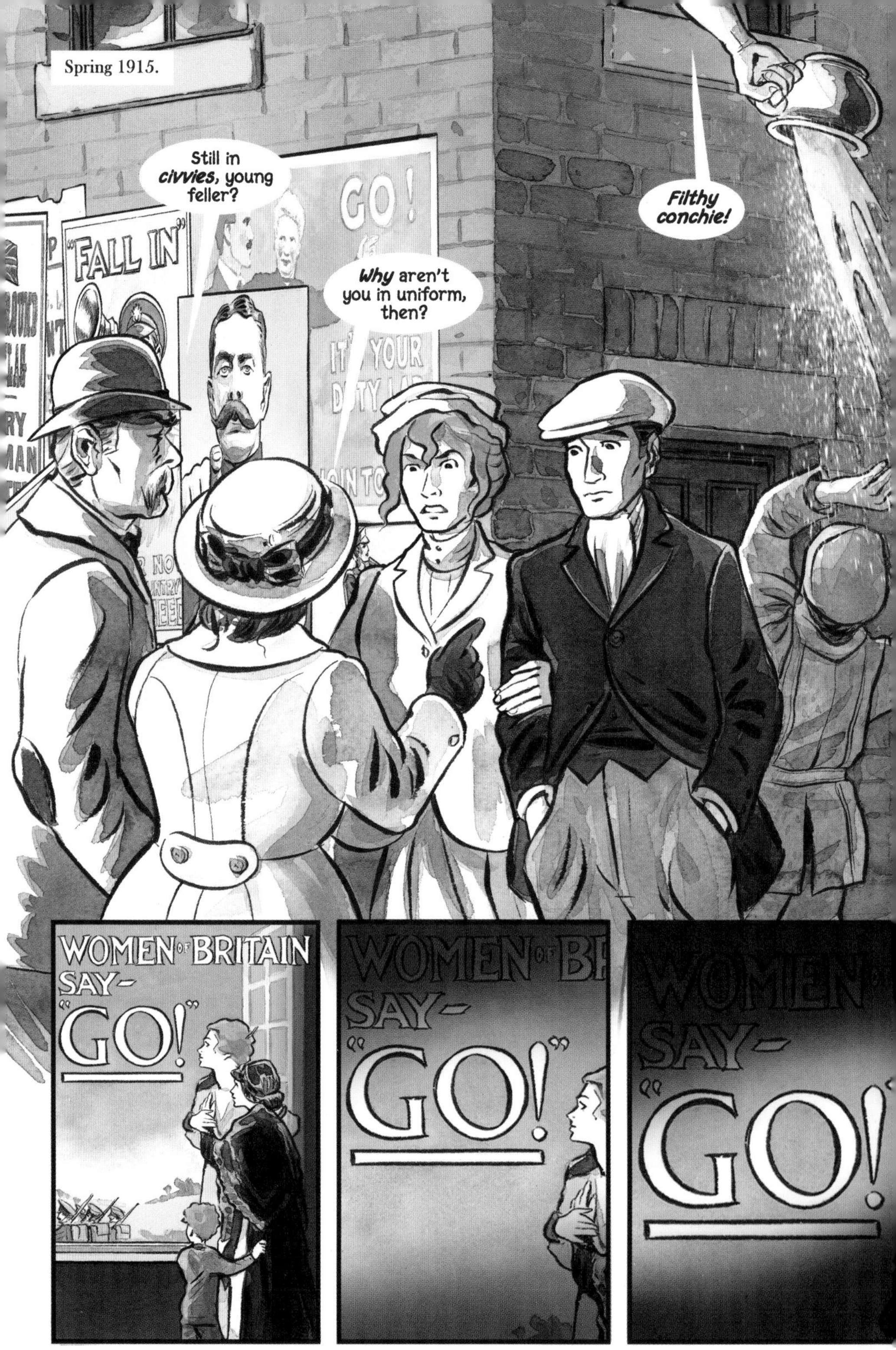
Spring 1915.
Still in *civvies*, young feller?
"FALL IN"
GO!
Why aren't you in uniform, then?
Filthy conchie!
WOMEN OF BRITAIN SAY - "GO!"

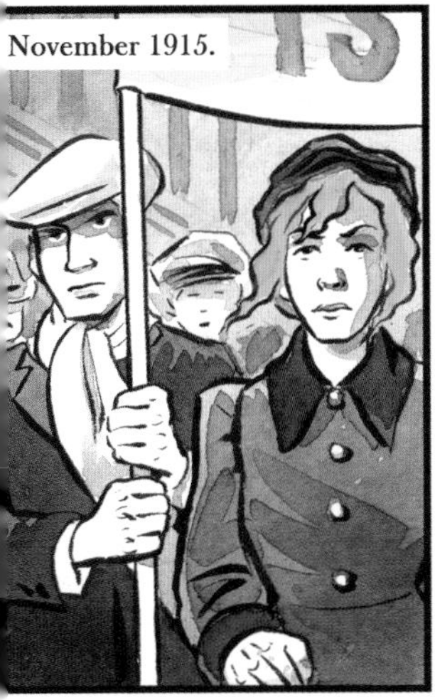
November 1915.

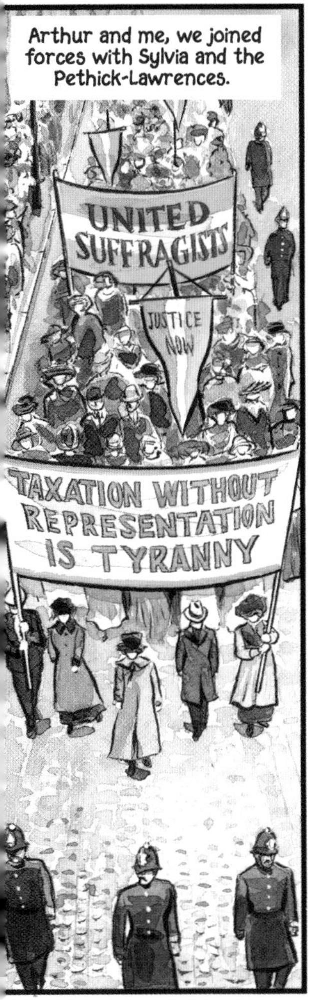
Arthur and me, we joined forces with Sylvia and the Pethick-Lawrences.
UNITED SUFFRAGISTS
JUSTICE NOW
TAXATION WITHOUT REPRESENTATION IS TYRANNY

"Votes for Women," November 19th, 1915. Registered at the G.P.O. as a Newspaper.

The War Paper for Women

VOTES FOR WOMEN

OFFICIAL ORGAN OF THE UNITED SUFFRAGISTS

VOL. IX. (Third Series), No. 402. FRIDAY, NOVEMBER 19, 1915. Price 1d. Weekly (Post Free. 1½d.)

THIS BIRD WON'T DROP WOMAN SUFFRAGE !

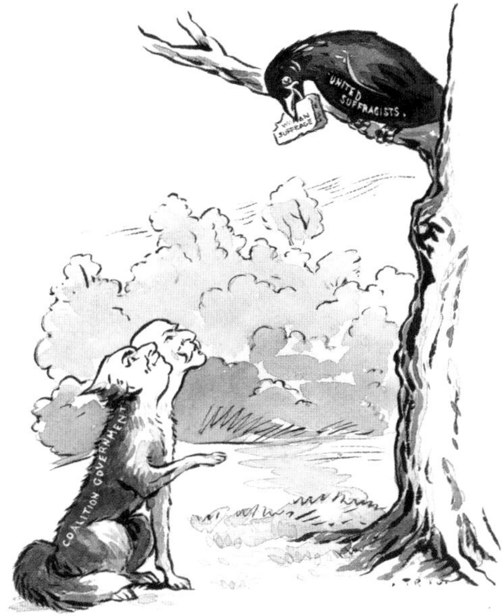
UNITED SUFFRAGISTS.
WOMAN SUFFRAGE
COALITION GOVERNMENT

The Government, while it praises Women's War Work, proposes to make a new register which will give more votes to men. Mrs. Pethick Lawrence, in a recent speech, said "Unless we take care, women will be once more in the position of the crow in the fable, who, tempted by the flattery of the fox, drops the cheese already in her mouth." United Suffragists are taking care!

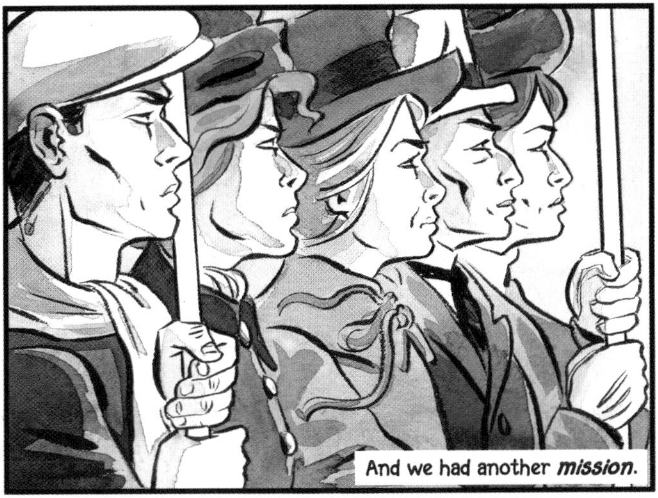
And we had another mission.

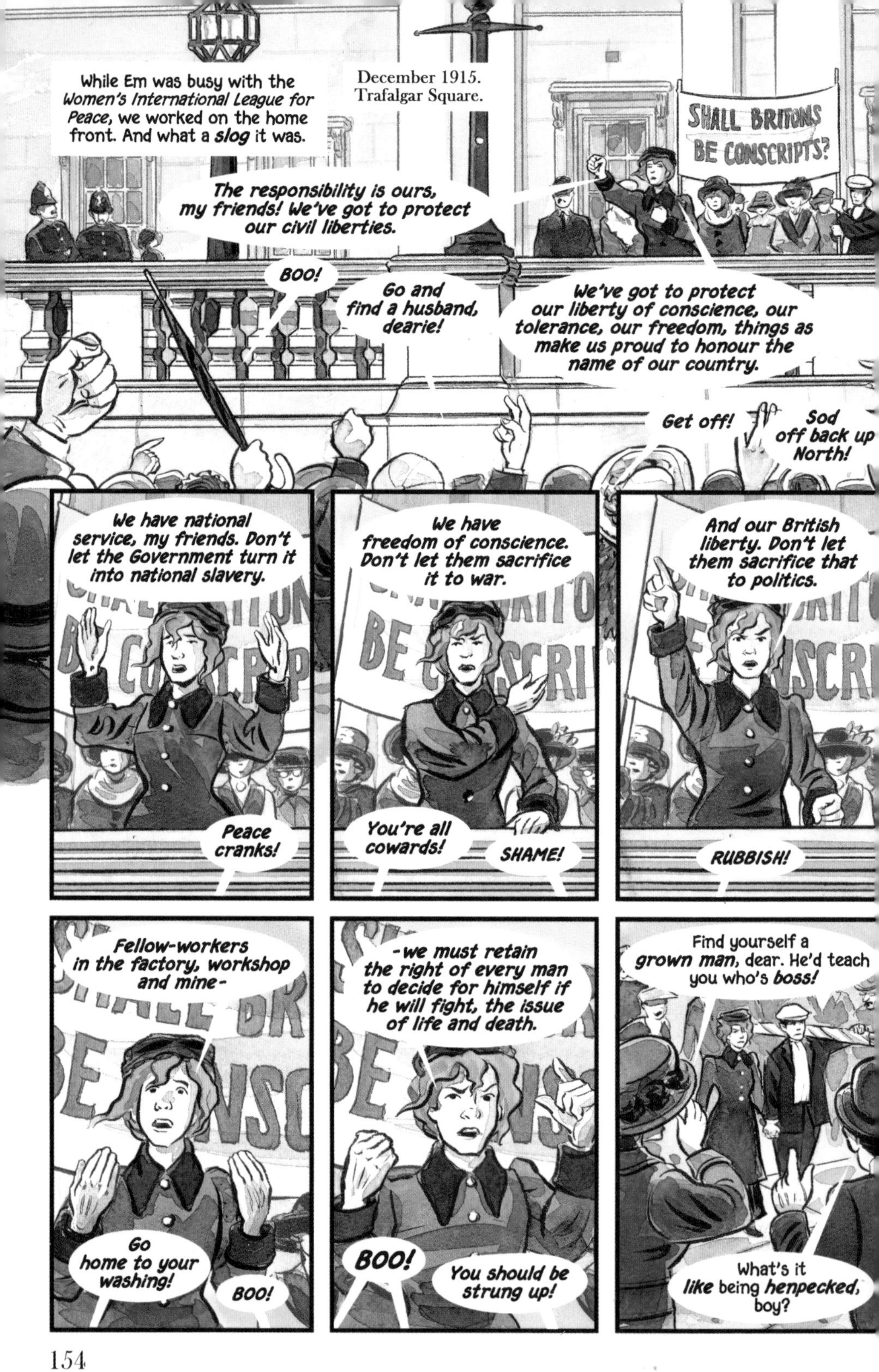
While Em was busy with the *Women's International League for Peace*, we worked on the home front. And what a *slog* it was.
December 1915. Trafalgar Square.
SHALL BRITONS BE CONSCRIPTS?
The responsibility is ours, my friends! We've got to protect our civil liberties.
BOO!
Go and find a husband, dearie!
We've got to protect our liberty of conscience, our tolerance, our freedom, things as make us proud to honour the name of our country.
Get off!
Sod off back up North!
We have national service, my friends. Don't let the Government turn it into national slavery.
Peace cranks!
We have freedom of conscience. Don't let them sacrifice it to war.
You're all cowards!
SHAME!
And our British liberty. Don't let them sacrifice that to politics.
RUBBISH!
Fellow-workers in the factory, workshop and mine-
Go home to your washing!
BOO!
-we must retain the right of every man to decide for himself if he will fight, the issue of life and death.
BOO!
You should be strung up!
Find yourself a *grown man*, dear. He'd teach you who's *boss!*
What's it *like* being *henpecked*, boy?

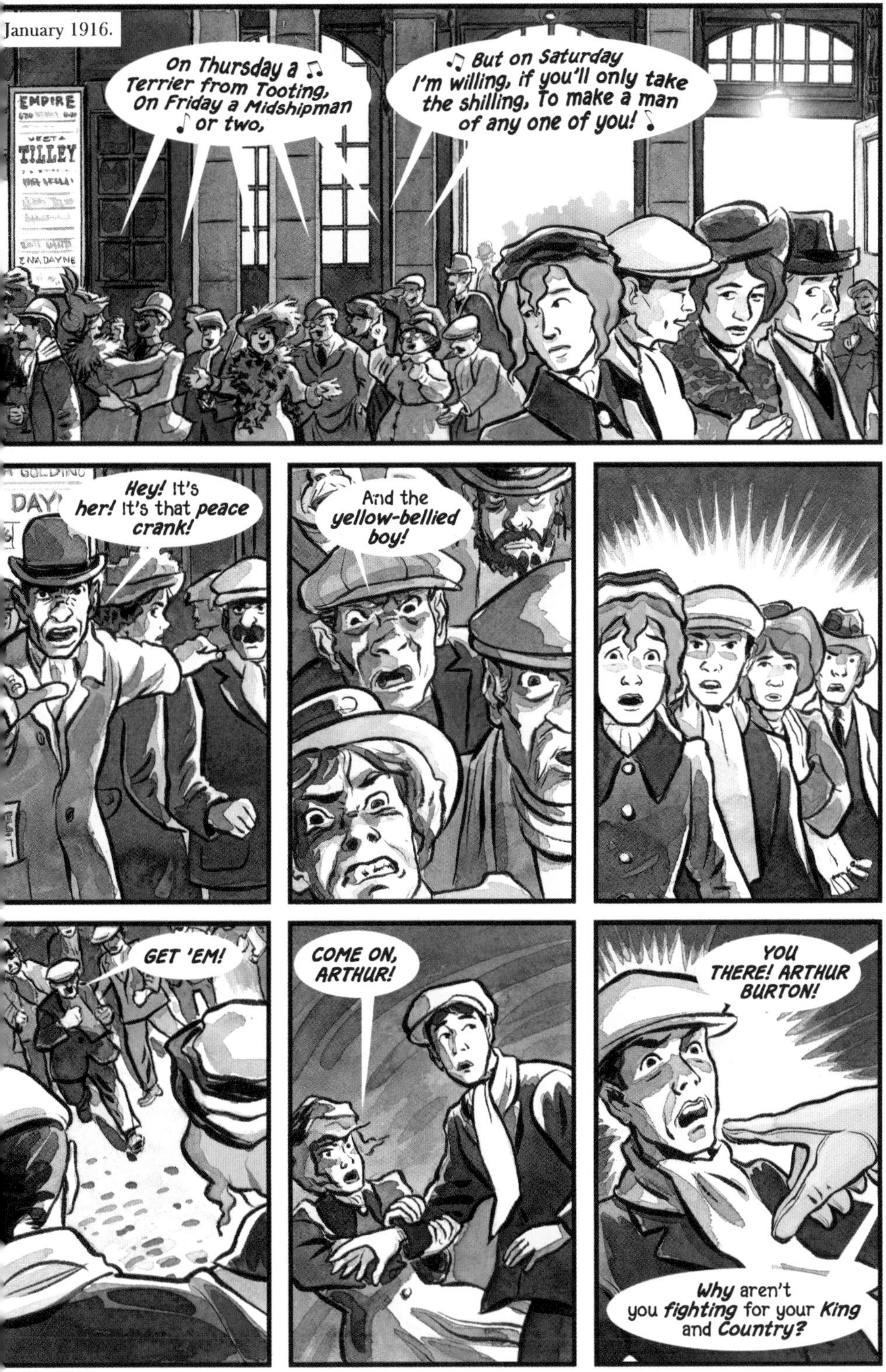

January 1916.
EMPIRE
VESTA
TILLEY
ENA DAYNE
On Thursday a ♫ Terrier from Tooting, On Friday a Midshipman ♪ or two,
♫ But on Saturday I'm willing, if you'll only take the shilling, To make a man of any one of you! ♪
Hey! It's her! It's that peace crank!
And the yellow-bellied boy!
GET 'EM!
COME ON, ARTHUR!
YOU THERE! ARTHUR BURTON!
Why aren't you fighting for your King and Country?

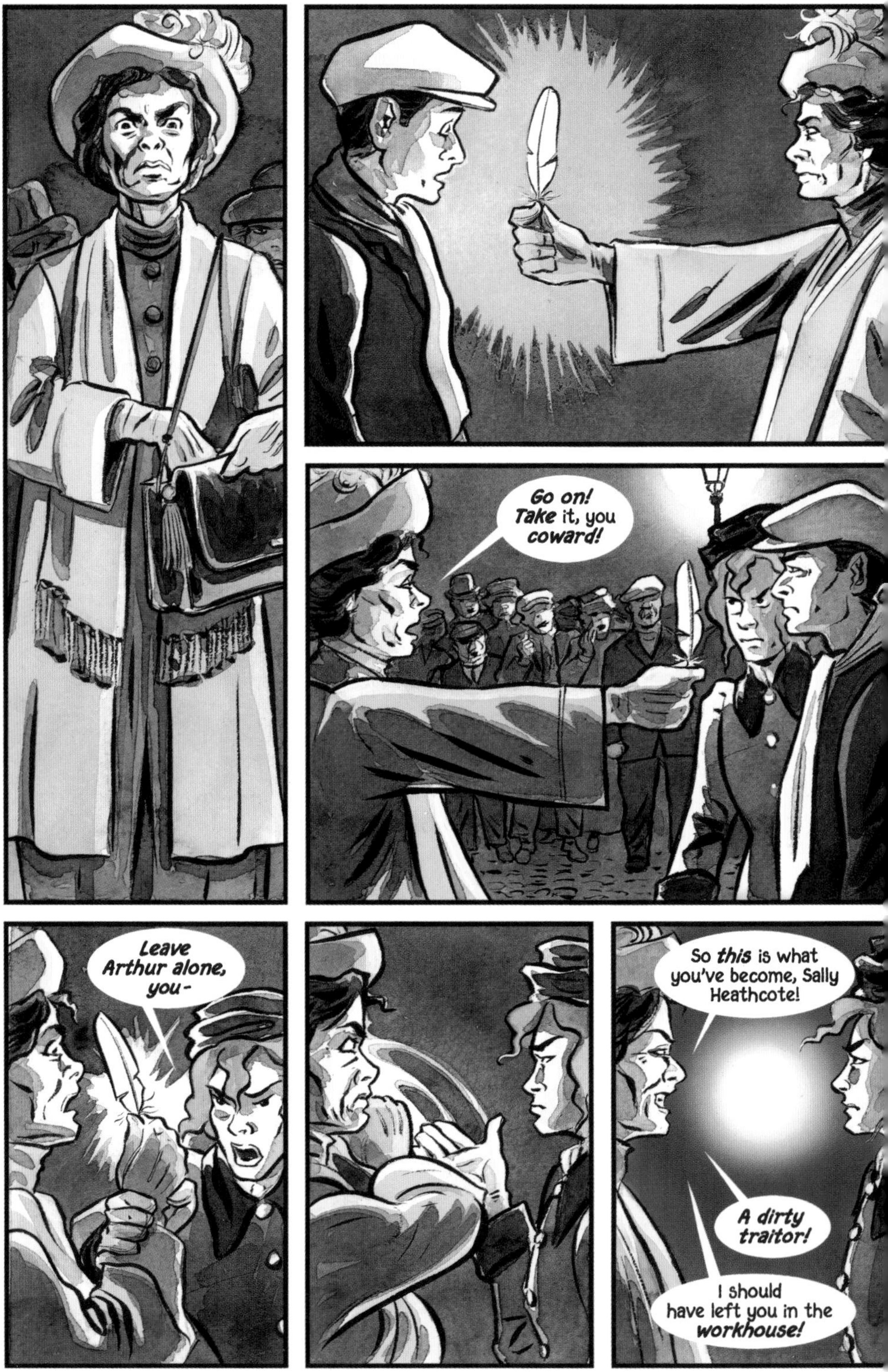
Go on! Take it, you coward!
Leave Arthur alone, you-
So this is what you've become, Sally Heathcote!
A dirty traitor!
I should have left you in the workhouse!

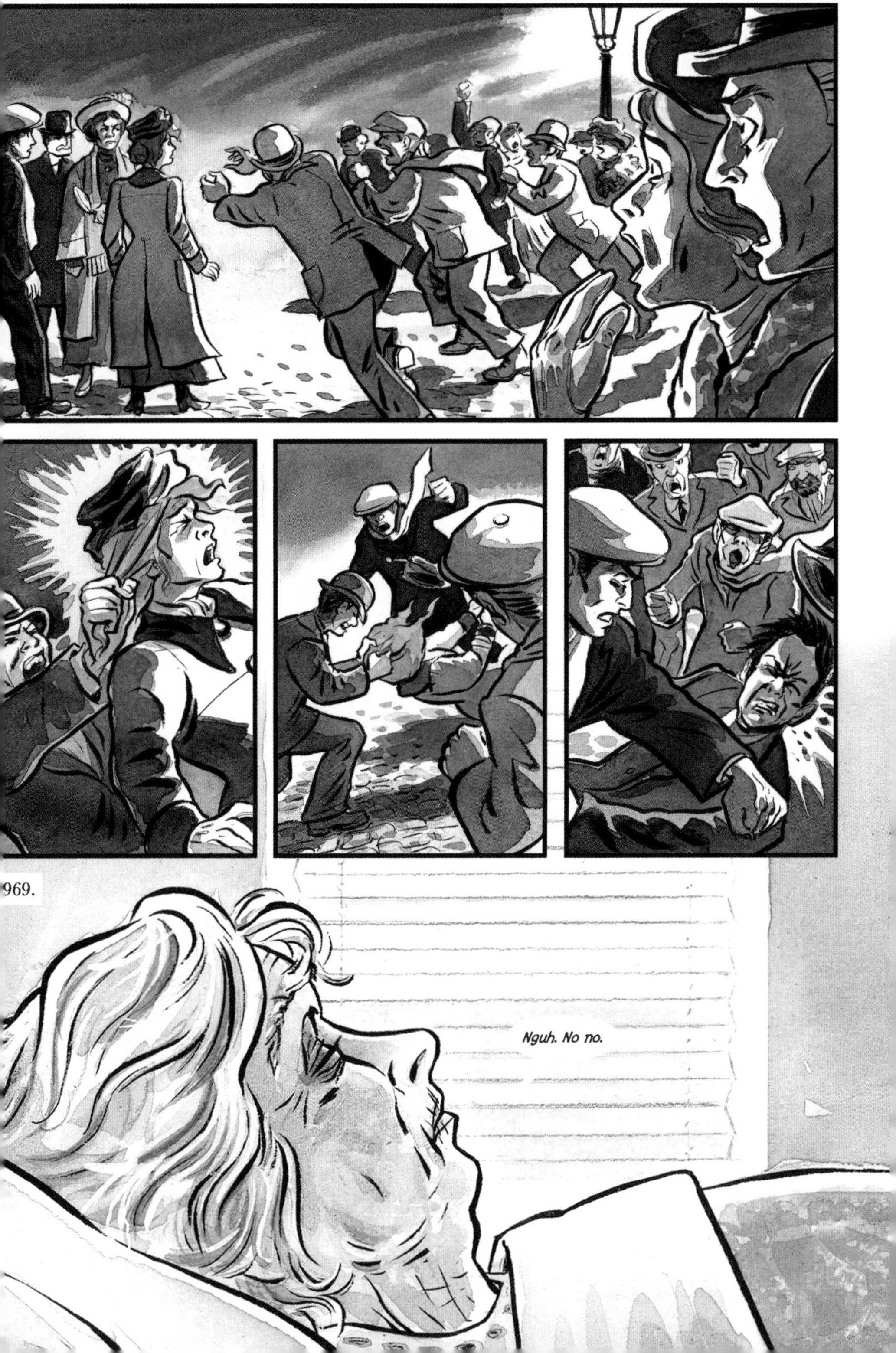
969.
Nguh. No no.

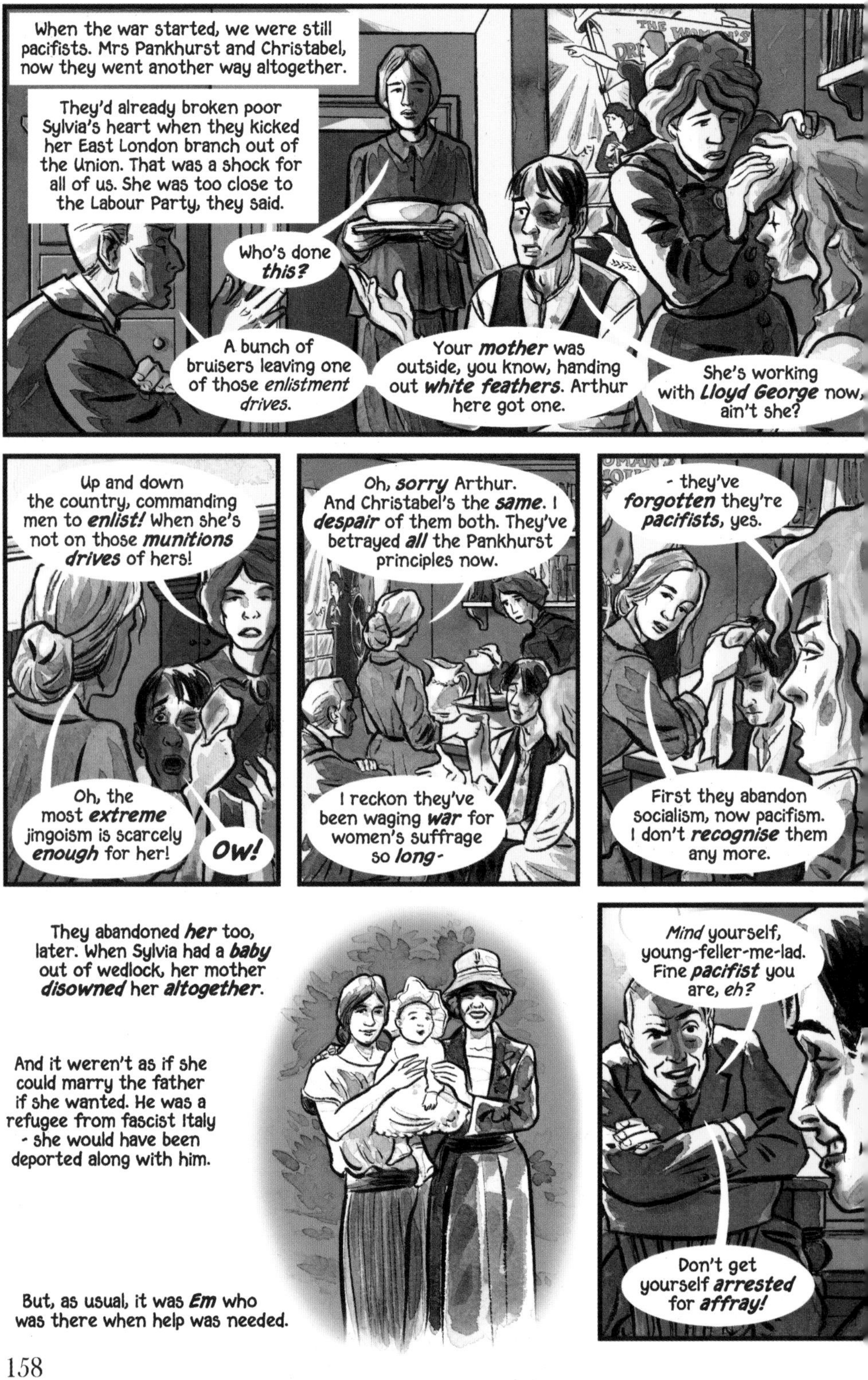
When the war started, we were still pacifists. Mrs Pankhurst and Christabel, now they went another way altogether.
They'd already broken poor Sylvia's heart when they kicked her East London branch out of the Union. That was a shock for all of us. She was too close to the Labour Party, they said.
Who's done *this?*
A bunch of bruisers leaving one of those *enlistment drives.*
Your ***mother*** was outside, you know, handing out ***white feathers***. Arthur here got one.
She's working with ***Lloyd George*** now, ain't she?
Up and down the country, commanding men to ***enlist!*** When she's not on those ***munitions drives*** of hers!
Oh, the most ***extreme*** jingoism is scarcely ***enough*** for her!
Ow!
Oh, ***sorry*** Arthur. And Christabel's the ***same***. I ***despair*** of them both. They've betrayed ***all*** the Pankhurst principles now.
I reckon they've been waging ***war*** for women's suffrage so ***long***-
- they've ***forgotten*** they're ***pacifists***, yes.
First they abandon socialism, now pacifism. I don't ***recognise*** them any more.
They abandoned ***her*** too, later. When Sylvia had a ***baby*** out of wedlock, her mother ***disowned*** her ***altogether***.
And it weren't as if she could marry the father if she wanted. He was a refugee from fascist Italy - she would have been deported along with him.
But, as usual, it was ***Em*** who was there when help was needed.
Mind yourself, young-feller-me-lad. Fine ***pacifist*** you are, ***eh?***
Don't get yourself ***arrested*** for ***affray!***

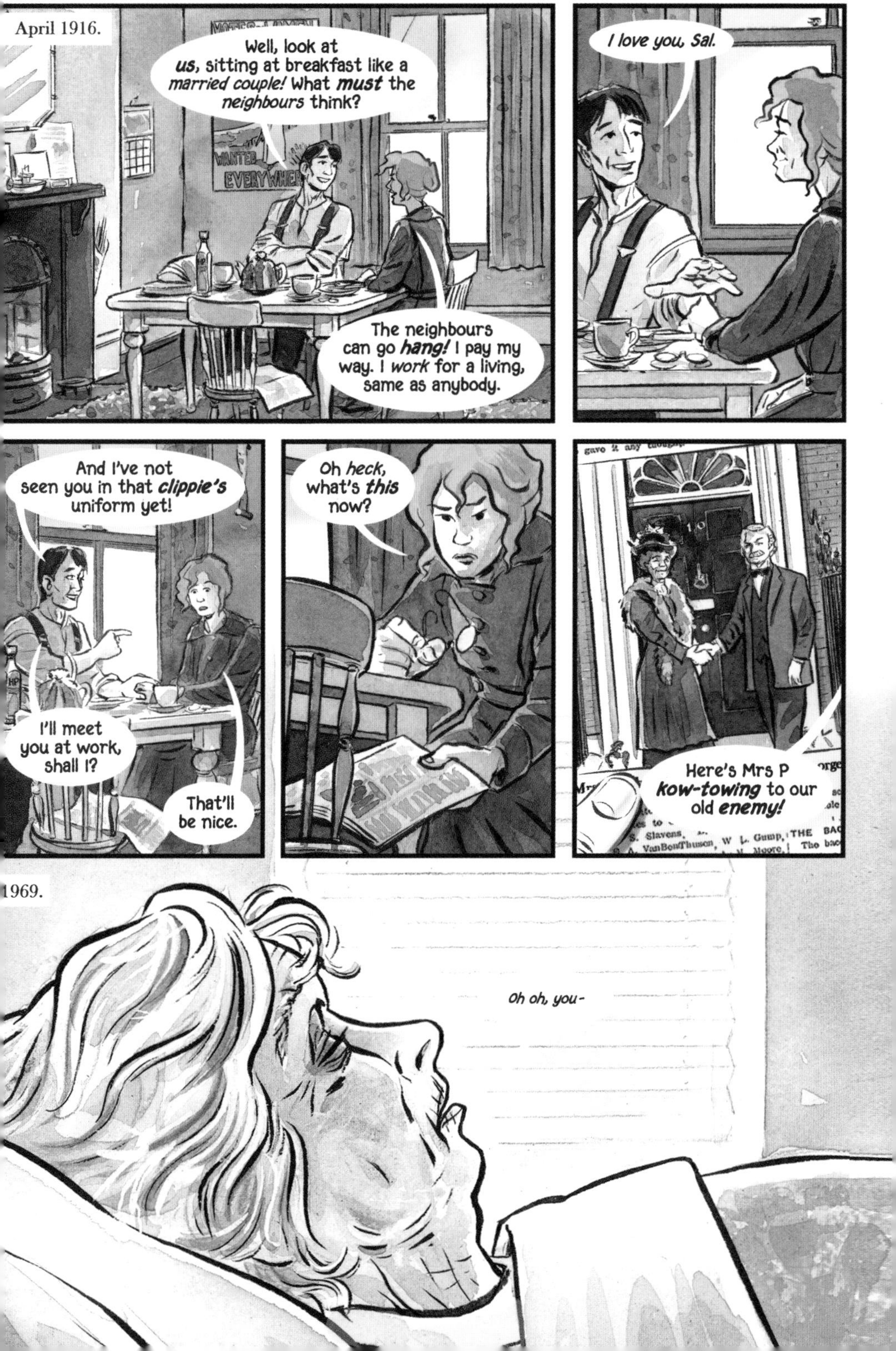
April 1916.
Well, look at *us*, sitting at breakfast like a *married couple!* What *must* the *neighbours* think?
WANTED EVERYWHERE
The neighbours can go *hang!* I pay my way. I *work* for a living, same as anybody.
I love you, Sal.
And I've not seen you in that *clippie's* uniform yet!
I'll meet you at work, shall I?
That'll be nice.
Oh *heck*, what's *this* now?
Here's Mrs P *kow-towing* to our old *enemy!*
1969.
Oh oh, you-

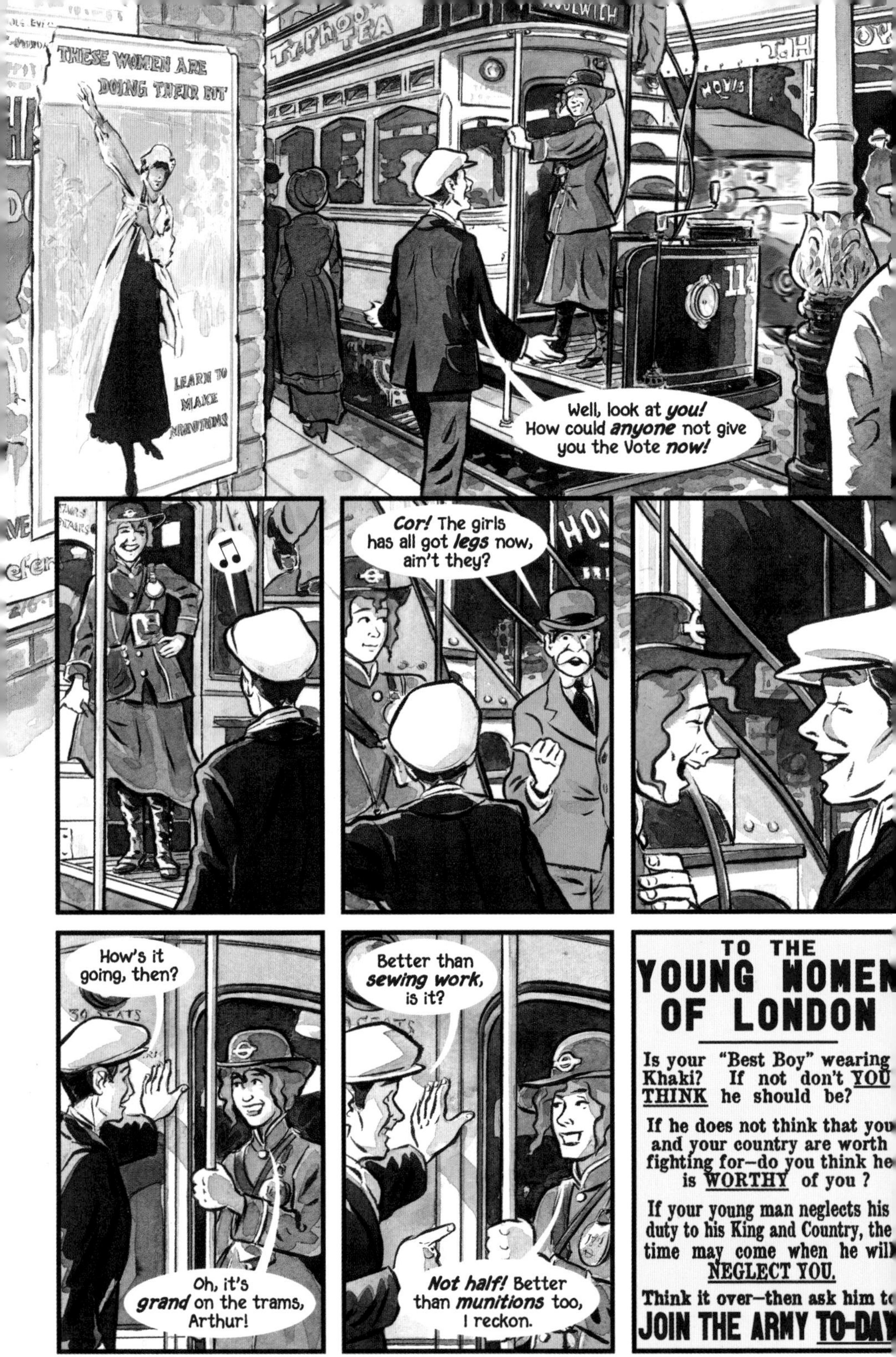
THESE WOMEN ARE DOING THEIR BIT
LEARN TO MAKE MUNITIONS
TYPHOO TEA
WOOLWICH
Well, look at *you!* How could *anyone* not give you the Vote *now!*
Cor! The girls has all got *legs* now, ain't they?
How's it going, then?
Oh, it's *grand* on the trams, Arthur!
Better than *sewing work,* is it?
Not half! Better than *munitions* too, I reckon.
TO THE YOUNG WOMEN OF LONDON
Is your "Best Boy" wearing Khaki? If not don't YOU THINK he should be?
If he does not think that you and your country are worth fighting for—do you think he is WORTHY of you ?
If your young man neglects his duty to his King and Country, the time may come when he will NEGLECT YOU.
Think it over—then ask him to
JOIN THE ARMY TO-DAY

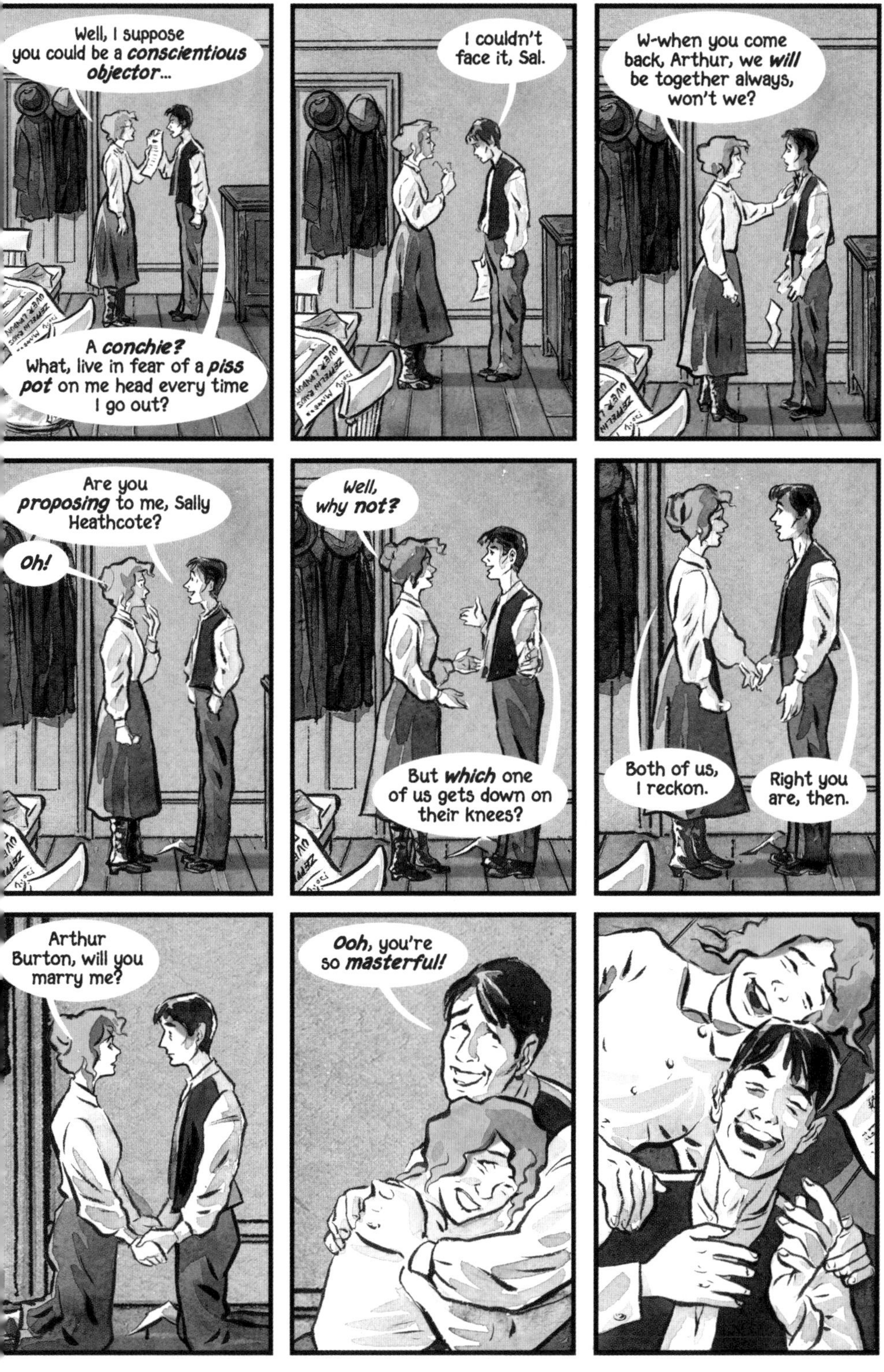
Well, I suppose you could be a *conscientious objector*...
A *conchie?* What, live in fear of a *piss pot* on me head every time I go out?
I couldn't face it, Sal.
W-when you come back, Arthur, we *will* be together always, won't we?
Are you *proposing* to me, Sally Heathcote?
Oh!
Well, why not?
But *which* one of us gets down on their knees?
Both of us, I reckon.
Right you are, then.
Arthur Burton, will you marry me?
Ooh, you're so *masterful!*

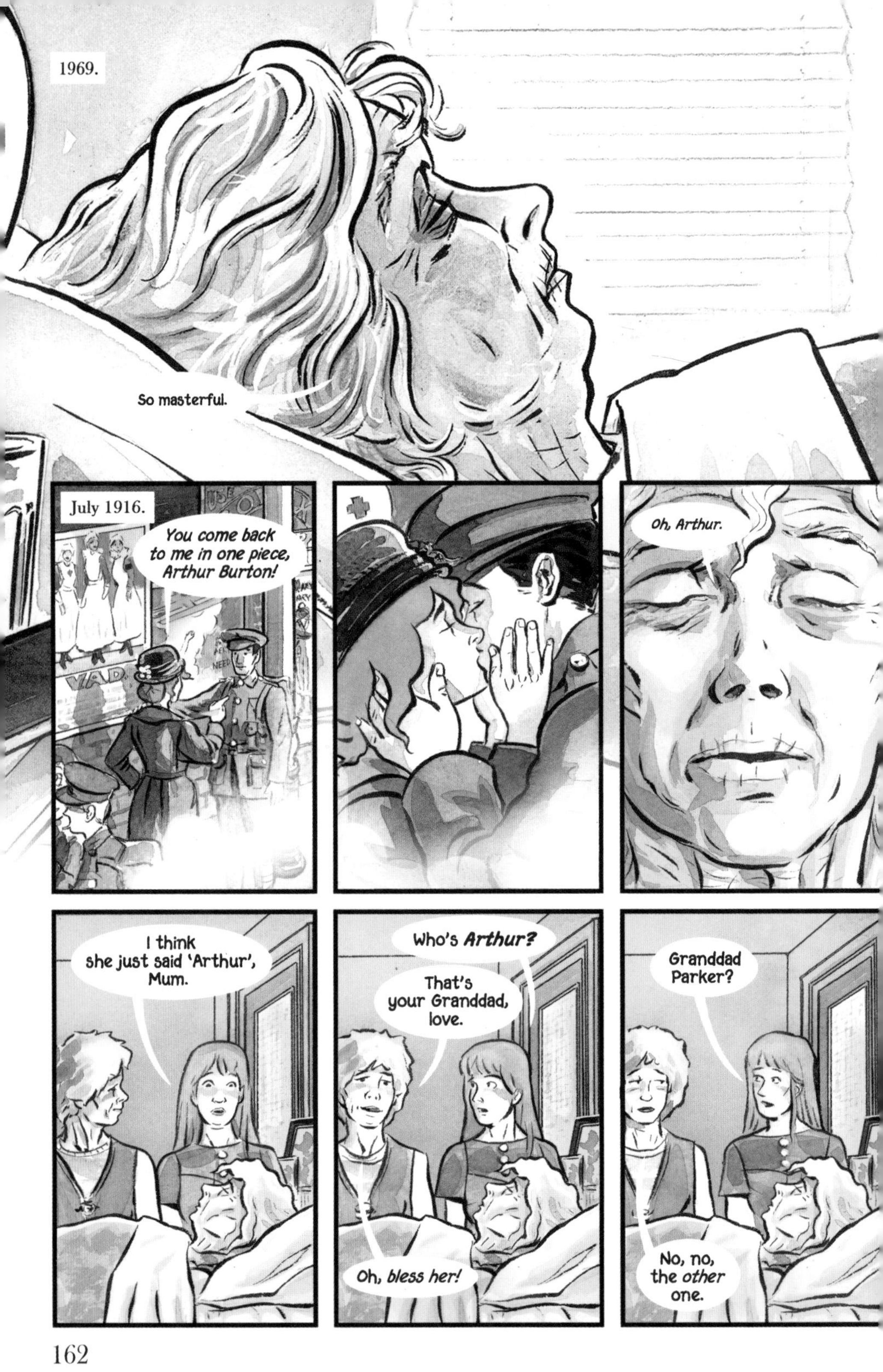
1969.
So masterful.
July 1916.
You come back to me in one piece, Arthur Burton!
Oh, Arthur.
I think she just said 'Arthur', Mum.
Who's *Arthur?*
That's your Granddad, love.
Oh, *bless her!*
Granddad Parker?
No, no, the *other* one.

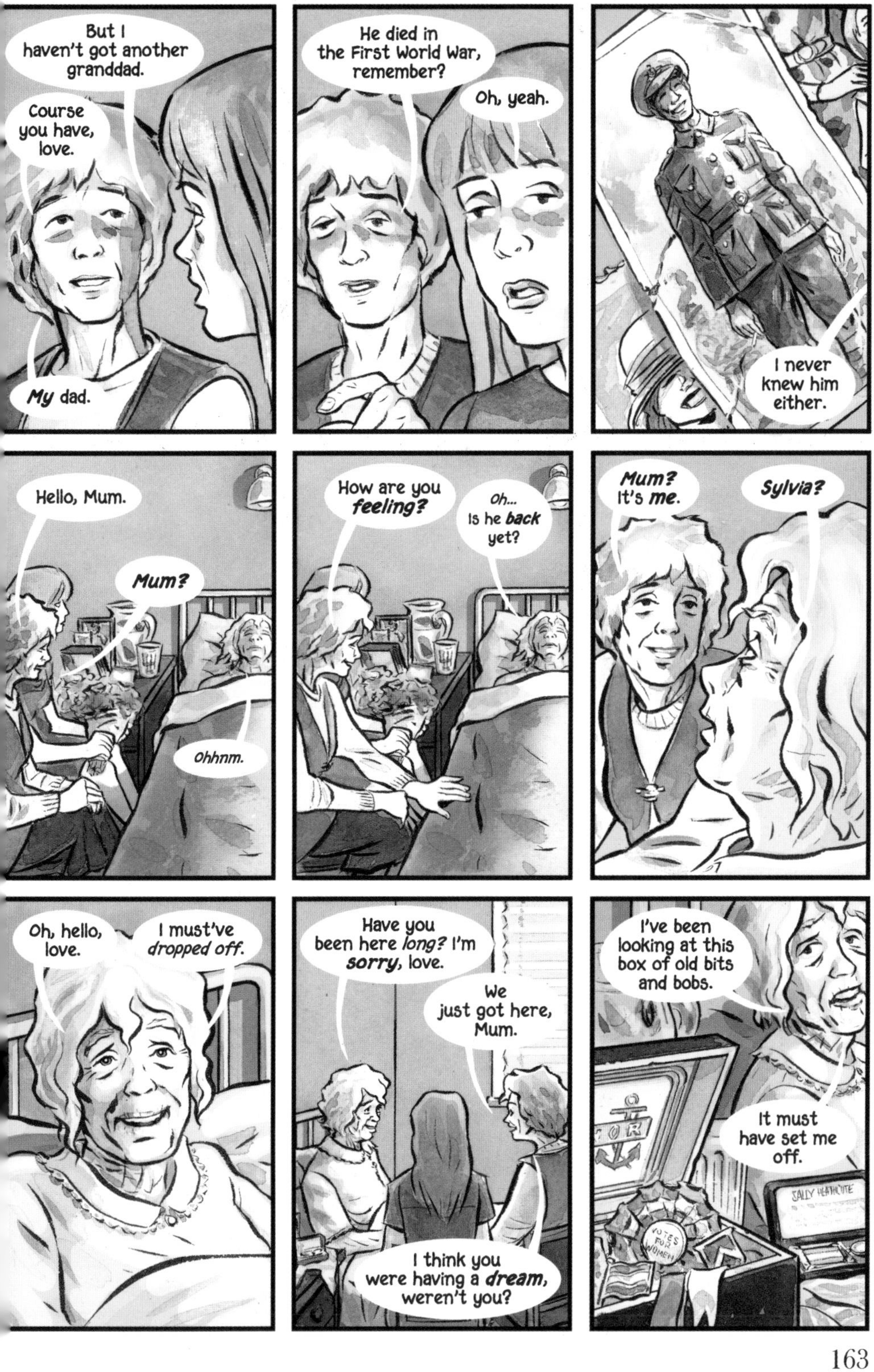
But I haven't got another granddad.
Course you have, love.
My dad.
He died in the First World War, remember?
Oh, yeah.
I never knew him either.
Hello, Mum.
Mum?
Ohhnm.
How are you feeling?
Oh... Is he back yet?
Mum? It's me.
Sylvia?
Oh, hello, love.
I must've dropped off.
Have you been here long? I'm sorry, love.
We just got here, Mum.
I think you were having a dream, weren't you?
I've been looking at this box of old bits and bobs.
It must have set me off.
SALLY HEATHCOTE
VOTES FOR WOMEN

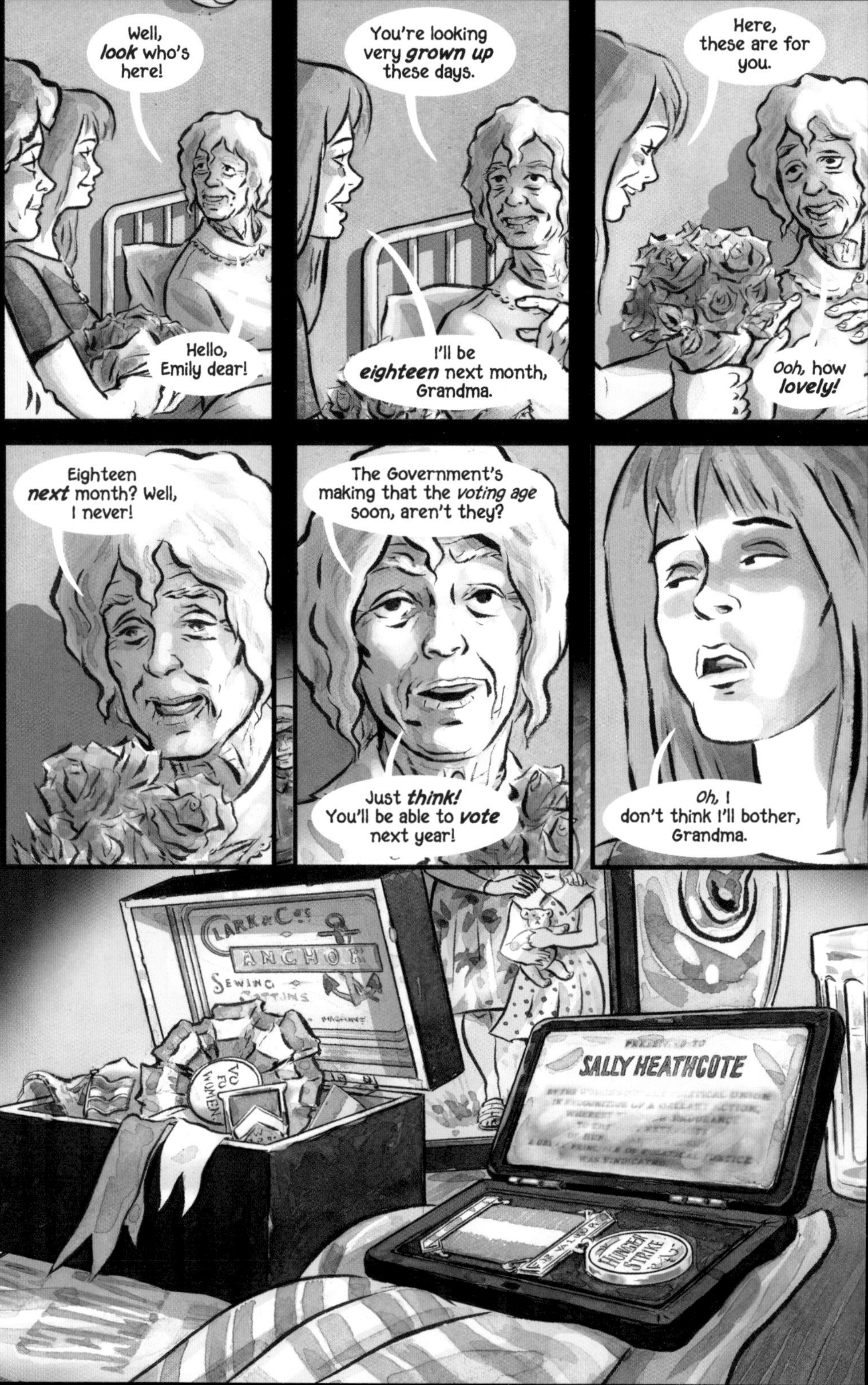
Well, *look* who's here!
Hello, Emily dear!
You're looking very ***grown up*** these days.
I'll be ***eighteen*** next month, Grandma.
Here, these are for you.
Ooh, how ***lovely!***
Eighteen ***next*** month? Well, I never!
The Government's making that the *voting age* soon, aren't they?
Just ***think!*** You'll be able to ***vote*** next year!
Oh, I don't think I'll bother, Grandma.
ANCHOR
SEWING
SALLY HEATHCOTE
HUNGER STRIKE

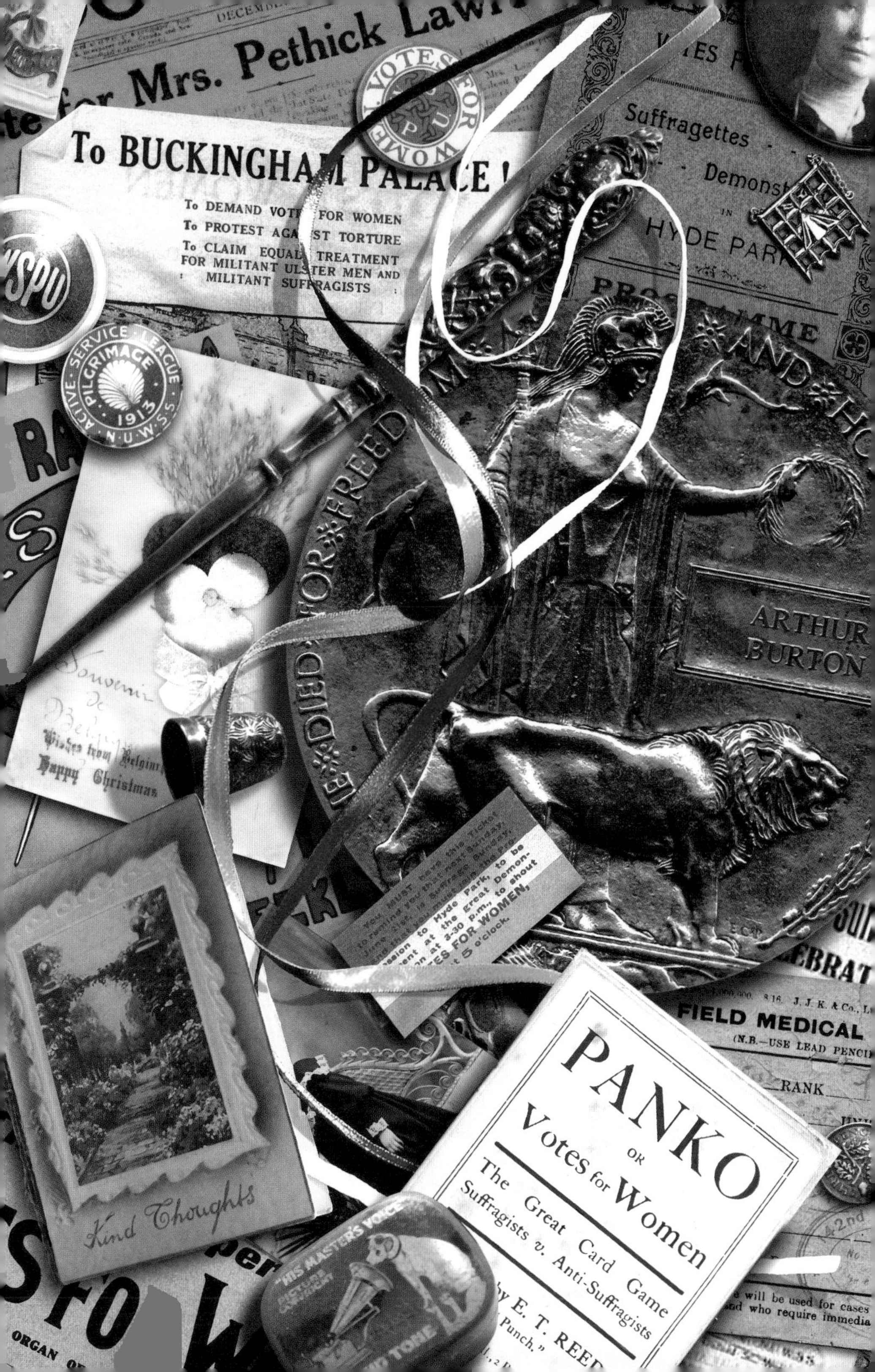
To BUCKINGHAM PALACE !
To DEMAND VOTES FOR WOMEN
To CLAIM EQUAL TREATMENT
FOR MILITANT ULSTER MEN AND
MILITANT SUFFRAGISTS
for Mrs. Pethick
VOTES FOR WOMEN
W S P U
Suffragettes
HYDE PARK
ACTIVE SERVICE LEAGUE
PILGRIMAGE
1913
N.U.W.S.S.
ARTHUR
BURTON
Souvenir de Belgique
Wishes from Belgium
Happy Christmas
Kind Thoughts
FIELD MEDICAL
RANK
PANKO
OR
Votes for Women
The Great Card Game
Suffragists v. Anti-Suffragists
HIS MASTER'S VOICE
ORGAN

1832 Representation of the People Act broadens the property franchise to include half a million 'Male Persons'.

1834 Poor Law Amendment Act does not exclude women from election of workhouse guardians.

1835 Municipal Corporations Act enfranchises property-owning 'Male Persons'.

1865 John Stuart Mill elected MP for Westminster. Franchise for women mentioned in election address.

1867 Second Reform Act. Two and a half million male householders now have franchise.

John Stuart Mill moves amendment to Representation of the People ('Household Franchise') Bill, urging removal of sex disqualification. Loses by 123 votes.

National Society for Women's Suffrage formed (branches in London, Manchester and Edinburgh).

1869 255 women's suffrage petitions to House of Commons.

Municipal Franchise Act extends vote to women ratepayers.

USA: State of Wyoming extends franchise to women.

1870 Limited property rights for married women in England, including the right to retain up to £200 of own earnings.

1881 Married Women's Property (Scotland) Act.

1882 Married Women's Property (England) Act.

1884 Third Reform Act. Five million male householders now have franchise.

1888 Creation of elected county councils with female franchise.

1889 Women's Franchise League formed.

1892 Independent Labour Party founded in Manchester.

1893 New Zealand extends franchise to women.

1897 Twenty societies amalgamated into the National Union of Women's Suffrage Societies. Millicent Garrett Fawcett elected President.

1900 Foundation of Labour Party, as Labour Representation Committee.

1901 Death of Queen Victoria.

1902 Australia extends franchise to women.

1903 Women's Social and Political Union formed in Manchester by Emmeline Pankhurst, from existing members of the Independent Labour Party.

1906 Finland extends franchise to women.

1907 *Votes for Women* launched by Frederick and Emmeline Pethick-Lawrence.
Qualification of Women (County and Borough Councils) Act entitles some women to enter local elections.

1908 First woman elected mayor: Elizabeth Garrett Anderson (Aldeburgh in Suffolk).

1909 'People's Budget' vetoed by House of Lords.

1910 Death of Edward VII.

1911 Coronation of George V.

1913 Norway extends franchise to women.

1914 War declared.

1915 Denmark and Iceland extend franchise to women.

1916 Military Service Act. Compulsory service for all men (18-41) regardless of marital status.

1917 Formation of Women's Army Auxiliary Corps.
Royal name-change from Saxe-Coburg-Gotha to Windsor.
'October Revolution' in Russia.

1918 Representation of the People Act. Franchise extended to all occupiers of rented property, including wives of householders, women householders and graduates over 30 years of age (12 month residency requirement removed).
17 women candidates in General Election, 1 elected: Constance Markievicz (Sinn Fein, Dublin).

1919 First sitting female MP: Nancy Astor (Conservative, Plymouth).

1928 Representation of the People (Equal Franchise) Act. Voting age for women lowered to 21.

1929 First woman Cabinet Minister: Margaret Bondfield (Labour, Wallsend).

1960 Sri Lanka: First ever woman prime minister, Sirimavo Bandaranaike.

1967 Sexual Offences Act decriminalises homosexuality.
Abortion Act decriminalises abortion.

1969 Lowering of voting age to 18.

1970 Equal Pay Act.

1973 Women allowed in the London Stock Exchange.

1975 Sex Discrimination Act.
Employment Protection Act makes sacking for pregnancy illegal.

These notes supply historical background detail that may be of interest, as well as identifying my sources. If you're reading this book for the first time, please *stop reading them now!* They are not needed to understand the story; in fact, they'll just distract you.

Some months after I'd settled on my eponymous heroine's name, I came across a book review in the WSPU's paper, *Votes for Women*. The book was called *Suffragette Sally*. Written by Gertrude Colmore and published in 1911, it weaves the stories of three fictional women into what were then very recent events in suffrage history. Each woman is from a different social class: a maid-of-all-work called Sally Simmonds; Edith Carstairs, a middle-class 'constitutionalist' who is gradually converted to militancy; and Geraldine Hill, an aristocrat who is clearly based on Lady Constance Lytton.

It's a coincidence that I came up with the same occupation and first name for my protagonist, but perhaps not altogether surprising. Domestic service was the most likely form of employment for a woman of no means before the First World War; Sally (from Sarah) was a common name then and it alliterates well with 'suffragette'.

Page iii.
The epigraph is taken from Emmeline Pethick-Lawrence's autobiography (Pethick-Lawrence 1938, pp215-239).

Page 1.
The image reworks a 1912 advertising poster design by Hilda Dallas, WSPU member and Slade student (Tickner 1987, p244).

Page 3.
The boxed medal bears the inscription 'Hunger Strike', the bar 'For Valour'. The inscription inside the lid reads as follows: 'Presented to SALLY HEATHCOTE by the Women's Social and Political Union in recognition of a gallant action, whereby through endurance to the last extremity of hunger and hardship a great principle of political justice was vindicated'. These medals were first awarded by the WSPU in August 1909.

Page 4.
The policeman's list of items and the text of the note are both authentic. Helen Craggs was apprehended by PC Godden of Oxfordshire Constabulary in the grounds of Nuneham Park and charged with attempting to set fire to the residence of Lewis Harcourt (Secretary of State for the Colonies and a well-known Cabinet 'Anti'). She was sentenced to nine months hard labour, but released after an eleven-day hunger strike (Crawford 2001, pp146-7; Rosen 1974, p169).

Page 5.
Asquith's rapturous welcome in Dublin is based on an account in the *Irish Times Online* (Collins 2012). The chief marshal is dressed up as the revolutionary hero Robert Emmet. Emmet led a rebellion against British rule in 1808, for which he was tried and hanged.

Page 6.
Mary Leigh and Gladys Evans sailed to Dublin from England ahead of Asquith's visit in July 1912. After other 'outrages' there, including acts of arson in the Theatre Royal, they were arrested and sentenced to five years (Rosen 1974, p170; Collins 2012). I now suspect that my account of Mary's hatchet hurling, based on these sources, like them may be complicit with police and press misrepresentation. I'm now more or less convinced (after continued research in the area) that my representation of this Dublin 'outrage' uncritically reproduces those sources. In Mary's own courtroom defence, she admitted that she 'put' the hatchet in the carriage but maintained she 'did not throw it ... Therefore it was impossible that Mr Redmond's injuries were received by her hand ... The hatchet was used in a symbolic manner' (*The Suffragette* Dec 20th, 1912, p152; Morley and Stanley 1988, p117). Votes coverage of the case maintains that her 'conduct of the case was truly magnificent' (*Votes for Women* August 16th, 1912, p742) and the charge of throwing the hatchet was dropped (Owens 1984, p61). However, I decided to leave the passage as it stands, otherwise the story's opening fireworks would have become something of a damp squib. There's news values for you.

Symbolic it may have been, but Mary's action had serious consequences for her Irish counterparts. The first window smashing by the Irish Women's Franchise League was in 1912, protesting about women's exclusion from the vote in the Home Rule Bill. The response from Nationalists and Unionists alike was vehement, despite their own use of far more extreme measures. Prior to Asquith's visit, ugly threats were issued to suffragists; it was made clear that suffrage demonstrations would be viewed as traitorous threats to the promise of Home Rule. Mary was vilified as 'The Virago with the Hatchet'; the IWFL announced that they had no prior knowledge of her intentions and that they abhorred 'the wicked actions of the English suffragettes'. Nevertheless Dublin became highly dangerous for women suspected of suffragist tendencies, who were liable to be the target of mob violence (Owens 1984, pp55-60).

Page 9.
The Government arranged to sell off the effects of house and garden by auction. The Pethick-Lawrences' friends flocked to buy up the items and return them. However, the sale only raised £300 towards the £1,100 court costs and they were also charged £5,000 for repairs to shop windows, all of which forced Fred into bankruptcy proceedings. The bankruptcy was eventually annulled but they had narrowly averted selling their home (Pethick-Lawrence 1943, pp101-2).

The full text of the telegram was too large to cram into the panel. Here it is in full:

> Dear Friends: You will understand the great happiness it gives us to be in our own country once more, fully restored to health and ready to take part again with you in the great battle for human liberty. On our arrival we learn with amazement the confirmation of a rumour that while we have been in Canada the Government burglars have entered our private house with intent to steal our belongings. To such underhand methods of fighting a political adversary our answer is open defiance. Unitedly - FW & E Pethick-Lawrence.

Page 11.
According to Em, it was Annie Kenney who persuaded her to attend her first WSPU meeting in 1906, really because she 'could not repulse her wistful eagerness'. Once there she was 'sucked into the whirlpool of the WSPU' as treasurer (Pethick-Lawrence 1938, pp147-152). Annie was a former factory worker who had been recruited by the Pankhursts in Manchester. She and Christabel commit the Union's first act of 'militancy' on p16.

Page 14.
The Pethick-Lawrences' return and expulsion from the WSPU is well documented, though their own accounts are very reserved. My main sources were Mitchell, D (1977, pp200-2); Raeburn (1973, pp180-3); Rosen (1974, pp172-77) and Pethick-Lawrence (1943, pp98-101). I have condensed the confrontation into a single episode. After this first confrontational meeting, Mrs Pankhurst crossed the Channel to France, where Christabel was hiding from the police, in order to persuade her to her point of view. Then, despite the risk of being spotted, Christabel travelled to London in disguise for a meeting on 14th October at which she backed up her mother's decision (Pugh 2008, p253). After this second confrontation, Fred and Em never saw Christabel or her mother again. 'The cleavage was final and complete,' Em remarks. 'From that time forward I never saw or heard from Mrs Pankhurst again, and Christabel, who had shared our family life, became a complete stranger. The Pankhursts did nothing by halves!' (Pethick-Lawrence 1938, p283)

Despite their separation, the Pethick-Lawrences never withdrew their public support for Mrs Pankhurst. When she was in financial difficulties after the war, for example, Em was among those who raised funds for her. In 1930, Fred helped raise finances for the statue of her in Westminster and gave her a warm tribute on its unveiling (Bartley 2002, p134).

Emmeline Pethick-Lawrence was affectionately nicknamed 'Pethums' (e.g. Ferguson 1958; quoted in Marlow 2001, p 269).

The image in the last panel is from the cover of *Votes for Women*, the issue in which the Union announced its impending move to larger premises (Sept 20th, 1912). It alludes to *Alice in Wonderland* as recently illustrated by Arthur Rackham (*Alice* had come out of copyright in 1907).

Page 16.
Christabel Pankhurst and Annie Kenney's first act of 'militancy', and subsequent imprisonment, brought the WSPU its first national press coverage. Christabel had learned useful lessons from the local socialist agitation in Manchester (Mitchell, D 1977, pp63-4; Pugh 2008, pp127-9; Rosen 1974, pp49-51).

Page 20.
'Voterettes on the Warpath' was a headline in the *Daily Express* (March 10th, 1906). There's a clipping of the article in a scrapbook of Emmeline Pethick-Lawrence's (now in the Women's Library archive). The term 'suffragettes' was coined in the *Daily Mail* (January 10th, 1906), in disparaging reference to the more militant suffragists. They took it up with enthusiasm nevertheless.

Page 21-3.
This entire episode (cabbages and all) is closely based on an account in Hannah Mitchell's autobiog-

raphy (Mitchell, H 1977). Oddly enough, in Em's account of the same event, it's Fred who's Adela's rescuer (Pethick-Lawrence 1938, p163). Hannah doesn't even mention that he was present.

Page 25.

Christabel's stage presence and handling of heckling is well documented (e.g. Mitchell, D 1977, pp92-3; Pugh 2008, pp176-80). Strictly speaking, she shouldn't be wearing the WSPU regalia of purple, white and green in this scene. They were only devised by Em in May 1908, while she was planning the pageantry for the 'Women's Sunday' demonstration in the following month. This and the next few pages represent year after year of ongoing activities by feminist activists, especially the WSPU, before the first physical militancy (the first stone thrown in protest was on 30th June 1908, aimed by Mary Leigh at a window of No. 10 Downing Street).

Em revered Christabel publicly, in the elevated language that was also a characteristic of her speeches, often with visionary subject matter and shaped by Victorian religious discourse. In 1908 she wrote an article about Christabel the 'maiden warrior' in anticipation of the latter's release from prison after a ten-week stretch (which turned out to be her last). Along with her mother and Flora Drummond, Christabel had been charged with inciting illegal behaviour (an exhortation to 'Rush the House of Commons' in a leaflet distributed in Trafalgar Square in October 1908). In this extract from Em's article, she likens Christabel to the heroic Wagnerian figure of Siegfried:

> Christabel! Christabel! As the dawn to the waiting earth upon whose breast have lain all night the chilling mists of tears, so are you dear to the hearts of women.
>
> Long, long, we waited for your coming. Too well have we learned the lesson of sorrow and of patience. Fear was upon us, and the anguish of womanhood had subdued us and brought us under submission.
>
> Then you came like the young Siegfried in his maiden might. Like him you took the broken pieces of the weapon of destiny, and welded them into 'Needful,' the magic sword. Like him, utterly without the knowledge of fear, you have gone forth to break the curse of terrible domination.
>
> Child of destiny! Spirit of the dawn! You will emerge undimmed even from the black recesses of a common gaol, for until the appointed time you are immune from the griefs which pierce and wound the hearts of those to whom has not been given at birth your magic armour . . .
>
> Maiden warrior! We give you rapturous welcome. Go forth with the fiat of the future, strong in your gladness and youth . . .
> (*Votes for Women* Dec 17th, 1908, p200)

And so on. With such writing, Em was partially responsible for Christabel's elevation to celebrity status. Her praise for Christabel's spirit in prison contrasts curiously with her subsequent remarks: 'We knew that imprisonment had a dread effect on all, but especially on Christabel, who seemed to lose vitality in isolation and confinement' (Pethick-Lawrence 1938, p205).

The customary greetings of prisoners on release were planned for the evening of 19th December 1908, to be followed by triumphal homecoming celebrations. However, the former were thwarted by the Home Secretary's early release of Christabel and her mother. No one came to greet them at the gates of Holloway and, it being Saturday evening, even Clement's Inn was empty – the Pethick-Lawrences were at their country house in Dorking. The Pankhursts took the train to Dorking to join them, where they stayed until after the

New Year. The victory celebrations took place as planned on 22nd December. The pageantry involved two brass bands, nine women on white horses, 200 women in white, all led by a young woman bearing the WSPU's tricolour flag (Pugh 2008, pp186-7; Rosen 1974, p113).

Page 26.
On the day of the opening of Parliament, a deputation went to the House of Commons with the intention of asking the Liberal Chief Whip to obtain a promise from the Prime Minister, Sir Henry Campbell-Bannerman (Pethick-Lawrence 1938, pp165-7).

Page 27.
The 'Woman Suffrage' article is from *The Times* (Oct 25th, 1906). The letter from Millicent Fawcett, leader of the NUWSS, appeared shortly afterwards (*The Times* Oct 27th, 1906). The exchange between Christabel and the judge is taken from the court proceedings (Raeburn 1973, p33).

Page 28.
The 'Dinner to Released Suffragists' article is from *The Times* (Dec 12th, 1906). At the dinner, Christabel is quoting from an article about a new soft toy: the teddy bear ('Fashion's Craze: America's Infatuation for "Johnny Bear"', *Penny Illustrated Paper* Dec 29th 1906). The discussion at the Pankhurst residence is compiled from a range of sources. For instance, Christabel's remark about socialist men is taken from an article of hers in the *ILP News* in August 1903 (cited in Mitchell, D 1977, p47).

The WSPU's 'At Homes' took place every Monday. With only five people present, the one in this scene is sparsely attended. Sitting at the table with Emmeline and Christabel Pankhurst are three other north-west suffragists: Teresa Billington, Hannah Mitchell and the elderly Elizabeth Wolstenholme Elmy.

Page 29.
According to Christabel's posthumously published account (Pankhurst 1959, pp79-80), Emmeline Pankhurst's resignation from her Registrarship was prompted by an anonymous complaint. She had received a letter from the Registrar-General, warning her that her activities risked jeopardizing her public appointment. At this point, no charge had been made against her and she had not yet participated in any of the demonstrations leading to arrests. Yet her prominence in public meetings reported by the press was apparently considered to be sufficient grounds for complaint. As a widow with a child of school age, the potential loss of income was a serious threat. It was the healthy finances of the WSPU and the Pethick-Lawrences' financial support that made her resignation possible (Pugh 2008, p153).

Page 30.
Victor Grayson became MP for Colne Valley in July 1907, though in fact he stood as an Independent Socialist candidate, with local Independent Labour Party (ILP) support. In his campaign he advocated revolution, which probably accounts for his success in Colne Valley at that time. There's an interesting profile online at Spartacus Schoolnet.

Page 33.
The *Votes* seller's exchange with a passer-by is the personal recollection of one Miss Marie Brackenbury, suffragette (personal papers, Museum of London, cited in Raeburn 1973, p44).

Page 34.

Emmeline Pethick-Lawrence chose the WSPU regalia of purple, white and green in May 1908 for the 'Women's Sunday' procession and rally that took place on 21st June. Green was for hope, purple for dignity, or sometimes courage, and white was for purity. They can of course be explained more prosaically with the demand, 'Give women votes' (green, white, violet).

My original plan for this scene was to build the talk around illustrations in coverage of the 'Women's Sunday' event in *Votes for Women*. This plan was thwarted, however. To my surprise, there wasn't a single image in the issue and little visual record of this early large-scale pageantry to be found anywhere. On later occasions, the suffragists presumably learned to orchestrate press photography more effectively as well as keeping a fuller record themselves. Two photographs that appeared in the *Illustrated London News* documented a promotional event on the Thames for the forthcoming demonstration. From a launch at Westminster, Flora Drummond used a megaphone to invite MPs on the terrace to the Hyde Park event. Other advertising included posters on buses and shop window displays.

The organisation of the event was prompted by Government denial of the widespread support that women's suffrage had: 'Members of the Government, when called upon to grant votes to women, have said that proof is lacking that women demand the vote, and have told women to hold demonstrations like those organized in the past by men. The Women's Demonstration ... will give the final answer to this argument, and will prove that there is a national demand for women's enfranchisement' (*Votes for Women* Apr 30th, 1908). 'General' Flora Drummond was the overall coordinator of the seven processions, which marched from Euston Station, Trafalgar Square, Victoria Embankment, Chelsea Embankment, Kensington High Street, Paddington and Marylebone Road. They converged on Hyde Park, complete with trumpets and bands, hundreds of banners and thousands of flags, all in the new purple, white and green regalia. There were twenty speaker platforms in Hyde Park, with life-size portraits on each (Rosen 1974, pp102-5).

Page 35.

The Maison Espérance tailoring establishment was first set up in 1897 by Emmeline Pethick (before she met and married Fred Lawrence) and Mary Neal at 155 Great Portland Street. A couple of years later it moved to Wigmore Street, Portman Square. I found the advertisement in a 1901 pamphlet by Mary Neal called 'Dear Mother Earth'. On the same page were ads for the Espérance Girls' Club and St Christopher's Boys' Club.

The Maison Espérance was founded with shareholder money. The initial plan to run it as a co-operative was abandoned; with domestic duties as well as paid employment, the workers weren't interested. Offering a guaranteed minimum wage of 15 shillings a week, it doubled their previous earnings and provided a degree of financial security that was rare in the seasonal industry of tailoring. As Em explains, 'We could arrange for constant employment only by making a personal appeal to our customers to give us orders out of season; and to their sympathetic response we owed our success' (Pethick-Lawrence 1938, p119).

Page 37.

Emmeline Pankhurst's speech here is an extract from a speech published in *Votes* (Oct 25th, 1912) after she had delivered it in the Albert Hall on October 17th, 1912. She was long-established as a public speaker by that time and I'm assuming she reused her own material a lot.

Page 38.
'Sing a Song of Christabel' is sung to the tune of 'Sing a Song of Sixpence'; the lyrics are from Mitchell, D (1977, p119). The song celebrates the 'pantechnicon raid' on Parliament in February 1908.

Page 40.
'Rise Up, Women!' is sung to the tune of 'John Brown's Body'; full lyrics can be found in Mitchell, D (1977, p96).

Page 47.
The image is loosely based on a page on 'The Strange "Suffragette" Outbreak in London' in The Sphere (Nov 3rd, 1906). We've turned it into a handy reference guide to some key women's suffrage figures.

Page 53.
The prices here are based on details in Pember Reeves (1979) and in Mitchell, H (1977) Mitchell was herself a seamstress. Her recollections of working as a dressmaker's assistant provide a first-hand account of sweated labour in Lancashire. Her hours at one establishment were from 8 a.m. to 8 p.m., often 10 p.m. or midnight on Friday and Saturdays, with Tuesday evening free – all for 8 shillings per week. No talking was allowed and there was a 1d fine for late arrival. The industry in London would have been much the same, whether in a dressmaking establishment or home-working like Sally. Homeworkers would have been supplied with fabric for each commission, but required to pay for thread, hire of machine and so on.

Page 55.
From two years old, Esther Knowles was a regular at the Espérance Girls' Club run by Mary Neal and Emmeline Pethick (Em's maiden name). When Esther left school, Em offered her a job as an office girl for the WSPU. She eventually became secretary to the Pethick-Lawrences and typed up Em's autobiography (*Radio Times* 1974).

Page 57.
I derived Fred's anecdote about Esther Knowles from her own account of starting work at Clement's Inn. In 1974, she was interviewed for a *Radio Times* special edition in conjunction with the showing of a new BBC series on suffragettes, 'Shoulder to Shoulder.' In her own words:

> When I left school at 14, Emmeline asked me if I would like to become an office girl at the WSPU offices at Clement's Inn, and, of course, I jumped at it. Fred Pethick-Lawrence was the editor of 'Votes for Women,' Emmeline the Union's treasurer. I went to work in the editorial offices for six shillings a week. After I'd been there a few days I realised that an office boy doing exactly the same job as I was being paid eight shillings a week. So I said to Fred, 'You are fighting for the equality of women and yet Harry Burton is getting two shillings a week more for doing the same job as me.' He roared with laughter and gave me a rise. (*Radio Times* 1974).

Page 61.
After the Hyde Park demonstration in June 1908, the WSPU launched a purple, white and green merchandising offensive. In January 1909, the Kensington branch opened the first retail outlet, in Notting Hill Gate. Numerous others subsequently opened throughout the country and thrived until the outbreak of war in 1914. There's a detailed entry on WSPU shops, offices and bazaars in Crawford (2001).

Page 62.

Elsie Howey was a very active unpaid organiser and fundraiser for the WSPU. She rode as Joan of Arc at Em's release in 1909 and again beside Emily Wilding Davison's coffin in 1913 (Crawford 2001). She was first arrested after the 'pantechnicon raid' on Parliament in February 1908 (referred to in 'Sing a Song of Christabel' on p38) and was one of the 'Women's Sunday' speakers in June of the same year.

Page 66.

The first hunger striker was Marjorie Wallace Dunlop, a sculptor and illustrator, on being re-fused political-prisoner status (the First Division). She was released after 91 hours. She took this step without any prior planning or consultation, but it quickly became normal practice (Rosen 1974, pp120-21).

Page 67.

Keir Hardie knew the elder Pankhursts through the newly formed Labour Party in the 1880s. They converted him to the cause of women's suffrage. As an MP in the House of Commons in 1909, he was vociferous in condemning the Government's treatment of suffrage prisoners, particularly the practice of forcible feeding. Spartacus Schoolnet has a profile.

On September 17th, 1909, Prime Minister Asquith was due to speak at a Liberal Party meeting in Bingley Hall in Birmingham. Because of the extensive disruptions caused by suffragette heckling, women were being excluded from all Liberal gatherings. Suffragette demonstrators had begun to resort to demonstrating outside, sometimes throwing stones at windows. On this occasion the whole street had been put under police cordon and women were not being allowed through. So Mary Leigh and Charlotte Marsh took another approach: they climbed on to the roof of a nearby house, armed with axes, then proceeded to remove slates and drop them in the direction of the police, Asquith and his car. A hose was turned on them, after which police climbed up to arrest them. They received tough sentences, with hard labour, so that if they gained early release by hunger strike the Government would have looked very foolish. So it was that Leigh and Marsh were subjected to forcible feeding in Winson Green Prison, Birmingham (Rosen 1974, pp122-3; Pugh 2008, p194).

Page 68.

On this page, the view from the carriage window in the main panel includes the white horse of Kilburn. It's in the North Yorks National Park, south of Thirsk, and can be seen as you travel north on the east coast main line. The horse was cut in 1857.

Pages 68-75.

This Newcastle episode is based on both Lady Constance Lytton's account (Lytton 2008) and contemporary coverage in the local press (*The Daily Chronicle*, Oct 9th and 11th, 1909). Con's autobiography, for example, supplied accounts of travelling north in a crowded third-class carriage, of a huge meeting that evening disrupted by howling students (p70) and of her con-versation with Emily Wilding Davison about the best way of attaching a slogan to a throwing stone (p72).

Con and the hatchet user (Jane Brailsford) were among the twelve who were convicted fol-owing arrest. They immediately went on hunger strike. This was an embarrassment to the Government, as Con was the daughter of a former Viceroy of India and Jane was the wife of a high-profile radical journalist. As a precaution, a physician was sent up from London to inspect them before proceeding with forcible feeding. They were both released without being subjected to the procedure.

Con was ashamed at this preferential treatment and, to draw attention to the class distinction it demonstrated, she resolved to carry out her next militant activity in disguise. Accordingly, in January 1910, she went to Liverpool (with Elsie Howey) and led a protest in the guise of a poor seamstress. In her disguise as 'Miss Jane Warton', she rather resembled the press caricature of the suffragette: poorly dressed, unattractive and ungainly. On imprisonment in Walton Gaol, Con again went on hunger strike. This time, as Jane Warton, she was declared healthy by the prison doctor and forcibly fed twice daily for a week. The press eventually learned of her identity and she was released on medical grounds. Her health was never really restored; within two years, she had suffered two strokes, while still in her early 40s.

Page 72.
The 'Handicapped' poster is based on Duncan Grant's entry for an election poster competition run by the Artists' Suffrage League. With W.F. Winter's 'Votes for Workers' (p64), it won joint first prize (Tickner 1987, p16). The 'Convicts, Lunatics and Women' poster depicts a 1908 design by Emily Harding Andrews, a member of the Artists' Suffrage League (Tickner 1987, p54).

Page 73.
The 'People's Budget' was one of the Liberals' key social reform measures in Edwardian times. Championed by David Lloyd George and Winston Churchill, it was the first ever British budget designed to redistribute wealth, by means of the introduction of higher bands of income tax, including a 'supertax' of the wealthiest, and a land tax. It was vetoed by the House of Lords (all landowners) on November 30th, 1909, forcing a General Election in January 1910. In April 1910, the Lords accepted a version of the budget without the land tax proposals. However, there were still bitter struggles between the Government and the Lords over plans for reform of the upper house. This forced another General Election in December of the same year. Both elections left the Liberal government weak and heavily dependent on the Labour and Irish Nationalist Parties for their majority (Liberal Democrat History Group website).

Page 76.
The political posters in the first panel were among the nine reproduced in a feature headed 'Politics By Poster' in *The Penny Illustrated Paper* (December 18th, 1909, p403).

A Conciliation Committee, chaired by the Right Honourable Earl of Lytton (one of Constance Lytton's brothers), drafted the text of a bill to placate supporters of women's suffrage by including one million women householders in the franchise: the Conciliation Bill. The relevant section of the text is quoted in Marlow (2001, p121).

Page 77.
Another version of the 'Miss Hissy' postcard appears to be poking fun at Christabel (popularly known as Chrissy). In it, the goose in prison plumage is asking 'Is a question of gander – I mean gender – to stand between us and the vote?' The version on this page seems to be a clever appropriation. Artists unknown.

Page 80.
This account of 'Black Friday' is based on numerous sources, principally Marlow (2001, pp125-9), Pethick-Lawrence (1938, pp249-50), Raeburn (1973, pp152-5) and Rosen (1974, pp139-143). The Westminster constabulary were accustomed to encounters with suffragists but on this occasion they had been deployed to police a miners' strike in Wales. Replacement police were drawn from other parts of London, particularly Whitechapel and the East End. They were under direct orders from the Home Secretary (Winston Churchill) to delay arrests, which had the presumably unintended effect of escalating the violence. At the end of six hours of repelling the demonstrators' attempts to enter Parliament on November 18th, 119 arrests had been made. For the purposes of Sally's story, I have conflated three days of violent clashes with police. There were further demonstrations on the 22nd and 23rd. There were actually no convictions following the arrests on 'Black Friday', because Churchill had ordered their release. But there were convictions following the 159 arrests made on November 22nd during the 'Battle of Downing Street', as their clash with police and crowds on that day came to be known.

Page 81.
Coverage in the press only mentioned injuries that were sustained by police, as in *The Times* extracts quoted. The press made no mention of the abusive treatment of demonstrators. Statements were collected afterwards, however. These were presented to the Home Office, with a demand for a public inquiry, in a document entitled 'Treatment of the Women's Deputations by the Police. Evidence collection by Dr Jessie Murray and Mr Brailsford forwarded to the Home Office'. No public inquiry followed.

The two men's report on the situation to Christabel is dialogue reported in Raeburn (1973, p154).

Page 85.
Before scripting Sally's prison ordeal, I reread Mary Leigh's statement on the forcible feeding she was subjected to in Winson Green Prison, Birmingham (*Votes for Women*, October 8th, 1909, p20) and also the autobiographies of Constance Lytton and Hannah Mitchell, both of which contain accounts of prison and forcible feeding.

Page 92.
Methods for forcibly holding a prisoner's mouth open while tube feeding varied from one institution to another. Written accounts from the period are a little vague in this regard, so we have imagined an Edwardian version of modern endoscopy practices.

Page 94.
The graffiti is mentioned in a shorthand diary kept by one Gladys Roberts of Leeds while serving a sentence in Holloway. She was one of the stone throwers in the first 'smash up' on June 29th, 1909 (Raeburn 1973, p105-6).

The YHB was a group of young unattached members of the WSPU, sworn to secrecy and to the performance of 'danger duty'. Founded by Mary Home in 1907, members were devoted followers of Mrs Pankhurst and Christabel and included Grace Roe, Jessie Kenney, Elsie Howey and Vera Wentworth. Meetings were held in a teashop on the Strand (Crawford 2001, p765; Pugh 2008, p168).

Page 97.
Elsie Howey suffered permanent injury to her larynx during forcible feeding. She required four months' treatment after her release and never fully recovered her voice (Crawford 2001, p297). The seated woman in the armchair reading *PIP* is Mary Leigh, the hatchet wielder in Dublin (p6).

Page 98.
Em eventually did run for Parliament with equal pay and nationalization on her campaign agenda. She was the Labour candidate for Rusholme, Manchester, in the 'khaki election' that took place on December 14th, 1918. She ran as a pacifist, speaking in favour of a just settlement in Europe and against the vindictive treatment of the defeated German people. This position won her the support of returning soldiers, but not of the civilian population: 'the electors that day voted, although they did not know it, for another world war' (Pethick-Lawrence 1938, pp322-3). In the end it was Fred who followed a career in politics, eventually serving as Secretary of State for India and Burma.

Page 99.
Sally is reading from Olive Schreiner's *Woman and Labour*, published in 1911. The book is dedicated to Constance Lytton. Con and Em both made her acquaintance, on separate occasions, on visits to South Africa.

Page 100.
Mrs Pankhurst's sister, Mary Clarke, wasn't the only woman to die from injuries sustained on 'Black Friday'. Sylvia names Cecilia Haig and Henria Williams as two other fatalities (quoted in Castle 1987, p87).

Page 105.
The image reworks a 1913 poster designed for the WSPU. Artist unknown.

Page 109.
The 'From Prison to Citizenship' banner was probably designed and worked by Clemence Housman. She was a highly skilled wood engraver and needlewoman who worked for the Suffrage Atelier (Tickner 1987, p71).

Page 110.
The revised Conciliation Bill was an electoral reform measure that retained the property qualification but extended it to women. The Government had been appearing to take it seriously, allocating time to debate it in the House, where it actually resulted in a majority in favour. However, Asquith and Lloyd George had resolved to block it at all costs. With grave concerns about it boosting the Tory vote, the Government 'torpedoed' it by introducing a new reform measure (Pethick-Lawrence 1938, pp257-8; Raeburn 1977, p164; Rosen 1974, pp143-50). The Manhood Suffrage Bill undertook to enfranchise all men, doing away with the property qualification, but still didn't include women.

I have based Em's speech in the Albert Hall on a circular she sent out on November 15th, 1911 (Raeburn 1973, p164).

Pages 111-13.
There is detailed coverage of the suffrage societies' meeting with the Prime Minister and Chancellor in *Votes for Women* (Nov 24th, 1911, pp116-19). The delegates' speeches are based on it.

Pages 114-15.
The headlines are from the front page of *The Times* (Nov 22nd, 1911). Em led the demonstration from Caxton Hall to Parliament Square, where a police cordon confronted them, leading to 223 arrests. Em was arrested for assaulting a policeman. In the transcript of her speech in defence, she claims that the constable was holding a fellow demonstrator by the throat and that she struck him twice with the back of her hand while calling to him to let her go. She was sentenced to one month's imprisonment (*Votes for Women* Dec 1st, 1911, p143). Christabel orchestrated the window-smashing spree separately, starting at the WSPU shop on Charing Cross Road, where hammers and bags of stones were supplied (Pugh 2000, p200; Rosen 1974, p154).

Page 116.
The police had warrants for the arrest of all four leaders: Emmeline and Christabel Pankhurst and the Pethick-Lawrences. They seized sheaves of documents for use in prosecuting them. Christabel eluded them; she no longer lived on the premises, having moved into a flat near Chancery Lane the previous November. Tipped off about the raid by Evelyn Sharp, she fled to a nursing home in Pembridge Gardens that was used by recuperating released prisoners. Then, disguised as a nurse, she took the boat train to Folkestone and crossed the Channel. She lived under the name 'Amy Richards' in Paris, issuing instructions to the WSPU from a distance, by means of weekly visits by the faithful Annie Kenney. She lived in France until war broke out in 1914 (Mitchell, D 1977, p180; Pugh 2008, pp237-8).

Page 117.
Both Emmelines were released on 24th June 1912, in poor health. Fred was discharged on the 27th, by which time he was over 50lbs lighter (Pugh 2008, p248). Emmeline Pankhurst joined Christabel in Paris on her release. Em Pethick-Lawrence wrote to a friend (George Lansbury) on July 3rd that she and Fred had 'both yielded to our medical advisors, backed up by our friends, and have promised to do no work and take no responsibility for at least three months. As soon as we are a little stronger we shall go abroad and live very quietly'. They planned to visit friends in Switzerland then Em's engineer brother in British Columbia. Just before leaving for Switzerland, they received a message from Mrs Pankhurst asking them to stop at Boulogne en route (Mitchell, D 1977, p197; Raeburn 1973, p180).

The original Joan of Arc image reworked here is attributed to an unknown artist called Poyntz Wright, presumably a pseudonym. Most of the cover cartoons for *Votes for Women* were executed free of charge by Alfred Pearse (signed A. Patriot). Pearse was a prolific illustrator for family journals and boys' adventure stories, who was presumably a supporter of the cause (Tickner 1987, p27).

Page 118.
Mrs Pankhurst and Christabel were set on a policy of 'civil war': 'If you do not accept Christabel's policy we will smash you!' (Mitchell D 1977, p296). The Pethick-Lawrences thought it was sheer folly not to capitalise on the groundswell of public sympathy. They were keen for Christabel to return and sensationally to challenge the Government to arrest her, an irresistible appeal to the public; and they were certain the Pankhurst plan would destroy the advantage they now

had. As Em explains, 'We considered it sheer madness to throw away the immense publicity and propaganda value that the demonstration followed by the State trial had brought to our cause … The people were eager to see us and to hear us and to support us' (Pethick-Lawrence 1938, pp277-278).

Page 120.
The leadership split was announced publicly in both *Votes for Women* and *The Suffragette*, as follows (in *Votes* it was headed 'Grave Statement By The Leaders'):

> At the first reunion of the leaders after their enforced holiday, Mrs Pankhurst and Miss Christabel Pankhurst outlined a new militant policy which Mr and Mrs Lawrence found themselves altogether unable to approve. Mrs Pankhurst and Miss Christabel Pankhurst indicated that they were not prepared to modify their intentions and recommended that Mr and Mrs Pethick-Lawrence should resume control of the paper *Votes for Women* and leave the Women's Social and Political Union. Rather than make a schism in the ranks of the Union, Mr and Mrs Pethick-Lawrence consented to this course. In these circumstances, Mr and Mrs Pethick-Lawrence will not be present at the Royal Albert Hall on October 17th.

The announcement was drafted by the four leaders at a second meeting in Boulogne in August, prior to the Pethick-Lawrences' departure for Canada.

Page 121.
There is a facsimile of Mrs Pankhurst's 'incitement' letter in some good learning materials for schools, available online at the National Archive. It's in a case study, 'Suffragist, Suffragette'.

Page 122.
The modus operandi (including wellies and hatpins) and the probable identity of two of the perpetrators are pieced together from the Metropolitan Police Report, reprinted in Marlow (2001, pp183-4) and from contemporary press coverage (*The Times*, February 20th, 1913; *Morning Post* February 20th and 21st, 1913).

Page 127.
The headlines on this page are from *The Morning Post*, February 20th, and *The Suffragette*, February 21st, 1913.

Page 129.
Fred's talk about the bailiffs here is drawn from his 'Government Burglars' article (*Votes for Women* Oct 11th, 1912, p10).

The Prisoners' Temporary Discharge for Ill-Health Bill was drawn up by the Home Secretary (Reginald McKenna) and hurried through Parliament before Mrs Pankhurst's trial. This 'Cat and Mouse Act' was put into force immediately, before receiving royal assent on April 25th. Mrs Pankhurst was released on licence on April 12th, to return in fifteen days. In defiance of the measure, she tore up the licence in front of the prison authorities. She was arrested and released ten times under the Cat and Mouse Act (Raeburn 1973 pp190-1, p249).

The measure did not replace forcible feeding altogether, as Em chillingly notes: 'Those prisoners who were not well known to the public could be tortured first by this process and re-arrested afterwards' (Pethick-Lawrence 1938, p295).

Page 131.

The press coverage of Mrs Pankhurst's trial is from *The Times* (April 4th, 1913, p4).

Before Emily's leap into a stairwell in Holloway in June 1912, she had been serving a six-month sentence since January, after setting light to pillar boxes in protest at the harsh sentencing of Mary Leigh. She was mostly in solitary confinement and being forcibly fed even though not actually on hunger strike (*Votes for Women*, May 10th, 1912, p500; Morley and Stanley 1998, p103, p158). Her account of the event appeared, edited, in *The Daily Herald* under the headline 'Desperate Leap: One Big Tragedy to Save Others.' Here's an extract:

> We decided that most of us would barricade our cells after they had been cleaned out. At ten o'clock on Saturday a regular siege took place in Holloway. On all sides one heard crowbars, blocks and wedges being used; men battering on doors with all their might – My turn came, and my door was forced open with crowbars. I protested loudly that I would not be fed by the junior doctor, and tried to dart into the passage. Then I was seized by about five wardresses, bound into a chair, still protesting, and they accomplished their purpose.
>
> In my mind was the thought that some desperate protest must be made to put a stop to the hideous torture. As soon as I could get out I climbed on to the railing and threw myself on to the wire-netting, a distance of between 20ft to 30ft. The idea in my mind was that one big tragedy might save many others; but the netting prevented any severe injury. Quite deliberately I walked upstairs, and threw myself from the top on to the iron staircase. If I had been successful I should undoubtedly have been killed – but I caught once more on the netting.
>
> I realised that there was only one chance left, and that was to haul myself with the greatest force I could summon from the netting on to the staircase. I heard someone saying, 'No surrender!' and threw myself forward on my head with all my might.

She sent it to *The Suffragette* as well, but they did not publish it until after her death, when it appeared in full, framed as an attempt at martyrdom (*The Daily Herald* July 4th, 1912; reprinted in Marlow 2001, p168; *The Suffragette*, June 13th, 1912, p577).

Pages 132-5.

Emily Wilding Davison was trampled on the Derby Day racecourse at Epsom on June 4th, 1913. Two WSPU flags were found pinned inside her coat. She died on June 8th, without having regained consciousness (Crawford 2001, pp161-2).

When she was carried off the racecourse, she also had her pockets full. She had on her person the return part of a rail ticket, notepaper, envelopes and stamps, a race card marked with her fancies up to the fateful 3 p.m. race and her helper's pass card for the WSPU Summer Festival in the Empress Rooms, Kensington, valid for 2.30 to 10.30 p.m. that day. It isn't clear that she was planning suicide. Indeed, she'd placed bets on horses and arranged to be an official at the festival later on (Morley and Stanley 1988, p130-1). According to locals in Longhorsley (the Northumberland village near Morpeth where Emily lived) she had been spotted at a horse-exercising track in the area, practising grabbing at the bridle of a passing horse. While this incident, as Morley and Stanley acknowledge, 'may be apocryphal', it is likely that she would have tried out such a hazardous course of action first. They conclude that she probably underestimated the speed of the Derby Day racehorses (Morley and Stanley 1988, p206 n47).

The return ticket has been taken as an indication that Emily was not intending a suicide attempt, but, as Crawford has pointed out, she would have had no option in the matter. The 'excursion train' ticket, which is what Emily was obliged to buy in order to travel from Victoria to Epsom Downs on Derby Day, would have been for the round trip.

Page 139.
The press and music-hall responses to suffrage activism were mixed, expressing both sympathy and mockery, as in the first two popular anti-suffrage songs here (Pugh 2000, pp227-9). The third number, that drives Sally out, was actually the first stanza from a verse submitted to the *Penny Illustrated Paper.*

Page 141.
A national 'Pilgrimage' through England was organised by the NUWSS in 1913 and took place from 18th to 26th July. There were eight routes starting from the North-east, North-west and West, culminating in a mass rally of 70,000 in Hyde Park (*Votes for Women*, July 25th, 1913).

Page 142.
Sylvia's East London Federation of the WSPU held two mass rallies in Trafalgar Square in July 1913. On both occasions Sylvia was out on licence under the Cat and Mouse Act and was rearrested. One strand I have not followed in detail is Sylvia's sustained East End activism, with numerous measures to help women workers (e.g. a mother and baby welfare centre and a cost-price canteen) and frequent marches (see e.g. Rosen 1974, pp270-6).

Page 143.
Olive Hockin really did lead the police to her by leaving papers bearing her address lying about on the scene. Her 'suffragette arsenal' consisted of wire cutters, a hammer, a tin of paraffin, a bag of stones, false licence plates and a bottle of corrosive fluid (Crawford 2001, p287).

In 1913, Scotland Yard began the practice of photographic surveillance (intelligence-gathering by means of covert photography with a telephoto lens), in order to monitor the movements of known militant suffragettes. Initially, in 1912, these were taken in Holloway exercise yard to record inmates who had evaded being photographed (Brown 2003; Casciani 2003).

Page 144.
There was 'some real progress' made in the Labour Party at their conference in Birmingham in January 1912: a resolution that no franchise reform would be acceptable if not including women. Readiness to face Liberals on the issue was confirmed by Ramsay MacDonald, the Party leader, in February (Pugh 2000, p264).

Asquith made his jibe about women and rabbits being 'naturally disqualified' from voting in a Commons debate in June 1913. My source was a letter of comment by George Bernard Shaw (reprinted in Marlow 2001, p200).

Page 150.
On March 10th, 1914, Mary Richardson infamously slashed a Velasquez painting known as the *Rokeby Venus*, in protest at the treatment of Mrs Pankhurst. The statement Mary issued to the WSPU was published in *The Times* (Mar 11th, 1914, pp9-10):

I have tried to destroy the picture of the most beautiful woman in mythological history as a protest against the Government for destroying Mrs. Pankhurst, who is the most beautiful character in modern history. Justice is an element of beauty as much as colour and outline on canvas. Mrs. Pankhurst seeks to procure justice for womanhood, and for this she is being slowly murdered by a Government of Iscariot politicians. If there is an outcry against my deed, let every one remember that such an outcry is an hypocrisy so long as they allow the destruction of Mrs. Pankhurst and other beautiful living women, and that until the public cease to countenance human destruction the stones cast against me for the destruction of this picture are each an evidence against them of artistic as well as moral and political humbug and hypocrisy.

There was indeed an outcry. 'Slasher Mary', as she became known, was widely vilified in the press. It's sometimes claimed that her action was specifically in retaliation for Mrs Pankhurst's rearrest the previous day. On an expired licence, Mrs Pankhurst had been smuggled into St Andrew's Hall, Glasgow, where she was due to speak from a platform protected with barbed wire that was hidden under flowers and flags. She was arrested after a pitched battle with the police, though, predictably, accounts vary as to who the aggressors were (Pugh 2008, p293).

According to Mary's autobiographical account of her deed, however, she wrote to Christabel outlining her plan and didn't proceed with it until permission came from Paris. 'The days, while I waited for her reply', she says, 'seemed endless' (Richardson 1953; quoted in Marlow 2001, p219).

Police were suppressing public gatherings by the WSPU, so the deputation to Buckingham Palace involved months of planning in secrecy. A very large empty house in Grosvenor Place, overlooking Buckingham Palace gardens, had been lent to them and 200 women gradually and surreptitiously gathered there (there are interesting first-hand accounts in Raeburn 1973, p229-31). Then, the day before, the WSPU distributed their customary handbill announcing their plans: 'To Demand Votes For Women', 'To Protest Against Torture', 'To Claim Equal Treatment For Militant Ulster Men And Militant Suffragists'. On the day of the demonstration The Times carried a small news item in announcing it (*The Times* May 21st, 1914, p5) then much more substantial coverage of the 'Suffragist Riot' the following day (*The Times* May 22nd, 1914, p8).

Page 151.

From June 1913 to June 1914 Sylvia was imprisoned and released ten times under the Cat and Mouse Act (Taylor 1993, p25). I've conflated several events in the first three panels on this page. From her invalid chair on the doorstep of Number 10, Sylvia persuaded Asquith to accept a deputation. But she was unable to attend herself, as she had been rearrested. The women's speeches and Asquith's actual, very wordy response are outlined in an article headed 'Working Women and The Vote. Mr Asquith's Sympathy. An East-End Appeal' (*The Times* June 22nd, 1914, p12).

Page 154.

Em was campaigning for peace but she was as galvanized as the rest of the population by the impulse to come to the aid of the nation at war. When war broke out she immediately joined the Women's Emergency Corps Committee and was soon involved in organising the care of Belgian refugees (Pethick-Lawrence 1936, p306).

Sally's anti-conscription speech is loosely based on a leaflet produced by the No-Conscription Fellowship entitled 'Shall Britons Be Conscripts?' (Online National Archives)

Page 156.

The white feather has long been a symbol of cowardice. An Order of the White Feather was formed in August 1914, as war broke out, in order to shame men into enlisting. Mrs Pankhurst and Christabel were both active members (Wikipedia).

In August 1914 Mrs Pankhurst and Christabel abruptly dropped the cause of female enfranchisement and never took it up again. They threw themselves instead into new roles as unofficial recruiting agents for the military and munitions, deflecting WSPU funds into the war effort and cultivating connections with Lloyd George when he became Minister for Munitions and later Prime Minister. The other two surviving Pankhursts – Sylvia and Adela – independently became peace campaigners (Pugh 2008, pp300-3, 324; Rosen 1974, p254). The Pethick-Lawrences, too, launched themselves into peace campaigning, while continuing with suffrage work until the full franchise in 1928. The former WSPU leaders' contrasting responses to the outbreak of war with Germany are quite striking and highlight how much their paths had diverged. Not only did Em not share Mrs Pankhurst's and Christabel's anti-German fervour, in 1919, after the war, she led a protest against the Hunger Blockade of Germany. She marched to Downing Street again, but this time leading soldiers who, unlike the civilian population, 'resisted the contagion of hatred' (Pethick-Lawrence 1938, p325).

Page 158.

In January 1914, Sylvia was commanded to sever her East London Federation's links with the WSPU, principally because of her continued collaboration with the Labour Party. Mrs Pankhurst had been recuperating in Paris since before Christmas. Sylvia was summoned to an unpleasant meeting there with her mother and sister. According to Sylvia's account, her sister objected to the democratic constitution of ELF: 'we do not agree with that'. Sylvia also notes that Christabel deplored her independent thinking: 'We do not want that: we want all our women to take their instructions and walk in step like an army!' The encounter isn't even mentioned in Christabel's autobiography, but it evidently distressed Sylvia greatly: 'I was oppressed by a sense of tragedy, grieved by her ruthlessness' (Castle 1987, p129-30; Pugh 2008, p286).

By the time war broke out, any Pankhurst family ties had been well and truly severed. The other sister, Adela, had been banished, in effect, to Australia. Sylvia complains about their mother in a letter to her: 'She takes the opposite view in everything. The most extreme jingoism is scarcely enough for her and I only look in wonder and ask: "can those two really be sane?"' (Pugh 2008, p307).

Sylvia's baby was born on 4th December 1927. The father was Silvio Corio, whom she had declined to marry because 'he is a refugee from fascism and I'm a Socialist, the government would deport us both to his country and we'd be shot'. Her mother refused to have any contact with 'the Scarlet Woman'. Sylvia named the child Richard Keir Pethick Pankhurst, after three people she considered to be her major influences: her father (the late Richard Pankhurst), her previous lover (the late Keir Hardie) and Emmeline Pethick-Lawrence (Pugh 2008, p403-4).

Page 160.

Sally has secured herself a job doing essential war work on the trams, but the vast majority of working-class women were in munitions. The popular press referred to them as 'Tommy's sisters' or 'munitionettes'. Their middle-class equivalents were mostly in the voluntary sector, doing a wide range of support work for the military. The VAD (Voluntary Aid Detachment) poster indicates some of the work required: 'nursing members', but also far less glamorous service roles as 'cooks, kitchen-maids, clerks, house-maids, ward-maids, laundresses, motor-drivers etc'. The prevailing image of women in the First World War is of care-workers, predominantly nurses, but, as Angela Smith points out, 'nursing was a role that was carried out by a very small number of women when compared with those working in munitions manufacture' (Smith 2008, p223). She attributes this false perception in part to the portrayal of nurses in memoirs by middle-class officers and to highly selective representations in war memorials.

Page 161.
Fred wasn't called up until 1918, when his age group came within the Conscription Act (he was 46). He became a conscientious objector and spent the last year of the war put to work as a farm labourer. He makes no mention of being the target for any chamber pots used as projectiles (Pethick-Lawrence 1943, p118).

Page 165.
So how did women finally get the vote? By 1916 a General Election was overdue, but huge numbers of men were away from their homes, either in the Armed Forces, coal mines or the munitions factories. This meant that they didn't satisfy the twelve-month residency qualification, so they couldn't register to vote. There was barely an electorate. The wartime coalition government could be extended for short periods, but some form of full-scale electoral reform was essential for an election to be a possibility at all.

Asquith delegated the task of drawing up proposals for such reform to a committee of backbenchers, with the intention of shelving the issue for the duration of the war. However, the Speaker's Conference into which this committee evolved produced unexpectedly rapid results. In January 1917 it reported its recommendations to Lloyd George, who was by then the new Prime Minister. The report proposed votes for all men over 21 and for women over 30 who were householders or university graduates, or who were wives of householders. This rather complicated compromise was evidently intended to limit the numbers of female voters to 'safe' levels! After 50 years of protracted struggle (the first Private Member's Bill in Parliament to propose the removal of the sex disqualification was John Stuart Mill's in 1867), a Bill enfranchising women had the Government's support and met with very little resistance. It passed into law in January 1918 as the Representation of the People Act.

It came about for a variety of reasons, but principally because the electoral system was not fit for purpose and in need of full-scale reform. It was widely accepted that soldiers and other citizens who had done active war service should, as Lloyd George put it, 'have a right to a voice in choosing the Government that sent them to face peril and death'; but the residence qualification was a hindrance. Another reason was that attitudes towards women's participation in the political life of the country were shifting, influenced by experiences of wartime conditions which had greatly extended the sphere of industrial service for women. A further, grim factor was that, by 1918, there were many thousands of households across the country that were unrepresented, because so many male householders had been casualties of war (Castle 1987, p138; Pugh 2008, pp321-3).

Mary Talbot, 2013

SOURCES

Atkinson, Diane 1992 *The Purple White & Green: Suffragettes in London 1906-14* Museum of London

Balding, Clare 2013 *Secrets of a Suffragette* BBC4 documentary, June 2013

Bartholomew's Reference Atlas of London and Suburbs 1908 http://mapco.net/bart1908/bart34.htm

Bartley, Paula 2002 *Emmeline Pankhurst* London: Routledge

Brown, Bill 2003 'Evelyn Manesta and the resistance to "modern" photographic surveillance' http://www.notbored.org/suffragettes.html Accessed 7/02/2011

Casciani, Dominic 2003 'Spy pictures of suffragettes revealed', BBC News Online. http://news.bbc.co.uk/1/hi/magazine/3153024.stm Accessed 18/05/2012

Castle, Barbara 1987 *Sylvia and Christabel Pankhurst* Harmondsworth: Penguin

Collins, Stephen 2012 'Celebrating momentous events that shaped the course of Irish history a century ago', Irishtimes.com http://www.irishtimes.com/newspaper/ireland/2012/0105/1224309833567.html Accessed 06/04/2012

Colmore, Gertrude, edited by Alison Lee 2008 *Suffragette Sally* Toronto: Broadview Press (first published by Stanley Paul in 1911)

Crawford, Elizabeth 2000 *The Women's Suffrage Movement: A Reference Guide, 1866-1928* London: UCL Press

Ferguson, Rachel 1958 *We Were Amused: Memoirs* London: Jonathan Cape

Liddington, Jill and Norris, Jill 1978 *One Hand Tied Behind Us: The Rise of the Women's Suffrage Movement* London: Virago

Lytton, Constance, edited by Jason Haslam 2008 *Prisons and Prisoners: Some Personal Experiences* Toronto: Broadview Press (first published by William Heineman in 1914)

Marlow, Joyce (ed.) 2001 *Votes for Women: The Virago Book of Suffragettes* London: Virago

Mitchell, David 1977 *Queen Christabel* Macdonald and Jane's Publishers Ltd

Mitchell, Hannah, edited by Geoffrey Mitchell, 1977 *The Hard Way Up: The Autobiography of Hannah Mitchell, Suffragette and Rebel* London: Virago

Morley, Ann and Stanley, Liz 1988 *The Life and Death of Emily Wilding Davison* London: The Women's Press

Owens, Rosemary Cullen 1984 *Smashing Times: A History of the Irish Women's Suffrage Movement 1889-1922* Dublin: Anvil Press

Pankhurst, Christabel, edited by Frederick Pethick-Lawrence 1959 *Unshackled: The Story of How We Won the Vote* London: Hutchinson

Pankhurst, Emmeline 1914 *My Own Story* London: Eveleigh Nash

Pankhurst, Sylvia 1911 *The Suffragette: The History of the Women's Militant Suffrage Movement 1905-1910* New York: Sturgis & Walton

Pankhurst, Sylvia 1977 *The Suffragette Movement: An Intimate Account of Persons and Ideals* London: Virago (first published in 1931)

Pember Reeves, Maud 1979 *Round About a Pound a Week* London: Virago (first published by G Bell & Sons Limited in 1913)

Pethick-Lawrence, Emmeline 1938 *My Part in a Changing World* London: Gollancz

Pethick-Lawrence, Frederick 1943 *Fate Has Been Kind* London: Hutchinson

Pugh, Martin 2000 *The March of the Women. A Revisionist Analysis of the Campaign for Women's Suffrage 1866-1914* Oxford: Oxford University Press

Pugh, Martin 2008 *The Pankhursts: The History of One Radical Family* London: Vintage

Radio Times 1974 'Shoulder to Shoulder', *Radio Times* Special, 30th March-5th April

Raeburn, Antonia 1973 *The Militant Suffragettes* London: Michael Joseph

Richardson, Mary 1953 *Laugh a Defiance* Weidenfeld & Nicolson

Rosen, Andrew 1974 *Rise Up Women! The Militant Campaign of the Women's Social and Political Union 1903-1914* London: Routledge & Kegan Paul

Smith, Angela 2008 ' "The girl behind the man behind the gun": women as carers in recruitment posters of the First World War', *Journal of War and Culture Studies* 1(3): 223-41

Taylor, Rosemary 1993 *In Letters of Gold: The Story of Sylvia Pankhurst and the East London Federation of the Suffragettes in Bow* London: Stepney Books

http://www.maryneal.org

http://www.historylearningsite.co.uk

http://www.liberalhistory.org.uk

http://www.nationalarchives.gov.uk

http://www.parliament.uk

http://www.spartacus.schoolnet.co.uk

http://en.wikipedia.org

http://womanandhersphere.com

Mary Talbot is an internationally acclaimed scholar whose academic publications include *Language and Gender*, *Media Discourse: Representation and Interaction* and *Language and Power in the Modern World* (with Karen Atkinson and David Atkinson). Her first graphic novel, *Dotter of her Father's Eyes* (with Bryan Talbot), won the Costa Biography Award in 2013.

www.mary-talbot.co.uk

Kate Charlesworth's strips, cartoons and illustrations have appeared in both mainstream and alternative publications for over 30 years. These include *New Scientist*, *The Guardian* and *Independent*, *Knockabout Comics*, *The Pink Paper* and the award-winning *Nelson*.

www.katecharlesworth.com

Bryan Talbot has written and drawn comics and graphic novels for over 30 years, including *Judge Dredd*, *Batman*, *Sandman*, *The Adventures of Luther Arkwright*, *The Tale of One Bad Rat*, *Heart of Empire*, *Alice in Sunderland*, and *Dotter of her Father's Eyes* (written by Mary Talbot) and his current *Grandville* series of steampunk detective thrillers.

www.bryan-talbot.com